P9-DWI-336

Also by Walter Russell Mead

Power, Terror, Peace, and War: America's Grand Strategy in a World at Risk

Special Providence: American Foreign Policy and How It Changed the World

Mortal Splendor: The American Empire in Transition

God and Gold

God and Gold

Britain, America, and the Making of the Modern World

Walter Russell Mead

Alfred A. Knopf New York 2007

This Is a Borzoi Book Published by Alfred A. Knopf

Copyright © 2007 by Walter Russell Mead

All rights reserved. Published in the United States by Alfred A. Knopf, a division of Random House, Inc., New York, and in Canada by Random House of Canada Limited, Toronto.

www.aaknopf.com

Knopf, Borzoi Books, and the colophon are registered trademarks of Random House, Inc.

Founded in 1921, the Council on Foreign Relations is an independent, national membership organization and a nonpartisan center for scholars dedicated to producing and disseminating ideas so that individual and corporate members, as well as policy makers, journalists, students, and interested citizens in the United States and other countries, can better understand the world and the foreign policy choices facing the United States and other governments. The Council does this by convening meetings; conducting a wide-ranging Studies program; publishing Foreign Affairs, the preeminent journal covering international affairs and U.S. foreign policy; maintaining a diverse membership; sponsoring Independent Task Forces; and providing up-to-date information about the world and U.S. foreign policy on the Council's Web site, www.cfr.org.

The Council takes no institution position on policy issues and has no affiliation with the U.S. government. All statements of fact and expressions of opinion contained in its publications are the sole responsibility of the author or authors.

Library of Congress Cataloging-in-Publication Data
Mead, Walter Russell.
God and gold : Britain, America, and the making of the modern world /
by Walter Russell Mead.
p. cm.
ISBN 978-0-375-41403-9
1. United States—Foreign relations.   2. Great Britain—Foreign relations.
3. Civilization, Modern—American influences.   4. Civilization, Modern—British influences.
5. United States—Foreign public opinion.   6. Great Britain—Foreign public opinion.
7. Great powers—History.   8. World politics.   9. Economic history.   I. Title.
E183.7.M47154 2007
327.73—dc2   2007029222

Manufactured in the United States of America

First Edition

To the memory of Scott Thorne O'Brien,
And to Lallie, Becca, Tim, and Michael

God moves in a mysterious way
His wonders to perform;
He plants his footsteps in the sea
And rides upon the storm.

—WILLIAM COWPER, 1779

Contents

God and Gold

Introduction

I n colonial Virginia a wealthy and well-connected planter's son once
asked his Anglican rector if it was possible to find salvation outside the
Church of England.

The rector struggled with his conscience; he could hardly claim that only
Anglicans get to Heaven—but he didn't want to encourage this well-born
young parishioner to associate with the dissenting riffraff and wandering
evangelists of the region.

After a few minutes of thought he was able to give the young man an
answer. "Sir," said the divine, "the possibility about which you enquire
exists. But no gentleman would avail himself of it."

Many Americans feel a little bit like that rector when confronted by discussions of American power. We know it's there and we know it's important—but the subject makes us uncomfortable. No gentleman—or, for that
matter, no lady—would bring it up.

This is a book about the meaning of American power for world history,
and I apologize. Most Americans probably do think that their country has a
unique world mission and that our success in domestic and foreign policy
has enormous implications for the rest of the world—but it still seems
unpardonably triumphalist to talk seriously about what this idea might
mean.

Americans tend to think both too much and too little about their country's rise to world power. They concentrate on what might be called the statistics of power, following indices that show the American lead in military
power, economic production, or various high-tech and scientific enterprises.
They congratulate themselves on the global spread of democratic ideals,
collecting statistics and rating countries based on their adoption of various
elements of democratic culture. They cheer the indicators—like the number

3

of American-trained Nobel Prize–winning scientists—that show the United States pulling ahead, and worry about statistics like the rising net national debt or the declining achievement of eighth-grade students on math tests that show American prospects in a less favorable light. Americans admire the prowess of their military forces and celebrate the popularity of their culture worldwide.

But while Americans spend a lot of time thinking about the *dimensions* of American power in the contemporary world, less thought is given to the *meaning* of that power. The United States has achieved an unprecedented leadership in an international community that faces unprecedented challenges. As the heir to centuries of Anglo-Saxon politics the United States supports, however inconsistently, a political and social philosophy based on free choice and private property, tolerance among religions founded in Protestant Christian values, and the idea that individuals—including women—have inalienable and equal rights which states must observe and protect. The United States is both a conservative power, defending the international status quo against those who would change it through violence, and a revolutionary power seeking to replace age-old power structures with market economics and democratic ideals. The political revolution that the United States supports involves radical change in countries as important as China, but even the political revolution pales before the economic revolution that the United States wishes to spread through the world. The United States seeks to make the world an ever more dynamic place—a place where an accelerating pace of technological change leads the world ever faster through the power of ever more flexible and dynamic private markets into ever accelerating "progress" toward an end we do not see.

This is an extraordinary ambition for the most powerful country in the history of the world—yet neither Americans nor anybody else has a very clear idea about the kind of revolution that American society seeks to bring about or about the consequences of this great revolutionary effort for the future of mankind.

Generally speaking, we have not thought deeply about the sources, foundations, consequences, or durability of American power; we do not, as a society, have a rich sense of the chief duties, risks, limits, privileges, and costs of the peculiar world position we have.

We can choose not to think about our power and its meaning for ourselves or for others, but we cannot make that power disappear and we cannot prevent decisions taken in the United States from rippling out beyond our borders and shaping the world that others live in and the choices that they make. Nor can we prevent the way that others see and react to our power from shaping the world we live in and affecting the safety and security of Americans at home.

Strong and Wrong

I start my analysis of American power with two observations: first, that the American international system and American power are in many ways continuations of a tradition of English-speaking power that goes back to the late seventeenth century. Since the Glorious Revolution of 1688 that established parliamentary and Protestant rule in Britain, the Anglo-Americans have been on the winning side in every major international conflict. The War of the League of Augsburg, the War of the Spanish Succession, the War of the Austrian Succession, the Seven Years' War, the American Revolution (Britain lost, but America won), the French revolutionary and Napoleonic wars, World War I, World War II, and the Cold War: these are the wars that made the modern world, and either the British or the Americans or both of them together have won every one of them. More than three hundred years of unbroken victory in major wars with great powers: it begins to look almost like a pattern.

Yet the second observation about Anglo-American power is also striking: that as their power has grown, the Anglo-Americans have more and more often been dead wrong about what their growing power and their military victories mean for the world.

That is, ever since Britain, having beaten back Napoleon's attempts at world empire, built what it hoped would be a lasting system of liberal prosperity and free trade in the late nineteenth century, Anglo-American writers and opinion leaders have seen, over and over, a stable and progressive world just ahead.

Writers captured this image as early as the eighteenth century. Bishop George Berkeley prophesied the rise and long duration of our English-speaking hegemony based in North America in his poem "On the Prospect of Planting Arts and Learning in America," published in 1752:

> Westward the course of empire takes its way
> The four first acts already past,
> A fifth shall close the drama with the day:
> Time's noblest offspring is the last.

The young poet Alfred Tennyson captured the vision in "Locksley Hall," a poem he published in 1842. Developing technology and commerce, fused with democratic liberty, would lead to universal peace.

> *For I dipt into the future, far as human eye could see,*
> *Saw the Vision of the world, and all the wonder that would be;*
>
> *Saw the heavens fill with commerce, argosies of magic sails,*
> *Pilots of the purple twilight, dropping down with costly bales . . .*
>
> *Till the war-drum throbb'd no longer, and the battle-flags were furl'd*
> *In the Parliament of man, the Federation of the world.*
>
> *There the common sense of most shall hold a fretful realm in awe,*
> *And the kindly earth shall slumber, lapt in universal law.*

Writing in *The Wall Street Journal* in 1993, Arthur M. Schlesinger quoted this poem to urge readers to support President Clinton's intervention in the Bosnian war. Tennyson's "noble dream" could be realized only if Americans were ready to use force, he argued—and reminded readers that Winston Churchill called this passage "the most wonderful of modern prophecies" and that Harry Truman kept a copy of the poem in his wallet.[1]

In 2006 Yale professor Paul Kennedy took the title and much of the spirit of his new book from the Tennyson poem: *The Parliament of Man* is a history of the United Nations that aims to show how the United Nations can grow closer to fulfilling Tennyson's hopes.[2]

By 1851, it had begun to look as if Tennyson's future had arrived. Thirty-six years had elapsed since the end of the Napoleonic Wars; major, all-out war between the great powers was beginning to look unthinkable. "It is of Thee, O Lord, that nations do not lift up the sword against each other nor learn war any more; it is of Thee that peace is within our walls and plenteousness within our palaces," the Archbishop of Canterbury prayed before the assembled dignitaries and throngs gathered in the Crystal Palace for the first day of the Great Exhibition. The Peaceable Kingdom had arrived; British power, progress, prosperity, and liberty were ushering in the universal rule of peace.

In mid-nineteenth-century Britain, Richard Cobden and John Bright articulated a more detailed vision than Tennyson's of just how the argosies of magic sail would usher in a millennial age of peace. Free trade, they argued, was one part of the answer; growing ties between what today we would call the civil societies of different countries would provide the rest. Free trade would promote peace between nations based on common interests and increasing prosperity. People-to-people contact, facilitated by international human rights and religious organizations, would remove the misunderstandings that led to war and create bonds of friendship as well. Following Jean Baptiste Say, who wrote that "the theory of markets will necessarily scatter the seeds of concord and peace," Cobden believed that the spread of market principles and free trade would create a peaceful order of free countries in Europe.

The older Tennyson was sadder and perhaps wiser; "Locksley Hall Sixty Years After," published in his old age, has a distinctly less positive tone. As Norman Angell wrote in *The Great Illusion,* published in 1910, while we are "quite prepared to give the soldier his due place in poetry and legend and romance," we are now beginning to wonder "whether the time has not come to place him, or a good portion of him, gently on the poetic shelf." The traditional activities of the soldier, according to Angell, "have in their present form little place in the world." Angell, like Tennyson, saw a link between the "magic sails" of commerce and the establishment of world peace. Economic integration and interdependence, he argued, meant that war would be ruinous for everyone involved. Because people are rational, wars would be increasingly rare and might already have died out. War, wrote Angell, "belongs to a stage of development out of which we have passed." Military power "is socially and economically futile."

The Great Illusion sold millions of copies and may be the best-selling book on international relations ever published; sales dropped off after August 1914, but new editions appeared in 1933 and 1938. Angell was championed by prominent British political leaders; the Garton Foundation was established to promote his ideas, and a series of workshops, lectures, and summer institutes were funded to expose scholars and thinkers to these promising concepts. The non-Anglo-Saxon world remained distinctly unimpressed: in France and Germany he gained few followers. In the United States, however, Angell became tremendously popular. Having moved to the United States when the First World War broke out, he is said to have influenced Woodrow Wilson's thinking and was a strong supporter of the League of Nations, receiving the Nobel Peace Prize in the year Hitler took power in Germany.

The catastrophe of World War I did not dent this optimism; it affirmed it. American tycoons like Andrew Carnegie and Henry Ford were more sanguine than ever. Just a year into the war, in November 1915, Carnegie declared, "The world grows better, and we are soon to see blessed peace restored and a world court established."[3] A month later, Henry Ford chartered a "peace ship" and, along with several pacifists, sailed to Europe "to crush militarism and get the boys out of the trenches. Our object is to stop war for all times."[4]

The war's grim end did nothing to sap America's cheerfulness. It is inconceivable, the *New York Times* editorialized on December 23, 1918, "that men of right mind and good conscience are going to oppose a League of Nations." Indeed, the horror of the past war made the establishment of permanent peace *more* likely, not less.

> Where five years ago there were a few seekers after righteousness, a few groups of men of foresight and forethought, lovers of their fellow-men, who dreamed and prophesied, there are now millions, literally hundreds of millions, who in the black shadow and blight and sorrow of this great war deeply feel and are resolved that this agony shall not be gone through again.

This was also Woodrow Wilson's view. The victory of the Allies in the war to make the world safe for democracy guaranteed the creation of a permanently peaceful and democratic world. For Wilson, this wasn't just pie-in-the-sky idealism. It was practical. It was necessary.

> What men once considered theoretical and idealistic turns out to be practical and necessary. We stand at the opening of a new age in which a new statesmanship will, I am confident, lift mankind to new levels of endeavor and achievement.

Subsequent presidential administrations would repeat the argument that the nation's values and interests had merged, making the idealistic course the only practical one. The Truman administration laid out the backbone of American Cold War strategy in NSC-68, a document particularly notable for its invocation of American ideals because it was highly classified: "In a shrinking world, which now faces the threat of atomic warfare, it is not an adequate objective merely to seek to check the Kremlin design, for the absence of order among nations is becoming less and less tolerable. This fact imposes on us, in our own interests, the responsibility of world leadership. It demands that we make the attempt, and accept the risks inherent in it, to bring about order and justice by means consistent with the principles of freedom and democracy." This theme reappeared in President Bush's second inaugural address: "America's vital interests and deep beliefs are now one. . . . Advancing these ideals is the mission that created our nation. It is the honorable achievement of our fathers. Now it is the urgent requirement of our nation's security, and the calling of our time."

Historical necessity was the wind in the sails of the new age of peace. After describing the past war as a contest between a system of oppression and one of freedom, Wilson told an audience in Paris:

> The triumph of freedom in this war means that spirits of that sort now dominate the world. There is a great wind of moral force moving through the world, and every man who opposes himself to that wind will go down in disgrace.

Wilson's success after World War I was no greater than that of Norman Angell and the Garton Foundation before it; Tennyson's "Parliament of man" obstinately refused to descend from the heavens. World War I was succeeded, not by a universal reign of peace, but by a rash of wars, murders, and ethnic cleansings. As the Bolsheviks crushed their opponents and proclaimed the Soviet Union, a bloody and cruel civil war across the old Russian Empire plunged millions into starvation and misery. The division of the German, Austro-Hungarian, and Ottoman empires across central and eastern Europe touched off more waves of fighting and refugees. A brutal war between Turks struggling to create a new nation from the Ottoman ruins and Greeks hoping to annex parts of what is now Turkey with large Greek populations led to hundreds of thousands of refugees and vicious fighting. "Free companies" formed out of the remnants of the disintegrating imperial German forces fought Communists, socialists, and non-German ethnic groups in the chaotic former eastern territories of the empire. Communist uprisings in Germany, Hungary, and elsewhere led to bloodshed, both from the Communists seizing power and from the forces that repressed them. In Italy, Mussolini's Fascist movement came to power; hopeful democratic experiments in much of eastern Europe fell to dictatorships of one kind or another. The United States Senate rejected the League of Nations; France engaged in a sordid politics of revenge against Germany; Germany's nascent democracy tottered as its economy collapsed.

Yet just a few years later, optimism revived and the "end of history" once more seemed to be at hand. As the 1920s rolled on, Tennyson's vision once again began to hover. The League might not be working as hoped, but the world was looking brighter. The 1920s were a relatively liberal era in Japan. In the Soviet Union, the rigors of war communism gave way to both a political and economic thaw under the New Economic Policy. Were the Soviets having a Thermidor? After the Dawes and Young plans restabilized European financial markets, prosperity returned to much of the war-torn continent. Support for the pro-democracy parties in Weimar Germany rose; Hitler looked increasingly like yesterday's man. From an outsider's perspective, it appeared that voting rights expanded and the middle class grew in Latin America.[5]

It was into this atmosphere that a group of prominent Americans made a revolutionary proposal that the nations of the earth agree to declare that war was illegal. The leading intellectual John Dewey and leading Protestant clergymen like John Haynes Holmes and *Christian Century* editor Charles Clayton Morrison supported the efforts of the American Committee for the Outlawry of War. These culminated in the famous Kellogg-Briand Pact declaring war illegal. Including India, eight of the original eleven to sign the treaty were English-speaking countries; the notoriously treaty-shy United States Senate ratified the treaty by a vote of 85 to 1.

Ultimately more than sixty-two nations solemnly signed it; the treaty is still in force. Technically speaking, war has been illegal for almost eighty years. This is, of course, a tremendous relief to all concerned.

Yet even this magnificent accomplishment failed to usher in the vision of Locksley Hall. Hitler took power in Germany; Japan turned from its brief experiment with liberalism to invade China; Mussolini defied the League of Nations to invade Ethiopia; the Soviet Thermidor of the New Economic Program mutated into the mass starvation and terror purges of the Stalinist era. A sadder but wiser Norman Angell wasn't fooled this time. He called, vainly, for the League of Nations to resist fascist aggression, and was one of a group of English dignitaries who welcomed exiled Ethiopian emperor Haile Selassie to London when the weak-kneed British government refused. As war clouds deepened, Angell sided with Winston Churchill in the Chamberlain years. War was no longer obsolete or fruitless; it was more terrible than ever, but also more necessary.

The end of history vanished during World War II, but as the Allied victory approached, the usual optimism began to reappear. Surely this time humanity had learned its lesson. Surely, now, we had learned that war was ruinous, costly, and unconscionably destructive. Surely Tennyson's "Parliament of man" would now be set up, and his "Federation of the world" would at last be established.

This time the planners of the Parliament of man went to San Francisco, where they wrote the charter of the United Nations. The American establishment, Republican and Democratic, sang hosannas to the promise of the institution that would guide the world into the long-awaited bright new age. President Truman mounted the podium at the opening session of the San Francisco conference and declared, "The world has experienced a revival of the old faith in the everlasting moral force of justice." California governor Earl Warren welcomed the council's delegates, assuring them, "You are meeting in a state where the people have unshakable faith in the great purposes that have inspired your gathering. We look upon your presence as a great and necessary step toward world peace. It is our daily prayer that the bonds of understanding forged here will serve to benefit all humanity for generations to come." The Layman's Movement called for national days of prayer as the charter was completed: "the largest mass outpouring in the history of the soul of man in search of God's help," as the Christian activist Wallace C. Steers called it. Joining the prayer movement were the American Legion, the Congress of Industrial Organizations, the National Association of Manufacturers, and the Mutual Broadcasting Company.

The chairman of the Senate Foreign Relations Committee, Tom Connally of Texas, called the charter "the greatest document of its kind that has ever been formulated." The senior Republican on the House Foreign Affairs Committee, Sol Bloom, called it "the most hopeful and important document in the history of world statesmanship." He went on: it was "the greatest and most hopeful public event in history." "The inexorable tides of destiny," he continued, were taking the world "towards a golden age of freedom, justice, peace, and social well-being." Future U.S. vice president Alben Barkley compared the U.N. charter to the Magna Carta, the Declaration of Independence, the Constitution, the Gettysburg Address, and Lincoln's Second Inaugural Address.

These hopes were disappointed when instead of a golden age of peace and prosperity, the world entered the Cold War under the shadow of nuclear annihilation. But when the Cold War ended, the same old notes were heard once again.

Francis Fukuyama, wiser than most, asked whether history was over, but carefully hedged the possibility that it might still have some nasty tricks up its sleeve. Others were much quicker to embrace the idea that with the collapse of the last Evil Empire, a golden age could finally begin. Democrats and Republicans talked about the "peace dividend," the money taxpayers would save as the U.S. was able to shrink the huge defense establishment constructed during the Cold War.

There was more. Now that socialism had failed, the whole world would grasp that free markets led to prosperity and that democracy made free markets work best. During the administrations of the first George Bush and Bill

Clinton, U.S. officials went around the world preaching the gospel of free markets, free trade, and free society. The secret was known; the Communist enemies of peace were defeated; all that we now needed to do was apply a few simple lessons and all would be well.

History has a nasty sense of humor. On September 11, 1990, eleven years to the day before the attack on the World Trade Center, President George Herbert Walker Bush addressed a joint session of Congress. As soon as Kuwait was liberated from the grip of Saddam Hussein, the new world could begin. The new era would be one in which

> [t]he nations of the world, East and West, North and South, can prosper and live in harmony. A hundred generations have searched for this elusive path to peace, while a thousand wars raged across the span of human endeavor. Today that new world is struggling to be born, a world quite different from the one we've known. A world where the rule of law supplants the rule of the jungle. A world in which nations recognize the shared responsibility for freedom and justice . . .

No doubt when and if the last fanatic terrorist in the Middle East lays down the last bomb, we shall hear once again that war is a thing of the past, and that the parliament of man is about to assemble and inaugurate the Federation of the world.

But pending that happy time, it is worth looking at one hundred fifty years of peaceable kingdoms that never quite seem to arrive. We win, we think we see the end of history, we're wrong. This, too, begins to look a little like a pattern.

And so this book addresses six key questions about the world we live in.

What is the distinctive political and cultural agenda that the Anglo-Americans bring to world politics?

Why did the Anglo-Americans prevail in the military, economic, and political contests to shape the emerging world order?

How were the Anglo-Americans able to put together the economic and military resources that enabled them to defeat their enemies and build a global order?

Why have the Anglo-Americans so frequently believed that history is ending—that their power is bringing about a peaceful world?

Why have they been wrong every time?

Finally, what does Anglo-American power mean for the world? How long is it likely to last, and what does three hundred years of Anglo-American power mean for the larger sweep of world history?

The Walrus and the Carpenter

The book begins with the first question and a look at the clash of civilizations that dominates the history of the modern world: the clash between the English-speaking powers of the United Kingdom and the United States and the various enemy nations since the seventeenth century who have fought against them to shape the world. The study of British history and culture has almost vanished from American schools today; as a result, many Americans are unaware of just how deep the similarities between the two countries go. Foreigners have a clearer idea about this, and often lump us together as the "Anglo-Saxon powers." This isn't about ethnicity; the term "Anglo-Saxon" today is used to describe a cultural heritage that continues to influence Britain and the United States. For more than three hundred years, the English and then the Americans have seen their wars against countries like France, Germany, Japan, and Russia as battles between good and evil, between freedom and slavery. During that same time, the enemies of the Anglo-Saxon powers have seen the Anglo-Saxons as cold, cruel, greedy, and hypocritical. The Anglo-Saxon powers fight under the banner of liberal capitalism; their enemies oppose it. The first section of the book reviews three hundred years of clashing civilizations, explores the common Anglo-Saxon culture of the United States and Britain, and examines the rise of an "anti-Anglophone" ideology among the various forces that have opposed the English-speaking powers from the time of Louis XIV to that of Osama bin Laden.

The Dread and Envy of Them All

It is unpardonably vulgar to say so, but in three hundred years of warfare, the English-speaking powers keep winning. To put this another way, either the British or the Americans or both have been on the winning side of every major war in which they have participated since the late seventeenth century. That history of victory shapes the world we live in; the second section of the book looks at the military, diplomatic, and economic strategies that led first Britain and then the United States to world power. It also outlines ways that Anglo-American civilization has shaped the world we live in. The Anglo-Saxon powers did not just win wars. They changed the way the world lives, thinks, and organizes itself as much as any of the great civilizations of the past, and the second section of this book describes some of the key features of the world of the Wasps.

Anglo-Saxon Attitudes

The third section moves to the third of the six questions: how were the Anglo-Americans able to put together the economic and military resources that enabled them to defeat their enemies and build a global order?

The decisive factor in the success of the English-speaking world, I argue, is that both the British and the Americans came from a culture that was uniquely well positioned to develop and harness the titanic forces of capitalism as these emerged on the world scene. This does not just mean that the British and the Americans were more willing and able to tolerate the stress, uncertainty, and inequality associated with relatively free-market forms of capitalism than were other countries in Europe and around the world— although that is true. It also means that the Anglo-Americans have been consistently among the best performers at creating a favorable institutional and social climate in which capitalism can grow rapidly. Because Anglo-American society has been so favorable to the development of capitalist enterprise and technology, the great English-speaking countries have consistently been at the forefront of global technological development. They have had the deep and flexible financial markets that provide greater prosperity in peace and allow government to tap the wealth of the community for greater effectiveness in war; the great business enterprises that take shape in these dynamic and cutting-edge economies enjoy tremendous advantages when they venture out into global markets to compete against often less technologically advanced, well-financed, and managerially sophisticated rivals based in other countries.

The book finds the roots of this aptitude for capitalism in the way that the British Reformation created a pluralistic society that was at once unusually tolerant, unusually open to new ideas, and unusually pious. In most of the world the traditional values of religion are seen as deeply opposed to the utilitarian goals of capitalism. The English-speaking world—contrary to the intentions of almost all of the leading actors of the period—reached a new kind of religious equilibrium in which capitalism and social change came to be accepted as good things. In much of the world even today, people believe that they remain most true to their religious and cultural roots by rejecting change. Since the seventeenth century, the English-speaking world or at least significant chunks of it have believed that embracing and even furthering and accelerating change—economic change, social change, cultural change, political change—fulfills their religious destiny.

What Hath God Wrought?

Building on these ideas, the fourth section looks at how the Anglo-American world synthesized its religious beliefs with its historical experience to build an ideology that has shaped what is still the dominant paradigm in the English-speaking world, the deeply rooted vision of the way the world works that lies behind the physics of Sir Isaac Newton, the political economy of Adam Smith, the constitutional theories of Thomas Jefferson and James Madison, and the biological theories of Charles Darwin. While many of these thinkers were not particularly or conventionally religious, their belief that order arises spontaneously, "as if by the workings of an invisible hand," from the free play of natural forces is a way of restating some of the most powerful spiritual convictions of the English-speaking world. The idea that the world is built (or guided by God) in such a way that unrestricted free play creates an ordered and higher form of society is found in virtually all fields and at virtually all levels of the Anglo-Saxon world. It makes people both individualistic and optimistic, and it climaxes in what many have called the "whig narrative"—a theory of history that sees the slow and gradual march of progress in a free society as the dominant force not only in Anglo-American history but in the wider world as well.

The fourth section of the book explores the implications of the golden meme for Anglo-American history and politics, and shows how the whig narrative creates the expectation of progress and the imminent sense of a triumphant end of history that is always, somehow, just around the corner.

The Lessons of History

The fifth and final section of the book addresses the final two questions: why Anglo-Saxon optimism has so often been wrong, and what three centuries of Anglo-Saxon success means for world history.

The section focuses first on the difference between the way that Americans think about their system and the way that system actually works in the world. That is, Americans think of liberal capitalist democracy as a way to promote social peace and stability. It does these things, but it also produces a great and still proceeding acceleration in the pace of social, economic, and technological change—not only for Americans, but for everyone in the world.

The acceleration of human technology and the increasing pace of historical and social change point to a much livelier future than the peaceful and prosperous stability that the whig narrative predicts. For one thing, the dynamism and change that Anglo-American and other advancing societies produce get quickly exported to other societies that do not welcome change and perhaps cannot cope with it. For another, the rise in American power—which Americans tend to think is self-evidently good not only for Americans but for everyone in the world—doesn't always look so good to those whose interests and ambitions are obstructed by it.

The section looks at the lessons that the "long view" of Anglo-American history may hold for American policy makers today. For the foreseeable future the United States is unlikely to lose its unique position in the global political system, but it is also unlikely to remain what some analysts have called a "unipolar" power. The section also looks at the challenge posed by radical Middle Eastern terrorists and compares that challenge with similar movements in the last two hundred years.

After reviewing some of the lessons that three hundred years of Anglo-American history hold for us today, the book ends by arguing that the world may indeed be heading toward an "end of history"—but the end we are approaching looks a lot more dramatic than the peaceful and restful paradise that the whig narrative has traditionally envisioned. Anglo-American civilization isn't leading humanity out of turbulence and chaos. Instead, powered by the belief that the way forward is the path of transcendence, America is leading the world in an accelerating rush toward a world very different from anything we have known or, perhaps, can imagine.

Conclusion

God and Gold, like my book *Special Providence: American Foreign Policy and How It Changed the World,* is a book about history, but it is not a history book. It is a book that reflects on history and tries to find meaningful patterns in the flow of events, but it does not try to present an authoritative and complete account of the historical events with which it deals. It is a book that touches on many subjects and doesn't pretend to offer the last word on any of them. A writer like myself who tries to write about subjects that involve many different disciplines suffers under the necessity of offending those to whom he is indebted. Without the work of specialists and scholars who do groundbreaking, in-depth research in many different subjects, a book like this would be impossible. Yet many of those specialists and scholars will feel that a general work like this one does not do full justice to the subtlety and sophistication of their work. They are right, and I apologize. From time to time when I feel particularly guilty about the way *God and Gold* skips over a rich and complex historical subject, I suggest other books that treat the subject in more depth, but the truth is that no single book can ever do full justice to the vast and rich scholarly literature in all the fields that need to be considered for a book of this kind.

Yet as I researched the background for this book, I was a little frustrated. There are a great many excellent books that take on various aspects of the Anglo-American ascendancy, but I have not found any recent books that address the whole subject in a serious way. There are books on the British empire; there are books on American foreign policy, but the topic of the common history of the two peoples in world affairs has not received the attention it deserves. In some ways, the best book on the subject remains Winston Churchill's *A History of the English Speaking Peoples,* published in 1956, but for all its many virtues that book is too old, too Anglo-centric, and too much influenced by the author's political agenda to meet the needs of a twenty-first-century public. Perhaps the next great history of the English-speaking peoples will be written by an Indian or a South African; it is work that needs to be done.

Part One

The Walrus and the Carpenter

One • With God on Our Side

On September 17, 1656, Oliver Cromwell, the Lord Protector, addressed the English Parliament to lay out his foreign policy, and he began by asking the most basic political questions: Who are our enemies, and why do they hate us?

There was, he then asserted, an axis of evil abroad in the world. England's enemies, he said, "are all the wicked men of the world, whether abroad or at home . . ."[1]

And, in the language of the seventeenth century, he said that they hate us because they hate God and all that is good. They hate us "from that very enmity that is in them against whatsoever should serve the glory of God and the interest of his people; which they see to be more eminently, yea most eminently patronized and professed in this nation—we will speak it not with vanity—above all the nations in the world."[2]

Cromwell went on to spell out for the Roundheads, as the partisans of Parliament had been known in the English Civil War, that the axis of evil had a leader: a great power which had put itself in the service of evil.

"Truly," said Cromwell, "your great enemy is the Spaniard . . . through that enmity that is in him against all that is of God that is in you." That enmity came from the origin of the Catholic religion in the primordial revolt against God, embodied by the serpent in the Garden of Eden. "I will put an enmity between thy seed and her seed," Cromwell said, citing God's curse on the serpent and the enmity He would fix between the Children of Darkness and the Children of Light.[3]

Cromwell's approach to world politics would resonate more than three hundred years later and three thousand miles away, when on March 8, 1983, U.S. president Ronald Reagan addressed the annual convention of the National Association of Evangelicals in Orlando, Florida. The Soviet

Union, he said, is "the focus of evil in the modern world."[4] And America was engaged in a test of faith against an adversary that had set itself against God. Citing Whittaker Chambers, the Communist-turned-informer, Reagan asserted that Marxism-Leninism is "the second oldest religious faith," first proclaimed by the serpent in the Garden of Eden when he tempted Adam and Eve to disobey God.[5] And like Cromwell, Reagan saw history as a struggle between spiritual forces. "I've always maintained," the president told the preachers, "that the struggle now going on for the world will never be decided by bombs or rockets, by armies or military might."[6]

Since the enmity between the Free World and the Empire of Evil was existential—the battle between the Children of Light and the Children of Darkness—it was also eternal, just like Cromwell's call for unrelenting war with Spain. One cannot make a covenant with the Father of Lies.

Catholic teaching, Cromwell warned Parliament, held that the pope has the power to forgive all sins. If Catholic princes made a peace treaty with England, the pope could absolve them from the sin of breaking their oaths whenever they pleased. As Cromwell summarized the matter, "The plain truth of it is, make any peace with any State that is Popish and subjected to the determination of Rome and the Pope himself, you are bound and they are loose . . . That Peace is but to be kept for so long as the Pope saith Amen to it."[7]

Reagan felt just the same way about Communists: they had a philosophical stance that expressly made it impossible to assume their good faith. The United States could not deal openly and honestly with the Communists, Reagan said, because "the Soviet leaders have openly and publicly declared that the only morality they recognize is that which will further their cause."[8] Their materialistic philosophy placed no absolute value on right action or truth and could absolve them of any crime because the end justified the means.

The similarities between the Cromwellian and the Reaganite arguments run deeper. Both leaders called their countrymen to a consensus foreign policy that would unify the nation. The arch-Republican Reagan offended some of his Democratic listeners by claiming to stand in the tradition of Democrat Harry Truman. Bipartisanship was an even more difficult concept for Cromwell's audience than for modern Americans. The "bipartisan foreign policy" of the Cold War was a staple of American political rhetoric in the last generation. In Cromwell's England, the concept of legitimate political parties was still struggling to be born; dissent and disloyalty were still seen as one and the same. Cromwell, who had recently led the parliamentary forces to triumph in a civil war that was concluded by the execution of the king, nevertheless wanted to make the point that all true Englishmen, royalist and republican, agreed on the evils of the Catholic threat. Queen Elizabeth, Cromwell pointed out, had supported the anti-Spanish policy, and in a phrase that must have shaken some of the rounder heads in the room, he praised the "famous memory" of the queen and—just as Reagan did with Truman—asserted a claim to stand in her tradition.

Evil empires throughout history have always trampled on human rights. American presidents during the Cold War routinely denounced Soviet mistreatment of dissidents and religious believers. Here again they were merely following in the footsteps of the Lord Protector. Cromwell's speech of 1656 chronicled Spanish atrocities: he referred to a messenger of the Long Parliament whom the Spanish cruelly murdered and noted that when the English ambassadors "asked satisfaction for the blood of your poor people unjustly shed in the West Indies, and for the wrongs done elsewhere, when they ask liberty of conscience for your people who traded thither,—satisfaction in none of these things would be given, but was denied."[9]

All we ask, Cromwell told Parliament, is liberty. Only that.

Describing the recent, failed negotiations with Philip IV, king of Spain, Cromwell wanted to show how reasonable, how moderate, the English demands had been. "We desired such a liberty as they [visiting English merchants in Spanish territory] might keep Bibles in their pockets, to exercise their liberty of religion to themselves and not be under restraint. But there is not liberty of conscience to be had . . ."[10]

Don Felipe, tear down that wall!

If empires of evil have much in common across the centuries, so too do alliances for good. America and its Cold War allies, like the Protestant allies of Cromwell's England, were fighting for more than their own—perish the thought—selfish interests. Their fight is the fight for good, right, and human rights everywhere.

"All the honest interests," said Cromwell, "yea, all the interests of the Protestants in Germany, Denmark, Helvetia, the Cantons, and all the interests in Christendom are the same as yours. If you succeed well and act well, and be convinced what is God's interest and but prosecute it, you will find that you act for a very great many people that are God's own."[11]

"America," Reagan told the evangelicals, "has kept alight the torch of freedom, but not just for ourselves but for millions of others around the world."[12]

Cromwell and Reagan faced other problems in common. There was more continuity to the Cold War than to England's long and intermittent contest with Spain, but both rivalries dragged on inconclusively for decades, sometimes in the foreground, sometimes on the back burner, with intervals of détente, reversals of alliance, and many changes in fortune. After the failure of the Armada in 1588, Spain could not attack England at home. English forces were never strong enough to wage sustained warfare on the Spanish mainland. Instead, the intermittent conflict moved indecisively through what we would now call the third world—the scattered colonial dependencies of the two powers and over the trade routes and oceans of the world. English hawks, often Puritans and merchants, wanted an aggressive anti-Spanish policy that would take on the pope while opening markets; moderates (often country squires uninterested in costly foreign ventures) promoted détente.

There was another problem—a domestic one. "And truly he [the Spaniard] hath an interest in your bowels," Cromwell told his audience. "He hath so. The Papists in England,—they have been accounted, ever since I was born, Spaniolised."[13] Ronald Reagan knew just what Cromwell meant, though with the changing fashions in metaphors he would have talked about a fifth column, rather than a Communist "interest in our bowels."

For almost a century, England had wrestled with the problem of how to treat its Catholic minority. Existing Penal Laws against Catholics had been tightened considerably after Pope Pius V excommunicated Elizabeth I in 1570 and declared her an illegitimate queen whom no Christian was bound to obey. The question for Elizabeth was how to tell the difference between Catholics loyal to the throne, or at least willing to live peacefully under it, and those actively engaged in plotting to murder the queen and plunge the country into civil war. The threat of invasion from Spain grew in the 1580s. Pressure on Catholics increased; it became illegal for a Catholic priest to set foot in England, and for any English subject to house or help a priest in any way. The penalty was death. There were also hefty fines for those who refused to attend Protestant services. When the Armada sailed from Spain in 1588, the noose tightened again. Local officials were ordered to imprison Catholics deemed a threat to security; enforcement of the laws relaxed once the threat of invasion had passed.[14]

Through the rest of Elizabeth's reign, the legal situation of Catholics would deteriorate or improve as the war with Spain grew more or less dangerous. Then an unprecedented attempted act of terrorism in 1605 led to a new and darker period for English Catholics in the reign of her successor.

On November 5, 1605, an extremist Catholic group put barrels of gunpowder beneath the Parliament building in London with plans to detonate the bomb when the Lords, Commons, and king were all gathered together. Although only a handful of Catholics were directly involved, and although the large majority of English Catholics probably opposed the so-called Gunpowder Plot, the old laws were brought back into force and new laws were quickly passed against a minority that was now perceived as more dangerous than ever. Anyone who refused to take an oath of allegiance to James I, which was worded in a way that was difficult if not impossible for conscientious Catholics to take, could be deprived of all landed property and imprisoned for life.

Up until the outbreak of the English Civil War in 1642 the situation of Catholics gradually improved; there was what would have been called a thaw in the cold war, and in the absence of security threats the enforcement of the laws against Catholics was relaxed. In 1632 an English Catholic was able to publish a group of sonnets in honor of the Virgin Mary; the works of at least one French Jesuit were translated into English and published at Oxford.[15]

The politics of religion grew increasingly fraught in England as the civil war approached. During the war, Catholics largely supported the Royalist side; Charles I, now king, was married to the Catholic French princess Henrietta Maria, and the increased tolerance of the Catholic minority during the 1630s was due to royal, not parliamentary, influence. The victorious Puritans were quick to retaliate; Catholics were punished for being both royalists and heretics. At least sixteen hundred had their homes and land confiscated.[16]

When Cromwell seized power in 1653, he relaxed enforcement of the anti-Catholic laws. After years of civil strife, England needed peace and stability; Cromwell hoped that compromise and toleration would stabilize the realm. The war with Spain changed that, as national-security-conscious conservative Protestants in Parliament demanded tough action against the minority.

About a month after Cromwell's evil-empire speech, a new bill was introduced. Anyone suspected of being a papist was to be summoned before a court to swear an oath of abjuration. This oath was much tougher than the one introduced after the Gunpowder Plot. No honest Catholic could possibly swear to it:

> I, [NAME], abhor, detest, and abjure the authority of the Pope, as well in regard of the Church in general, as in regard of myself in particular. I condemn and anathematize the tenet that any reward is due to good works. I firmly believe and avow that no reverence is due to the Virgin Mary, or to any other saint in heaven; and that no petition or adoration can be addressed to them without idolatry. I assert that no worship or reverence is due to the sacrament of the Lord's Supper,

or to the elements of bread and wine after consecration, by whomsoever that consecration may be made. I believe there is no purgatory, but that it is a popish invention; so is also the tenet that the Pope can grant indulgences. I also firmly believe that neither the Pope, nor any other priest can remit sins, as the papists rave.[17]

Those who refused to swear to this oath immediately lost two-thirds of all their goods; and a second refusal to swear would lead to the confiscation of two-thirds of their remaining goods, and so on. In the past, Catholics had been able to avoid the penalties by settling their estates on their wives. No more: the loopholes were nailed shut.

The law was controversial, even at the time. Lambert Godfrey, a lawyer representing the county of Kent in Parliament, saw the law as an abomination: "I know no difference between it and the Inquisition, only one racks and tortures the purse, the other the person."[18] Lambert was eloquent, but the bill passed—with only forty-three votes dissenting. It proved very useful in separating Irish Catholics from their homes.

CROMWELL HAD ANOTHER PROBLEM that would be echoed during the Cold War. The grand battle against papistry occasionally forced him into strange alliances, even into alliances with papists. Truman found himself aiding Marshal Tito, the Yugoslav Communist leader. In the case of both Nixon and Reagan, opposition to Communist Russia led to improved relations with Communist China; Cromwell found himself trying to explain why Catholic France was a worthy ally against Catholic Spain.

Once again similar problems found similar answers. As Truman and his successors noted that Yugoslav Communists were independent of Moscow, Cromwell claimed that France was in fact independent of the papacy and so able to conclude treaties on its own. Cromwell also argued that his secret correspondence with France's Cardinal Mazarin would result in improved treatment of Protestant dissidents in that country; the prospect of improved human rights in China was constantly held out by uncomfortable American presidents justifying the twists and turns of the Cold War. To make Cromwell's position even more difficult, Mazarin pointed out that his ability to improve the treatment of Protestants in France might well depend on Cromwell's success at making life more tolerable for Catholics in England.

Anyone trying to understand English policy under Oliver Cromwell would have many of the same problems that face historians attempting to understand American policy during the Cold War. Cromwell attacked the

Catholics in Ireland and their Spanish allies for murdering an estimated twenty thousand Protestants in Ireland between 1649 and 1652, but his own forces in Ireland committed brutal crimes that have not lost their power to shock.[19] Similar controversy arose during the Cold War, when the United States supported dictatorships that were sometimes as murderous as the Communist regimes it opposed. Was Cromwell "sincere" in his opposition to Spanish Catholicism, or was the ideological element of his foreign policy a devious ploy to build public support for an aggressive, expansionary pursuit of English national interests? When Cromwell decided to help the Protestant Dutch against the Spanish, he did so in alliance with the Catholic king of France—and only after securing the Channel port of Dunkirk as payment for his services. Was he a religious zealot fighting God's wars or a shrewd statesman advancing England's interests?

Cromwell probably would have said that the two elements of his policy—the fight for God's religion and the fight for English national interests—fit together, and that this in itself was a sign of God's providence. By doing good and fighting papists, England would do well and earn riches. What was good for God was good for the commonwealth, and vice versa. This comfortable synthesis presumably won the uncritical support of many English people at the time.

Whatever Cromwell's private views, his policy undoubtedly attracted the support of people who did not care much about his religious convictions. Many of the English soldiers in Ireland were likely more interested in the redistribution of Irish farmlands than in theological controversies. No doubt some of their commanders and backers were consciously and cynically using the ideological climate of the time to enrich themselves through what would normally be criminal methods. There were ship captains and crews who welcomed the opportunities to prey on Spanish commerce more than they welcomed the prospect of advancing the Protestant cause. There were, on the other hand, many hard-nosed warriors for the faith who held material gains in contempt, and these Calvinist counterparts of the John Birch Society's hard-liners sometimes shook their heads over Cromwell's willingness to compromise the heavenly fight against popery in return for some passing temporal advantage, just as the Birchers ranted against "accommodation" of anything Communist.

"Realism" and "idealism" were woven together in Cromwell's England; only God Himself could disentangle the dark- and light-colored threads that ran through the history of the period. England's friends were more likely to attribute her policy to her high moral convictions; her enemies were more likely to credit her national interests. Both interpretations can find support in the record of what Cromwell said and of what England did in the long fight against Spain's evil empire.

Spain was not the last evil empire to confront the English-speaking world. Satan was fortunately vanquished in the land of Cervantes, but no sooner was he driven from the Escorial than he took up residence in the then rising halls of Versailles. From 1689, when the British called William of Orange to the throne to replace the overthrown James II—a Catholic—England found itself locked in a series of wars against France as long and as dangerous as the earlier struggle with Spain. The English writer Joseph Addison made the case against France in an essay published in 1707 that updated Cromwell's arguments for a more secular time.

"The French are certainly the most implacable and the most dangerous enemies of the British nation," he wrote. "Their form of government, their religion, their jealousy of British power, as well as their prosecutions of commerce, and pursuits of universal monarchy, will fix them for ever in their animosities and aversions towards us, and make them catch at all opportunities of subverting our constitution, destroying our religion, ruining our trade, and sinking the figure which we make among the nations of Europe."[20]

They were, in other words, an evil empire determined on global conquest; they could not be trusted; they employed secret agents of subversion in Britain itself; and they had far-reaching plans to undermine Britain's prosperity and prestige.

But England's cause was of course greater than her own narrow interests. Addressing liberty as a goddess, Addison echoed Cromwell's cry that liberty was all the English sought:

> *Thee, goddess, thee, Britannia's Isle adores:*
> *How has she oft exhausted all her stores,*
> *How oft in fields of death thy presence sought,*
> *Nor thinks the mighty prize too dearly bought! . . .*[21]

More than that, for Addison as for Cromwell, England's cause was the cause of many beyond her boundaries.

> *'Tis Britain's care to watch o'er Europe's fate,*
> *And hold in balance each contending state,*
> *To threaten bold presumptuous kings with war,*
> *And answer her afflicted neighbours' pray'r.*[22]

The war against the Sun King and his evil allies and successors, like the war against Spain, dragged on for decades. It was sometimes hot and sometimes cold; and much of it was fought out in the third world, including battles between American colonists and the Indian allies of France.

Once again, to defend freedom it became, or at least seemed, necessary to curtail it. The position of Catholics in England had, despite some occasional rough moments, gradually improved once Cromwell was replaced by the secretly Catholic Charles II and his openly Catholic brother, James II. Laws against Catholics still existed, but the kings used their pardoning and dispensing powers to enable Catholics to participate more freely in public life than at any time since the first Penal Laws had been passed under Elizabeth I.

That changed after James II fled to France. Louis XIV received him with royal honors, and promised that French forces would help restore him to the throne of his fathers. An invasion fleet took James to Ireland, where the largely Catholic population rose to support him.

The Jacobite war (partisans of James were known as Jacobites) in Ireland soon came to an inglorious end. "Madam, your countrymen ran from the battle," the defeated James announced to an Irish supporter as he hastily returned from the failed campaign. "Sir," she replied, "you seem to have won the race." Neither the threat from France nor the threat of new Jacobite risings ended with James's defeat, however.

Although the pope, in his capacity as the ruler of the Papal States in Italy, was a military ally of William III in the wars against France, and although news of James II's defeat at the Battle of the Boyne was celebrated at the Vatican, Catholics were regarded as nearly universally loyal to the old king; once again they were driven from public life and subjected to new pressures and fines. In 1715 a Jacobite rebellion occupied much of Scotland; alarmed Protestants saw it as a Catholic crusade. The old Penal Laws were dusted off, the oaths taken out of the libraries, and under long-prepared emergency plans, Catholics and suspected Catholics were presented with oaths swearing allegiance to the Protestant George I, the present king, and abjuring the claims of the pope. The consequences of refusal were severe; to start with, Catholics' movements were restricted, their horses and arms were to be confiscated, and anyone suspected of "disaffection" was to be preventively detained.[23]

When war with the French broke out again in the 1740s, fear that the Catholic minority within would side with the Catholic enemy outside led to new restrictions and persecution. Anti-Catholic mobs stormed through the

streets, burning effigies of the pope and the grandson of James II, known as
the Young Pretender, and sometimes attacking suspected Catholics. Once
again the magistrates went on their rounds to Catholics and suspected
Catholics, oaths in hand. Once again, horses and arms were taken from
those who refused to swear; other penalties loomed.

The one city in the British Empire where the Catholic mass could be
openly celebrated at this time was the Quaker metropolis of Philadelphia.
Everywhere else the Penal Laws were enforced, lest the Catholic fifth column link up with the French.

The evil empire of the absolute kings of France was finally defeated in
1763. Satan turned his coat but did not change his house, and by 1791 he
could be found in command of the conquering troops of the French Revolution. Finding Catholicism no longer adequate to his purposes, Satan threw it
overboard and embraced the secular philosophy of revolutionary France.
The evil empire had once been conservative and Catholic; during the French
Revolution it became secular and modern. Under Napoleon it shifted,
briefly, from atheism back to Catholicism—but all this twisting and turning
did Satan no good. British observers saw the same horrifying spectacle
that Cromwell had once denounced: an evil empire at war with all that
was right.

As the great Irish statesmen Edmund Burke and the younger William Pitt
so sagely observed, the evil empire was guilty of the same familiar crimes:
violations of human rights, a program for universal monarchy, plotting subversion in Britain, and a perfidious faithlessness that made negotiations dangerous and peace impossible.

On February 1, 1793, Pitt—who had, at twenty-three, become the
youngest person in the history of Britain to become prime minister—
warned Parliament about the danger of Jacobin France:

> They take every opportunity to destroy every institution that is most sacred and
> most valuable in every nation where their armies have made their appearance;
> and under the name of liberty, they have resolved to make every country in sub-
> stance, if not in form, a province dependent upon themselves, through the des-
> potism of Jacobin societies . . . France has trampled under foot all laws, human
> and divine. She has at last avowed the most insatiable ambition, and greatest
> contempt for the law of nations, which all independent states have hitherto pro-
> fessed most religiously to observe; and unless she is stopped in her career, all
> Europe must soon learn their ideas of justice—law of nations—models of gov-
> ernment and principles of liberty from the mouth of the French cannon.[24]

The long wars began when Britain—shocked! *shocked!* by the execution of Louis XVI in 1793—began to organize coalition after coalition against France. One hundred years before, Cromwell's England had been the nation of regicides and its enemies the upholders of monarchical legitimacy; fortunately both God and the Devil rose to the occasion and made the necessary adjustments of principle.

During the generation of hostilities that followed, Britain and its allies fought wars with France and its allies in the third world; decades of hostilities were once again punctuated with intervals of détente.

It was not, of course, enough that this satanic ideology challenged Britain in foreign wars. There was a Jacobin interest in England's bowels: a nest of radicals, liberals, committees of correspondence, and others promoting dangerous ideas in the heart of Britain itself. Pitt's government rose to the challenge.

There were more trials for sedition in 1792 and 1793 than in the previous eighty-seven years; the poet and artist William Blake was tried (and acquitted) for sedition after telling a trespassing soldier, "Damn the King, and damn all his soldiers, they are all his slaves." In late 1792 the French revolutionary government offered its "fraternal assistance" to foreigners struggling to overthrow their own kings and tyrants; riots erupted across much of northern England and Scotland in response. When war broke out in 1793, British government action against internal enemies, real or perceived, stepped up.

In May 1793 the government seized the papers of the corresponding societies—networks of liberal and radical activists—and suspended habeas corpus. When this proved insufficient, the Treasonable Practices Act and the Seditious Meetings Act were introduced, setting severe limits on freedom of speech and assembly throughout the country. Under these so-called Gagging Acts, even legal assemblies could be ordered dispersed by magistrates; the penalty for resisting such an order was death. A lawyer was sentenced to eighteen months in prison for saying, "I am for equality . . . Why, no kings!" The publisher of Thomas Paine's *The Rights of Man* was sentenced to eighteen months in prison as well; Paine had to flee to France but was tried in absentia and convicted of seditious libel.

Meanwhile, the authorities set up what William Wickham called "a System of Preventative Police." The Alien Office kept close tabs on suspicious foreigners; the Post Office and Customs Service checked for subversive materials; local magistrates watched over the behavior of questionable organizations and individuals operating in their districts.

Not since the height of the anti-Catholic religious frenzy had Britain adopted such severe measures against dissent, and they were bitterly criticized by opposition members of Parliament, but, defenders of the new measures argued, not since the days of the Catholic threat had Britain been so endangered by an enemy within. The Gagging Acts passed by overwhelming majorities.

In this war, where Britain fought side by side with traditional Catholic monarchies against the new revolutionary danger, Catholicism did not look like so much of a threat. Almost immediately following the French defeat in 1763, the slow emancipation of British Catholics began. The Penal Laws stayed on the books but were seldom enforced; the Quebec Act of 1774 was the first parliamentary law providing tolerance for the Catholic religion since Bloody Mary died.

The liberalization for Catholics continued even as the crackdown on left-wingers gathered force. In 1791 and again in 1793 Parliament passed Catholic relief acts that removed all civil penalties for the practice of the Catholic religion. Further concessions were made to Irish Catholics in 1801. The radical French revolutionary Jacobin, not the Jacobite, was the enemy in the bowels of Pitt's Britain, and Pitt himself did everything he could to persuade a recalcitrant George III to give Catholics full equal rights with their Protestant fellow subjects.

Napoleon hated the Jacobins almost as much as Pitt did, but Napoleon's universal empire was as much a danger to Britain as the Jacobin Revolution. As such, Pitt was able to detect the common features in the two challenges, and as early as February 3, 1800, he was making the argument that Napoleon's regime could never be trusted or bargained with, as it exhibited "[a] perfidy, which nothing can bind, which no tie of treaty, no sense of the principles generally received among nations, no obligation, human or divine, can restrain."[25] Like the Spanish Hapsburgs and the French Bourbons before him, Napoleon sought to set up a universal monarchy, was the enemy of liberty and human freedom worldwide, and hated English values and culture: the fight against him was the fight of all mankind.

As it happened, it took the combined efforts of almost all mankind to defeat Napoleon once and for all, but at last Satan in the guise of Napoleon was banished to St. Helena, and the victors assembled to establish a new world order. At the Congress of Vienna in 1815 the British worked with the Catholic monarchs of Europe to establish a political order that would safeguard their thrones; the Hapsburgs and Bourbons were now pillars of the European order, and the British wanted them shored up.

For most of the next century, Satan gave Britain a rest. The British had a few anxious moments as the occasional French government cast covetous eyes on the old Austrian Netherlands, joined briefly to the Dutch Netherlands in 1815 and then, after 1831, independent as Belgium in the safe hands of Queen Victoria's uncle Leopold. Russia also seemed to flirt with the Evil One from time to time, now glancing toward Constantinople, now toward Britain's frontiers in north India.

Yet despite the occasional alarms, no new evil empire appeared until the closing years of the nineteenth century, when Kaiser Wilhelm II assumed the role once played by Philip II, Louis XIV, and Napoleon I. The die was cast in August 1914, when the kaiser's forces did something that had brought Britain into European wars ever since the reign of Good Queen Bess: they invaded the Low Countries, striking at Belgium.

The British prime minister at the time, Herbert Asquith, was never a spellbinding speaker, but his speech to Parliament on the declaration of war against Germany brought the old themes back:

> I do not believe any nation ever entered into a great controversy—and this is one of the greatest history will ever know—with a clearer conscience and a stronger conviction that it is fighting, not for aggression, not for the maintenance even of its own selfish interest, but that it is fighting in defense of principles the maintenance of which is vital to the civilization of the world.[26]

Asquith's chancellor of the exchequer, David Lloyd George, made a fuller case on September 19, 1914. Lloyd George began by quoting a speech of Kaiser Wilhelm to German forces leaving for the front. "Remember that the German people are the chosen of God," the Kaiser (allegedly) said.

> On me, on me as the German Emperor, the spirit of God has descended. I am His weapon, His sword, and His viceregent. Woe to the disobedient! Death to cowards and unbelievers!

Lloyd George knew what this meant. For some of the men around the Kaiser, at least, this was the call of a new and wicked religion. This, in Lloyd George's words, is what the Kaiser and his minions thought:

> Treaties. They entangle the feet of Germany in her advance. Cut them with the sword. Little nations. They hinder the advance of Germany. Trample them in the mire under the German heel . . . Britain. She is a constant menace to the predominancy of Germany in the world. Wrest the trident out of her hands!

Lloyd George could see where this was headed.

> More than that, the new philosophy of Germany is to destroy Christianity—
> sickly sentimentalism about sacrifice for others, poor pap for German
> mouths . . . Liberty goes, democracy vanishes, and unless Britain comes to the
> rescue, and her sons, it will be a dark day for humanity.[27]

Satan had once again taken up the sword, and was advancing to destroy
Christian civilization, small nations, the British navy, and the liberties of
England.

The old pattern became even clearer as the Germans aggressively
marched through Belgium. Eager to mobilize public opinion at home and to
win neutral support for their cause, the British publicized a series of shocking allegations about German atrocities. Lord Bryce, former British ambassador to Washington and good friend of Theodore Roosevelt, issued a report
documenting that, for example, in the Belgian town of Haecht,

> [s]everal children had been murdered; one of two or three years old was found
> nailed to the door of a farmhouse by its hands and feet, a crime which seems
> almost incredible, but the evidence for which we feel bound to accept.[28]

An eyewitness in Malines is quoted as reporting that as German soldiers
advanced,

> I saw a small child, whether boy or girl I could not see, come out of a house. The
> child was about two years of age. The child came into the middle of the street so
> as to be in the way of the soldiers . . . [T]he man on the left stepped aside and
> drove his bayonet with both hands into the child's stomach, lifting the child into
> the air on his bayonet and carrying it away on his bayonet, he and his comrades
> still singing. The child screamed when the soldier struck it with his bayonet, but
> not afterwards.[29]

Most, if not all, of these allegations were discredited after the war.

WORLD WAR I MARKED an important stage in world history, and not
just because it was such a devastating and gruesome conflict. When the
United States declared war on imperial Germany in March 1917, the two
largest English-speaking nations, the two heirs of Cromwell and the Glorious Revolution, were fighting side by side for the first time since the French

and Indian War, when the American colonies had still been part of the British Empire.

The years of angry separation had seen the two English-speaking powers on different sides of the barricades from time to time, but the apple hadn't fallen far from the tree. Like the British, the Americans saw their struggles as wars against an evil empire—even if at times that empire was centered in London. Even at the height of their war of independence, Americans did not believe that British civilization was an evil civilization; it was recognizably their own civilization and therefore obviously good. But they did argue that the American Revolution was the latest round in the eternal civil war between good and evil within the British world itself. For the colonists, English history was a long battle between traditional English values—the rule of law, the rights of the people, the limits on the power of the king to tax and to raise armies—and the sinister and corrupt forces of a dissolute and immoral court. Runnymede, where King John in 1215 had been forced to sign the Magna Carta to recognize the rights of at least some of his subjects, was a battle in the American Revolution, according to this thinking. So were the battles of the English Civil War when Cromwell and the freedom-loving Roundheads broke the power of the corrupt (and suspiciously pro-Catholic) Cavaliers. The name revolutionaries pinned on the loyalists, Americans who sided with George III and Lord North in the war, was Tories: a name originally given to the Irish Catholic forces who fought with the Jacobites against William III.

In the American Civil War, both Northerners and Southerners looked to English history to justify and explain their actions. The North compared itself to the Roundheads; the South claimed to represent the chivalry and aristocracy attributed to the Cavaliers—while somewhat paradoxically defending its rebellion by citing the precedents of the English Civil War, the Glorious Revolution, and the American Revolution. In the South, the federal government was compared to the British kings who abused their power; when the government abused its position, the citizen had a right to rebel.

Edward Everett, the former Massachusetts governor who gave the principal speech at Gettysburg on the day Lincoln delivered his famous address, spoke for the North. The Earl of Russell, a member of the House of Lords who like many British aristocrats sympathized with the Confederacy, had recently pointed to the Southern rebellion as justified by the precedents of 1640 and 1688; Everett begged to differ, pointing out to his lordship that the cases were very different. On the greatest battlefield of the American Civil War, at an event commemorating the thousands of Union soldiers who gave their lives there, it seemed perfectly appropriate and fitting both to Everett and his appreciative audience to present an intricate argument about the legitimacy of the Confederate rebellion based on the facts of English history. The South compared its rebellion to the American Revolution? But the Americans, Everett pointed out, weren't represented in Parliament in 1776. The South, on the other hand, was well represented in the American government at the outbreak of the Civil War.

> What would have been thought by an impartial posterity of the American rebellion against George III, if the colonists had at all times been more than equally represented in Parliament, and James Otis and Patrick Henry and Washington and Franklin and the Adamses and Hancock and Jefferson, and men of their stamp, had for two generations enjoyed the confidence of the sovereign and administered the government of the empire? . . .

The South claimed to be fighting for the principles of constitutional liberty against the North—like the English rebels against Charles I in the English Civil War and James II at the time of the Glorious Revolution. But that analogy, too, was false.

> The Puritans of 1640 and the Whigs of 1688 rebelled against arbitrary power in order to establish constitutional liberty. If they had risen against Charles and James because those monarchs favored equal rights, and in order themselves "for the first time in the history of the world" to establish an oligarchy "founded on the corner-stone of slavery," they would truly have furnished a precedent for the Rebels of the South, but their cause would not have been sustained by the eloquence of Pym or of Somers, nor sealed with the blood of Hampden or Russell.*

Noting that "litanies of every church in Christendom" agree with those of the Church of England in praying to God to deliver us from "sedition, privy conspiracy and rebellion," Everett went on to cite the precedents of the Wars of the Roses and the English Civil War to show that a nation once divided in civil conflict could be fully restored.

IN THE WARS of the twentieth century, the Americans and the British would fight side by side. In these wars, the American government as well as

---

* John Pym, John Somers, John Hampden, and William Russell were heroes of the English Civil War who successfully opposed King Charles I's persecution of Protestant dissenters and his dissolution of Parliament.

the British echoed the arguments of Cromwell, Addison, and Pitt. Wilson and Lloyd George, Churchill and Roosevelt, Thatcher and Reagan all drew from the rich tradition of evil empire–bashing as they sought to mobilize public opinion to face the challenges of their day.

Like his unscrupulous predecessors, Wilhelm/Hitler/Hirohito/Stalin/ Brezhnev was implacably opposed to all that is good; his wicked philosophy freed him from all moral restraints; his forces were guilty of violations of human rights and of the law of nations; the fight against him was the fight of all decent people; even the unlikeliest alliances against him had merit; he aimed at nothing short of global domination and had recruited a dangerous fifth column that sought to undermine Britain and America from within. Whether he spoke Russian, German, or Japanese, or sported the eagle, the swastika, the rising sun, or the hammer and sickle on his armband, neither the tactics nor the goal of the Evil One ever changed.

Both the British and the Americans added a new set of arguments in the twentieth century: the common origins, common values, and common destiny of their two countries. Building on the historical memories and connections that Everett evoked at Gettysburg, leaders of both countries spoke of the deep ties between them. Benjamin Strong, the head of the Federal Reserve Bank of New York at the time, told the story of the Anglo-American tradition and the long battle against tyranny to a group of Liberty Bond salesmen soon after the American entry into World War I:

> [F]or substantially four hundred years we English-speaking people, and those from other countries whom we have adopted, have been developing our institutions based upon that foundation of constitutional law. For forty years . . . Germany, filled with lust for power, has been building up a great military structure, on an entirely different theory of personal autocratic government, and so they have come into conflict . . . [T]he question is, which is going to win? That is the greatest problem the human race has ever faced—constitutional government against personally organized military government with the Kaiser at its head.[30]

American politicians were perhaps slightly less eager to make this argument than their British counterparts; Franklin D. Roosevelt for one was too good a politician ever to forget the importance of the Irish vote.

But when it came to bashing evil empires, the Americans quickly showed they could dish it out as well as the Brits. Former secretary of state Elihu Root called World War I "this great struggle between the principles of Christian civilization and the principles of pagan cruelty and brutal force." For J. P. Morgan, the situation was similarly stark: "The whole German

Nation had started out on the war with the cry of 'world domination or anni-hilation,' and we recognized that world domination by Germany would bring complete destruction of the liberties of the rest of the world."[31]

Woodrow Wilson's war message to Congress stressed similar themes: Germany was the enemy of all mankind. She had "put aside all restraints of law or humanity"; her attacks on "hospital ships and ships carrying relief to the sorely bereaved and stricken people of Belgium" showed "reckless lack of compassion or principle." Germany was fighting "a war against man-kind." Germany's crimes "cut to the very roots of human life."[32]

Evangelist Billy Sunday put it more plainly: "Christianity and Patriotism are synonymous terms, and hell and traitors are synonymous."[33] The pastor of Henry Ward Beecher's historic Plymouth Congregational Church in Brooklyn gave close to four hundred lectures on German atrocities in Bel-gium and elsewhere.[34]

The German enemy of all mankind, like the Napoleonic, Jacobin, Bour-bon, and Hapsburg enemies of old, had an interest in the bowels of both Britain and America. On the day after war was declared, Parliament gave the government the authority to issue regulations concerning the treatment of enemy aliens. Under the Alien Restriction Act, the British government required all enemy aliens to register and prevented them from owning arms, explosives, radios, and cars; even homing pigeons were banned. Bars and restaurants frequented by enemy aliens could be closed; more than thirty thousand such aliens were ultimately interned.

In the United States, where German immigrants were, after the British, the largest single ethnic group in the country, the war on the enemy within also reached extraordinary levels.

In April 1917, all males older than fourteen who were still "natives, citi-zens, denizens, or subjects" of the German Empire were declared enemy aliens; the next year, Congress extended this category to include women and girls over fourteen. Under regulations issued by Woodrow Wilson the day Congress declared war, enemy aliens could not own firearms, aircraft, or radio equipment. They could not "attack" United States government policy in print. They could live only in areas permitted by the president and they could be removed on the order of the president. New regulations issued in November prohibited enemy aliens from entering the District of Columbia, or approaching facilities including railroads, docks, and warehouses. Enemy aliens could not travel by air. The attorney general was authorized to issue any restrictions on alien travel he saw fit, and to require aliens to regis-ter weekly with local authorities.[35]

The Espionage Act of 1917 further tightened the screws. Just as the

British examined the mail for subversive publications during the revolutionary and Napoleonic wars, the U.S. Postal Service could refuse to deliver anything that, in its judgment, willfully obstructed the war effort.[36] *The Nation* magazine was banned from the mails under this edict, as were more than a dozen socialist publications. The Trading with the Enemy Act gave the postmaster additional censorship powers; explaining it to newspaper editors, Postmaster Albert Sydney Burleson asserted that publications could not

> say that this government got in the war wrong, that it is in it for the wrong purposes, or anything that will impugn the motives of the Government for going into the war. They can not say that the Government is the tool of Wall Street or of the munitions makers . . . It is a false statement, it is a lie, and it will not be permitted.[37]

Apparently this was not enough. In May 1918 the Sedition Act strengthened existing legislation and made it a crime to "interfere with the success of the national forces," to obstruct the sale of government bonds, or to say or do anything that cast aspersions on the cause of the United States or favored that of the enemy. A quarter of a million volunteers signed up to help the forerunner of the FBI identify traitors and spies across the country. German Americans were stoned, beaten, flogged, harassed, jailed, ostracized, and jeered. The teaching of German in public schools was banned in several states, and the burning of books in the German language was widespread. A German American socialist was barred from taking his seat in Congress due to his antiwar stance and the strong Austrian accent which, disloyally, he continued to use. The House of Representatives voted 311 to 1 not to seat him.

The enemy in our bowels was purged and the Kaiser joined Napoleon, Louis XIV, and Philip II in the hall of failed conquerors, but evil wasn't finished with us yet. Within a generation of the kaiser's fall, Franklin D. Roosevelt described the new Nazi threat to the American people in a nationally broadcast "Fireside Chat" in the closing days of 1940.

> The Nazi masters of Germany have made it clear that they intend not only to dominate all life and thought in their own country, but also to enslave the whole of Europe, and then to use the resources of Europe to dominate the rest of the world . . . In other words, the Axis not merely admits but the Axis proclaims that there can be no ultimate peace between their philosophy of government and our philosophy of government . . . [T]he United States has no right or reason to

encourage talk of peace, until the day shall come when there is a clear intention on the part of the aggressor nations to abandon all thought of dominating or conquering the world.

This utterly evil regime came equipped with the traditional fifth column operating in the United States that would have to be dealt with. Roosevelt was ready:

> Let us no longer blind ourselves to the undeniable fact that the evil forces which have crushed and undermined and corrupted so many others are already within our own gates. Your Government knows much about them and every day is ferreting them out.

During the Second World War, U.S. surveillance of and restrictions on enemy aliens would in many cases be tougher than those imposed in the First; the internment of Japanese Americans, including many full citizens, was an unprecedented step in American history.

WHEN PRESIDENT GEORGE W. BUSH addressed a joint session of Congress nine days after the terrorist attacks on the World Trade Center and the Pentagon in September 2001, the old logic could be heard once again. It was an eternal war we were fighting: "Freedom and fear, justice and cruelty, have always been at war, and we know that God is not neutral between them."[38]

Osama bin Laden, whom President Bush has since referred to as "the evil one," and his Al-Qaeda organization seek the old goal: world domination. "Its goal is remaking the world—and imposing its radical beliefs on people everywhere."

Our fight is the fight of good people everywhere—a fight for the rights of the Afghan people, for the freedom of Muslims, for the safety of all people of goodwill. Al-Qaeda's "interest in our bowels" had to be contained; alliances with governments of dubious moral credentials like Russia and Pakistan were enlisted in the common cause.

In 2001, as the heir of an Anglo-American tradition that had seen off one enemy of freedom after another for half a millennium, Bush was conscious of the history behind the new war. Al-Qaeda had made itself the heir of Nazism and totalitarianism, he said, and it would follow their path "all the way, to where it ends: in history's unmarked grave of discarded lies."[39] Despite some eloquent dissents, Congress quickly passed the Patriot Act, giving the government new powers against any possible fifth column inside the United States; Britain soon followed suit with tough new laws against those who organized or supported terror from the shelter of mosques.

The old firm was back in business; the war against the Evil One was once more under way.

Two • On the Beach

P ope Gregory the Great, it is said, once saw some handsome slaves for sale in the market at Rome. When he asked what nation they came from, he was told they were *Angli,* Angles, or as we would now say, English. *Non Angli,* the witty pope replied, *sed angeli:* not Englishmen, but angels. History does not record whether he bought.[1]

Sixteen centuries later, with four hundred years of struggle between the English-speaking world and the great European powers behind them, few Europeans would share that papal view. *Non angeli, sed Anglo-Saxones* would be the likely reply today to anyone making Gregory's mistake: Those aren't angels—they are Anglo-Saxons.

Despite the long and close association with the mother country, Americans are frequently amazed and less frequently pleased to discover that foreigners often class us with the British. To be called an Anglo-Saxon power grates on the American ear; Americans are too conscious of their ethnic and cultural diversity to welcome a label that appears to identify the entire country with a far from universally popular pebble in the national mosaic. Moreover, admiring testimonies to the Anglo-Saxon characteristics of the American people have generally been double-edged. Historically, the term was used in American discourse to separate the "good" old-stock Americans from "inferior" and presumably dangerous minorities and immigrants. This is not a set of ideas Americans want to revive, and rightly so.

Nevertheless, the term is used today not only by many Europeans to refer to both the Americans and their British cousins, but also by Latin Americans, Africans, and Asians. We should not be surprised; with the rise of a great English-speaking transatlantic republic to supplement and ultimately replace the British Empire that had so long held the balance of power in Europe, continental Europeans (and, increasingly, Japanese, Chinese, and other non-European observers) began to use this new term to describe this joint force in world affairs.

During the Cold War, when American power permeated the world while British influence steadily diminished, the term faded out of use, generally replaced by "Yankee." But as Britain became more assertive, more self-confident, and more clearly aligned with the United States under Margaret Thatcher and her successors, the old term staged a comeback, and it is once again a commonplace of diplomacy to talk about the Anglo-Saxon powers at, say, the U.N. Security Council.

Often, when they talk about us, what they have to say isn't very nice.

Their view of us was best expressed in English, strangely enough, in "The Walrus and the Carpenter," the poem that Tweedledee and Tweedledum recite to Alice in *Through the Looking-Glass.*

As the poem opens, the Walrus and the Carpenter—who, we can suppose, allegorically and respectively represent Britain and the United States—have worked themselves into a typically Protestant and Anglo-Saxon froth of transcendental idealism. The state of the world's beaches can no longer be borne:

> *They wept like anything to see*
> *Such quantities of sand:*
> *"If this were only cleared away,"*
> *They said, "it would be grand."* [2]

Foreign opinion is often bemused by the way in which the Anglo-Saxon powers are so frequently troubled by the existence of conditions that are almost as old as humanity and likely to be just as long-lived. Bribery, protectionism, cruelty to animals, smoking, sexual harassment in the workplace, the excessive use of saturated fats in cooking, unkind verbal epithets for low-status social groups, ethnic cleansing: in much of the world things like these are deplored, but a vigorous and puritanical attempt to suppress them altogether is viewed, not entirely unreasonably, as a cure that can be worse than the disease. This is not the approach of the Anglo-Saxons, and it is not the approach of the Walrus and the Carpenter. Democracy must reign around the world. Vice must be suppressed at all costs. All beaches must be cleared of sand.

What Continentals take to be the surreal quality of the Anglo-Saxon mind is only heightened by the "practical" proposals, bristling with statistics and projections, that the reformers bring to their self-imposed and impossible task. Perhaps, the Walrus might put it today, the community of nongovernmental organizations (NGOs) can solve the world's problems if they have enough resources and time.

> *"If seven maids with seven mops*
> *Swept it for half a year,*
> *Do you suppose," the Walrus said,*
> *"That they could get it clear?"*
> *"I doubt it," said the Carpenter,*
> *And shed a bitter tear.*[3]

Having established their idealistic credentials, they go on to something slightly more practical: inviting the oysters of the beach to go for a walk with them—a kind of league, one might say, for general philosophical and social advancement. Except for the oldest and wisest, the mollusks come running.

The oysters and the Anglo-Saxons stroll along the still-sandy beach with one another, until a comfortable spot is found for conversation.

> *"The time has come," the Walrus said,*
> *"To talk of many things:*
> *Of shoes—and ships—and sealing-wax—*
> *Of cabbages—and kings—*
> *And why the sea is boiling hot—*
> *And whether pigs have wings."*[4]

This agenda is eerily similar to an agenda that might be proposed today for an international gathering. It begins with trade in manufactured goods, moves to transport, goes on to services (sealing wax was used on legal documents) before briefly touching on agricultural products. There is talk about political reform, a discussion of global warming, and the session ends with a discussion about whether it is proper to produce genetically modified animals.

But the pleasant social gathering has a hidden agenda: the Walrus and the Carpenter are planning to feed. The reaction of the oysters reminds one of the reactions of developing countries to the discovery that the World Trade Organization (WTO) trade agreements opened their markets to the exports and the corporations of the developed world, but sharply limited their ability to export key products in agriculture and textiles. "Feed?" they asked.

> *"But not on us!" the Oysters cried,*
> *Turning a little blue.*

"After such kindness, that would be
A dismal thing to do!"[5]

The Walrus is troubled, and wonders if they have done the right thing. The pragmatic Carpenter has no time for this, muttering only in reply, "The butter's spread too thick!" This only moves the Walrus to a more dramatic display of idealistic concern:

"I weep for you," the Walrus said:
"I deeply sympathize."
With sobs and tears he sorted out
Those of the largest size . . .[6]

The poem ends with the beaches unswept and the oysters eaten. Somewhat shocked, Alice says she liked the Walrus best. At least he was a little sorry for the oysters.

But, said Tweedledee, he only cried so the Carpenter wouldn't notice him grabbing the largest ones.

"Then I like the Carpenter best—if he didn't eat so many as the Walrus," said Alice.

"But he ate as many as he could get," Tweedledum replied.

"Well," said Alice, "they were *both* very unpleasant characters."

Today the poor old moth-eaten Walrus has lost his once-formidable tusks and it is generally the Carpenter who makes the most moving speeches as he sorts the tastiest morsels into a pile, but otherwise the portrait remains uncannily accurate—at least when the subjects are viewed from an unflattering angle.

The British role in suppressing the slave trade was endlessly gratifying to British opinion, a nineteenth-century forerunner of American human rights policies. This did not, however, prevent Brazilian sugar producers in particular from noting that Britain's inspiring moral conversion occurred at just the time when Britain's sugar-producing colonies feared the increasing competition from more efficient, slave-importing plantations springing up in Brazil.

Today, when countries like Brazil and the Philippines contemplate the similarly inspiring American movements against third world sweatshops and tuna nets that kill dolphins, their admiration for our naïve and unworldly idealism is at least slightly tempered by their sense that such policies would redound to the benefit of American textile workers and tuna companies in much the same way that limiting Brazilian slave imports once benefited British colonial sugar producers.

This is also the way many Asian businessmen felt about the Anglo-American advocacy of capital market liberalization when, after the financial crash of 1997–98 brought about in part by rapid, unregulated capital flows, English-speaking investors scooped up Asian assets at fire-sale prices.

Fairly or not, the psalm-singing, pocket-picking emissaries of the Anglo-Saxon world are met with suspicion wherever they go. So many beaches unswept; so few oysters uneaten. It begins to look almost like a pattern.

The Trueborn Englishman

However we judge the morality and intentions of the Walrus and the Carpenter, Americans should learn from the rest of the world and accept that we are one of the Anglo-Saxon powers. This isn't an *ethnic* slur. When Europeans, Latin Americans, and Asians call us Anglo-Saxons, they aren't asserting that all or even most of us are descended from the tribesmen who accompanied the Saxon chiefs Horsa and Hengist in their sixth-century descent on the beaches of Kent. Nor are they describing a genetic heritage destined to rule the world or a privileged American ethnic group that spends its free time blackballing the applications of immigrants deemed too pushy, swarthy, and/or garlic-eating for prestigious suburban country clubs. Rather, they are pointing to a psychology and a culture: a set of ideas and values about how the world works. It is as a cultural term, not an ethnic one, that "Anglo-Saxon" has any meaning today, and, to the extent that it denotes ideas and values found throughout the English-speaking world to greater or lesser degrees, it still has a descriptive utility.

It is sometimes shocking to find out how others see you. Southerners traveling abroad are often horrified to be called "Yankees"; Jews in Los Angeles wrestle uneasily with their local status as "Anglos." Madeleine Albright, Condoleezza Rice, and Colin Powell might not be descended from Ethelred the Unready any more than Walter Lippmann or Martha Stewart (of Polish descent). It doesn't matter. Wasp is a state of mind today, and most Americans live there.

Americans have, for the most part, stopped teaching British history in their schools. This is a mistake; the American colonies were part of the British Empire from 1607 to 1783. Not until the year 2021 will Texas have been part of the United States this long. California must wait for 2024,

Hawaii until 2074. Eight English kings, three queens, and two lords protector reigned over the American colonies;[7] there are still some Americans alive who remember the days when British history through 1689 was considered part of, or at least a prologue to, American history.

Addicted to theories of exceptionalism but a little weak on facts, American historical lore tends to accentuate the differences between the United States and Great Britain. Anglophiles contrast the supposed sophistication and Old World realism of British policy against the allegedly naïve idealism and blundering moralism of the Americans. Anglophobes generally paint the same picture but draw an instructive and satisfying comparison between the high moral tone, democratic social order, and progressive political agenda of the United States and the corrupt schemes of the class-ridden British.

In reality, the two Anglo-Saxon powers have shown a more consistent balance of realism and idealism in their policies than many of us like to admit. It is, at least to Americans, a remarkable and little-appreciated fact that historically it was the British who considered themselves if anything too moral, while the Americans were, they believed, canting hypocrites whose pretensions to morality were mere cover for their grasping appetites. "How is it," asked Samuel Johnson during the American Revolution, "that we always hear the loudest yelps for liberty among the drivers of negroes?"[8] As Britain rose toward the zenith of world power, its press and politicians felt that the overscrupulous nature of the British evangelical conscience sacrificed the national interest for abstract and fugitive moral goals. They did not see any such inhibitions among their Yankee cousins. We can still hear that high and sometimes irritatingly nasal note of whiny self-righteousness today among Canadians who, accepting the undoubted superiority of American military power, feel that their distinctive contribution to the alliance can and should be a quality in which Americans are poor, while Canada is specially, even uniquely rich—morality. (One of the most annoying things for foreigners about Americans is that we sometimes sound to them the way Canadians sound to us.)

Greater familiarity with the British background to American history would help Americans understand just how deep the cultural and political ties between the two societies are. Many of the values, ideas, and attitudes that Americans think are part of America's unique exceptionalism actually came to us from Great Britain. In particular, the ideas and attitudes behind the Glorious Revolution have left a deep and abiding mark on American political culture as well. The Declaration of Independence, to take only one example, was closely modeled on the English Declaration of Right. Americans justified their overthrow of George III with the same arguments the English used to justify *their* overthrow of James II.

Daniel Defoe, best known today as the author of *Robinson Crusoe,* was a strong supporter of the Glorious Revolution. As Jacobites continued to oppose the postrevolutionary government, they pointed to the large number of Dutch officials that the new king brought with him from Holland, and complained that "trueborn Englishmen" were not getting a fair shake under the new regime.

This was too much for Defoe, who wrote a satirical poem in reply, "The True-Born Englishman," that became a best seller. In it, Defoe lays out a view of British society and British politics that exposed his opponents as out-of-touch elitists—and incidentally shows how much common ground exists between British attitudes in 1701 and American ideas today.

Defoe begins by showing that the idea of "trueborn Englishmen" is an illusion. England is, he says, a nation of immigrants—there is no English "race." Those who take pride in their pure English ancestry have lost touch with their own origins.

> *Forgetting that themselves are all deriv'd*
> *From the most Scoundrel Race that ever liv'd,*
> *A horrid Crowd of Rambling Thieves and Drones;*
> *Who ransack'd Kingdoms and dispeopled Towns.*
> *The* Pict *and Painted* Briton, *Treach'rous* Scot,
> *By Hunger, Theft, and Rapine, hither brought.*
> Norwegian *Pirates, Buccaneering* Danes,
> *Whose Red-hair'd Off-spring ev'ry where remains*
> *Who join'd with Norman-French compound the Breed*
> *From whence your* True Born Englishmen *proceed.*

Moreover, the poet continues, since the Normans arrived, immigrants have continued to flood into England—and those immigrants were by no means the best. Defoe's metaphor is more startling than the conventional American image of a melting pot: he compares England to a chamber pot, a septic tank where all of Europe's sewage flowed and merged.

> *We have been* Europe's *Sink, the Jakes where she*
> *Voids all her Offal Out-cast Progeny.*

By long tradition, England has welcomed the tired, the poor, the huddled masses longing to breathe free:

From our Fifth Henry's time, the Strolling Bands
Of banish'd Fugitives from Neighb'ring Lands
Have here a certain Sanctuary found:
Th' Eternal Refuge of the Vagabond.

The persecuted and oppressed are welcome, no matter their religion or even their crimes:

Religion, God we thank thee, sent them hither,
Priests, Protestants, the Devil and all together:
Of all Professions, and of ev'ry Trade,
All that were persecuted or afraid;
Whether for Debt, or other Crimes they fled.

We lift the lamp beside the golden door. But the English immigrants, like the Americans, quickly assimilated into the melting pot. The latest immigrants, hundreds of thousands of refugees from Europe's wars of religion, are now, Defoe writes, planting families

Whose Children will, when Riper Years they see,
Be as Ill-natur'd and as Proud as we:
Call themselves English, Foreigners despise,
Be Surly like us all, and just as Wise. [9]

Defoe was right about the influx of immigrants, and England's openness to immigrants was a significant force in making the country richer and more advanced. David Landes notes that Dutch immigrants had brought new weaving and drainage techniques to sixteenth-century England; the English financial industry was substantially aided by Sephardic Jews fleeing seventeenth-century persecutions in the Spanish Empire and elsewhere, and the influx of French Protestants (Huguenots) fleeing that country's worsening religious persecutions in the late seventeenth century included disproportionate numbers of skilled trade and financial workers. [10]

Defoe's England was American in other ways as well. While France, Austria, and Spain gloried in their aristocratic families with their thousand-year-old family trees, nobility in England was based more on accomplishment than family worth.

Wealth, howsoever got, in England makes
Lords of Mechanicks, Gentlemen of Rakes:

> *Antiquity and Birth are needless here;*
> *'Tis Impudence and Money makes a Peer.*

Donald Trump would have been at home in Defoe's England—and would no doubt have become Lord Jersey or perhaps the Duke of Vegas. Sir Jerry Springer, Lord Sharpton, Dame Madonna: the possibilities are as endless as they are diverting. Meanwhile, Defoe tells us, the English of his day were independent-minded (*"For* Englishmen *do all Restraint Despise"*), egalitarian, and litigious.

> *The meanest* English *Plow-man studies Law,*
> *And keeps thereby the Magistrates in Awe;*
> *Will boldly tell them what they ought to do,*
> *And sometimes punish their Omissions too.*

More than that, when Defoe comes to give the English theory of government, he lays out the basic ideas of the Declaration of Independence. When a ruler trespasses against the rights of subjects, they have the right to overthrow him.*

When kings fail to govern in the interests of their subjects, they lose their legitimacy, and their subjects have a natural right to rebel. When the American colonists declared that George III had forfeited his right to rule over them, it was to thinkers like Defoe and to texts like these that they pointed. The colonists were Englishmen, with the rights of Englishmen, and the determination of Englishmen to defend their rights.

Horsa and Hengist

Defoe believed that there was such a thing as the English people, but that their identity did not come from racial purity. Genealogy doesn't make a

---

* *And punishing of Kings is no such Crime,*
  But Englishmen ha' done it many a Time . . .
  Titles are Shadows, Crowns are empty things,
  The Good of Subjects is the End [the proper task] of Kings;
  To guide in War, and to protect in Peace:
  Where Tyrants once commence the Kings do cease:
  For Arbitrary Power's so strange a thing,
  It makes the Tyrant, *and unmakes the King.*

person English; a set of shared values does. Those values have deep roots in the history of the British Isles, but by choosing to share those values and participate in a community shaped by them, the immigrant or refugee can start a new and English life.

> *Fate jumbled them together, God knows how;*
> *Whate'er they were, they're true-born English now.*

This rowdy and litigious community—surly, snarky, enterprising, self-reliant, and free—is what Defoe meant by the English, and it was this community and these values that English writers and thinkers in his era meant by Anglo-Saxon. The identification of the Anglo-Saxons with a race, a genetic rather than a cultural identity, came later—as the "scientific racism" of the Victorian era reflected on its past, and as "the Anglo-Saxon race" became a protagonist in the social Darwinist struggle for survival and competition against other races.

Coming out of the experiences of the English Civil War, the Whigs of Defoe's era did not believe that in fighting the divine right of kings they were part of a forward-looking revolution against tradition. They were fighting for traditional values against modernizers and usurpers. They looked back to the institutions and laws of the Germanic tribes as described by Tacitus and as found in crumbling and moth-eaten old books of English custom and law, and argued that the Anglo-Saxons in the seventh and eighth centuries were a free people, and that England owed its liberty and its most important institutions to these ancient traditions.

The English common law, the limits on the rights and powers of the king, a popular assembly with the right to make laws and withhold assent to taxes—these were, the Whigs argued, part of the good old English constitution. As historian Reginald Horsman reports in *Race and Manifest Destiny: The Origins of American Racial Anglo-Saxonism,* these ideas crossed the Atlantic with the American colonists. "Coke on Littleton" (from the *Institutes* of Sir Edward Coke) was the essential legal text in American legal education; Coke argued that Anglo-Saxon law was the basis for English freedom. Feudalism was rejected as a Norman import; the Anglo-Saxon farmers had been free yeoman farmers, not cringing peasants. (Patrick Henry wrote his resolution against the Stamp Act on the flyleaf of a copy of the Coke book.)[11] French writers like Montesquieu and the once-popular historian Paul de Rapin-Thoyras also traced English freedom to the Anglo-Saxon past. Written in 1771, *A Historical Essay on the English Constitution* was a pamphlet much read and discussed in both

Britain and the colonies. Its author took the Anglo-Saxons to new heights, writing that

> [i]f ever God Almighty did concern himself about forming a government for mankind to live happily under, it was that which was established in England by our Saxon forefathers.[12]

These ideas were particularly intriguing to Thomas Jefferson, a lifelong proponent of Anglo-Saxon studies and values. Thanks to Jefferson's influence, the University of Virginia was for many years one of the few places in the United States where students could learn to read *Beowulf* in the original. Jefferson seems to have believed all his adult life that laws of the Anglo-Saxon era were based on natural rights; it was the evil Norman Conquest that introduced kings, priests, feudalism, and the whole apparatus of corruption and tyranny. He composed a grammar book to help young Americans learn the Anglo-Saxon language, hoping that they would "imbibe with the language their free principles of government."[13]

The Anglo-Saxons were particularly on Jefferson's mind in the summer of 1776. According to John Adams, the great seal of the United States as proposed by Thomas Jefferson had two sides. On one was "the children of Israel in the wilderness, led by a cloud by day and a pillar of fire by night; and on the other side, Hengist and Horsa, the Saxon chiefs from whom we claim the honor of being descended, and whose political principles and form of government we have assumed."[14] Jefferson's odd—and very Anglo-American—mix of radicalism and conservatism were at work when he asked that same summer:

> Has not every restitution of the ancient Saxon laws had happy effects? Is it not better now that we return at once into that happy system of our ancestors, the wisest and most perfect ever yet devised by the wit of man, as it stood before the 8th century?[15]

In the years after American independence, the bond of a common Anglo-Saxon identity was important for those promoting Anglo-American friendship and cooperation. After the U.S. Civil War, these views were often wrapped in social Darwinism; writers would call for the Anglo-Saxons to unite so as to prevail in the inevitable racial strife with other breeds. Before that time, the ideas of a common identity and a common, world-conquering destiny for the English-speaking nations were already very common. An American reviewer of Macaulay's *History of England* wrote:

We too are English, and all the far-descended honors of the English name are ours by inheritance . . . our race reads lessons to the world in philosophy, in science, in mechanical skill, in the arts of government, in Christian morality . . . we are far behind in the light and frivolous arts.

The Anglo-Saxon mission was, the reviewer wrote, "like that of the Jews in Canaan, 'to subdue the land and possess it.'"[16]

Providence had left unclear exactly how much land the Anglo-Saxons were meant to possess, but many writers were suggestive. "If the Anglo-Saxons of Great Britain and the United States are true to each other and to the cause of human freedom," Abbot Lawrence wrote in 1850 while serving as American minister to Britain, "they may not only give their language, but their laws to the world, and defy the power of all despots on the face of the Globe."[17] Another contemporaneous writer believed that "no power on earth should build dock-yards or support navies, except the Anglo-Norman Race, its kindred and allies."[18] Robert Walker, who served as secretary of the treasury in the Polk administration, believed he knew where things were heading.

A time shall come when the human race shall become as one family, and that the predominance of our Anglo-Celt-Sax-Norman stock shall guide the nations to that result . . . this great confederacy would ultimately embrace the globe we inhabit.[19]

This consummation was, he believed, foretold in the Bible.

Commerce, the English language, democratic political institutions, and the Christian religion: these were the blessings the Anglo-Saxons would bring to the world; these were also the instruments that would allow them to rule it.

Three • How They Hate Us

Josef Joffe, the publisher-editor of the German weekly *Die Zeit,* tells of a fifteen-year-old German schoolboy in Hamburg who in 2003 wrote the following letter to his local newspaper.

> A pleasant place in the woods. Brown squirrels are happily jumping from branch to branch. But suddenly a black squirrel darts in and begins to hunt down the brown members of his species. The first black squirrels were slipped in here from America. Ever since, their number has ballooned . . . Now, they are almost as numerous as European squirrels. They are displacing our beloved Browns . . . Americanization in the animal kingdom.[1]

The most frightening stories of black squirrels do not come from western Europe, or from the United States (where black squirrels are rare and, where they exist, are often descended from populations imported from Canada), but from the Russian far east, where a recent BBC report carried the story of a pack of black squirrels who killed a dog and ate it.[2] Naturalists in Russia and elsewhere are skeptical. The urban legend that aggressive black squirrels are driving out their more civilized rivals (stories of black squirrels attacking grays in the United States, attacking browns in Europe) is without serious scientific foundation as naturalists report no unusually aggressive behavior among the blacks.

The truth behind the young Hamburger's concern is that the American gray squirrel (*Sciurus carolinensis*) is gradually replacing the European red squirrel (*Sciurus vulgaris*) in parts of its range. However, the grays are not hunting down and killing the reds; the preferred habitat of the red squirrel is shrinking as coniferous forests in Europe shrink; gray squirrels compete more successfully in deciduous forests and urban parkland.

The spread of *Sciurus carolinensis* in Europe is not a unique or isolated phenomenon. With the growth in human travel and trade, animal species—sometimes hitchhiking, sometimes introduced on purpose—are also spreading from their native habitats. *Sciurus vulgaris* is not the only loser in this process. In the United States, many European animal and plant species and subspecies have exploded over the landscape and driven out native populations. *Sus scrofa,* the European wild boar, has become a major pest in many American forests; *Sturnus vulgaris* (the European starling) and *Lymantria dispar* (the European gypsy moth) are among the other invasive species described on a United States Department of Agriculture Web site.[3] *Caulerpa taxifolia,* also known as Mediterranean clone weed and killer algae, was accidentally bred in the Stuttgart Aquarium. Rather than eradicate this horror at the source, the Stuttgart Aquarium spread it around until it reached the Oceanographic Museum of Monaco and was discharged into the Mediterranean. German-spawned killer algae has now turned thousands of acres of seafloor into wasteland and has recently been detected in American waters.

The young writer in Hamburg, innocent of context, has moved from concrete and perhaps troubling facts—the decline of the European red squirrel and more broadly the consequences for biodiversity of the increasing movement of animal species around the world—to a melodrama planted firmly in fantasy. Vicious American invaders are destroying innocent and playful Europeans. They are hunting them down and killing them.

ANOTHER EUROPEAN who worried about the displacement of his "beloved Browns" was Robert Ley, the Nazi official Hitler appointed head of the German Labor Front. "Oliver Cromwell always called on God in the midst of his atrocities," wrote Ley in 1942, "and viewed his devilish soldiers as the chosen people of God. Churchill and Roosevelt have learned the methods of the bestial hypocrite Cromwell by heart, and have proven that nothing, absolutely nothing has changed in the English-American world over the past three hundred years."[4]

German left-wingers can be equally scathing. A 1953 list of approved terms for describing Britain advised German Communist orators to select from among the following: "Paralytic sycophants, effete betrayers of humanity, carrion-eating servile imitators."[5] Other recommended terms included arch-cowards and collaborators, gang of women-murderers, degenerate rabble, parasitic traditionalists, playboy soldiers, conceited dandies.

The Party of Democratic Socialism, the successor party to the German Communists, includes speakers who today would find some of the epithets they used in their old Communist days fit for Tony Blair; meanwhile, "Anglo-Saxon capitalism" remains as much a bugbear as ever for this party, with speakers claiming that this social model leaves "only winners and losers" and that while European capitalism has social safety nets, such nets "do not exist in America."[6] These people are not saying that America's nets are less generous than Europe's, or less extensive; they are saying that none exist at all. And these cannibal black winner squirrels, it is clear, are hunting down the Europeans from branch to branch, and soon none will be left.

Hatred of all things Anglo-Saxon is an old and honorable tradition in much of the world. Anglophobia was the most common form in the nineteenth century, when the British Empire was the world's most powerful state and Britain possessed the world's most dynamic and advanced economy; anti-Americanism is the preferred form today. But regardless of the immediate target, from the far left to the far right, from communists, fascists, Nazis, Catholic clerics and theologians, secular traditionalists, radical Jacobins and fanatical royalists, a torrent of vituperation has poured over the Anglo-Saxon world from the age of Cromwell to the present. And just as the centuries of rhetoric from Anglo-Saxon leaders has had certain common elements, so too the attacks on the Wasps by their enemies have had their continuities.

WHEN THE WALRUS and the Carpenter invited the oysters to accompany them on their walk, some of the mollusks did not accept.

> The eldest Oyster looked at them,
> But never a word he said:
> The eldest Oyster winked his eye,
> And shook his heavy head—
> Meaning to say he did not choose
> To leave the oyster-bed.

This oyster was probably French. Long before President Jacques Chirac led U.N. opposition to the 2003 Anglo-American invasion of Iraq, it was France that had longest and most consistently opposed the Anglo-Saxon empire-builders; it is France that has thought hardest and most deeply about what is wrong with them, and it is France that has most often attempted to defeat or at least contain them.

The modern rivalry goes back to the late seventeenth century, when England was the chief obstacle to Louis XIV's plans to dominate Europe.

The great Catholic preacher and theologian Bossuet denounced "*La perfide Angleterre*" in a sermon preached at Metz in 1682.[7] Louis himself remarked dismissively that "England is a little garden full of sour weeds."[8]

The American Revolution and the Napoleonic Wars saw an intensification of the sense of a profound and principled conflict between the two countries. The English saw themselves fighting for liberty; the French saw it as a war between civilization and plutocratic barbarism. "Vile and insolent" was Robespierre's verdict on the neighbors.[9] "In my capacity as a Frenchman, a representative of the people, I declare that I hate the British . . . We shall see if a people of merchants is a match for a people of farmers."[10]

In French eyes, the Franco-British rivalry was a replay of the ancient battles between the pious, land-based, and civilizing empire of Rome and the cruel, money-grubbing, maritime and commercial power of Carthage. An anti-British song to be sung to the tune of "La Marseillaise" attacked "This ambitious Carthage / Supporter of perverse émigrés,"[11] blaming the British for all the domestic woes then afflicting France.

Napoleon's seizure of power only intensified the rivalry and the hatred. "England's greed and ambitions are finally out in the open," said an 1803 article over Napoleon's name in the official French newspaper, *Le Moniteur Universel,* that once again sounded the anti-Punic theme. "One single obstacle stands in the way of her policies and her ambitious course—victorious, moderate, prosperous France; her vigorous and enlightened government; [and, Napoleon ventures to say it himself] her illustrious and magnanimous leader . . . But Europe is watching. France is arming. History is recording. Rome destroyed Carthage!"[12]

The Carthaginian motif would reappear during World War II. The Vichy radio journalist Jean Herold-Paquis made daily broadcasts during the German occupation of France and every day repeated his slogan: "England, like Carthage, must be destroyed."[13]

France supported the American colonies against Britain in the hope that the noble and virtuous American farmers would side with their French liberators against the British merchants who preyed on them both. These hopes were soon disappointed; the more one looked at the Americans, the more like the British they were. Talleyrand, exiled in America during a particularly nasty phase of the French Revolution, reported back with the painful news that the Americans and the British, however much they might talk of their differences, were essentially one and the same. Every Englishman who goes there is at home, said Talleyrand; no Frenchman ever is.[14] "In truth," wrote a disillusioned Ernest Duvergier de Hauranne in 1864, "this is no longer America: it is England, and the country is correctly named New England."¹⁵

Only as America became more powerful would the connection between the Anglo-Saxon powers begin to disappear from French thought; in the twentieth century Anglophobia would gradually retreat from the foreground of French (and, more generally, of Latin) minds, while hatred and fear of the Yankee would loom ever larger. The Northern victory in the Civil War, followed by the shocking defeat of the French-backed "Emperor" Maximilian Hapsburg in 1867 in Mexico, sent waves of fear and hostility through a French society beginning to think in terms of a global contest between the peaceful, civilized Latins and the brutal, remorseless, and horrifyingly powerful Yankee "race." The Spanish-American War—from the French perspective a brutal attack by the brash Yankees on the soft and friendly Spaniards—accelerated the transition in France and in Latin America from Anglophobia to anti-Americanism as the dominant fear.¹⁶

"I ACCUSE THE UNITED STATES of being in a permanent state of crime against mankind," wrote the novelist Henri de Montherlant, member of the Académie Française. Freud was more moderate: "A mistake; a gigantic mistake, it is true, but a mistake none the less."¹⁷ "I don't hate America, I regret it!"¹⁸

Not only in France, but in many parts of the world, opposing the Anglo-Saxons and their various programs of beach-sweeping and world order is the common ground of both the right and the left. Traditionalist Catholics, populists, and socialists across Latin America share this core set of values; to some degree the political relationship among these three forces has historically been a competition to see which of them offers the best hope of defeating or frustrating the Wasps. Karl Marx, Charles Baudelaire, and Pope Pius IX did not agree on very many subjects, but the danger of the Anglo-American juggernaut was a topic on which they could all sing from the same hymnbook. One can see the same pattern in Iran and throughout the Arab world, where secularists, socialists, and Islamic radicals have sought to shape a resistance to British and American power.

It is hard to know what to call this self-conscious, systematic hatred and fear of and opposition to Anglo-American civilization and power. It is a kind of meta-ideology, a mother of ideologies that breeds children on the left and on the right. It is more than mere anti-Americanism and more than Anglophobia, although it includes both.

Although it is one of the most powerful forces shaping world history, it does not have a name. "Waspophobia" comes as close as anything to describing it: a fear and hatred of the political, social, and economic basis of Anglo-American civilization. Whatever we call it, the hatred and fear of white Anglo-Saxon Protestants and of all their doings is one of the motors driving the world.

To be a Waspophobe, it is not enough to hate England, or America, or even to hate them both. Like Robert Ley, a Waspophobe needs to have an integrated view of the Anglo-American presence in the world, to believe that Anglo-American civilization is evil at its core and to see this inner evil as manifesting itself in the policies and practices of the Anglo-Saxon states.

For Maxim Gorky, apologist of Lenin and Stalin, America was "[a] machine, a cold, unseen, unreasoning machine, in which man is nothing but an insignificant screw!"[19] For the Waspophobe, whether of the right or the left, whether traditionalist Catholic or fundamentalist Muslim, Gorky's description of America captures the essential nature of Anglo-American civilization: a cold, inexorable machine that cares nothing for the individual.

Cruelty and greed in the service of an inflexible, absolute, and utterly inhuman will to power, made more formidable by an insolently arrogant hypocrisy and exuding an irresistible but intolerable vulgarity: that is what our enemies since the seventeenth century have seen when they looked our way.

EXTRAORDINARY AND HEARTLESS CRUELTY is where it all begins. Heroes of the English wars against Spain—like Sir Francis Drake,[20] Sir Walter Raleigh, and John Hawkins[21]—could be and often were portrayed as pirates whose raids on Spanish territory demonstrated a rapacity and a disregard for the laws of warfare that later generations would ascribe to the Anglo-American "air pirates" who rained destruction down on the cities of Europe in World War II. (Vichy propaganda produced a poster saying that "They always return to the scene of the crime" after the English bombed Rouen, the city where Joan of Arc was burned at the stake.)[22]

A Spanish chronicler described Drake's behavior in Santo Domingo, where Queen Bess's favorite sailor led a raid and his men "bitterly offended our Catholic piety by their insults to the most revered images of our Lord and the Holy Virgin, cutting off arms and legs, using them for seats or burning them to cook their food . . . Two old and infirm monks, who, not having the strength to run away . . . were taken out and hanged in the public square for their protest against such acts."[23]

Those seeking to make atrocity propaganda against Anglo-Saxon powers have never had far to look. Cromwell's campaigns against the Irish were shocking even by the standards of the time. The suppression of the Scots Highland clans in the late seventeenth and early eighteenth centuries was, partly due to the popularity of the novels of Sir Walter Scott, a great scandal in the European world. The Glencoe massacre, when troops loyal to William III spent twelve winter days as guests of Scottish Highlanders before murdering the entire village, horrified European opinion in an age of atrocity. In peace and war England's policies in Ireland were a shame and a horror for most of modern times. The extermination of native peoples in the many non-European lands settled under Anglo-Saxon leadership provided continental critics ample ammunition to attack any claims to moral superiority coming from the Walrus and the Carpenter. The horrors of the African slave trade and plantation slavery in the antebellum South, Sherman's march through Georgia (part of an American South which French opinion at the time erroneously believed to be ethnically "Latin"), the British use of concentration camps to warehouse Boer noncombatants, the post-Reconstruction racial policies of a South now discovered to be aggressively Anglo-Saxon rather than romantically Latin: all these elements made up a portrait of a race whose lust for power was matched only by its lust for gold (and, of course, in modern times for oil).

Attacks on the barbarity of the Anglo-Americans in war continued through the twentieth century. German propagandists attacked the British naval blockade and the resulting famines and food shortages across Europe in the two world wars as deliberate attempts to murder millions of innocent civilians—much as sanctions on Iraq between the two Persian Gulf wars were attacked as cold-blooded efforts to use the suffering of helpless women and children as a political weapon. The Anglo-American terror bombings of the Second World War, climaxing in the American nuclear attacks on Hiroshima and Nagasaki, were cited by Germany and Japan during the war, and by Communists after it, to stir up hatred and resentment against the perpetrators. The international press brimmed with atrocity stories during the Korean and Vietnam conflicts, some based on facts, others concocted by Soviet and Communist propagandists and disinformation offices. Reports of American mistreatment of prisoners in Abu Ghraib and Guantánamo after the overthrow of Saddam Hussein, as well as detailed accounts of the suffering of civilians on such Iraqi battlefields as Falluja, are more recent installments in this long list of abuses. As President Mahmoud Ahmadinejad said, in a response to President George W. Bush in early February 2006 that blends classic Soviet Cold War propaganda with distinctively Iranian ideas:

These are people whose arms are submerged up to the elbows in the blood of other nations. Wherever there is war and oppression in the world, they are involved. These people channel their factories to the production of weapons. These people generate wars in Asia and Africa, killing millions and millions of people, in order to help their production, employment, and economy. These are people whose biological laboratories manufacture germs, and export them to other countries in order to subjugate other peoples. These are the people who, in the last century, caused several devastating wars. In one world war alone, they killed over 60 million people.[24]

A Syrian journalist had a similar perspective. "Murdering is genetically ingrained in American culture," writes Dr. Husnu Mahalli in *Yeni Safak*, a Turkish newspaper said to have ties to the government.

> Let's return to [the subject of] Fallujah . . . Americans are using Iraqi civilians as human shields to protect themselves . . . One can expect no less from the faithless, treacherous, murderous Americans . . . After bombing the mosques of Fallujah, the American soldiers desecrate them by urinating on and soiling their walls. After raiding homes, American soldiers strip the women and girls naked and molest them . . . The Americans want to obliterate the human values of all peoples of the region. Just like [Israeli prime minister Ariel] Sharon, the Americans want to denigrate and humiliate us, and defile our honor. The Americans, together with Sharon, want to drag us into hopelessness and despair in order to enslave us.[25]

The theme of Anglo-Saxon cruelty in the service of Anglo-Saxon greed becomes one of the key organizing principles that many observers use to make sense of mysterious events. "Beslan: Responsibility of Slaughter Points Towards the Anglosaxons" ran the headline of an article published on September 27, 2004, by a self-identified nonaligned news source, Voltairenet.org, about an incident in which three hundred Russian schoolchildren died in a Chechnya-related terrorist attack. Russian military analysts, some quoted by name, argue that the horrific event was part of a wider Anglo-Saxon plot to further U.S. and British interests in the northern Caucasus. Ruthless, greedy, cruel, far-reaching: the hidden hand of the Anglo-Saxon menace is everywhere, even hunting down children to feed its lust for oil.[26]

Unfortunately, claims of Anglo-Saxon atrocities are not always as paranoid and unrealistic as this; far from it. But the distinctive mark of the Waspophobe is not a hostility toward Anglo-American atrocities. It is not

Waspophobic to oppose evil. Many of the greatest leaders of the English-speaking world have denounced and fought these evils. William Wilberforce was not a Waspophobe when he attacked slavery; Charles Dickens was not Waspophobic in exposing the conditions in England's factories and workhouses. William Gladstone was not Anglophobic when he sought home rule for Ireland; Martin Luther King Jr. was not anti-American when he fought segregation. Many of the journalists who have exposed wrongdoing by British and American forces in various wars have done so out of patriotism; they are surgeons trying to save the patient, not ax murderers trying to kill it.

And, of course, if Anglo-Americans can be appalled by and oppose the various evils and crimes of their respective countries, there is nothing wrong with foreigners noting that these evils exist, and deploring and opposing them. It was not necessarily Waspophobic to oppose U.S. wars in Vietnam or Iraq; it does not take a Waspophobe to believe that the American Indians were not treated well.

The Waspophobe, as opposed to the humanitarian, sees these atrocities as more than incidents in military history. They are signs of the beast within, windows into the soul of the Wasps—into the terrible and vacant cruelty that lurks in the Anglo-Saxon heart. They are not excesses, blunders, or regrettable misjudgments by young soldiers in the heat of action. To Waspophobes they are coldly calculated, deliberate crimes, committed for gain, and they reveal as nothing else can the bottomless moral depravity at the core of what Anglo-Saxons so hypocritically refer to as their "civilization" and "culture."

ATROCITY BEGINS AT HOME. For many observers, the cruelty with which the Anglo-Americans have pursued power abroad reflects the inner dynamic of Anglo-American society, and, historically speaking, the cruelty goes back to the dawn of modern English history. Karl Marx, writing against the comfortable assumptions about the rise of capitalism found in the works of Adam Smith, wrote about the process of "primitive accumulation" in English history. The English Reformation, the wars against the Stuarts, the rise of parliamentary government, and the development of English "liberties": these were the means by which the English gentry plundered the peasants, he said. The landowners drove the peasants off the land by enclosing it; the urban capitalists paid starvation wages to desperate ex-peasants faced with starvation. Catholic and traditionalist writers, like Hilaire Belloc and

G. K. Chesterton, joined Marx's attack. They countered the Whigs, the successors of those who supported the overthrow of James II, who developed a view of an England led to freedom and prosperity through enlightened Protestantism. This became known as the "Whig myth." For the anti-Whigs, the story of modern Protestant England was the story of a crime.

On both the left and the right, a host of writers portrayed the English Reformation as an unscrupulous land grab, less motivated by religion than by the desire of the rulers of Tudor England to seize the wealth of the Catholic Church. It marked the start of the process by which the gentry dispossessed the peasants of their traditional land rights in order to set up a heartless and godless capitalism. In England, they drove them off the land by enclosing the traditional common lands to the benefit of the aristocracy; in Scotland the Highlanders were murdered and flogged off the land after the failure of Bonnie Prince Charlie's rebellion of 1745. In Ireland the Catholic peasantry was relentlessly persecuted, dispossessed, exploited, transported, and hanged from the reign of Elizabeth I through that of George V.

For committed Waspophobes, the military and political cruelty of the Wasps was in the service of the systematic and overwhelming greed that is the dominating feature of Anglo-American society. It was not that one particular landlord oppressed the peasants and stole their land, or that a particular factory owner exploited his workers: the English land system and factory system depended on theft and exploitation in order to work.

For Waspophobes, capitalism, at least in the fierce dog-eat-dog form that appeared in eighteenth-century Britain, was a system of theft and inhumanity. Again, it was not just the Marxists who thought this. Catholic intellectuals recoiled from a brutal system they believed abolished all the protections and human features that medieval society had developed. In 1792, the Inquisition placed *The Wealth of Nations* on the Index of Forbidden Books. It was easy to demonstrate that the fierce competition of what would come to be called the Anglo-Saxon capitalist model, which included such traditional concepts as a "just price," was unusually cruel.

Again and again, continental Europeans drew attention to the unbridled greed of the Anglo-Saxon world, the "new Carthage" of Jacobin and Napoleonic lore. Carthage was a mercantile, seagoing society; its merchants were famous for their wealth and (in a time when Romans still prided themselves, somewhat inaccurately, on their indifference to material goods) their avarice. Carthage was also renowned for cruelty; the god Moloch was worshipped there, and his rites included burned offerings of infants.

"The store the English set by wealth is such that when they want to express their admiration for anyone, they say he's worth a great deal of money and they even stipulate the sum," wrote the French traveler Joseph Fiévée in his 1802 *Lettres sur l'Angleterre.*[27] De Tocqueville, whose overall favorable opinion of American democracy substantially reduced his reputation in France, put the Americans in the same camp—in spades: "[O]ne usually finds that love of money is either the chief or a secondary motive at the bottom of everything the Americans do,"[28] he wrote. "The American will describe as noble and estimable ambition that which our medieval ancestors would have called base cupidity."[29]

Less sympathetic observers were more brutal. Of the very many testimonies to this disagreeable element in the national character, let these early nineteenth-century observations by Felix de Beaujour lay out the usual indictment:

> The American never loses an opportunity of enriching himself. Gain is the subject of all his discourse, and the lever of all his actions; so that there is scarcely a civilized country in the world in which there is less generosity of sentiment, less elevation of soul and less of those soft and brilliant illusions which constitute the charm of life. There a man weighs everything, calculates all, and sacrifices all to his own interests. He lives only in himself, and for himself, and regards all disinterested acts as so many follies, condemns all talents that are purely agreeable, appears estranged to every idea of heroism and of glory, and in history beholds nothing.[30]

Waspophobes believe that for Anglo-Americans, committing atrocities in pursuit of monetary gain is second nature. Indeed, by this way of thinking, their cruelty and greed form the basis for their unscrupulous and exploitative international system. The Irish exile Arthur O'Connor wrote propaganda for Napoleon and gave a description of the British Empire that in many interesting respects matches the indictment that opponents still make of America's world system: "An island at one extremity of Europe, with a population of scarcely eleven million, she bestrides the other three-quarters of the earth; one foot on the vast continent of America, the other upon the Indies, she consigns Africa to eternal barbarism and slavery, that the produce of the Antilles may swell the list of her imports."[31]

Britain exploits this position to collect "by a mixed system of commerce, exaction, plunder and tribute" commodities which she sells to Europe at inflated, monopoly prices, so that even those countries that remain "territorially free" are "maritimely enslaved" by the empire. For Waspophobes, not much has changed since the time of Napoleon; Noam Chomsky could scarcely put it more clearly.

Carthage survived, and Napoleon landed on St. Helena, where he continued to reflect on the shortcomings of the perfidious isle. "I have paid dearly for the romantic and chivalrous opinion which I had formed of you," he regretfully said, forgetting apparently his earlier comment that "[t]he English have no exalted sentiments. They can all be bought."[32]

Napoleon's empire perished, but O'Connor's analysis of the global consequences of the Anglo-American power system has echoed through generations of Waspophobic commentators who have argued that the Anglo-American system produces wealth in the English-speaking world *because* it produces poverty in what is now the third world—even as it depresses the wealth and the comfort of European rivals. In subsequent decades and centuries, O'Connor's analysis—natural and perhaps even inevitable for a thoughtful Irishman at the time—appeared obvious and irresistible to Indians, Latin Americans, Frenchmen, Germans, Ottomans, Egyptians, and many others who chafed under the restraints and bridled against the limits imposed by the British imperial system. Lenin's analysis of imperialism, Hitler's analysis of global politics, the political strategies of Stalin and Mao all incorporate these core views as surely as they inform the speeches of Venezuela's Hugo Chavez or Zimbabwe's Robert Mugabe.

Some observers deplored the British; some hoped to imitate them. Kaiser Wilhelm II felt that Germany needed colonies to break the stranglehold of the British system; Japan needed an empire in China to become, as Japanese nationalist intellectuals wanted, "the Britain of Asia." Other Japanese looked to the United States; they called for a "Monroe Doctrine for Asia" that would give Japan the same kind of power monopoly in its region that the United States enjoyed in the Americas. Hitler's theory of Lebensraum, the idea that Germany needed a vast hinterland so its population could grow to the size necessary to maintain a great power in the long run, was based on his observation of what the settlement of the United States, Canada, Australia, and New Zealand had done for the Anglophones.

But whether you wanted to fight them or to follow their example to become a world power, the story was clear: first the British and then the Americans built global empires on the basis of cruelty and greed.

Societies this degraded could not, of course, produce a decent culture or quality of life, and a long line of non-Anglophone observers have described and analyzed the shocking cultural poverty of the English-speaking world. Again, the French were in the lead. "The English take their pleasures sadly, after the fashion of their country," wrote the duc de Sully in his memoirs in 1638.[33]

The old Carthage had no high culture; neither did the new. "I have read [Shakespeare]," said Napoleon to his advisers in 1803. "There is nothing that comes anywhere near Corneille and Racine. It's impossible to finish reading any of his plays; they are pitiful . . . France need not envy England anything."[34]

"[T]he English are the most uncivilized people in Europe," wrote Joseph Fiévée.[35] "The lack of sociability you find in their nature has three main causes: one, the high regard they have for money; two, the boredom they feel in the presence of women; three, the exaggerated opinion they have of themselves, which borders on mania."

The Americans were worse. The French premier Georges Clemenceau famously observed that "America is the only nation in history which miraculously has gone directly from barbarism to degeneration without the usual interval of civilization."

The Anglo-American world was a horrifying mix of Puritanism and permissiveness, a ghastly blend of parsons and prostitutes. The dreary dullness of the English sabbath and the stuffy hypocrisy of Victorian England were frequently noted by European visitors. Few social experiments have been greeted with such gales of laughter as America's fling with Prohibition.

On the other hand, the fierceness of the American appetite has caused both alarm and amusement. French visitors were horrified at the spread of chewing gum, seen as a diabolical American exercise to make the jaws ever more formidable and the appetite ever more keen. That the contemporary United States is both the world's fattest country and the home of obsessed nutrition nazis and food cranks is the cause of a great deal of merriment around the world. Nothing could be more Anglo-Saxon than a fat health nut on a perpetual treadmill of crackpot diets.

It was not, however, the simple gracelessness of Anglo-Saxon society, the brashness of the women, the hypocritical stuffiness of the morality, the brutality of sports like football, or the weirdness of such activities as cheerleading that struck Continentals most forcefully. It was the vulgar popular culture, already visible in British music halls, that would exemplify both the hideous depths to which the Anglo-Saxon world had fallen and the existential threat that world presented to everything good, true, and beautiful in Europe itself.

This perspective was brilliantly described by the Uruguayan essayist and critic José Enrique Rodó (1872–1917), whose *Ariel* has helped shape a century of Latin American response to the United States. We once thought, says

Rodó, that the English were bad—their positivism, their pragmatism, their single-minded focus on acquisition to the neglect of higher culture and values was and is appalling. But the Americans, he says, are much worse—they are Englishmen with the good qualities left out and the bad qualities swollen to fill up the vacuum. England's aristocracy protects English society from the worst consequences of its mercantile classes, but in America "the spirit of vulgarity encounters no barriers to slow its rising waters, and it spreads and swells as if flooding across an endless plain."[36]

The Soviet writer Genrikh Volkov placed the source of the problem in the core structure of the American capitalist system: "its hostility to man, the individual, to spiritual culture in general, its Shylock passion to utilize for the sake of profit not only a man's blood but also the living soul and his beating heart."[37]

Having taken its Shylockian pound of flesh, the American system then offers "compensations" to its exhausted, confused victims: "cheap literature, shocking movie and television hackwork, low-quality shows, pornography, narcotics and hallucinogens."[38]

Alexander Solzhenitsyn and Soviet apologists like Volkov disagreed over many matters, but on the subject of American culture they were as one. Parts of Solzhenitsyn's famous 1978 address to Harvard's graduating class could have come from Volkov's pen as the great dissident characterized American popular culture as a stultifying mixture of "the revolting invasion of publicity . . . TV stupor, and . . . intolerable music."[39]

Sayyid Qutb, the renowned ideologue of the Muslim Brotherhood and a seminal figure in the history of Muslim anti-Americanism, had similar views on the American culture he witnessed. He starts with a description of the American girl:

> The American girl is well acquainted with her body's seductive capacity. She knows it lies in the face, and in expressive eyes, and thirsty lips. She knows seductiveness lies in the round breasts, the full buttocks, and in the shapely thighs, sleek legs—and she shows all this and does not hide it.

The American male in his way is no better.

> This primitiveness can be seen in the spectacle of the fans as they follow a game of football . . . or watch boxing matches or bloody, monstrous wrestling matches. . . . This spectacle leaves no room for doubt as to the primitiveness of the feelings of those who are enamored with muscular strength and desire it.

Put them together, even at a chaperoned dance in the basement of a church, and terrible things start to happen.

> They danced to the tunes of the gramophone, and the dance floor was replete with tapping feet, enticing legs, arms wrapped around waists, lips pressed to lips, and chests pressed to chests. The atmosphere was full of desire . . . [T]he minister . . . advanced to the gramophone to choose a song that would befit this atmosphere and encourage the males and females who were still seated to participate. And the father [*sic*] chose.* He chose a famous American song called "Baby, It's Cold Outside."[40]

This hideous underculture, revolting but somehow dangerously seductive, puritanical and yet salacious, has been horrifying foreigners for nearly two centuries. During much of that time Anglo-American culture was more repressed on sexual subjects than literature and the arts in other parts of the world; compare Balzac and Zola to Thackeray and Trollope. It was the social, not the sexual, license of British and American culture that shocked so many foreign observers: the degree to which the lower orders and women were involved in the production and the public consumption of culture, and the disparity between the relatively weak high culture and the vibrant and growing popular culture.

Anglo-American high culture, where it existed at all, was seen to be "philistine": hostile to the fine arts, an enemy of the subtle. The upper classes of the English-speaking world were more likely to ride and hunt than to attend operas; the lower classes increasingly dominated the cultural scene through music halls, vaudeville, and, beginning at the turn of the twentieth century, movies.

Mass production and technologies like the phonograph magnified the impact of the populist and vulgar low culture of the English-speaking world. For the first time, popular culture could travel. With the rise of the movies, ordinary people all over the world could see the American lifestyle for themselves: the uppity women, the independent working people and farmers, the young people ready to start lives of their own without deference to tradition or parents. Cultural products designed for the American mass market began to pour out in a steady stream, with unwelcome political and social consequences for elites and traditionalists everywhere.

---

* A Muslim feeling his way through the subtleties of Christian nomenclature, Qutb apparently uses both Protestant and Catholic terms (minister and father) to refer to the same person.

From the era of ragtime and jazz into the era of hip-hop, American music has also been seen as a sign of cultural disaster and a menace to European civilization. The danger has often been seen in racial and ethnic terms. Georges Duhamel, a member of the Académie Française and the author of, among other works, *America: The Menace* (1931), wrote that "North America has inspired no painters, kindled no sculptors, brought forth no songs from its musicians, except for the monotone Negroes."[41]

The renowned social critic Adolf Hitler was building on this preexisting European analysis when he once noted, "Everything about the behavior of American society reveals that it's half Judaised and the other half negrified."[42] As the Nobel Prize–winning Norwegian novelist Knut Hamsun so elegantly expressed it, "Instead of founding an intellectual elite, America has established a mulatto studfarm."[43]

Even as Europeans denounced American racial policies as cruel and unjust, they feared the contagion of America's African side. The racial subtext in a fearful 1950 *Der Spiegel* article on American music is not hard to read; this sultry, rhythmic music from the slums had turned American youth into "haunted medicine men of a jungle tribe governed only by music." An article on Elvis Presley suggested that his primary appeal was to "wild barbarians in ecstasy" and to "primitive human beings."[44]

More recently, it is in the Arab world where one finds the ability to hate America because it mistreats black people—and to despise America because it is so full of black people. A recent Saudi newspaper cartoon presented Secretary of State Condoleezza Rice in the stereotypical and exaggerated caricature of the Negrophobic imagination, with Star of David earrings to add to the horror.[45] Sayyid Qutb called jazz "this music that the savage bushmen created to satisfy their primitive desires, and their desire for noise on the one hand, and the abundance of animal noises on the other."[46]

Hoping to defend their musical accomplishments, American intellectuals and their allies abroad pointed to jazz as a way that American popular music could ultimately acquire some intellectual respectability. Theodor Adorno of the Frankfurt School was unimpressed: "Anyone who allows the growing respectability of mass culture to seduce him into equating a popular song with modern art because of a few false notes squeaked by a clarinet; anyone who mistakes a triad studded with 'dirty notes' for atonality, has already capitulated to barbarism."[47] The American mass culture "proclaims the stupor of tolerated excess to be the realm of freedom," Adorno wrote.

For the Syrian parliamentarian Dr. Muhammad Habash, the vulgarity of American popular culture is related to what he believes are the Nietzschean

foundations of American life. "I personally view him," Habash writes of
Nietzsche, "as the philosopher of American administrations and philosopher of American policy." In particular, Habash cites a dictum of Nietzsche's as the basis for American policy in the world today: "If we want to
build our culture we must crush the weak, oppress the weak, crush them,
climb all over their corpses. We must fulfill this duty in order to build our
culture."[48] This is not, Habash tells us, an attack on American culture; after
all, Nietzsche is a well-esteemed philosopher.

For Habash, American popular culture is more than a business; propagat-
ing violence and degradation through culture implements the Nietzschean
project of American society as a whole.

> The culture that is exported today, through Hollywood, for example, is a culture
> of violence, a culture of films ending usually with the policeman bleeding and
> the robber hugging his lover and smoking a cigar. These images glorify cruelty,
> glorify force, glorify the man who is victorious because of his might and his
> weapons.[49]

Carthage had been founded by suspiciously Semitic émigrés from the
neighborhood of ancient Judea, and the Waspophobe—like Hitler and
Stalin—will often be an anti-Semite as well. G. Volkol's attack on the "Shylockian" nature of Anglo-American society slyly hinted at a theme of growing importance among the enemies of the Anglophones.

A long European tradition now flourishing in the Muslim Middle East
associates the godless capitalism of the Anglo-Saxons and their acolytes
with the rise of Jewish power. King Edward I forced the Jews out of Britain
in 1290; they returned under Cromwell and, though still often marginalized
and suspected, played an increasing role in British life from the seventeenth
century forward. The triumphal nineteenth-century entry into British politics of Benjamin Disraeli—Christian by faith but openly proud of his Jewish
ancestry—raised eyebrows across Europe. By the end of the nineteenth century, and especially at the time of the Boer Wars, which much European
opinion interpreted as an attack on virtuous farmers ("Boer" is a Dutch
word meaning farmer) to protect the interests of Jewish plutocrats, the link
between the Jews and Anglo-American capitalism was self-evident to many
observers.

This theme appeared in the anti-Dreyfusard propaganda of the French
Catholic and nationalist right early in the twentieth century and became
something of an obsession of the French right between the wars. The "dera-
cinated," "cosmopolitan" Jew was ideally suited to function in the deraci-

nated, cosmopolitan spew of Anglo-Saxon society, where no value but money was believed to reign. Here, once again, America was a worse England: when Fanny Trollope came to define the distinctive marks of the Yankee, she noted that in his love of lucre, the Yankee resembled "the sons of Abraham."[50]

Anglo-Saxon capitalism, continental critics argued, quickly degenerated into plutocracy, and the democratic institutions and values on which the Anglo-Saxons prided themselves were only a façade. A handful of billionaires pulled the strings behind the scenes—and these financiers and plutocrats were, of course, often Jewish. Nazi agitators delighted in detailing the connections, real or invented, that linked Franklin Roosevelt to "the Jews": Roosevelt had a Jewish secretary of the treasury, and Secretary of State Cordell Hull was married to a Jew. Winston Churchill was another attractive target. The anti-Semitic Lord Alfred Douglas—whose outraged father initiated the process that brought Oscar Wilde to grief because of Wilde's relationship with the young Lord Alfred—charged that Churchill had received £40,000 from the Jewish financier Sir Ernest Cassel for providing inside war information that allowed Sir Ernest and his associates to make a speculative windfall. Douglas sued a newspaper for libel when the newspaper called this story a fabrication and testified in court that Churchill,

> this ambitious and brilliant man, short of money and eager for power, was trapped by the Jews . . . his house was furnished for him by Sir Ernest Cassel.[51]

Douglas won a derisory judgment of one farthing (one-fourth of a penny) and, furious, went on to publish thirty thousand copies of a pamphlet that accused Churchill of being under Cassel's influence. Douglas was arrested for criminal libel, and the case went back to court, now with Douglas as the defendant. More details of Churchill's relationship with the rich, German-born financier emerged. Cassel had invested Churchill's writing and lecturing income, and had given him a cash wedding present worth almost $40,000 in 2006 U.S. dollars. Cassel had also furnished a "small library" for Churchill at his London house on South Bolton Street.

No wrongdoing on Churchill's part was ever shown, but rumors of subterranean financial links between Churchill and Jewish financiers would persist and be revived by the Nazis in the 1930s.[52]

During the 1920s and 1930s, French opinion fumed about the presumed power of the Jewish financiers in the United States, and over American demands for the repayment of the French war debt. "*Oncle* Shylock" replaced "*Oncle* Sam" in many French minds, and anti-Semitism and anti-liberalism merged, not for the last time, into a picture of the hated Judeo-Saxon power. "Henceforth the world will be governed by the Anglo-Saxon peoples, who, in turn, are swayed by their Jewish elements,"[53] mourned a group of European critics of the 1919 Treaty of Versailles. This lament can now be found on an Islamist Web site.

Once again it would not only be the Nazis who saw Jewish hands in this new and alarming manifestation of the Anglo-Saxon threat. The success of Jews in Tin Pan Alley and Hollywood—something like the success that, today, new generations of African American artists and entrepreneurs are achieving in those fields—struck many European observers as yet another sinister sign of the Anglo-Saxon/Hebraic synthesis. Plutocracy and vulgarity linked with unappeasable greed and an inflexible, uncompromising will to power: this is how the Anglo-Saxons appeared to those who confronted them.

That Jews flocked to Hollywood, that many prominent studio heads, actors, writers, and producers were Jewish, and that these first- and second-generation immigrants were so quickly able to assimilate into the cultural power structure of the Anglo-American world inflamed Waspophobic opinion and tightened the link between hatred of Wasps and hatred of Jews. The two groups were clearly hand in glove, engaged in some great conspiracy to destroy the moral fiber of the world while subjecting its peoples to the savageries and barbarities of Anglo-Saxon-Jewish "culture" and capitalism at its worst.

The World of the Waspophobe

The true Waspophobe hates America because it is an insolent sea of vulgarity in which a triumphant and unrestrained rabble heedlessly treads underfoot the complex and subtle achievement that only the cultivated minority can support; he also hates America because it is a land of hideous inequality where the all-powerful plutocrats trample the silently suffering and impoverished masses into the dust. He hates America because it hates pleasure and sex like the Puritans of old; he hates America because its decadent hedonism has commodified sex. The Waspophobe at one and the same time can hate American militarism and brutal use of force while despising the cowardice of the American people and their unwillingness to fight and die for what they believe in. The American must be hated because he is indifferent to the world, wrapped up in his own concerns to the exclusion of all else; he must be resisted because he is inflexibly and permanently determined to impose his values on the rest of the world. One despises America as a contemptible, exhausted, decadent society; one resists it because it is voraciously dynamic and expansive. The American is naïve and unworldly; the American is insinuating and sly. The American is a God-besotted Holy Roller; the American is the cynical Jewish manipulator with no values either religious or secular. The American is a fat and lazy couch potato like Homer Simpson; the American is the shrewd and relentless businessman who ruthlessly strips his opponents of their assets by a superintelligence both icy and malign. The American male is a reckless, quick-drawing cowboy trampling over all restraints and civilized norms; the American male is a feminized weakling under the thumb of his domineering wife. The American woman is a slut and seducer who sleeps with any man she can find; the American woman is a hatchet-faced, ice-cold Amazonian man-killer with no trace of femininity left. America is a soft and pathetic land of whiners and twelve-steppers, narcissistically preoccupied with its emotional problems; it is a brutal land of machines where winners eat losers and solidarity and sympathy are crushed underfoot. America oppresses and suppresses its noble black minority; America is a degraded and mongrelized society whose popular culture spews African filth over the world's vulnerable youth. America endangers the peace of the world by an unworldly idealism that fecklessly threatens the stability of the international system; America foments war by policies so ruthless and inhuman that they generate mass outrage and resistance all over the world. America is evil because it is fundamentalist and Christian; it is evil because it is ruled by the Jew.

Anti-Americanism in this mode is more than a sentiment; it is an all-encompassing if not always coherent worldview. The writers Ian Buruma and Avishai Margalit relate it to a phenomenon they label "Occidentalism"—the many attempts by European and non-European writers and political thinkers to develop a coherent counterideology to various aspects of the eighteenth-century Enlightenment. Occidentalism shares with Waspophobia a systematic hatred and detestation of liberal capitalist modernity; the difference between them is that while the Occidentalist may not identify either Britain or America (or both) as the primary source and power of this hated modernity, the Waspophobe does.

Ironically, France is often the major villain for non-Waspophobic Occidentalists. The German Romantics who fought to free German culture of the hated influence of the French Enlightenment, Algerian rebels against French cultural and political domination, and Catholic traditionalists opposing secular modernity and the radical Jacobin tradition of not only the separation of church and state but the marginalization of the church by the state have all seen the French Revolution (aided by the Freemasons and the Bavarian Illuminati) as the source of the evils troubling the human race. Farther east, Russian intellectual history is full of Occidentalists—pan-Slavs and others—who reacted against what they saw as the cold, cruel light of the German Enlightenment to preserve the rich inner world of the Russian soul. In Central Asia there are Occidentalists who want to eliminate the hated westernizing influence of Russia.

Over time, however, as American political, economic, and cultural power has come to replace and to tower over French, German, and Russian power in the world, Occidentalism is becoming more closely linked to Waspophobia—just as the British have progressively been replaced by the Americans as the Great Satan of the Waspophobic imagination. Occidentalism as such is unlikely to disappear, but the focus on America is likely to heighten. To the Occidentalist, America will be hated as the purest expression of a tendency found throughout the West and indeed throughout the world. The Waspophobe will hate the rest of the West because it is the part of the world most penetrated by the values and ideas of American society and which most closely resembles the United States; the Occidentalist will hate America because it is there that the despised ideologies and values of the West find their purest expression and their political champion.

Also among the Occidentalists and the anti-Americans must be counted the anti-Semites. The Occidentalist and the anti-American hate the Jews because the Jews and/or the Israelis are allies of the West or of the Americans; the anti-Semite hates the West and the Americans because they are the slaves of the Jew.

For all three groups of modernity-haters, America and all it stands for are more than an annoyance. The United States, its culture, its way of life, and its values are a menace to those well beyond its frontiers. The menace is omnipresent, total, and terrifying. A Moroccan feminist scholar described the feeling of Arab men during the 1991 Gulf War when Mecca came under the protection of the American air force:

> The enemy is no longer just on earth; he occupies the heavens and the stars and rules over time. He seduces one's wife, veiled or not, entering through the skylight of television. Bombs are only an incidental accessory for the new masters. Cruise missiles are for great occasions and the inevitable sacrifices. In normal times they nourish us with "software": advertising messages, teenage songs,

everyday technical information, courses for earning diplomas, languages and codes to master. Our servitude is fluid, our humiliation anesthetizing.[54]

Under contemporary conditions America is everywhere that the goods of the modern consumer economy penetrate and everywhere that electronic waves can carry the messages of the contemporary media. In virtually every country of the world powerful sections of both public opinion and the elites have bought into a program of "Americanization"—economically if not politically. Imperialism is no longer a question of conquest or settlement. There is a spiritual aggression, a conquest based on consumption, like the fear that obsessed some French intellectuals after World War II that the Marshall Plan would subject France to "Coca-colonization."

"Has America left a place in our lives that it did not corrupt for us Muslims?" writes the Egyptian Tareq Hilmi. In the U.N., the World Bank, and the IMF and in the GATT, the United States uses the international system to divide, weaken, and exploit the hapless Muslim world. Yet there is hope. The bigger they are, the harder they fall. Quoting the "well known economist, Lyndon LaRouche," Hilmi looks forward to an imminent financial crisis and collapse. The ordination of "Sodomite" bishops in the Anglican Communion is additional grounds to believe that the Anglo-American catastrophe, so long and unaccountably delayed, may now be at hand.[55]

Today's systematic anti-Americans see the various aspects of an increasingly weighty American presence in the world as part of the old "manifest destiny" Anglo-Saxon plan for world domination.

Their fears are not totally without foundation. Whether one listens to politicians like George W. Bush talk about America's mission to promote democracy around the world, or one listens to American feminist organizations eager to promote a certain type of gender relations around the world and resolved to use American government pressure to help them to do it, whether one reads Pentagon planning documents that stress the need for the United States to ensure that no country ever seeks to reach military parity with it, or whether one pays attention to American businesses seeking to penetrate new markets while noting that Americans continue to dominate and control the Internet despite international opposition, the non-American can be excused for wondering whether there are ways to reduce America's global influence.

For the anti-American, these and other signs of American power are more than disturbing. They are signs of a mounting, dangerous threat to all that is valuable in human life. There is, as usual, a long French tradition that identifies the triumph of America with the triumph of the machine over life, but here it is the German philosopher Martin Heidegger who has best expressed the anti-American view. American culture and life, "American-ism" in Heidegger's thought, is the hideous final destination on humanity's road away from a meaningful way of life. America reduces life to the consumption of meaningless products and the experience of meaningless events, and human relationships are emptied of everything worthwhile. This is the vision of a nongeographic but still imperial America that seduces one's wife over the television, that steals one's son and one's daughter via the movie and the video game.

In the early 1930s Heidegger saw the Soviet Union and the United States as twin evils: both in their way expressed the triumph of the machine and of instrumentality over real human life. For a time, at least, Heidegger went so far as to see Nazi Germany as Europe's best and even noblest protection from the twin threats. Like Robert Ley, like the young German squirrel fancier, Heidegger feared for the beloved browns at the claws of the aggressive black squirrels. After the end of the Nazi period, Heidegger concluded that the Marxist machine, for all its evil, was less dangerous than the American; he hoped that an intellectual dialogue with Marxism could open a new road to an effective anti-American coalition.

Heidegger's vision remains central to much European and Latin American anti-Americanism today on both the left and the right; thinkers in the Muslim world have reached similar conclusions by slightly different thought processes. It appears today that some elements among the remnants of the Marxist left, radical Greens, miscellaneous postmodern radicals of various hue, and radicalized Muslims are searching for a way to unite around the only issues that connect them: hatred of liberal capitalist modernity, Israel, and the United States of America.

In October 2002, Osama bin Laden issued a message to the American people that summarizes most of the themes that the enemies and the opponents of the Anglo-Saxons (and their Jewish associates) have endorsed over the generations. Calling Americans a people of "fornication, homosexuality, intoxicants, gambling, and usury," and "the worst civilization witnessed in the history of mankind," bin Laden delivers a multipronged indictment.

The constitutional separation of church and state violates the authority of God. Usury, the basis of the American economy, has allowed the Jews to take control of the media, and made Americans their servants. Americans identify sexual immorality with personal freedom—and left President Clinton's immoral acts in the Oval Office unpunished. Americans gamble. They exploit women like consumer products while claiming to support the liberation of women. Commercialized, commodified sex permeates the American economy and culture. American scientists invented and spread AIDS. American pollution is destroying the world—and even so, the United States has refused to ratify the Kyoto Protocol. American politics only pretends to be democratic; it is actually a plutocratic system, with Jews behind the scenes pulling the strings. America is the most violent society in the history of the world, dropping nuclear weapons on Japan among many other crimes. American hypocrisy is without compare; American democracy is reserved for the privileged white race. America has no respect for international law, though it wants to impose such laws on others. The Patriot Act and other harsh measures after 9/11 fully expose the hypocrisy of America's claims to stand for human rights.[56]

ALTHOUGH ANTI-AMERICANISM has replaced Anglophobia as the dominant paradigm among Waspophobes, the Walrus and the Carpenter, along with the Jew, still haunt the beaches of many imaginations in the world. Speaking of Britain and America, Osama bin Laden told an interviewer that "[i]t is well known that the policies of these two countries bear the greatest enmity towards the Islamic world."[57] He later returned to the theme:

> I say that there are two sides in the struggle: one side is the global Crusader alliance with the Zionist Jews, led by America, Britain and Israel, and the other side is the Islamic world.[58]

The Shi'a Iranians also still see the old partnership at work, and are prepared to resist it. Reporting on the establishment of a new Iranian organization to export its revolution on an international basis, a London-based Arabic-language newspaper reported that a "theoretician" for the Iranian Revolutionary Guards described plans for future actions against Iran's primary enemies:

> Haven't the Jews and the Christians achieved their progress by means of toughness and repression? We have a strategy drawn up for the destruction of Anglo-Saxon civilization and for the uprooting of the Americans and the English.[59]

Iranian president Mahmoud Ahmadinejad struck a similarly optimistic tone in a 2005 speech, predicting that, as a result of their apostate ways, Iran's enemies would fall: "Today, it is the United States, Britain, and the

Zionist regime which are doomed to disappear as they have moved far away from the teachings of God. It is a divine promise."[60]

The oysters are eaten, the beaches unswept—and the Walrus, the Carpenter, and their Jewish paymasters need to be called to account.

THOSE OPPOSED TO ANGLO-SAXON CIVILIZATION and order have long sought to oppose the Anglo-Saxon powers militarily, politically, and culturally. The need for a pan-European union against this menace figured prominently in the arguments of four centuries of continental statesmanship. Charles V and Philip II of Spain tried and failed to unite Europe under the banner of Catholic orthodoxy against the heretics of the foggy isle. Napoleon urged the subjects of his empire to support his effort to overturn the ancient tyranny of the perfidious shopkeepers; French intellectuals were calling for a European union against the Anglo-Saxon threat that would include even the hated German enemy after 1870. Both the Kaiser and Hitler called for European solidarity with Germany in its selfless stand against the Anglo-Saxon menace. Communist propaganda did everything it could during the Cold War to alienate Europe from its Anglo-Saxon protectors. In post–Cold War Europe, enthusiasts for the European Union have argued that only a united Europe can be resolute and strong enough to stand against the insidious American forces of globalization and the Anglo-Saxon social model. Jean-Paul Sartre brought Heidegger's anti-American thought into the mainstream of postwar European Marxism, where it played a role in efforts by the Communists to disrupt the western alliance in the Cold War. Today the ideas if not the systematic philosophy of Heidegger, this secular German ex-Nazi long popular among western Communists, enjoy a new vogue in the Muslim Middle East among some who find his principled anti-Americanism a useful tool as they, in their turn, seek an effective means of opposing and destroying the threatening American system and its proliferating works.

AND SO, for four hundred years, two discourses have been taking shape. The Anglophones have seen themselves as defending and sometimes advancing liberty, protecting the weak, providing opportunity to the poor, introducing the principles of morality and democracy into international life, and creating more egalitarian and more just societies at home and abroad. Their enemies have looked at the same set of facts and seen a ruthless assault on every kind of social and moral decency.

One can argue whether these ideological differences were a cause of the frequent wars between the Anglophones and their neighbors or whether they were a consequence, whether we fought because we hated each other or hated each other because we fought.

There are, of course, many shades of nuance. Not all Waspophobes are anti-Semites; not all Anglo-Saxons hate high culture. There are Waspophobes in the Anglosphere and Waspophiles in France.

Yet on the whole it is difficult to avoid the conclusion that something very real and very important has been at stake in these frequent conflicts between the English-speaking societies and their neighbors and rivals. It is, at bottom, a religious conflict.

"We worship God by loathing America," writes Tareq Hilmi, latest in a long line of Anglophobes and anti-Americans to reach this conclusion.

Our enemies, said Oliver Cromwell, "are all the wicked men of the world, whether abroad or at home, that are the enemies to the very being of this nation . . . from that very enmity that is in them against whatsoever should serve the glory of God and the interest of his people; which they see to be more eminently, yea most eminently patronized and professed in this nation—we will speak it not with vanity—above all nations in this world."

They can't both be right.

The Long War

The conventional narrative of the rise of a unified "West" disguises one of the oldest and most bitter clashes of civilization in world history: centuries of warfare between the Anglo-Saxons and continental Europe. During the long years of struggle, almost as much ink as blood has been spilled in the quarrel between the Anglo-Saxons and their opponents in Europe and, increasingly, beyond it. The Anglo-Saxon world has something to learn from its critics; the oysters have a point. Much of what "they" have said about "us" is true and important. We can and should learn from it.

Still, beneath all the hypocrisy and the humbug, the crimes and the greed, something very real was at stake in the Wasp wars. There really was a difference between the liberal empires of the Anglo-Saxon powers and the illiberal ones on the continent, and whatever the faults on the Anglo-Saxon side, there has been surprisingly little demand for the restoration of Catholic absolutism, Jacobin terror, Napoleonic megalomania, Prussian militarism, the sadistic lunacies of Nazi Germany and imperial Japan, the blood-drenched "scientific" fanaticism of Lenin, the murderous paranoia of Stalin and Mao, or the mind-numbingly sterile bureaucratic oppression of Leonid Brezhnev. One feels somehow that when and if the bigotry and terrorism of fanatics like Osama bin Laden and the Ayatollah Khomeini are consigned like these others to the dustbins of history, the world will feel equally little desire to exhume and revive the doctrines and practices of these latest opponents of Cromwell and his heirs.

As one struggles to make sense of this long war, there is something else to reflect on: victory.

Since the time of Elizabeth I, the Anglo-Saxons have not only fought wars with illiberal opponents in Europe and beyond but they have won them. First Britain and then the United States rose to a global power and cultural dominance never before seen. It is perhaps bad manners to say so, but that does not make it less true. The Anglo-Saxon powers have established the most extensive, powerful, and culturally significant hegemony that history records—and this in the teeth of bitter opposition by rich and powerful states capable of waging both military and ideological campaigns against the Anglo-American order. The Anglo-Americans have gone from strength to strength, from riches to riches, while their opponents suffered ignominy and humiliation until they learned to accommodate themselves to the Anglo-Saxon order.

As Cromwell, but not Martin Heidegger, would put it, from the seventeenth century to the present day, the Evil One and his minions on earth have hated the English-speakers and sought to break their pride and humble their power. Mighty axes of evil have risen against the Anglophones, and the greatest concentrations of armed force and economic power ever seen have combined against the English-speaking world—and they have failed. Drake singed the beard of the king of Spain; Cromwell helped break his heart. Marlborough defeated the armies of Louis XIV; the elder Pitt destroyed the empire of his heir. The younger Pitt organized resistance to Napoleon. Wilson and Lloyd George stood against the Kaiser; Roosevelt and Churchill crushed the Nazis and brought fire down from heaven to punish Germany's crimes against the world. Truman contained Stalin; Reagan lived to see Gorbachev fall.

In all these wars the Anglophones had allies. There have always been countries, often the smaller and weaker ones, who believe with Addison that the Anglophones are the power that will "answer the afflicted neighbor's prayer." Yet there have been repeated moments when the Anglophones stood alone or nearly so: when all of Europe lay under a nightmarish single power—when a Stalin, a Hitler, a Napoleon, or a Louis seemed on the verge of triumph. The votaries of totalitarian ideologies were confident and exulting; the Anglo-Americans were scornfully dismissed as outmoded and irrelevant. The Dark Lord was triumphant, the alliances broken, the Dark Tower rose to the sky and the fear-laden, poisonous smoke of Mount Doom overlay Middle Earth.

Yet always in the end, somehow, the tricksy little hobbits win. The Tower falls and the Shire blooms. Narnia rises and the witches flee.

This is the biggest geopolitical story in modern times: the birth, rise, triumph, defense, and continuing growth of Anglo-American power despite continuing and always renewed opposition and conflict. The last ingredient necessary to understand the bitter rage and fanatical hatred of the most determined enemies of that system today is this history of successive triumphs. For the Waspophobe, history has been headed in a catastrophically wrong direction since the seventeenth century; every confrontation leaves the Anglo-American system stronger and more powerful than the last. Resistance is necessary; resistance is futile. Underneath the screams of hatred and defiance from men like Osama bin Laden and Abu Musab al-Zarqawi lurks the knowledge that the tide of history has flowed toward the English-speakers for a long time now.

The rest of us, looking back across four hundred years of Anglo-American power, ask what it means. Apparently this: God is a liberal; the Devil is not. It might be difficult to get Cromwell, Truman, Addison, and Pitt to agree on a precise definition of what they were fighting for, but for want of anything better, Reagan's 1987 cri de coeur from Berlin will do: "Mr. Gorbachev, tear down this Wall!"

That God is a liberal has been the great fundamental conviction of the English-speaking powers since the English Reformation, and, if history is the mirror of Providence, they were right. Every century since the sixteenth has seen the Anglo-Americans face imposing, illiberal opponents, and each century has seen the Anglo-Americans and their world order stronger at the end than it was at the beginning. The Anglo-Americans have sought to build a global trading system based increasingly on liberal democratic capitalism; their enemies have resisted and tried to build walls that would protect their societies from the disruptive effects of Anglo-Saxon practices and ideas. Those walls have a way of coming down; the Anglo-Saxons believe that this pattern reflects the way God, or at least the forces of nature, want the world to work.

In the words of Robert Frost: "Something there is that doesn't love a wall."

Nothing in the history of the modern world is as enduring or as important as the development and rise of the Anglo-American world order. Since Good Queen Bess called upon Sir Francis Drake to sail out against the Spanish Armada, almost everything has changed: technology, society, politics, culture, religion. The last four hundred years have seen unprecedented changes proceed at accelerating rates.

But something hasn't changed. The basic structure of world politics that was dimly emerging under Elizabeth and Cromwell—a liberal maritime empire opposing the consolidation of illiberal hegemonies on the Eurasian mainland—matured and persists. True, the exhausted Walrus lies panting in the surf, only occasionally rising on arthritic flippers to bark out sharp words of advice ("Now, George, this is no time to go wobbly!" as Margaret Thatcher told the first President Bush in the run-up to the first Gulf War); but the Carpenter—once just a glint in the eye of Queen Bess—still patrols the sandy shores, with one eye cocked for the Devil, and the other on the deep blue sea.

Part Two

The Dread and Envy of Them All

When Britain first, at heaven's command,
Arose from out the azure main,
This was the charter of the land,
And guardian angels sang this strain

"Rule, Britannia! Britannia rule the waves;
Britons never, never, never shall be slaves."

The nations, not so blest as thee,
Must, in their turns, to tyrants fall:
While thou shalt flourish great and free,
The dread and envy of them all.

—*James Thomson*

Four • The Protocols of the Elders of Greenwich

W aspophobes are right about one thing: the Anglo-Americans do in fact have a secret master plan to dominate the world, and they have been following it faithfully for three hundred years. During that time Britain and the United States have been willing and able to adhere to a unique approach to world politics that has consistently led the English-speaking powers to greater success in world affairs than their rivals.

This Anglospheric grand strategy has not always been conscious. To some degree it is embedded in the assumptions, habits, and institutions of the English-speaking powers. Ronald Reagan did not study the speeches of Oliver Cromwell to plan his attack on the evil empire of his day; George Kennan did not develop his strategy for containing Communism by studying the economic and political strategies of the Duke of Marlborough in Queen Anne's War.

Although many British and American statesmen were aware that they shared a distinct approach to world power, the Protocols of the Elders of Greenwich, the secret Anglo-Saxon plan for global power, were never written down. No secret society whispered the master plan down the ages. By doing what came naturally, by following the logic of their geography, culture, and society, the British and then the Americans happened on a way of managing their affairs in the world that provided for a flexible and durable form of global power suited to their circumstances while committing them to a less difficult set of tasks and conflicts than other leading powers have faced.

Yet in retrospect, one can clearly see a basic approach to global politics and world power that has informed the foreign policy of the Anglo-Saxon hegemons. The core geopolitical power strategy of the English-speaking world can best be described in the words of Admiral A. T. Mahan. Describing the rise of British power in its seventeenth- and eighteenth-century wars against France, Mahan wrote about the rise of an "overwhelming power, destined to be used as selfishly, as aggressively, though not as cruelly, and much more successfully than any that had preceded it. This was the power of the sea."[1]

However, if the Anglo-Saxon powers have carried out a sea-power strategy, they didn't invent it. Trading empires were known in ancient times, and the Athenians recognized themselves as a sea power in their long contest with the land power of Sparta. Mahan himself wrote at length about how the Romans had to build a superior sea power to overcome their enemies in Carthage. More recently, the Venetians and Genoese had built extensive maritime empires based on a mix of capitalistic enterprise and naval power.

The modern version of sea power was invented by the Dutch. The system of global trade, investment, and military power that the Dutch built in the seventeenth century was the envy and the wonder of the world at the time, and many of its basic features were adopted by the British and the Americans in subsequent years. That Dutch system was like version 1.0 of the operating software on which much of the world still runs. At the turn of the eighteenth century the British introduced version 2.0; there were several incremental upgrades along the way until the Americans introduced version 3.0 after the Second World War.

In each version, sea power has built up global systems of trade and might; this maritime order has played an increasingly important role in world history since the Dutch first developed it. It is not too much to say that the last four hundred years of world history can be summed up in ten letters. As leadership in the maritime order shifted from the United Provinces of the Netherlands to the United Kingdom and finally to the United States, the story of world power goes U.P. to U.K. to U.S.

"I Have Always Honored the King of Spain"

It all started in the Low Countries, a collection of provinces in northwestern Europe now divided among the Netherlands, Belgium, and France. The region had long been among the most prosperous and advanced places in Europe. Wool cloth was one of the few things that medieval Europe produced which the rest of the world was eager to buy; the ability to purchase high-quality fleeces from England, to reprocess them into both fine and coarse fabrics, and, with the help of Italian traders, to sell them in the rich markets of the urban Middle East provided the Low Countries with centuries of prosperity and laid the foundations for sophisticated industrial production and technically advanced shipbuilding.

In the late Middle Ages these rich provinces were under the feudal leadership of dukes of Burgundy until January 1477, when the Duke, Charles the Bold—also known as Charles the Terrible—died in an unsuccessful attempt to retake the city of Nancy. Charles has been called the last embodiment of the feudal spirit; in any case, with his death the Low Countries passed to the legacy-hunting Hapsburg dynasty, because Charles's only surviving heir was married to Maximilian I of the Holy Roman Empire.

Intrepid matchmaking soon brought the Hapsburgs another bonanza: Maximilian's son married the daughter (and heir) of Ferdinand and Isabella of Spain. Under Maximilian's grandson Charles V (1500–1558), the Hapsburgs ruled much of Europe as well as the New World empire rapidly acquired by the Spanish conquistadors. The Low Countries went from being the most important possession of the dukes of Burgundy to being a small but rich part of a far-flung empire involved in all the tumults and struggles of European politics.

It started off smoothly enough. The Hapsburgs taxed the wealthy burghers of the Low Countries—but the vast imperial government was good for business, too. The superior soldiers, shipbuilders, traders, and merchants of the Low Countries played a major role in the burgeoning Hapsburg empire, and much of the gold plundered from the Americas found its way to the burghers of Amsterdam.

Over time, however, relations between the world-girdling empire and its Low Countries subjects deteriorated. The Low Countries objected to taxes that went to far-off wars, like the struggles between the Hapsburgs and the Ottomans in Hungary and the Mediterranean. For the merchants and nobles of the increasingly restive provinces, these wars were bad for trade; being taxed to pay for wars that hurt your trade was not a good bargain. When Charles V abdicated in 1556, the Hapsburgs' Austrian and Spanish possessions were separated again. Charles left his son Philip the thrones of Naples and Milan, Sicily, the Netherlands, and Spain; Philip's brother Ferdinand received the imperial crown. When Philip II tried to reorganize and centralize the administration of his still sprawling domain, his Low Countries subjects resented the loss of local control over their own affairs—and resented the foreign governors and soldiers sent to enforce Hapsburg orders.

The Reformation made things worse. The Dutch in particular tended toward the Protestant cause, and the doctrines of John Calvin found a ready hearing there. The Hapsburgs, patrons of the Spanish Inquisition, wished to enforce strict Catholic control over their empire.

What became known as the Dutch revolt broke out in 1568; although interrupted by truces it was not finally settled until the United Provinces won formal independence eighty years later in the Treaty of Westphalia. Like the American revolutionaries before July 1776, the first Dutch rebels claimed to be loyal subjects of Philip II, fighting only his evil counselors. The Dutch national anthem still contains the plea of their first revolutionary leader: "I have always honored the king of Spain." This phase did not last long and the Dutch revolt soon developed into the first European war that could be called a world war as the Dutch, building their naval power and their worldwide trade, fought Hapsburg forces in China, the East Indies, and Brazil.

In the earliest stages, the war was a desperate struggle for survival. Fearing that a Hapsburg victory against the Dutch would lead to a Spanish conquest of England (Mary I, "Bloody Mary," as she became known to Protestants following the religious persecutions of her reign, had obligingly named Philip II as her heir following their marriage), Elizabeth I sent English troops to defend the Dutch Republic. That provocation eventually launched the Spanish Armada in 1588, and it marked England's tentative entry into the struggle for global supremacy that it would ultimately win.

Disappointed but not daunted by his failure to inherit the English throne from Mary, in 1580 Philip II was fortunate enough to have inherited Portugal and its vast overseas empire from another dead wife, Princess Maria Manvela.* The combined might of Spain and Portugal was turned against the Dutch; they suffered shattering defeats and the loss of the southern portion of the country.

But they did more than survive. Even as they fought off Spanish, Portuguese, and occasionally French and English rivals, the Dutch built version 1.0 of the maritime system. Dutch trade, financial institutions, ingenuity, and science startled the world: the first modern joint stock companies, the first stock exchanges, the first great speculation bubble (the tulip mania of the 1630s), the arrival of religious tolerance and even liberty combined with major scientific and technological advances to unleash an extraordinary period of affluence and power. The Dutch "golden age" was the wonder of the century in Europe; its artistic accomplishments, its military triumphs, its

---

* Philip also had a claim to the throne through his mother, Isabella, daughter of King Manuel I of Portugal.

scientific feats, and its social traditions of liberty and tolerance still command our respect today.

The tiny Dutch Republic (about the size of Maryland) built a navy that, at its peak, dominated the oceanic trade routes of the world. With 168,000 sailors staffing 10,000 ships, Dutch commerce each year carried goods worth more than one billion francs.[2] The Dutch East India Company drastically curtailed Portuguese power in the Far East and founded a Dutch empire that would last there until the twentieth century. At one point the Dutch seemed poised to take Brazil from the Portuguese as well, while their North American colony of New Amsterdam looked ready to become a pillar of Dutch power in what is now the United States. The Dutch established a colony at Cape Town, and hardy if narrow-minded descendants of the Dutch colonists would defy both the British Empire and world opinion in the twentieth century. The financial market at Amsterdam was the center of world commerce; as late as 1803 Dutch financial markets played a central role in the financing of the Louisiana Purchase.

Seventeenth-century travelers were astonished at the affluence and the independence of even the common laborers in the United Provinces. As Jews from Portugal and Protestants from France poured into the Netherlands, bringing their skills and sometimes their wealth with them, the Dutch boasted that they were becoming a melting pot and a society open to the best talents from all over the world. When the bigoted colonial administrator Peter Stuyvesant tried to ban Portuguese Jewish refugees from settling in New Amsterdam, he was sternly rebuked by the Dutch West India Company—and the Jews were admitted. Wealthy merchants married into aristocratic families, and penniless laborers pushed their way into the trading elites as Dutch society developed the kind of social mobility that had been rare in feudal Europe—but would become increasingly common in the emerging world system. Rich young Dutchmen and their less wealthy but more learned tutors set off on the first version of the "grand tour," visiting universities and points of interest across Europe. Scholars flocked to Amsterdam to enjoy the freedom and intellectual stimulation they could not get at home; Dutch universities became renowned centers of scholarship and debate. Artists flourished as wealthy patrons provided the kind of support that in the past came only from princely courts. Dutch scientists and scholars astounded the world with discoveries and inventions.

A new kind of society and a new kind of power had appeared in the world. An open, dynamic, and capitalist society generated innovations in finance, technology, marketing, and communications. Those innovations offered the open society enormous advantages in world trade. The wealth

gained in this way provided the basis for military power that could withstand the largest and mightiest rival empires of the day. This basic formula
of an open society, world trade, and world power was the power secret of the
sea kings and the major driving force in the history of the last four hundred
years.

Westward the Course

The Dutch invented the system, but they could not maintain their place at its
center. World politics took a different turn, and the center of the emerging
maritime order crossed the North Sea to London as the seventeenth century
gave way to the eighteenth.

The problem was France. Reviving from a prolonged period of weakness
as a series of brilliant rulers replaced the weak government and civil wars of
the past with an absolute monarchy and a powerful, centralized state, as
Spanish power waned, France sought to dominate western Europe on land
and to use that power and wealth to project its power on a global scale. On
the sea, the English and the Dutch were sometimes divided by an increasingly bitter rivalry over the riches of the global sea trade and sometimes
driven together by a sense of common danger from France. Fear of Spain
had kept France friendly to the United Provinces; as that fear faded during
Spain's long decline, France sought to take the southern, Catholic half of the
Low Countries from the slipping grasp of the Spanish Hapsburgs. Any significant French advances in the neighborhood posed a mortal threat to
Dutch independence; the stage was set for the next installment in Europe's
long history of war.

The key French strategy during much of this phase was to keep England
weak and divided. Spain was in decline. The German lands were still weakened and exhausted from the devastating wars that followed the Reformation. With England out of the picture, France's only possible rival in western
Europe was the Dutch.

As long as the Stuarts reigned in London, keeping England weak was relatively straightforward. Supporting Charles II and James II in their attempts
to rule without Parliament usually worked very well. The Stuart kings
depended on the money and support they received from Paris, and never had
the resources or the authority to challenge French policy. Sometimes Louis
XIV would drag a weak and divided England into his quarrels with the

Netherlands; at other times the English would stay neutral as France sought to bring overwhelming military pressure against the tiny republic.

The French policy of divide and rule failed definitively in 1688–89 with the overthrow of England's last Catholic and Stuart king, James II. The stadtholder of the leading Dutch provinces, William III of Orange, was married to Mary, James II's eldest (and Protestant) daughter. As a powerful Dutch fleet landed in England, James's elite supporters, like John Churchill, Viscount Cornbury, and the Earl of Clarendon, deserted to the Protestant cause, and the Dutch leader and his wife gained the throne. After tense and complex negotiations William of Orange began to reign as William III, holding power jointly with his wife.

William's first task was to bring the British, the Dutch, and all the other countries worried about the rise of French power into what became known as the Grand Alliance. This alliance, with no more than the usual defections and changes, would endure through two wars until the Treaty of Utrecht in 1713 established a new order in Europe. Louis XIV was a tough opponent, and the War of the League of Augsburg and the War of the Spanish Succession were both grim and difficult affairs. In the end, though, the Anglo-Dutch alliance prevailed over the French.

Within the alliance, however, it was the British who gained. The two powers were roughly equal when the Dutch fleet installed its stadtholder as king of England in 1688–89; by 1713 the rising British Empire had clearly replaced the Dutch Republic as the senior partner in the firm. Not until Franklin Roosevelt led the United States to replace the British Empire as the leading power in the maritime system while defending the British against their German and Japanese enemies would any power make such deft use of an alliance.

Admiral Mahan argues that sea power was the key to both British victories—over their Dutch allies as well as their French enemies—during these wars. The problem for the Dutch was that their desperate need to defend their homeland against a French invasion forced them to concentrate their military efforts on land armies, leaving relatively little for the fleet. The British had no such problems, and their naval preponderance over the Dutch grew during the wars. In William's war councils, British admirals took precedence over their Dutch colleagues, and the naval strategy tended to follow British instincts.

Like the Dutch, France suffered from divided resources during the war. Distracted by his own heavy commitments on land, Louis XIV was unable to concentrate effectively on building the naval power that would have allowed him to defeat Britain by sea and make France, not Britain, the leading power in the emerging global system.

In the spring of 1689 French ships carried James II to Ireland, yet during the climactic phases of the Irish war, the French navy was afraid of battles at sea and failed to reinforce James's faltering expedition. As the War of the League of Augsburg progressed, French sea power dwindled; France's commerce was ruined and a lack of funds ultimately forced Louis XIV to starve his navy of needed supplies.

The War of the League of Augsburg ended in 1697 in a compromise peace, but the contest between France and England was only beginning. Its shape became clearer just a few years later with the outbreak of the War of the Spanish Succession.

This war began when Louis XIV, taking an idea from the Hapsburg playbook, combined clever genealogical arguments with asute political maneuvers to have his grandson named as the heir to the Spanish throne after the last of the increasingly enfeebled Spanish Hapsburgs died in 1701. Horrified by the thought of a union between the weak but huge Spanish empire and the aggressive power of France, Britain joined Austria, the Netherlands, and most of the German powers in another world war.

This war did not turn out as well for France, especially as the brilliance of allied generals like the Duke of Marlborough and Prince Eugene helped defeat French forces by land even as the French fleet vanished from the seas. Although political bickering in Britain and disputes among the allies allowed France to escape the worst consequences of its defeats, the Treaty of Utrecht that ended the War of the Spanish Succession in 1713 was a great success for the British and, to a lesser extent, for the Dutch. Not only was Louis's grandson forced to partition his inheritance in Europe, giving up enough additional territory in Italy to greatly weaken France's overall position, but naval power allowed Britain to make major gains around the world. The Dutch were pleased to see the Spanish Netherlands (what is now Belgium) pass into the much weaker grip of the Austrian Hapsburgs, removing the threat of direct French invasion of the Dutch homeland.

The biggest gains were at sea, however, and they were won by the British. The Treaty of Utrecht gave Britain Gibraltar, then and now the key to naval power in the Mediterranean. Britain also picked up the island of Minorca, a useful Mediterranean naval base. In North America its conquests were greater, with the French abandoning significant portions of Canada and acknowledging British claims to much of the rest. By keeping both the Dutch and the French largely occupied, the war helped the British solidify their growing power in India. As for South America, the British received the morally dubious but economically lucrative *asiento,* a license to import slaves into the Spanish colonies that de facto opened other enormous trading opportunities. The slow but inexorable replacement of Spanish power by British throughout Latin America arguably begins from this time. Similarly, the war solidified the Anglo-Portuguese relationship; British traders would enjoy increasingly close and profitable relationships with Portuguese territories through the ensuing decades. Meanwhile, the French state emerged from the war in worse financial shape than ever; it was less capable than before of sustaining a naval rivalry with the British, and Britain's economic advantage was beginning to grow.

As the French prepared for the negotiations that would ultimately result in the Treaty of Utrecht, the first secretary of the Ministry of Foreign Affairs warned that it would be a fatal error to allow the English any enterprising outposts in the Pacific:

> One can be sure that, however deserted it may be today . . . if it came into English hands, one would see there, in a few years, a large number of inhabitants, built-up ports, and the greatest entrepot of European and Asian manufactures, which the English would then purvey to the kingdoms of Peru and Mexico.[3]

This nightmare would ultimately be realized with Singapore and Hong Kong, cities that the British founded which gave new energy and impetus to commerce throughout the Pacific basin.

As version 2.0 of the maritime system took shape, new features were added to the Dutch design. One was the concept of the balance of power. The phrase first began to appear in this period of multipolar rivalry; by the end of the War of the Spanish Succession it had become a basic building block of the European political system. Mentioned in the Treaty of Utrecht, the European balance of power became a principle of legitimacy in international politics; countries had a right and indeed a duty to act when necessary to preserve it.

For Britain, the establishment of a European balance of power was a major strategic victory. Vexed and challenged by rival land powers, Britain's potential competitors would always have to divide their resources between land and sea forces. Britain, protected by the English Channel and the British navy, could ensure its superiority at sea.

In the future, any European country that wished to challenge Britain's global maritime order would first have to defeat all its rivals and potential rivals on the continent. Britain, of course, would not stand idle while those wars went on. Invoking the principle of the balance of power, Britain could and would intervene to make it difficult and perhaps even impossible for great continental powers to dominate Europe enough to set off on a career of global conquest.

Anglo-American diplomacy in Europe has followed these lines ever since, joining or forming coalitions of the weaker countries against the strongest. When President Truman organized NATO in the early stages of the Cold War, dropping our World War II ally the Soviet Union to include a weakened West Germany in our new coalition, he was following a diplomatic strategy that the first Duke of Marlborough understood very well.

The Americans have globalized this traditional British approach, typically promoting the weaker states against the strongest as its allies in any geostrategic theater. Today, for example, the United States continues to work toward the emergence of a stable balance of power in Asia, building new partnerships with old enemies like Vietnam. During the Cold War, Washington saw the USSR as the great threat to the balance of power in Asia, and lined up all the allies it could to balance it, including both China and Japan in its coalition. From World War I through 1949 the United States took a different tack following the same balance-of-power logic and sided with China against Japan.

The balance of power is a universal factor in international relations; all countries, not merely the British, the Americans, and the Dutch, have used it. What makes its use unique in the maritime system, however, is the way that the maritime powers have linked and leveraged it with a global strategy that, over time, has brought increasing rewards.

Ever since the reigns of King William and Queen Anne, the chief object of Anglo-American strategy has been global. The balance of power in Europe freed both Britain and the United States from the tyranny of neighborhood. They have not, like Germany and France, swapped provinces such as Alsace-Lorraine back and forth with the varying fortunes of war. For the Anglo-Americans, the great prize has been and remains the construction of a global system that meets their economic and security needs.

Less by a process of deep strategic reflection than through trial and error and the struggles of trade and economic interest in domestic politics, the British from the late seventeenth century forward saw with increasing clarity that the key to world power was not supremacy on the battlefields of Europe. Medieval English kings fought with their French rivals over duchies like Normandy and Anjou. Increasingly, such goals looked primitive and futile to their modern successors; the sometimes half-conscious, sometimes frankly acknowledged goal of the empire-building British state in modern times was to fashion a world system, not conquer a duchy.

The Britons who laid the foundation of the most powerful global empire ever created saw the rivalries of Europe less as a game to play than as a strategic asset. Let France and Prussia duke it out on the Rhine; let Austria and Prussia batter one another bloody over Silesia, an irregular, slightly sausage-shaped territory now part of Poland that is roughly equal to the combined area of Connecticut and Massachusetts. While they were busy with one another, England would build a global economic system that would leave all rivals in the dust. As Thomas Pelham-Holles, Duke of Newcastle-upon-Tyne and prime minister under George II and George III, once remarked, "Ministers in this country, where every part of the World affects us, in some way or another, should consider the whole Globe."[4]

In Anglo-American strategic thought, there is one world composed of many theaters. The theaters are all linked by the sea, and whoever controls the sea can choose the architecture that shapes the world. The primary ambition of Anglo-Saxon power is not dominance in a particular theater; it is to dominate the structure that shapes the conditions within which the actors in each of the world's theaters live. European policy, Asian policy, African policy, Middle Eastern policy: these policies are all means to an end. The end is control of the system that binds them all together.

Where they can, the Walrus and the Carpenter have sought to dominate whole regions and hemispheres—the British Empire in India, the United States in the Western Hemisphere. But where that is not possible, or not possible at a feasible cost, they have been happy to accept a balance of power in key theaters. A global power does not need to dominate every region to secure its goals. Some theaters can be ignored; in others a rival or partner can be allowed control. In some, one can set up a system of one's own; in others, a favorable balance of power secures one's key interests.

In Mahan's sense, sea power is more than a navy. It is more than control of strategic trade routes. It means using the mobility of the seas to build a global system resting on economic links as well as on military strength. It means using the strategic flexibility of an offshore power, protected to some degree from the rivalries and hostilities of land powers surrounded by powerful neighbors, to build power strategies that other countries cannot counter. It means using command of the seas to plant colonies whose wealth and success reinforce the mother country. It involves developing a global system that is relatively easy to establish and which, once developed, proves extremely difficult to dislodge.

THE TREATY OF UTRECHT left what was known, after the 1707 Act of Union between England and Scotland, as the (United) Kingdom of Great

Britain as the leading power of the rising maritime system. Another century of war would put that system to the test until Napoleon's final defeat at the battle of Waterloo left Great Britain the undisputed master of its universe.

The next round of the military struggle began in 1739 after Spanish officers boarding a British ship trading illegally in Spanish waters allegedly struck off the ear of Robert Jenkins, the ship's captain. When the aggrieved captain waved a jar containing his mistreated ear at a session of the House of Commons, Prime Minister Robert Walpole had no political choice but to declare war against Spain. The desultory War of Jenkins's Ear had few lasting consequences; Portobello Road in London was named for an ultimately pointless victory British forces achieved in Panama. The young colonial patriot Lawrence Washington, the future U.S. president's half brother, named the family home in Virginia Mount Vernon after Admiral Sir Edward Vernon, who won the Portobello engagement, and a dinner in honor of Vernon's triumph provided the occasion for the first public performance of "God Save the King." That song would not, however, displace the more traditional "Roast Beef of Old England" as the popular national anthem until the end of the century, and the results of the War of Jenkins's Ear were otherwise not very great. The war was gradually absorbed into the larger and, from the standpoint of Britain, almost equally pointless War of the Austrian Succession in which, after a great deal of mayhem and slaughter, Austria yielded Silesia to Prussia. During the war Bonnie Prince Charlie succeeded in landing in Scotland with a small group of supporters; he roused the Highland clans in a desperate dash into England and forced the panicked return of the small British army in Europe, but the French fleet was too weak to support him and the venture failed.

The more serious challenge Britain faced during this period was a renewed French attempt to build a rival global system. From early and unpromising beginnings, British power had grown considerably in India. Many fortunes were made as the British East India Company built an increasingly important trading empire. With fortified trading stations in Bombay, Calcutta, and Madras,* the British looked forward to steady growth in profits and power.

There was, however, the problem of the French. Arriving in India soon after the British, the French established trading posts and political relationships of their own. By 1740 the French trade, though only half the size of Britain's, was considerable, and the ably led French traders were competing with the British for favors and influence in important Indian courts.

* Known today as Mumbai, Kolkata, and Chennai.

The once-powerful Moghul Empire was rapidly declining, and better armed, organized, and trained European-led forces were demonstrating increasing military superiority over the various Indian states. It was becoming clear that either Britain or France would play a leading role in India's future—but it was far from clear which of the two would predominate.

In North America also, the French had recovered from their losses in the War of the Spanish Succession. In population and general economic development, the British colonies on the Atlantic seaboard rapidly outstripped the French settlements in Canada. Even so, French explorers had mapped out much of the strategic Mississippi and Ohio valleys while the English-speaking settlements still clung to the coastal plains. To worried strategists in Britain, and to optimists in France, it appeared possible that, with the help of Indian allies, the French would succeed in settling the Mississippi and Ohio, confining the British to their narrow strip along the coast.

The growth of French global power was also reflected in the Caribbean, where the brutal exploitation of slaves on the sugar plantations produced one of the major economic engines of the age. The French possessions on Hispaniola were fertile and vast. French sugar rapidly drove the English from European markets, and the trade of Britain's American colonies was increasingly attracted to flourishing French outposts like Guadeloupe and Martinique.

British and French forces and their native allies began to clash around the world, with conflict breaking out in both India and America. What Americans know as the French and Indian War began in 1754 as colonial American troops under the young militia officer George Washington clashed with a French garrison near the Ohio River. The first battle of the war took place on July 3 in heavy rain. After eight hours of fighting, the French forced Colonel Washington to surrender for the first and last time in his life—ironically on July 4. The French press would later vilify him as a coward who acted contrary to the laws of war, and Washington retreated over the mountains back to his home in Virginia.

The first, American stages of the conflict were quite satisfactory from the French point of view. The squabbling and disorganized American colonials were unable to mount an effective military campaign; professional British generals unfamiliar with the terrain and the conditions of frontier war led their lumbering armies into successive defeats. Washington recrossed the mountains in 1755 with General Edward Braddock, but another crushing defeat that July sent him back to Mount Vernon one more time, where the contrasts between his military record and that of Admiral Vernon at Portobello must have begun to look rather daunting.

The sparks thrown off by these distant colonial engagements fell on a European scene where fire was ready to break out. The rise of the formerly insignificant kingdom of Prussia to great power status had destabilized European power relations. France and Austria, formerly bitter enemies, overcame their differences and joined with Russia to crush the upstart. If successful, this coalition would unite Europe under anti-British powers; Britain needed to protect its overseas empire from the French while helping Prussia. As the fighting spread, in May of 1756 Britain declared war on France, and the war officially began.

French victories in North America continued through 1755, but as the war went worldwide, the new British leader, William Pitt, decided to assemble the full resources of the maritime system for an all-out global war against the French. Pitt was an extraordinary figure at an extraordinary moment. Known as "the Great Commoner" because, unlike most leading British politicians of the era, he did not have and, apparently, did not seek a noble title, Pitt came to public notice when he accepted the position of paymaster-general, one of the most lucrative offices in the British government—and promptly and ostentatiously refused to accept the very large customary bribes, fees, and other emoluments that went with it.

Pitt not only stood for a more modern, efficient, and meritocratic state; he had an instinctive understanding of global strategy and the maritime system. The Pitt family fortune was established by Thomas Pitt, who set out to trade illegally in India in defiance of the East India Company monopoly. The outraged company agents fined and imprisoned the interloper, but he was so determined and canny that the company ultimately gave up. They put the fox in charge of the chicken coop: they made him the governor of the company post at Madras. While ensconced there, Pitt bought a 410-carat diamond despite its surprising checkered past (the man he bought it from maintained that he had bought it from an English sea captain who had stolen it from a slave who had smuggled the stone out of the mines in a wound in his leg). Pitt realized a considerable fortune from the sale of the diamond (cut to 136 carats) to the French regent, who placed it among his country's crown jewels. Stolen in the French Revolution, it was later recovered, and Napoleon subsequently wore it on the pommel of his sword. It can still be seen in the Louvre.

With the fortune he made in India, Thomas—who soon became Sir Thomas—acquired control of the "rotten borough" of Old Sarum. Once a prosperous country town, by the time of Queen Anne Old Sarum mainly consisted of a few uninhabited ruins dotting a grassy hill near Stonehenge. Fortunately what it lacked in population it made up in parliamentary representation, and the empty borough retained a seat in the House of Commons.

In effect, this seat became the property of the Pitt family, and ensured that William Pitt could face the electorate with calm and equanimity whatever the political weather.

But this also meant that Britain in 1757 had a prime minister who understood how an open society and unfettered capitalist enterprise enabled a country and its citizens to succeed in global competition. He saw how this economic power could translate into military and political power.

As no one before him, Pitt understood the full shape and nature of British power. He understood that he was fighting a world war, and that Britain's twin advantages were its global sea power and its prosperous economy. He determined to use the one to increase the other, and, taxing the British people as never before, he used Britain's credit rating and its financial markets to borrow sums that boggled the minds of his contemporaries. He spent lavishly to bring Britain's military power to a new peak of size and efficiency. With one hand, he sent prodigal subsidies to help Britain's desperate Prussian ally to survive its encircling enemies in Europe. With the other, he ordered armies and fleets to the major theaters in the global war: India and America.

Bankrupting the enemy while crushing him: this was the strategy that Ronald Reagan would use against the Soviet Union in the 1980s. Reagan attacked Soviet economic interests by placing sanctions on its economy and the economies of its satellites; he sent military aid to the USSR's enemies and opponents from Central America to Afghanistan. And, while doing all this, he inaugurated a high-tech arms race that the Soviet Union could not win. The American economy became a decisive weapon of war, as Britain's had been against France under Pitt.

In India, the Seven Years' War in 1756 came at the height of an escalating Anglo-French struggle to control the south. Determined efforts by resourceful French agents had built a network of alliances with local rulers, and the French nourished hopes of driving the British out of their lucrative trading post in Madras. A string of island bases—Reunion, the Seychelles, Mauritius, Madagascar—could shelter French forces and trading ships making the long run from Europe. For the French as for the British, communication with their home base was the key to their local strength. Weapons and supplies had to come from the homeland; without secure communication home trade withered and died, and without trade their local power would do likewise.

Pitt's navy drove the French flag from the Indian Ocean. As the final contest for supremacy between French and British agents in India began, the French were completely cut off—while the British had secure lines of communication and supply. Victory did not come in a day, but the better-supplied, better-funded, and better-equipped British and their allies gradually prevailed against the French. By 1760 French power in India was broken for good. A few forts and bases remained, but France would never again face Britain on equal terms anywhere in Asia. Britain would go on not only to build an empire in India, but to dominate the lucrative China trade. Up through the Second World War, Britain would still be reaping the fruits of its Indian victories under Pitt.

In America also, the maritime system gave Britain a superiority that could not be withstood. The early French victories in the Ohio Valley proved fruitless. Inexorably British and colonial pressure moved against Quebec. Indian tribes friendly to the French weakened as rifles and ammunition became scarce; the British blockade prevented new supplies from entering French Canada. With their markets in Europe blockaded, French traders and their Indian allies watched their beaver pelts piling up on the wharves. British traders and their allies enjoyed higher prices as French products vanished from world markets.

The British could dispatch new forces and new supplies to the conflict zone at will. Pitt, who believed that America was the place where the French empire could be finally and utterly crushed, was determined to do everything needed to break France's grip on the St. Lawrence, Ohio, and Mississippi valleys. The massive forts that guarded the approaches to French Canada and haunted the dreams of New England fell one by one to British assault. Quebec and Montreal fell as outnumbered French forces gallantly resisted superior and better-supplied British adversaries.

The orgy of conquest continued. Spain made the mistake of entering the war; a British fleet occupied Havana and Florida. The sugar islands of Guadeloupe and Martinique fell in their turn. British forces dismantled French power in India as showers of wealth fell on a few lucky officers of the British East India Company.

Despite all this, Pitt was not fully pleased by the end of the war. Shocked by the escalating cost and growing skeptical about the benefits of further conquests, the House of Commons and the new king, George III, replaced Pitt in 1761 with Lord Bute, who promptly signed a compromise peace in 1763 that restored some of France's lost territory and gave Cuba back to Spain.

In Europe, Britain's ally, Prussia, was saved at the last minute when the anti-Prussian Empress Elizabeth was succeeded in Moscow by her pro-Prussian son. After thirteen years of devastating wars, Prussia kept Silesia. Otherwise, it was more or less status quo ante in Europe, for whose inhabitants, as Fred Anderson notes in his book *Crucible of War,* "six years of heroic expenditure and savage bloodshed had accomplished precisely nothing."

Britain, on the other hand, had built a global empire, suffering fewer casualties than Prussia lost in keeping, and Austria lost in failing to gain, their disputed sausage in the Polish hills.

Five • French Toast

T he French, who remained the most powerful of the continental European states after the Seven Years' War, took note of the strategy that Britain had used in the war—and they were by no means reconciled to defeat. In the next rounds of their long war with Britain, the French understood that the maritime system was the basis of Britain's power, and they paid increasing attention to the integration of naval power and trade in Britain's grand strategy.

As Voltaire put it:

> What has made England powerful is the fact that from the time of Elizabeth, all parties have agreed on the necessity of favoring commerce. The same parliament that had the king beheaded was busy with overseas trading posts as though nothing were happening. The blood of Charles I was still steaming when this parliament comprised almost entirely of fanatics passed the Navigation Act of 1650.[1]

Both Louis XVI, whose financial and military support enabled Britain's thirteen American colonies to win their independence, and Napoleon, who shook British power to its foundations as the leading French actor in the wars that convulsed Europe from 1791 to 1815, knew that Britain could not be defeated until its maritime system was successfully challenged.

In the first of these conflicts, France succeeded in enabling the American colonies to separate from the British motherland. British power in India also received a serious setback when British forces were forced to accept a compromise peace with Tipu Sultan, the ruler of Mysore and an ally of France. These setbacks were real, but when British power recovered and even grew in the wake of the American Revolution, the maritime system had demonstrated another of what would prove to be its core characteristics: resiliency. Once established, the maritime order has successfully resisted every attempt to overturn it.

Britain's victory in the Seven Years' War left most European powers worried about the danger that a too-mighty Britain could pose to the European balance of power. The Dutch feared Britain's global supremacy; Spain feared for the safety of its own global empire. Both were happy to follow France into a new round of warfare against the British colossus. This triple alliance would previously have struck fear into the heart of enough other European powers that the global struggle in the Americas and the Indies would have spawned a major land war in Europe. This time, however, there was relatively little fear that a French victory in America would overturn the balance of power in Europe, and the Netherlands, France, and Spain were free to engage in a global struggle against Britain without worrying about simultaneously fighting expensive land wars at home. Prussia, Russia, and Austria were quietly digesting the territories each had gained with the first partition of Poland and beginning to look forward hopefully to a second course. These countries were not particularly interested in assisting the British by attacking the French, and when Russia did finally take an interest in the American war, it was to form a League of Armed Neutrality that worked against British interests.

Sea power played a decisive role at every stage of the American Revolution. It was Britain's command of the sea and of its maritime order that allowed George III's forces to fight the war at all, and it was Britain's enormous wealth that enabled it to recruit and pay the Hessian mercenaries who provided up to one-third of its American troop strength. Sea power dictated Britain's war strategy as British fleets seized the major American coastal cities and sought to pacify the country by sending forces outward from the major urban centers and ports.

More than once the strategy came close to working. In the early years of the war, Washington's Continental Army, proudly mustered on Cambridge Common to drive the British from Boston, was forced out of New England, out of New York, out of New Jersey, and out of Philadelphia into the barren and windswept encampment at Valley Forge. Without French loans and the help of friendly financiers in revenge-minded Amsterdam, the Continental Army might well have dissolved.

Yet ultimately it was sea power that won the war for the rebels. Without land enemies to worry them, the French were able to assemble and deploy a fleet that could, temporarily, prevail against British naval forces in American waters. The arrival of the French fleet off Yorktown transformed Lord

Cornwallis's fortified camp into a prison; Cornwallis was forced to surrender to a Franco-American land army, and the British were forced to concede defeat in a major international conflict for the first time since the Glorious Revolution. From 1783 to the present day, however, the British have not had to repeat the experience.

Ironically, the outcome of the American Revolution testified to the strength of Britain's maritime system. In part this was because the principal French geopolitical hope for the war was thwarted. The French hoped that the new American republic would be an ally against Britain and the maritime system. In fact, the United States of America soon developed into a pillar of that system.

There were other factors as well. One was that the French continued to labor under their economic disadvantages. The cost of the American war was ruinous to the French monarchy. Ultimately the debts from the war would contribute materially to the financial crisis that forced Louis XVI into a series of steps that led to the French Revolution. Meanwhile, the French war debt strained the French budget. Louis was unable to follow up his military victory by continuing to build up his fleet; French finances dictated retrenchment, not further advance.

At the same time, Britain's defeat was not total. After losing to the French and the Americans in North America, the British were able to recover lost ground in India very quickly after the war. A major naval victory near Guadeloupe returned the British to control of the Atlantic. The French naval predominance at Yorktown was a fluke, not a trend. Additionally, during the war, the British managed to administer a thorough defeat to their Dutch former allies. The Fourth Anglo-Dutch War, which coincided more or less with the American Revolution, resulted in sweeping British victories in the Far East. When the Dutch agreed to terms in 1784, they regained (briefly) control of Ceylon, but the British kept territorial gains in India and extracted new trade privileges in the Dutch possessions in what is now Indonesia. Victory created a political and economic crisis in France that enfeebled the government; defeat had the same consequence for the Netherlands.

Victory made British power grow; defeat could not undermine it. This was where the maritime system stood when the French Revolution produced the greatest challenge the British would face until Adolf Hitler planned an invasion across the English Channel.

The Great Antagonist

At first most European observers thought that the French Revolution would weaken France further. As the Estates General passed a series of edicts that abolished feudalism, as royal power shrank, and as mobs took control of the Parisian streets, it appeared that the central authority on which French power rested was breaking down. The trained officers in the armed forces were generally loyal to the old regime. The common soldiers and some of the lower-ranking officers might support the revolution, but they presumably lacked the tactical and logistical skill required for the complex warfare of the time. More than that, with the collapse of the old regime, the authority of the government weakened throughout the countryside. Peasants seized the châteaux of their erstwhile lords; committees of notables took over municipal government from the royal authorities. The state was in a shambles, and French credit, always a delicate flower, withered and drooped as the paper currency of the revolutionaries inflated toward worthlessness.

To near-universal surprise, the French revolutionary state quickly proved to be one of the most formidable military powers in the history of the world. Defeating an invading army of Prussians and Austrians in September 1792, the forces of the French Revolution quickly occupied what is now Belgium.

This was something the British had to oppose. The ports of Belgium and the mouth of the river Scheldt are strategically located opposite Britain's most important lines of communication. Since Elizabeth I sent troops to help the hard-pressed Dutch rebels stave off Spanish attacks on the Netherlands, one of the main elements of Britain's balance-of-power policy toward Europe had been to keep Belgium out of the hands of a powerful rival state. It would be Germany's invasion of Belgium in 1914 that brought Britain into World War I.

In November 1792 the French swept into Belgium. From that point on, Britain—where many had early on welcomed the overthrow of the French monarchy—was the most determined enemy of the revolutionary power.

Early the next year the British put together their first coalition against the revolution; final victory would come only with the seventh. In the meantime, the French, soon under the inspired leadership of Napoleon Bonaparte, challenged the maritime system as never before.

Both the Dutch and the British versions of the maritime system depended on the existence of a balance of power in Europe. When Louis XIV became so powerful that he threatened the Dutch homeland with invasion, the Dutch were no longer able to maintain the sea power that is vital to the maritime system, and the English were able to seize the leadership of the order. In subsequent wars, Britain held a global advantage because France was never able to concentrate all its resources on its navy; it was always hemmed in by land powers to its rear. In the one war in which the U.K. faced a France that had no worries by land, the U.K. lost.

Under Napoleon, the French systematically demolished the European balance of power. The conquest of Belgium was only the start. There were retreats as well as advances in the 1790s, but French power, like a flooded river, was over its banks and sweeping out on all sides. By 1799, when Napoleon overthrew the increasingly ineffective civilian government to install himself as "first consul," the French had conquered the Netherlands as well as Belgium, had occupied much of western Germany on both banks of the Rhine, and had taken control of large chunks of Italy.

Sea power was still crucial. When Napoleon invaded Egypt, apparently as a first step toward challenging British power in India, the British navy defeated the French fleet at the Battle of the Nile. Napoleon's army conquered Egypt and invaded Palestine, but without naval support the campaign was futile. Unable to bring his troops with him across seas dominated by the British navy, Napoleon returned home by stealth and mounted the coup that made him consul.

The string of European victories continued as the French crushed the Austrians in the battle of Hohenlinden. In 1802 the British and French reached a peace agreement that recognized Napoleon's vast conquests. War broke out again the following year, and on December 2, 1804, Napoleon brought the captive pope to Notre Dame, where he crowned himself emperor.

Britain now faced something new: a single great land power that dominated the European continent.

By the time he seized the imperial crown, Napoleon had as clear an understanding of the dynamics of world power as any of his predecessors. Since the beginning of the wars of the French Revolution, two successive coalitions had risen against France. Each had been defeated, yet each time British gold revived the fortunes of France's enemies and helped them recruit new armies to replace the ones lost on the field, and British manufacturing prowess provided them with arms and munitions. The coalitions against France were like the Hydra of Greek myth: Napoleon could lop off head after head, yet as long as Britain, the heart of the beast, lived, the heads grew back again and again. What to do?

Napoleon's first plan was to strike Britain at home. In 1798–99 the

French had tried the usual method of encouraging the restless "Celtic fringe" (chiefly Scotland and Ireland) to rebel and sent weapons and troops to support the Irish rebels under Wolfe Tone. As usual, the support was not enough to enable the undertrained and poorly equipped rebel forces to do more than annoy and harass the British government. After renewed war broke out in 1803 Napoleon tried something more dramatic: he assembled an army of invasion in Boulogne and built transports to carry them over the English Channel to England.

With the resources of western Europe at his disposal, and with the help of Spain, Napoleon put together a fleet that, he hoped, would give him at least temporary mastery of the English Channel. Admiral Rochambeau's superiority in American waters had lasted only a short time, but it had been enough to force Cornwallis to surrender and end the American war.

This was the moment when the British maritime system faced its greatest test to date. After very complex sailings, countersailings, and blockades, a Franco-Spanish fleet of thirty-three ships was utterly smashed and defeated by twenty-seven British ships under Lord Nelson at the Battle of Trafalgar. Nelson died in the battle, but twenty-two of the thirty-three Franco-Spanish ships were lost; all the British ships survived.

"I do not say, my Lords, that the French will not come," First Lord of the Admiralty John Jervis had said to the House of Lords in 1801. "I only say they will not come by sea."

They didn't. Even before Trafalgar, Napoleon had turned to a second plan to defeat the sea empire: he would weld Europe together into a single mass and use the total power of a united Europe to wage an economic war that would bring Britain to its knees. Smashing the third and fourth coalitions within months, Napoleon defeated Austria, Russia, and Prussia once again in a series of devastating battles (Austerlitz, Ulm, Jena, and Auerstadt) that rank among his most spectacular victories. On November 21, 1806, Napoleon announced the Berlin Decrees: an attempt to starve Britain's commerce and therefore its power by closing off Europe to British trade.

It was a formidable threat. At the time, Napoleon's French empire and its allies, willing or unwilling, covered most of the continent. The British economy was already experiencing the rapid changes and growth of the Industrial Revolution; the loss of all principal foreign markets had great potential to disrupt the economy and diminish the government's ability to prosecute the long and, so far, almost entirely unsuccessful war with France.

Failing an invasion, the Continental System, as Napoleon called his alternative to Britain's maritime system, was the only strategy that offered much hope of ending British resistance—and as long as Britain was unconquered,

Napoleon's European land empire wasn't safe. Britain's worldwide trade and its rapidly expanding and industrializing economy made the country rich enough to build more and more coalitions against the French (as long as its foreign markets were unaffected); as long as Britain stood, France was locked in an endless war of attrition that prevented the consolidation of Napoleon's power and the creation of a stable European order under French hegemony. After 1806, Napoleon's grand strategy was to maintain the Continental System as his best hope to defeat Britain once and for all and to ensure the permanence of his vast new empire.

This turned out to be expensive. The incentives for Europeans to trade with the British—and with the rest of the world, for Britain controlled Europe's access to global markets—were high. Not only was widespread, organized smuggling increasingly popular; local elites in many countries, hard-hit in their pocketbooks by the Berlin Decrees, began to reconsider their policies of collaboration with France. Yet because the Continental System demanded universal compliance if it was to work, Napoleon found himself working harder to enforce the edicts as support for his rule began to wane.

The Continental System would also involve Napoleon in the two wars that ultimately brought about his defeat: the Peninsular War in Portugal and Spain and the invasion of Russia.

A weak country fearing Spanish power by land and trying to protect a large and scattered global empire against predators like the French and the Dutch, Portugal had turned to the British for help throughout the seventeenth and eighteenth centuries. Trading links between the two countries were close, and British and Portuguese merchants enjoyed cooperative partnerships throughout the world. Portugal had no desire to join Napoleon's Continental System, but Napoleon could not tolerate such a large gap in his blockade.

From a military point of view, Portugal posed no threat to Napoleon's power. It was an isolated and poor kingdom on the fringes of Europe; yet as a trading partner of Britain it was a threat. In one of the two most fateful decisions of his career, Napoleon decided to force the Portuguese to comply.

At first things went well. By December 1807, Napoleon's forces had occupied Lisbon and most of the country. But then things began to come unglued. The Portuguese royal family escaped with British support and continued fighting the war from Brazil. ("This is what ruined me," Napoleon would write years later when, from his exile on St. Helena, he looked back over the events of his life.) The delicate political situation in Spain crumbled as the feeble and incompetent government of Queen Maria Louisa's lover, Manuel de Godoy, named prince of peace in 1795, was overturned in a coup. Anxious to ensure stability, Napoleon took the opportunity to overthrow the Spanish royals (relatives of the deposed Bourbon dynasty in France) and install his own brother Joseph as king of Spain.

The Spaniards may not have loved their ineffective Bourbon rulers, but they hated the idea that foreign troops should replace them with the puppet of an upstart Corsican dictator. A guerrilla war against the French broke out across Spain; seizing the opportunity offered by unrest in both Portugal and Spain, the British landed forces to begin what history knows as the Peninsular War. The long and costly conflict would tie down French forces for years and give Arthur Wellesley the military experience he would put to good use when he finally defeated Napoleon at the battle of Waterloo.

None of this was necessary in strictly military terms. A handful of troops in the Pyrenees could have protected France no matter who ruled Spain, and in any case, had Napoleon's war with Portugal not destabilized the Iberian situation, the Prince of Peace might have long continued Spain's pro-French policy with the royal cuckold Charles IV benignly indifferent.

It was the strategic need to overcome Britain's mercantile and sea power that helped draw Napoleon into this quagmire. The same need contributed to the disastrous decision to invade Russia.

Drawing the Russian czar, Alexander I, into the Continental System was critical to Napoleon's anti-British strategy. Russia was not only a significant trading country with a history of economic links with Britain dating back to the Elizabethan period; its military and diplomatic weight was necessary to secure support for the system among the other Baltic powers. Indeed, Napoleon rejoiced when Russia joined his system after the 1804 Treaty of Tilsit; when Sweden refused to join, Russia invaded and conquered Sweden's eastern territories (modern Finland) and forced the Swedes to comply.

Yet the Continental System was profoundly unpopular in Russia. Trade with Britain was profitable; in any case, with France so dangerously strong, many Russian patriots saw little advantage in a foreign policy that strengthened France against the one country still able to keep it in check.

Czar Alexander had been forced into his alliance with Napoleon after successive defeats of Russia and Austria at Austerlitz and Friedland had deprived him of any possible continental allies against the all-conquering French. However, as Napoleon continued to extend his influence eastward—reestablishing a quasi-independent Poland, annexing various pieces of the Baltic seaboard to the French colossus—Alexander realized that peace gave him no security against Napoleon's ambitions. Russian ships renewed a clandestine, unofficial trade with Britain, and Russia considered ways of rebuilding some sort of united European front against the Bonaparte state.

It was to nip this rebellion in the bud that Napoleon assembled the largest army the world had ever known and marched it into Russia. Following a chain of reasoning which would ensnare and destroy Hitler more than a century later, Napoleon's failure to cross the English Channel led him into a ruinous invasion of Russia.

The Peninsular War and the destruction of the French army (only about 2 percent of the eight hundred thousand troops who marched into Russia came out still ready for battle) led to Napoleon's fall and his exile. But beyond that, Britain emerged from the Napoleonic Wars with an extraordinary prestige and power that would be matched only by that of the United States following similar victories in the wars of the twentieth century. With France morally exhausted, bled white, and back under the rule of the unpopular Bourbon dynasty, for decades there was no power capable of playing the role of great antagonist to the maritime system. Satan, banished from Versailles, would find no place to base himself until the rising power of Wilhelmine Germany began to disturb the European balance late in the nineteenth century.

Not only had Britain's global trade prospered during the long wars while the trade of its antagonists had been hampered and harried from the seas, but Britain had used, as usual, the opportunities of war to select a choice few bases and colonies around the world. More than this, the war years promoted Britain's economic and technological lead over its neighbors. The years of the French revolutionary and Napoleonic wars, from 1791 to 1815, were years in which Britain's economic lead widened as never before. The Industrial Revolution would expose Britain to new challenges, and ultimately it would strengthen a new round of antagonists eager to snatch the crown of global supremacy from Britannia's head, but in the immediate aftermath of the Napoleonic Wars, Britain's geopolitical prestige was enhanced and fortified by the radical and growing disparity between British industry and its less mechanized, less efficient continental rivals.

After more than a century of almost constant warfare across the globe, much of it against countries with larger populations, larger economies, and greater natural resources, the United Kingdom had emerged stronger, richer, and more securely established at the center of a geopolitically dominant and economically ascendant maritime system.

A century later, Britain would begin to yield its dominant position within the maritime system to the rising power of the United States; nevertheless, up until the present day this system that the Dutch invented, that the elder Pitt made the greatest empire in the world, and that the younger Pitt and his colleagues defended against Napoleon, has continued to drive the process of world history.

Time and time again, the Anglo-Americans have suffered terrible defeats in Europe and Asia; time and time again, they have turned to their command of the global system to deny its resources to their enemies—and to acquire the resources they need to raise up new coalitions to replace the ones that have fallen apart.

The Anglo-Americans' enemies gradually go bankrupt; all their victories on land never seem to make a difference. Napoleon conquered Europe from Moscow to Madrid—but he could never strike at the heart of British power, and her wealth, annually renewed by her overseas trade, enabled her to support her weakened allies and carry on the war through final victory. For three years, Hitler beat Britain and its allies everywhere he faced them—yet after three years of dramatic, historic victories it was Hitler who worried more about losing the war than Churchill did. When the Germans briefly overran American camps during the 1944 Battle of the Bulge, a German general realized that the war was lost when he saw that American privates were getting chocolate cakes from their families back home. With Germany desperate for every ounce of fuel, every bite of food, the Americans had enough food and enough shipping capacity to send birthday cakes across the ocean to ordinary soldiers.

When General Winfield Scott developed a version of this strategy for the Civil War, the American press had called it the Anaconda plan. Union sea power cut the South off from foreign trade, while protecting the world-ranging commerce of the North. By the end of the Civil War, Southern money was worthless, the Southern economy was ruined, and confederate armies in the fields were short of weapons, clothing, and food. The North, by contrast, was richer at the war's end than at the beginning.

George Kennan called it containment when he revived the classic sea-king strategy for the Cold War. American and British sea power would contain Soviet influence on the mainland of Eurasia, while the subsidized NATO allies in Europe and Japan in Asia added their weight to the western alliance.

It was a coalition strategy when Pitt used it against the French Revolution and Napoleon; the French won battle after battle, overthrew coalition after coalition, and in the end, exhausted and impoverished, surrendered to Britain and its allies.

During all these many wars, while the continental powers wore one another out with titanic, ruinously expensive struggles on land, the Anglo-Saxons occupied themselves with the crown jewel of their power strategies: they entrenched themselves more deeply than ever in the global system by stealing the colonies of their warring rivals. The British forced France out of India and North America using this technique; they used it to take the Cape Colony from the Dutch. They used the Napoleonic Wars to destroy the Spanish empire in the Americas; in World War I they turned the Germans out of Africa and the Turks out of the Arab Middle East; in World War II it was the Italians' turn. Sometimes the lands the British grabbed belonged to their enemies; sometimes, whoops, they belonged to their allies, but over time the British systematically dismantled rival colonial empires.

The United States, which had always resented the European colonial empires, did the same thing during the Cold War. Adamant U.S. opposition to British rule in India was one of the reasons the British had to give it up after World War II. The U.S. forced the Dutch out of what is now Indonesia by threatening to withhold Marshall Plan aid. The Suez Crisis of 1956 meant the end of the British and French empires in the Middle East when the United States forced the United Kingdom and France to abandon their attack on Nasser's Egypt.

Yet the United States did not create a new colonial empire for itself on the British model after the Second World War. Instead, it followed the pattern the British established when they helped the South Americans free themselves from the Spanish and the Portuguese. America supported independence drives in the former colonies, and then allowed the new states to enter the global economic system the U.S. was building. The drawback of empire had always been that you had to conquer countries first and then keep them down; the advantage of an order is that people choose freely to belong.

Order or empire, it isn't just the turf. It's the trade routes, the market share, the financial markets, and the relationships. When the wars are over and the other countries come back into world markets, they find the Anglo-Americans better ensconced than ever. Thus armed with the spoils of the last war, the Anglo-Americans have entered each great international power struggle better equipped for victory.

It's a simple plan, but it works. At least, it's been working since the Dutch first figured it out four hundred years ago.

Six • The World Was Their Oyster

In 1815, while Wellington was orchestrating the final defeat of Napoleon in the battle of Waterloo—as Napoleon, once again, was trying to invade the Low Countries—the great transatlantic offshoot of the British Empire, the United States, was growing and industrializing rapidly as it slowly recognized the benefits of working within Britain's maritime system. Even after Britain's technological and economic lead began to narrow later in the nineteenth century, the onrushing torrent of American progress and development would keep the English-speaking world at the forefront of world power and events.

With Britain as the world's only truly industrial and global power, British capital and British trade were the first to begin to draw the vast non-Western world into the global capitalist economy on a mass scale. Even as British emigrants populated Canada, Australia, and New Zealand, British conquerors, administrators, and investors transformed India, and British traders and navies battered down the walls within which China sought to preserve unchanged an ancient way of life. In the New World, British influence helped destroy Spain's vast empire in Latin America as the Portuguese royal family consolidated a new one in Brazil. In both regions, British investment, British trade, and British political influence played a growing role as the power of the old colonial masters faded away. Throughout the world, British missionaries began to preach the gospel in the unlikeliest places; that Christianity is a global religion today is in considerable part due to the efforts begun then.

The foundations, in other words, of the world we know today had been well and truly laid, and as the British took advantage of their opportunities after Waterloo, they began to carve the cultural, economic, and political channels in which world affairs to a very large degree continue to flow.

Americans are familiar with the story of the westward expansion, population growth, and economic development of their own country during the nineteenth century, but it is worth placing these events in the larger context of the dramatic rise in the power and reach of the maritime system of which the American expansion was a vital part—but only a part.

THE END OF THE NAPOLEONIC WARS saw two linked historic movements that have had a profound influence on present politics. One was the enormous flow of emigrants from the British Isles to the United States, Canada, Australia, and New Zealand. The second was the unprecedented wave of investment that brought more and more of the world, both within and beyond the expanding boundaries of the British Empire, into ever closer economic and political relations. Together, these flows helped create important new geopolitical realities and strengthened the maritime system around the world. The Anglosphere, the group of countries where English is the native language of a substantial majority of the population and where social values and culture are largely shaped by Anglo-Saxon values, remains an important fact of world politics. Canada, Australia, and New Zealand fought alongside Britain in both world wars from start to finish; all the English-speaking nations fought in the Cold War as well. Australia is the only country in the world which sent military forces to fight side by side with the Americans in the Korean War, the Vietnam conflict, and the two wars with Iraq.

The British made a conscious effort to avoid repeating the mistakes that led to the American Revolution. Beginning with Canada, London developed plans that gave the growing settlements of English-speakers overseas the kind of rights that the American colonists had sought in vain. Never again would an English-speaking "daughter" society have to use force to break away from the mother country. And for the next century and a half Britain could count on the support of these countries when danger came.

The Great Diaspora

When Napoleon sailed into exile on the remote British outpost of St. Helena, the only significant English-speaking population beyond the British Isles was made up of the citizens of the United States—a country which fought the War of 1812 against Britain in the closing stages of the Napoleonic Wars.

The countries that the British Empire once knew as the "white dominions"—Canada, Australia, and New Zealand—did not yet exist. The Cape Colony, nucleus of the future South African colonies of the empire, had been only recently snatched from the Dutch, and few of its inhabitants, whatever their color, knew anything of the English language. The foundations of the indigenous English-speaking community in India had yet to be laid; few inhabitants of India had learned the language of the latest imperial invader to set up new dominions on the subcontinent.

In all of these places and others, the long interval between the Anglo-French wars of 1689–1815 and the Anglo-German wars between 1914 and 1945 saw an extraordinary series of developments. Again, in the conventional narratives of world history, this is often confounded with the quite separate and much less significant episodes of European imperialism in the same era. That is like, as Mark Twain would say, confusing the lightning with a lightning bug. The Germans, Belgians, and Italians made colonies during this period; the French did a little more, but not much. The British made a new kind of world.

The greatest difference between the British Empire and the tentative ventures of other states in the era was the rise of the self-governing, English-speaking colonies. Like the thirteen colonies that broke away, the English colonies of the nineteenth century had a variety of histories and were established for a variety of purposes. But this second wave of colonization, coming almost two hundred years after the Pilgrims landed at Massachusetts Bay, was one of the ways that the British, having risen to become the world's leading power in their wars against the French, went on to make a durable imprint.

Political refugees from the United States helped kick-start the rise of English Canada when an estimated ninety thousand Loyalists fled and settled mostly in the Canadian Maritimes during and immediately following the American Revolution. (Not all of them stayed, but "late Loyalists" kept arriving until about 1812.) But massive emigration from the United Kingdom to Canada started only after the fall of Napoleon restored safety to the seas—and even then it was not until after about 1830 that the economic dislocations of the Industrial Revolution led many British people to try their fortune in a new country. While many British immigrants continued to choose life in the United States, a significant stream went to Canada and moved inland past Quebec and Montreal into what remains today the heartland of English Canada—Ontario.

Until the midcentury gold rush in Australia, Canada was the fastest-growing colony of what is often called "the second British Empire." For this reason, and because ominous signs of restlessness could be found in its mixed and sometimes dissatisfied population, it was Canadian affairs that led the British to think seriously about new ways to organize their overseas settlements. In 1838 the Earl of Durham was dispatched to Canada in the aftermath of a series of rebellions. Accompanying him was Edward Gibbon Wakefield, a convicted felon who had served three years in prison for seducing a young heiress to elope with him. The marriage was dissolved by an act of Parliament, and Wakefield went to prison—it was, after all, his second offense. The higher moral tone of Victorian society would deny Wakefield a career in the public eye, but as one of Durham's staff he was able to get his ideas into the influential Durham Report that guided British policy toward Canada over the next generation. Wakefield, his less flamboyant writing partner, Charles Buller, and the Earl of Durham told the British authorities that moving toward responsible government was the way to keep the Canadians peacefully in the empire. It was more than this. To paraphrase Britain's Lord Ismay on NATO, it would keep the Anglo-Canadians in, the Americans out, and the French Canadians down.*

The British succeeded reasonably well at all three of these goals, and by 1867 Canada was beginning to emerge as a pro-British, Anglophone-dominated federation increasingly responsible for its own affairs. Anglo-Canadian identity and culture were then, and remain now, recognizably related to the identities and cultures of England, Scotland, Ireland, the United States, Australia, and New Zealand.

The empire was becoming an Anglosphere.

Wakefield was also influential in the development of the smallest of the new English-speaking countries, and the latest to get started. In 1838, when Lord Durham was working to pacify angry Indians, French Canadians, and Irish rebels in Canada, there were less than three hundred European settlers living in what is now known as New Zealand. The original Polynesian inhabitants, the Maoris, managed to put up a fierce enough resistance that they compelled the British to recognize substantial portions of their land and political rights. In the 1840s settlements were planted despite occasional conflict; two settlements in particular, Christchurch and Otago, were inspired by Wakefieldian ideas of planting British culture in the colonial territories.

---

* Lord Lionel Ismay, NATO's secretary general from 1952 to 1957, said the organization was founded to keep the Americans "in," the Soviets "out," and the Germans "down."

Christchurch was named for one of the colleges of Oxford, and was intended as a model Anglican town, complete with bishop. Otago was Church of Scotland, and similarly planned. The bishop left rather quickly and unhappily, but otherwise, the two settlements prospered and still retain something of their original character. By 1852, although the English-speaking population was small, it was already demanding "home rule." This was granted; like Canadians, New Zealanders would ultimately have their own parliament and their own laws while continuing to remain part of the wider English-speaking world.

The founding of an English-speaking society in Australia is to some degree a consequence of the American Revolution. Once the Atlantic colonies were independent, they were no longer available as dumping grounds for convicts. With upward of two hundred crimes technically punishable by death, and with a large, restless, and often lawless pauper population and no capability to build or sustain enough prisons to hold all the criminals, the British authorities were anxious to find a new place of exile for criminals sentenced to "transportation." What better place to put them than Australia—as far as possible from the British Isles? That the settlement would provide a basis for British sea power in the South Pacific was an additional consideration. The first fleet sailed from London with 730 convicts in May 1787. By 1830, 58,000 more had joined them, including 8,000 women.

The continuing influx of convicts, including both common criminals and political criminals associated with various Irish and labor uprisings, meant that even by the standards of a frontier society, early Australian life and government were brutal and harsh. William "Mutiny on the *Bounty*" Bligh served as governor; the prison within a prison of Norfolk Island was one of the most horrifying places on the planet.

From this harsh and unpromising start, yet another free society with a responsible government would grow. Even before the home government had stopped shipping convicts, the British Parliament, determined not to repeat the mistakes that had lost America, was granting more home rule to Australian provincial assemblies. Here too Edward Wakefield's ideas bore fruit as organized settlers in family groups populated much of South Australia. A wave of mid-nineteenth-century gold strikes threatened to submerge the family-friendly side of Australian life as drifters and dreamers from all over the world rushed to the goldfields and boosted Australia's economy, population, and crime rate. Yet responsible, democratic self-government and self-policing (once the police stopped deserting en masse to dig for gold) soon restored order, and Australia continued its cheeky progress toward full self-government as one of the most democratic and egalitarian societies in the world.

TO GRASP THE IMPORTANCE of the English-speaking offshoot societies for the power and wealth of the maritime system, one must consider the strategic depth and resources that the U.S., Canada, Australia, and New Zealand provided and still provide. Add to this the resources and trade that these far-flung, vast, and wealthy countries bring to the system. Timber, pitch, and tar from America gave British ships advantages in the eighteenth century. The gold of America, Australia, Canada, and South Africa was a major factor in the rise of the banking system and capital markets of the English-speaking world to levels that gave these countries long-term economic advantages whose consequences are still felt today. The cotton of the American South, the wheat of Canada and the American North, the mutton and wool of Australia and New Zealand: a cornucopia of resources and opportunities poured out over astonished inhabitants of the English-speaking world, helping to enrich these countries to unprecedented levels.

These lands did much more for the maritime system. Access to them provided the British with an outlet for the malcontents at home who might otherwise have threatened domestic stability. Instead, the most talented and promising (and therefore, under certain circumstances, the most dangerous) found ways to get themselves out to the new colonies, where they often as not became pillars of society and, therefore, staunch pillars of the maritime system. More than twenty million people emigrated from the British Isles between 1812 and 1914; the large majority settled in the United States and most of the rest went to the white dominions.[1]

More than this, for nearly two centuries the promise of these lands has called some of the most talented, industrious, and enterprising of the world's people to leave their homes to make a new home in the English-speaking world. Scores of millions of Germans, Russians, Poles, Italians, Greeks, Norwegians, Swedes, Portuguese, Mexicans, Arabs, Africans, Indians, Pakistanis, Chinese, and Japanese have flocked and still flock to the English-speaking world, there to add their talents and their ambitions to the common stock. The ability of the overseas English-speaking societies to welcome and assimilate vast numbers of immigrants from all over the world remains a key factor in the continuing strength of the United States (and other countries) to the present day.

The British triumphs over the Hapsburgs, Bourbons, and Bonapartes made this possible and enabled the English-speaking world to become the richest and most powerful political, economic, and military force the world has yet known. And as the English-speaking world began to harvest the wealth and the opportunities that these conquests provided, the sea powers grew yet stronger and richer, and their global position became more enviable—and also more secure.

There were victims, of course. The aborigines of Australia and Tasmania, the American and Canadian Indians, and even the relatively fortunate Maoris of New Zealand might well wish that the Walrus and the Carpenter had never left the beaches of Kent. A rosy glow of nostalgia and myth that now softens the edges of the processes of emigration and exile that push as much as pulled millions of famine-struck Irish and dispossessed and starving peasants from all over Europe should not blind us to the exploitation and hardship that the emigrants faced when they landed, whether at Montreal, Ellis Island, Sydney, or Auckland. Nor should we forget the discrimination and exclusion that limited the opportunities of Asians to reach these fabled lands.

Alabaster cities do indeed gleam throughout the English-speaking world, but it is hard to argue that they are, in the words of "America the Beautiful," "undimmed by human tears."

The Other British Empire

The most obvious difference between the British lightning and the lightning-bug empires that various European countries patched together in the nineteenth century is that no other empire contained anything comparable to the Anglophone dominions. But even if we turn from these new Albions springing up across the Atlantic and Pacific to the more conventional forms in which the nineteenth century measured imperial wealth and success, the empires of Britain's continental rivals were, by contrast, cheap tinsel and gimcrack.

The sturdiest and most durable rival was, as might be expected, the empire of the French. Banished from the high seas by the British triumphs in the long wars, the French nevertheless reached across the Mediterranean to put down roots in North Africa, where, particularly in Algeria, the French colonial presence would be long-lasting, influential, and hard to pull up by the roots. Later French conquests in West Africa and above all in Indochina were substantial in area, and French cabinet ministers and schoolchildren could gloat over large areas of the map painted a satisfying Gallic blue, but in extent, wealth, and strategic significance the French overseas empire was eclipsed and surpassed by British pink.

The British empire at its peak—which was not reached until after World War I, when for the last time the British were able to make the traditional harvest of the choicest territories of their defeated German and Ottoman foes—covered more than one-fourth of the earth's land surface and included more than one-quarter of the world's people. First and foremost, Britain controlled the fabulously wealthy subcontinent of India, including the present-day countries of India, Pakistan, Bangladesh, Sri Lanka, and Burma. If Sir Thomas Pitt sold the regents' diamond to the French royal house, the almost equally grand Koh-i-Noor was taken from the Sikh kingdom of Punjab when it fell to British arms; the commanding British general popped the diamond into a box, put it in his pocket, and was able to deliver it to Queen Victoria, who placed it among her crown jewels.

Britain controlled the lands on or near the principal sea routes from London to India. Napoleon's defeat left Britain with present-day South Africa, the strategic key to the traditional route around the Cape of Good Hope. Britain also had a string of naval bases across the Mediterranean from Gibraltar to, ultimately, Alexandria and Suez. As the Suez route, both before and after the digging of the canal, began to eclipse the Cape route, British power rapidly penetrated Egypt and its satellite, the Sudan, as well as the Arabian Peninsula and the Persian Gulf.

The Strait of Malacca, the crucial sea route that leads from the Indian Ocean into the South China Sea and the Pacific, was similarly bordered by reassuringly pink-colored land on the map. The strategic harbor of Singapore, founded by Sir Thomas Stamford Raffles in 1809 as a trading station, quickly became what it remains—the major trading entrepôt between India and China. (This despite the best efforts of the local tigers that, in the early years of the British settlement, averaged about one human kill per day.)

Hong Kong, taken from the Chinese after the morally corrupt but undoubtedly effective Opium War, proved equally valuable as trade in opium and other commodities made fabulous fortunes for British and Chinese trading houses.

In Africa the British Empire was put together haphazardly, but here too the British territories were generally superior to those of their rivals. Egypt was the continent's most populous country; British South Africa had the best gold and diamond mines, as well as the land most suitable for European settlement. Zanzibar was a key strategic point on the east coast of Africa; fertile and oil-rich Nigeria on the west is today the home of one out of every four sub-Saharan Africans. After British adventurers snatched up the German East African colonies during World War I, Britain controlled an unbroken string of land reaching from the Cape of Good Hope to the mouth of the Nile.

The Invisible Empire

Travelers passing through the former British Empire still frequently have the chance to visit and marvel at the extraordinary botanical gardens organized by the British in places like Durban, South Africa, and Nairobi, Kenya. Usually beautifully laid out and often still meticulously maintained, these gardens are more than testimonies to the British love of gardening, or even to the spirit of scientific curiosity that guided naturalists like Charles Darwin on their expeditions. The cultivation of useful plants was one of the characteristics of the British empire and indeed a key to its success.

Sugar, even more than tobacco, had been the great engine of British imperial and colonial prosperity in the eighteenth century. So important were the sugar islands to the world economy at the time that, given the choice of the return of either Canada or the sugar islands of Martinique and Guadeloupe after its defeat in the Seven Years' War, the French scarcely hesitated before choosing the islands.

The poppy was another plant in the British imperial garden to play a great role in the rise of the empire. The insular consumers of Qing-dynasty China were uninterested in the consumer products the British had on offer—but opium found a ready market, and the British were ready to supply it. With the global vision and power that their mastery of the seas gave them, the British began by purchasing the opium in what is now Turkey, and sailing it around the Cape of Good Hope to China. When the British began to cultivate the intoxicating blooms of the poppy in India, months were cut off the trip, and the Turkish growers were cut out of the market.

More innocently, British botanical know-how identified tea plants growing wild in the hills along what is now the Burmese-Indian frontier; British-owned tea plantations in Ceylon (now Sri Lanka) were soon competing effectively with Chinese producers in the world market.

The commercial rubber tree, *Hevea brasiliensis,* is as its name suggests a native of South America. Today, however, about 90 percent of natural rubber worldwide comes from plantations in Asia. At a time when the rubber market was a key to Brazilian prosperity, it was British botanists acting under the orders of the India Office in London who got *Hevea brasiliensis* seeds out of the country. First they were grown at Kew Gardens; then they were taken to Ceylon and to the botanical garden at Singapore. The rubber plantations of Malaya would be a key source of British prosperity until Malaysia attained independence in 1963.

With the world's largest collection of territories spanning every climate zone on the planet, united to the world's greatest system of finance and trade and equipped with the talents of a good proportion of the world's best scientists and most resourceful entrepreneurs, the happy and prosperous Walrus found that the world was indeed Britain's oyster in the century after Napoleon fell.

It was not by accident that the British were well placed to understand the cultivation and uses of *Hevea brasiliensis* and its remarkable sap. Long before Columbus, Aztec and other Indians used the sap of the rubber tree in various ways. The first Europeans to report extensively on its properties were members of a French expedition that visited South America between the wars of the Spanish and Austrian successions. In 1736 the explorer Charles-Marie de La Condamine sent samples to Europe, and new uses for this substance were gradually discovered. Ever a bridesmaid but never a bride, France did not enjoy the kind of uninterrupted access to tropical products that might have allowed its early lead to develop.

It was two Britons who took the next step. In 1820 Thomas Hancock found a way to make large sheets of rubber; the Scottish inventor Charles Macintosh developed a process that allowed a layer of rubber to be placed between two sheets of wool. The mackintosh and the modern rubber industry were born.

British relations with Brazil could not have been better at the time. The British fleet had escorted the royal family of Portugal out of Napoleon's grasp over the Atlantic in late 1807 as Napoleon sought to extend the grip of his Continental System. Arriving in Rio early in 1808, King John VI declared Brazil a coequal part of the Portuguese empire and repaid the British by opening Brazil's ports to British commerce. The treaty, written to British specifications, set tariffs on British exports to Brazil lower than exports from Portugal and, quite unusually, contained the requirement that "the Present Treaty shall be unlimited in point of duration, and that the obligations and conditions expressed or implied in it shall be perpetual and immutable."[2]

The trip to Rio had been unpleasant. The fleas were so bad on John VI's ship from Europe that the women, including the royal princesses, had to cut their hair to relieve themselves of the pests.[3] Rio was a welcome relief to the royal family; John delayed his return to Portugal until political problems there made his return a matter of urgency in 1821. He left his son Dom Pedro as regent in Brazil. As the Portuguese Cortes worked to return Brazil to colonial status and, significantly, to abridge its right to trade with other countries, including Britain, the prince first refused an order to sail to Lisbon, and then proclaimed, with tacit support from both his father and London, that Brazil was an independent empire and that he, now Dom Pedro I, was its emperor. The perpetual and immutable treaty was saved.

Despite spats over subjects ranging from Uruguay (whose independence from both Brazil and Argentina was supported by Britain) to the slave trade, Britain's economic and political relations with Brazil remained strong, and British enterprise and British capital were deeply entrenched in the new South American empire.

In similar ways, British influence dramatically increased throughout Latin America. Spain had always viewed British and indeed all foreign traders with suspicion. When Spanish power collapsed during the Napoleonic Wars, British traders were quick to take advantage of the Spanish Empire's declining ability to enforce trade regulations. Both British and American traders increased their business in Latin America, but the British—with the larger economy and, thanks to the way that Brazil juts out so far to the east, with a location closer to the major Latin cities south of the equator—were far better positioned to become the dominant trading partner in the region.

Thomas Cochrane, the tenth Earl of Dundonald, was a British admiral whose adventures Patrick O'Brian used as a partial model for his Aubrey/Maturin novels. Temporarily dropped from the British naval list after attempting to make money in the financial markets by abusing his naval position to spread false rumors about the abdication of Napoleon, Cochrane accepted an invitation from Chile's revolutionary government (led by the interestingly named Chilean hero Bernardo O'Higgins) to help in the war against Spain. After O'Higgins and Cochrane destroyed Spanish naval power on the west coast of the continent, securing the independence of Chile and Peru, Cochrane went on to perform a similar service for Brazil in the naval conflict over its independence from Portugal. The intrepid admiral went on to help the Greeks in their (British-backed) campaign for independence from the Ottoman Empire until 1828, and, having been returned with full honors to the naval list in 1832, he was buried in Westminster Abbey when he died in 1860.

Meanwhile, the independence of the Latin American countries was assured when, as Hancock and Macintosh were improving their rubber processes, the British government made clear that it would not permit the newly restored French Bourbons to help their Spanish cousins repossess their American empire. The Americans chimed in with the Monroe Doctrine, but in Paris and Madrid it was the British voice that counted. Less than a decade after Napoleon's fall, Britain had replaced Spain and Portugal—its two closest allies in the war with Napoleon—as the predominant power in Latin America. For the next century British capital would take the lead in building the railroads and industries and developing the resources of much of the region, and even today the mark of British influence remains clear.

What Britain had in the nineteenth century, and what the United States has today, was a complex mix of power and influence. Brazil was never formally part of Britain's empire, and Brazil sometimes opposed British policies when the interests of the two countries clashed. Britain did not have a monopoly on commercial, political, or intellectual influence in Brazil. French ideas and French companies were also active and, boosted by immigration to the more temperate provinces in the Brazilian south, Germany was a growing presence as late as the start of the Second World War. Yet the British position was unique—and when British power began its irreversible decline, the growing power of the United States deepened the ties between Brazil and the Anglo-Saxon world.

Britain's invisible empire covered more of the world than Latin America. The networks of investment and trade that centered on London spanned the globe, and in places like Beijing, Constantinople, Tehran, and Bangkok, the voice of the British ambassador and the business leadership of the British community was heard very clearly. Some governments were more independent of British influence than Brazil, others were much less so, but no country could match Britain's worldwide influence.

The importance of this wider empire can be seen in the figures for Britain's foreign investment. Between 1815 and 1880, British investors are believed to have invested approximately £6 billion abroad (something like $350 billion at 2006 prices); only about one-sixth of this sum was placed inside the British Empire, India included.[4] British investment was a major source of capital in Europe; beyond it, Britain was the chief source of foreign capital in North America (including the United States), Africa, Asia, Latin America, and Australia throughout the nineteenth century.

THERE ARE OTHER MEASURES of influence. In 1847 a Portuguese citizen with a Jewish background, David Pacifico, was living in Athens. His house was burned in an anti-Semitic riot as the Greek police stood by and did nothing to stop the mob. Because Pacifico had been born on the

British possession of Gibraltar, he had a claim to British citizenship as well, and asked for Britain's support in claiming compensation from the Greek government.

The British foreign minister, Lord Palmerston, backed Pacifico to the hilt, telling Parliament that a British citizen should be able to say, anywhere on earth, "*Civis Britannicus sum,*" like St. Paul proudly asserting his Roman citizenship at his trial, and "in whatever land he may be, shall feel confident that the watchful eye and the strong arm of England will protect him against injustice and wrong."

Many British intellectuals and politicians rolled their eyes at "Pam's" bluster and fuss, but the assertion of British power and pride went over well with voters. With a balance of power in Europe, with Asia, Latin America, and Africa lagging far behind European technology and political organization, and with North America still half empty, Britain had indeed achieved on a global scale the kind of power that Rome once held around the Mediterranean.

Britain's rulers were not omnipotent; far from it. Britain could maintain a balance of power in Europe through most of the nineteenth century, but it could not dictate to any of the great European powers. The rise of Japan gave Britain a dangerous rival in the Far East; increasingly, the Walrus left matters in the Western Hemisphere to the Carpenter's discretion. As the long and peaceful century between the fall of Napoleon and World War I went on, Russia and Germany posed increasingly serious challenges to British power in Europe and even beyond. By the turn of the twentieth century, Britain's global supremacy was looking more fragile with every passing year.

Yet sea power had won the day. For two hundred years Britain defied great rival powers, and when British power was no longer sufficient to maintain the maritime system, the United States was there to carry on.

Seven • The Sinews of Power

In 1692, the House of Commons faced a long and expensive war with France—the richest nation in Europe, with a population and an economy far larger than Britain's. The government needed money, and lots of it, but it wouldn't be easy to get. Government finance in those days was extremely primitive and uncertain; treasury records were kept on notched sticks, and goldsmiths served as the closest thing to a banking sector. The revolutionary government of William III was on thin ice with the country gentry, traditionally loyal to the House of Stuart, whose head, James II, William had just overthrown. In the seventeenth century, taxes on land were the most important source of revenue. Since the country gentry were the main owners of land, increasing their already burdensome taxes to fund a war against a man many of them thought was still the legitimate king of the realm seemed like a bad idea. Higher taxes do not increase public support for unpopular wars.

On the other hand, many traders and merchants in London had lots of cash and no safe place to invest it. Stock markets at the time were turbulent and unsafe; sounder investments tended to be illiquid, tying up cash for long periods of time. The traditional method of European governments facing financial crises was to extort money from merchants under the thin guise of forced loans. John Morton, chancellor of England in the reign of Henry VII, had perfected the technique of impaling merchants on a dilemma now known as Morton's fork. Visiting a merchant who was living large, with lavish entertainment, fancy clothes, and lots of retainers, Morton would tell the merchant that since he was so obviously rich, he must have plenty of money to lend to the king. Visiting a merchant who lived abstemiously, Morton would note that anyone who saved so much money must have plenty to lend to the king.

These techniques had never been popular with merchants, and after Charles II precipitated the first modern financial crisis in English history by suspending government payments for a year (the 1672 Stop of the Exchequer), the credit rating of the government was lower than ever. Back in the days of John Morton, Henry VII had been able to rely on the Court of Star Chamber to bring recalcitrant Englishmen to understand the wisdom of complying with royal requests; Star Chamber had, however, been abolished, and William III, a politically weak foreigner on a shaky throne, could not compel the merchants to support him; he had to persuade them.

The leaders of the government developed a plan. Special excise taxes would be levied on alcoholic beverages; the government promised to dedicate these new revenues to the interest on a special government loan. That looked good to the merchants, and a million pounds came in to the Exchequer. The squires were pleased, the army and navy were paid and supplied, and the merchants were glad to get 10 percent interest on a relatively safe and liquid investment.

Two years later, Parliament chartered the Bank of England to manage and organize the growing national debt. (The idea came from a Scotsman whose checkered résumé included a trip to the West Indies—he said as a missionary; others said as a pirate.) Those who contributed money to a government loan would receive dividend-paying stock in the bank; the bank would lend money to the government but operate as a commercial bank discounting bills of exchange and performing various other services. Over the years the bank came to play a larger and larger role in the commercial life of the country, ultimately evolving into the first great central bank.

From the very beginning, the national debt that the bank made possible was viewed with the greatest possible alarm. As the historian Thomas Babington Macaulay wrote with the perspective of one hundred fifty years, Britain's national debt "ever perplexed the sagacity and confounded the pride of statesmen and philosophers."

At every stage in the growth of that debt the nation has set up the same cry of anguish and despair. At every stage in the growth of that debt it has been seriously asserted by wise men that bankruptcy and ruin were at hand. Yet still the debt went on growing; and still bankruptcy and ruin were as remote as ever.

The Bank of England was set up to raise money for the wars against Louis XIV. By the time Louis XIV died, the national debt had grown from its original million pounds to more than fifty million. Macaulay reports the tortured lamentations that ensued:

[T]hat debt was considered, not merely by the rude multitude, not merely by foxhunting squires and coffeehouse orators, but by acute and profound thinkers, as an incumbrance which would permanently cripple the body politic.

Yet ruin didn't quite arrive. As the nation struggled and strained under this unprecedented, this crippling burden, Macaulay notes, "trade flourished wealth increased: the nation became richer and richer."

Next came the War of the Austrian Succession in 1740, and the debt rose to £80 million. Then came the extraordinary expenses of the Seven Years' War; the debt reached £140 million. Now, surely, the end was at hand. Macaulay summarizes the arguments of the brilliant philosopher and historian David Hume writing about this mountain of debt. Hume pointed out that the madness of the British leadership in assuming such a debt was greater than the madness of the Crusaders who thought to gain salvation by conquering the Holy Land. It was, after all, impossible to prove that conquering the Holy Land did *not* lead to salvation—but, Hume's argument continued,

[i]t was possible to prove by figures that the road to national ruin was through the national debt. It was idle, however, now to talk about the road: we had done with the road: we had reached the goal: all was over . . . Better for us to have been conquered by Prussia or Austria than to be saddled with the debt of one hundred and forty millions.

Writing in 1767 the well-known Scottish economist Sir James Steuart—whose works would be read with great admiration and interest by the German philosopher Georg Friedrich Hegel—trenchantly warned:

If no check can be put to the augmentation of public debts, if they be allowed constantly to accumulate, and if the spirit of the nation can patiently submit to the natural consequences of such a plan, it must end in this, that all property, that is income, will be swallowed up by taxes.[1]

But ruined as it was, instead of groaning under this crushing load of debt, England perversely prospered more than ever. As Macaulay wrote:

Cities increasing, cultivation extending, marts too small for the crowd of buyers and sellers, harbours insufficient to contain the shipping, artificial rivers joining the chief inland seats of industry to the chief seaports, streets better lighted, houses better furnished, richer wares exposed to sale in statelier shops, swifter carriages rolling along smoother roads.

Blind to this paradox, the terrified government of George III cast about for ways to reduce the catastrophic weight of this impossible debt. The solution seemed obvious: since the American colonies were flourishing and wealthy, why not spread the debt burden by taxing the colonists?

This decision, driven in large part by foolish fears about the national debt, not only led to the loss of the American colonies, but the miserable, lost war of the American Revolution added another £100 million to a debt that was already, people thought, unsustainably huge. Now a reduced empire with no colonies to tax would have to pay the interest on £240 million. Surely the end was near.

Yet again ruin was predicted; yet again it failed to come. Then came yet another round of wars, worse wars than ever. The wars against revolutionary France and Napoleonic France were waged for a generation, and at their end a shocked British government was left holding a national debt of £800 million. The cries of ruin and bankruptcy reached new heights; yet again something very strange happened. Far from collapsing, exhausted and depleted, under this unprecedented burden, Britain, Macaulay writes,

> [w]ent on complaining that she was sunk in poverty till her wealth showed itself by tokens which made her complaints ridiculous. The beggared, the bankrupt society, not only proved able to meet all its obligations, but, while meeting those obligations, grew richer and richer so fast that the growth could almost be discerned by the eye. In every county, we saw wastes recently turned into gardens: in every city, we saw new streets, and squares, and markets, more brilliant lamps, more abundant supplies of water: in the suburbs of every great seat of industry, we saw villas multiplying fast, each embosomed in its gay little paradise of lilacs and roses.

Those who worried about the national debt may have been wrong in their predictions, but their concern was understandable. Historian Niall Ferguson estimates that the British national debt as a percentage of gross domestic product (GDP) during the French wars reached levels that would still shock us today. At the end of the American Revolution, the British national debt stood at 222 percent of GDP; at its peak in 1822 it was at 268 percent of GDP.[2] Britain's ability to bear this load, and to flourish while bearing it, was one of the wonders of the world.

Without Britain's ability to borrow and service these astronomical levels of debt, it could not have prevailed in the long series of wars with France. The cost of war exploded between 1689 and 1815; the War of the Spanish Succession tripled Britain's annual government spending. By the time of the

American Revolution, the annual cost of wartime government had quadrupled again.[3] As the historian John Brewer puts it, "Most eighteenth-century wars ended when the protagonists neared financial exhaustion."[4] Budget deficits were endemic in this period; the French government is believed to have run a deficit in every year between 1610 and 1800, with the exception of the period from 1662 through 1671.[5] If France could have matched Britain's skill at handling government finance and the public debt, there is little doubt that the French, not the British, would have prevailed. The distinguished economist Jean-Baptiste Say, sent by the restored Bourbon government of Louis XVIII after the Napoleonic Wars to discover the reasons for Britain's strength, started his report by stating that England's strength was not primarily due to its military power but to its wealth and credit.[6]

The secret of British financial success lay not just in its ability to borrow; Britain was also better than its rivals at the art of taxation. It may shock some American conservatives to hear this, but during the century in which the British defeated the French, laid the foundations of the world order that still exists today, and began the Industrial Revolution that would reshape the world, they were considerably more heavily taxed than the French. The British debt system was largely borrowed from the Dutch—it was called "Dutch finance" for many years—but its revenue system was its own. Taxes were higher, more uniform, and more centrally and professionally gathered and controlled than in either the United Provinces or France.

The Glorious Revolution of 1688 was not only a revolution for liberty; it also unleashed a period of rapidly climbing taxes as Parliament ultimately proved willing to grant monarchs greater resources now that the old battles between Parliament and the Crown were safely over. Overall, taxes are believed to have grown from something like 3.5 percent of national income under Charles II in the mid-seventeenth century to 16 percent in Queen Anne's reign early in the eighteenth century and to 23 percent during the American Revolution. All this pales in comparison to the Napoleonic Wars, when up to 35 percent of the national income was taken in tax.[7] These levels of taxation were about twice the levels in France during this time—before the Glorious Revolution, the government in London is believed to have received about 20 percent as much revenue as Louis XIV at Versailles—but the poorly designed, poorly administered French taxation system yielded comparatively less revenue. That the French failed to develop a professional and reliable system of state finance like the Bank of England added to their troubles.

Joseph Addison described the British funding system in a 1711 essay published in *The Spectator,* a magazine of personal essays and observations that had a role in its time comparable to that of some weblogs today. The essay, recounted as a dream, relates how Addison found himself in the great hall where the clerks and directors of the Bank of England toiled, but instead of bankers he saw a beautiful young woman seated on a golden throne. Her name was Public Credit; copies of the Magna Carta and recent acts establishing limited religious freedom and a Protestant monarchy and guaranteeing the sanctity of government debt hung on the walls instead of the pictures and maps that were found there by day. Behind her throne was a "prodigious Heap of Bags of Money" rising to the ceiling; gold coins covered the floor and rose to pyramids at her right and left. She had, Addison heard in his dream, the Midas touch; she could convert anything she wished into gold.

For all her wealth and abilities, Public Credit was an extremely nervous young person. Clerks at her feet were handed dispatches from all over the world with the latest news; she listened intently to everything they said, and quickly grew pale and sickly if anything alarmed her.

As Addison watched, six figures entered the room in three groups of two. Tyranny and Anarchy, Bigotry and Atheism, the young Stuart pretender to the throne and the "Genius of a commonwealth"—the spirit of those who wanted to go back to the commonwealth of Oliver Cromwell. When Public Credit saw them, she "fainted and died away at the sight." Instantly the bags of money shrank into burlap scraps on the floor, and the great heaps of gold turned into ledgers and accounting records.

Fortunately, six very different figures entered the room: Liberty, Monarchy, Moderation, Religion, the young prince destined to become George I, and "the Genius of Great Britain." As soon as these figures appeared, Public Credit awoke from her swoon, the money bags were once again stuffed with banknotes, and the ledgers and accounts once again became heaps of gold coins.

Addison's allegory summarizes the way the British system worked. The Bank of England was possible because English society was based on long-established traditions of liberty and law. Because parliamentary government was felt to be legitimate and responsive to public opinion, the people at large would consent to the taxes it imposed to honor the obligations that the government made. Tyranny would destroy this bond between government and people, and even if a despotic ruler tried to maintain the financial system, the debt of an illegitimate government was a riskier investment.

Meanwhile, the bank did more than vacuum up capital from private investors and hand it over to the government for wars. The debts of the government became assets for the bank. Because people believed that the government would honor and meet its obligations, government and bank securities could be held by private investors as assets, and used, for example, as collateral for other loans and investments. The bank facilitated flows of private credit by discounting the bills of exchange of reliable firms, enabling companies to raise money based on anticipated future earnings. A stably funded national debt facilitated investment and commercial enterprise in the right hands; Britain's funding system made its economy more prosperous while still providing resources to the state. Despite rising taxes, debt, and one war after the other, Britain's GDP is estimated to have tripled between the Glorious Revolution and the battle of Waterloo.[8]

More than that, the bank united the country around its institutions and values. Any threat to the bank's existence and to the conditions that promoted its health would cause financial panics and immense losses. Concretely, as the bank's organizers and Addison knew very well, the Bank of England depended on the continued exclusion of James II and his heirs from the throne. The bank had been formed to prosecute a war against him; as king he would obviously refuse to repay loans made for that purpose and bank stock and bank paper would be worthless. The economic consequences of the collapse of the bank would be catastrophic for virtually every significant financial interest in Britain. Over time, as more investors saw that bank stock and paper were good investments, the circle of those with an economic stake in the bank's success, and therefore in the political arrangements based on the revolution of 1688, continued to grow wider and more influential.

Government debt, historically a source of weakness, had been transformed into an instrument of strength. The more King William and his successor, Queen Anne, borrowed, the more money they had to fight wars—and the more they united an ever more prosperous country behind them. And because a last-minute revision to the law authorizing the bank made it illegal for the king to borrow money from it without parliamentary approval, no new king could use access to the bank's financial power to rule without the House of Commons.

Alexander Hamilton deliberately reproduced both the political and economic consequences of the Bank of England when he designed the First Bank of the United States—and the system worked as effectively in the United States as it did in Britain. Daniel Webster, like many Americans unwilling to acknowledge in public just how much the United States owed to the mother country, said that Hamilton

> smote the rock of the natural resources, and abundant streams gushed forth. He
> touched the dead corpse of the public credit, and it sprang to its feet. The fabled
> birth of Minerva from the brain of Jove was hardly more sudden or more perfect

than the financial system of the United States as it burst forth from the conception of Alexander Hamilton.[9]

In fact, the financial system that burst forth from Hamilton's brain was already almost a century old.

For Addison and Macaulay, this system was both efficient and *moral*. It required morality to work, and it rewarded morality with power. This is why Addison includes Religion and Moderation among the "good" apparitions and Atheism and Bigotry among the "bad." Atheism, in Addison's view, undercuts even commercial morality; bigotry leads to faction and discord.

Macaulay's analysis is rooted in Addison's. In describing the way that the new funding system strengthened Britain, he notes: "That strength—and it is a strength which has decided the event of more than one great conflict—flies, by the law of its nature, from barbarism and fraud, from tyranny and anarchy, to follow civilization and virtue, liberty and order." Public Credit is a fragile being; the conditions have to be just right for her to emerge and flourish. But where those conditions exist, a stable funding system and a mighty central bank will raise up a power that can defy all its foes.

As a practical matter, Britain's mastery of the arts of credit and trade was a key factor in its victories against France, and foreign observers noted with astonishment that while the wars of the eighteenth century left France—a larger and fundamentally wealthier country than Britain—impoverished and its finances ruined, Britain's prosperity only increased. Voltaire in particular understood how the superiority of British institutions and practices provided a solid basis for British power. He noted in pained admiration:

> Posterity will very probably be surprised to hear that an island whose only produce is a little lead, tin, fuller's-earth and coarse wool, should become so powerful by its commerce, as to be able to send, in 1723, three fleets at the same time to three different and far distanced parts of the globe. One before Gibraltar, conquered and still possessed by the English; a second to Porto Bellow, to dispossess the King of Spain of the treasures of the West Indies; and a third into the Baltic, to prevent the Northern Powers from coming to an engagement.[10]

Voltaire relates with equal parts admiration and chagrin an incident in the War of the Spanish Succession when Britain's Hapsburg ally Prince Eugene of Savoy had brought an army over the Alps to defend Turin from a French attack. Lacking the money for supplies and a siege, he wrote to some

English merchants nearby; in ninety minutes they responded with a loan of £5 million, which enabled him to defeat the French and save the city. Without the commercial prosperity that the bank helped bring to Britain, those merchants would scarcely have been able to extend such a loan; without utter confidence in the financial probity and resources of the government they would not have wished to.

At the close of the Seven Years' War, Isaac de Pinto wrote: "The utter and inviolable punctuality with which the interest on [English bonds] has always been paid, and the Parliamentary guarantee have established England's credit to the point that it has been able to borrow sums that have surprised and astonished Europe."[11]

The national debt had been turned into a national asset promoting the rise of a healthy and flourishing system of private credit; the well-being and survival of the British revolutionary regime was indissolubly linked with the prosperity of the chief powers and interests of the country; the new balance of power between Parliament and the Crown was safely protected from royals tempted to abuse the vast powers that the new system created. With such safeguards in place, Britain—by no means the largest or wealthiest economy in the Europe of the day—was uniquely placed to finance the wars that shook its rivals and enabled it to conquer the world. The blushing, swooning virgin on her golden throne crushed Louis and Napoleon and gave Great Britain the means to establish its maritime order.

Private Credit

The Bank of England was the foundation of both the public and the private credit systems of the English-speaking world, and would hold that role through the French wars into the twentieth century, when the Federal Reserve System of the United States replaced her at the helm. The edifice that rose and is still rising on that system, comprising capital markets and the commercial and consumer financial industries of the English-speaking world, remains to this day among that world's most powerful bulwarks and instruments. Through the development of the British economy, the rise of the United States to global economic predominance, the extension of British and American power and influence to much of the world, and much else besides, the Anglo-Saxon financial system has shaped, and continues to shape, the world we live in today.

This financial system, originally modeled in many ways on the Dutch system it eventually replaced, was already beginning to coalesce before the Bank of England was established, but the foundation of that bank helped provide the private financial system the stability and support that would enable it to flourish beyond anyone's expectation.

There was nothing new in principle about the global system of finance that the British established. Roman, Chinese, Arab, Italian, German, and Dutch bankers had already operated intercontinental financial systems that allowed merchants to transact business thousands of miles from home. The era of Italian banking supremacy in particular left deep marks on Britain itself. Lombard Street, named for the Italian bankers who once frequented it, remained the financial center of London until late in the twentieth century. Yet for all the sweep and daring of these earlier systems, nothing in previous history compares with the sophistication, flexibility, and scale of Anglo-Saxon finance. What the Germany of Bach, Beethoven, and Brahms is to music, what the Italy of Michelangelo, Raphael, and da Vinci is to painting and sculpture, that is what London and New York are to finance. To the initiates who understand the complexities and subtleties of the discipline of finance, three hundred years of insight, invention, and unremitting toil have erected a monument to the ingenuity of human thought that may be unequaled in any discipline in any land. The bankers, accountants, investors, traders, and corporate officers whose joint efforts brought this system forth have changed the world far more profoundly than virtually any of their contemporaries.

At its core, finance concerns itself with the efficient allocation of resources. The Anglo-Saxon supremacy in modern finance means that to an extent unprecedented in the history of the world, the Anglo-Saxon world has brought the allocation of resources to the highest pitch of efficiency. Superior state finance gave Britain decisive advantages in the military contest with France; superior private finance has made the English-speaking world supreme in virtually every field of commerce for most of modern history. The political and military advantages of this supremacy are incalculable; they continue to shape world history even today.

The intellectual complexity of the subject of Anglo-American finance and its ramifications across every field of industry and politics make its history a topic for a lifetime of research and reflection. Such a lifetime would be well spent and well repaid, but for our current purposes we must content ourselves with just a quick glance.

. . .

LINKING THE WORLD OF STATE FINANCE with the private econ-
omy was the province of a few great financial firms. At one level, companies
like the House of Morgan and Barings Bank handled the affairs of sovereign
states. The House of Barings not only provided the financing that allowed
the United States to complete the Louisiana Purchase at the beginning of the
nineteenth century; its Paris representative helped lower the asking price to
a level compatible with the bank's ability to handle the transaction.[12] Following France's disastrous defeat in the Franco-Prussian War in 1871, the
House of Morgan helped stabilize the new French government by organizing a syndicate that provided the new republic with $50 million.[13] In 1895
and again in 1896 the House of Morgan, which came to act unofficially as
the central bank of the United States, provided the finance that kept the dol-
lar on the gold standard. Theodore Roosevelt turned to Morgan to finance
the purchase of France's $40 million of assets on the Isthmus of Panama
that would allow a canal to be built there under the American flag.[14] The
$500 million syndicated loan that Morgan helped organize in 1915 provided
the financial backing without which both Britain and France would have
been hard-pressed to continue fighting World War I.[15]

But if their heads were in the clouds, negotiating on equal terms with the
heads of governments, the financiers' feet were planted on the terra firma of
the private economy. It was from their activities as commercial bankers and
investment managers that the banks acquired both the resources and the repu-
tations that enabled them to manage state finance. And it was their success
in facilitating private commerce and investment, both domestically and
internationally, that made the banks and the countries that housed them so
potent.

The primitive state of British financial markets at the time of the formation of the Bank of England in 1694 rapidly improved as both investors and
"projectors" (those who proposed new companies and projects to the public
hoping for investment) became more sophisticated and experienced. Joint
stock companies, ancestors of the modern corporation, were once rare; they
became more common and, slowly and with many missteps, they became
safer vehicles for investment. Bit by bit and piece by piece in an ongoing
process, the modern framework of securities law, shareholder rights, disclo-
sure requirements, and the regulation of securities markets has been gradually and painfully established. New financial techniques were introduced
and found unexpected uses; new abuses prompted new reforms.

International investment on a large scale dates back to the early nineteenth century, when the common legal systems and cultural heritage of
Britain and the United States combined with the economic dynamism of the

two countries to build what would grow into the most complex and systematic form of economic interdependency yet seen. The Americans were developing a vast continent with untapped resources and were chronically short of money; British investors were flush with the profits of the Industrial Revolution and their global trading system and wanted to invest them at higher rates than could be earned in their home market. The trend began when British investors led the way by purchasing stock in the First and Second banks of the United States; indeed, fear that British investors would profit too much from the banks was one of the arguments used by their political opponents to block the renewal of their charters.

Following an American financial crisis in the 1830s which saw many private companies and even state governments default on their financial obligations, British banking firms, led by Barings, became much more actively engaged in monitoring the performance of American securities and their issuers. At the same time, a new generation of financiers with roots in the United States established offices in London, the better to entice British capital into the burgeoning American market while profiting from the commercial trade of London, financial center of the world. Foremost among these American-born transatlantic bankers was George Peabody. Born to a middle-class family in eastern Massachusetts, Peabody was the first large-scale American philanthropist, giving away what was then the colossal sum of $8 million to charities on both sides of the ocean. Peabody had no children of his own, and J. P. Morgan, the son of his banking partner, ultimately took over the firm, renamed it in accordance with the custom of the times, and placed it among the most important financial firms not only in American history, but in the history of the world.

The commercial and investment business of the Anglo-American banks prospered greatly. The rapid industrialization and economic growth in Britain and America created both an urgent need for capital and an abundance of opportunities for profitable investment. Despite frequent scandals and panics, British capital poured into the American economy during the nineteenth century, building railroads and steel mills and laying telegraph and cable wires. Barings Bank was responsible for £34 million worth of American railway stocks between 1865 and 1890; with some prompting from Morgan it also took a leading role in the first stock flotations for what became AT&T and its subsidiary the New York Telephone Company.[16]

The relationship between Morgan and Barings points to another important development. Unlike other recipients of British investment such as Argentina and Brazil, the United States had the combination of skills, cultural values, and laws that allowed American firms and institutions to act as equal partners and, ultimately, to compete on equal terms with the British in the financial markets of the world.

By the end of the nineteenth century, British investment in the United States had reached staggering levels. British citizens saved about £160 million per year in the 1890s; a considerable portion was invested in the United States. Large investment funds pooled capital from many sources to invest them in various overseas ventures, often with restrictions on the percentage of the fund that could be invested in any one particular company.

Other aspects of the financial industry grew and became more complex in parallel with the developments in banking. Insurance in particular became a major force in the world. Collecting premiums that allowed companies to make their futures more predictable by managing risk, insurance companies also became sophisticated investors and fund managers, placing capital where it was likely to earn the best returns. Insurance today is a $3.3 trillion global business; like banking, insurance had a long history before the Anglo-Saxon world took it up, but also like banking it owes its modern scale and scope to the emerging financial markets of seventeenth-century London. A desire for fire insurance after the 1666 Great Fire led to what many consider the first modern property insurance market. Britain's growing sea trade led to the establishment of a marine insurance business in a London coffeehouse in the revolutionary year of 1688. The proprietor of the coffeehouse, Edward Lloyd, moved his business to Lombard Street in 1691; Lloyds of London remains today the world's largest issuer of marine insurance. North America is the world's largest insurance market, and Great Britain, with less than 1 percent of the world's population, is still responsible for more than 9 percent of total insurance issued worldwide.

Consumer Credit

The financial infrastructure of the Anglo-American world is not limited to the needs of governments and corporations. That Americans held more than half of the 1.3 billion consumer credit cards in the world according to a 2003 study is only one consequence of a financial system that has penetrated into the lives of individuals and families and supported the formation of small business on an unprecedented scale. (The country with the second-largest number of consumer credit cards in the 2003 study was Great Britain.)[17]

The development of modern household finance began in seventeenth-century Britain. Changes in the law allowed landed property to be "settled"—made essentially inalienable. Paradoxically, perhaps, this increased the market of those willing to borrow against the income from their landed property rather than sell off some of their acreage. Country squires needing to raise marriage portions for their offspring could mortgage some of their income while preserving the estate for the future.

The establishment of a stable, funded debt by the Bank of England further widened the scope of household finance. Merchants and shopkeepers could and did "speculate in the funds," and not even the searing losses of individual investors in the stock market frenzy known as the South Sea Bubble quashed public interest in the possibilities of investment. The liquid market in government debt also provided a basis for weighing the risks of different financial products, allowing individuals to purchase life insurance and annuities with more assurance and more manageable risk. Risk-averse investors could take the low returns but minimal risks of government bonds; others could chase higher rewards from equities and private debt paper. It is from this period onward that even modestly successful middle-class shopkeepers and others could begin to plan a secure retirement.

Though the modern insurance industry developed in Britain, nineteenth-century America saw its widespread democratization. Life insurance, fire insurance, theft insurance, burial insurance: on an unprecedented scale even poor Americans were insuring themselves against the vicissitudes of life as the nineteenth century wore on.[18]

The opening years of the nineteenth century witnessed another momentous development: In 1807, Cowperthwaite and Sons, the first furniture retailer in New York, opened its doors, and five years later it inaugurated the practice of allowing purchasers to pay for their furniture in installments. "Hire purchase"—allowing people to rent furniture with an option to buy—was introduced in London in 1830.[19]

As new and more complicated and expensive but also very desirable products appeared on the market, the need for installment credit grew. Manufacturers and merchants were as eager to find ways to make their goods affordable as consumers were to find ways to buy them. The existence of a sophisticated system of commercial finance allowed manufacturers and retailers to manage their cash flow to accommodate a stream of small payments from customers over time; the conditions for a mass consumer market based on household credit began to take shape.

The typical American household in the nineteenth century was a family farm; as Lendol Calder shows in *Financing the American Dream: A Cultural History of Consumer Credit,* farm appliances and sewing machines helped popularize and institutionalize the new credit system. Starting in the 1850s, farmers could buy Cyrus McCormick's Virginia reapers with a down payment of $35 with a balance of $90 due after the harvest. Although he offered a discount for cash purchases, two-thirds of his customers bought on credit.[20]

The same decade saw sewing machines offered to both rural and urban households on the installment plan. The Singer company began to offer credit terms in 1856. Sales tripled immediately, and Singer was the national market leader in the industry within a decade. The machines could be bought for a $5 down payment, with $3 to $5 monthly payments—and interest charged on the unpaid balance.[21] By 1876, Singer had sold more than a quarter of a million sewing machines, accounting for roughly half of all sewing machine sales.[22] This success was noted by other manufacturers and retailers, and consumer credit became increasingly widespread. In every year after 1896 the per capita personal debt level of Americans steadily rose;[23] levels exploded in the 1920s when the total amount of outstanding debt more than doubled.[24] Though the Depression led to a temporary setback, the modern American economy was set on its current path of consumer-led, debt-financed growth. The automobile led the way with two out of every three cars in America bought on credit as early as 1926; other breakthrough electric consumer products of the era, including refrigerators, radios, and vacuum cleaners, played a role as well.[25] Other forms of consumer lending also grew rapidly as licensed, regulated lending companies challenged traditional loan sharks and others for the business of small businesses and working-class households. A New York City investigation in 1911 estimated that 35 percent of city employees (who are generally better-than-average credit risks) owed money to illegal lenders; nationwide, 20 percent of urban workers were believed to resort to illegal lenders at least once a year.[26] The development of a formal small-loan industry transformed the picture for millions who had previously been unable to get credit from regulated companies. Household and small business loans written by licensed lenders increased from $8 million in 1916 to $255 million in 1929.[27]

The credit bureau, a company that facilitates the expansion of credit to the mass market by providing lenders with (usually) reliable information about the past financial records of consumers, is another peculiarly American institution with deep roots in our history. Like Elizur Wright, who is known as the father of life insurance, Lewis Tappan was an ardent abolitionist and social reformer. Beginning in 1841 Tappan built a national network of agents recruited mostly from the ranks of the abolitionist movement. (Abraham Lincoln was one of the two thousand he recruited.) Tappan's agency claimed it could locate any individual anywhere in the United States within seven days, and it kept extensive reports on the personal and financial habits of those who entered its orbit. Coining terms like "bad egg" and "good for nothing" that became an integral part of the American language, Tappan's network was a massive enterprise that added seventy thousand names to its records in one year alone.[28]

There is something disagreeable about industrial-strength snooping like that pioneered by Tappan and now carried out by the major credit agencies. Yet such agencies on balance have increased rather than restricted the access of ordinary Americans to credit and, by allowing lenders to make better decisions and reduce their losses, reduced the cost of credit for responsible borrowers. But whether one approves of such enterprises or not, their development at such an early date on such a wide scale is one of the more telling illustrations of the rise of a consumer-oriented financial system in the English-speaking world.

Housing was then and remains today the largest single expense for most working families. From the earliest days of European settlement, the prevalence of the single-family farm meant that most Americans were homeowners. But urban Americans began to purchase or build homes on credit relatively soon. The first building societies were organized in Philadelphia in 1831, and by the end of the nineteenth century there were approximately 1.6 million households enrolled in almost six thousand building and loan associations spread over the country. Typically, the members of these societies would repay a large loan for a purchase such as a house or a lot in monthly installments over a period of time. The installments included principal, fees, dues, and interest.[29] From these humble beginnings would grow the American system of home finance, a system which has generated substantial wealth for ordinary American families, provided most Americans with the largest and most valuable asset they own, underwritten the development of America's capital markets as a sophisticated secondary market in mortgage-backed securities took shape, helped scores of millions of Americans move to the suburbs, and helped define the American dream.

The Bank of America

If the story of the Bank of England shows how Anglo-American achievements in finance laid the foundations of the global maritime order, the story of the Bank of America shows how the financial potential of that order was unleashed to transform the lives and habits of consumers all over the world. The trends in consumer credit, small-business loans, and opening financial markets generally to middle- and lower-income households that had been taking shape on both sides of the Atlantic for two hundred years came together in a unique financial institution that remains one of the largest and most profitable banks in the world.

The origins and nature of the Bank of England and the Bank of America could not have been more different. The Bank of England, though originally proposed by a scruffy adventurer, was shepherded into existence by courtiers and peers. From its earliest days it was intimately linked to the British establishment and royal family; its business dealings were with the best established blue-chip companies.

The Bank of Italy, as the Bank of America was known until 1930, was founded by A. P. Giannini, the self-educated son of Italian immigrants. Giannini's father, a laborer, was killed in a fight when Giannini was seven. The future banker grew up as a porter and laborer among the Italian grocers, laborers, and small businesses of San Francisco's North Shore. Over the years he built a reputation for integrity and reliability, and also formed judgments about the character of the small-business people around him. At the age of thirty-one, he was able to persuade investors to entrust him with $150,000; this was the seed capital for what, renamed the Bank of America in 1930, would become the world's largest bank by the time of his death.

Giannini's business model was as simple as it was revolutionary. His reputation for integrity allowed him to persuade suspicious immigrants to entrust their savings to his bank; he lent those savings to the small-business people whose character and judgment he could trust. Giannini's bank was built on both depositors and borrowers that the more established financial institutions considered too small and too marginal to work with.

The great San Francisco earthquake struck when the Bank of Italy was two years old. Concerned about the possibility of fire, Giannini drove a mule wagon to the bank, loaded up the $2 million in gold coins and his records from the vaults, covered the gold in crates of vegetables, and drove home to the suburbs. Most of the city's other banks, and their records, were destroyed in the ensuing fire. Within days of the quake, Giannini reopened his bank on a wharf in the harbor, and from his improvised office behind a plank balanced on two barrels he made reconstruction loans to his clients, paid out balances to needy depositors, and lent money to the ship captains in the harbor, so they could sail north to Seattle and Portland to stock up on the lumber needed to rebuild San Francisco.

In the next four decades, Giannini and his bank would midwife the birth of modern California. He helped usher the film industry to California. Before Giannini, filmmakers could not get bank loans. Banks lent on collateral. What kind of collateral could a film company offer to offset the costs of production? Giannini found an answer: the film shot each day. The emerging film colony of Hollywood clustered around this farseeing banker and the cheap and available financing he offered. Over the years he would finance the formation of United Artists, the making of *Snow White,* and the construction of Disneyland.

Giannini's most important innovations and achievements, however, proceeded from his core insight that providing financial services to ordinary Californians was the key to success. Giannini's bank popularized the thirty-year, self-amortizing home mortgage, the lending product that put home ownership within the grasp of average American working families and that would become the model for federal housing policy. In a very real sense, Giannini and his bank created the modern American suburban lifestyle that defined first California and then the nation. The thirty-year mortgage put consumers in homes. Giannini also provided consumer credit for both automobile dealers and purchasers, and Bank of America was the leader in installment loans for ordinary workers. Bank of America helped towns and cities develop and place the bond issues that allowed them to build the roads and sewer and water infrastructure that made new subdivisions possible. The interest on the bonds would be paid by the higher land values as the new tracts were filled with houses sold to consumers on thirty-year loans.

The extraordinary growth of the Hollywood dream factory as well as the popularization of the American dream of suburban home ownership and a family car were the consequences of Giannini's revolutionary approach to democratic finance. The revolution continued after his death: Bank of America was the first bank to issue consumer credit cards. This card, ancestor of the Visa card that is still the world's most popular credit card, took democratic banking to new frontiers of both accessibility and profitability, and unleashed a movement that is still spreading around the globe.

Like Addison and Macaulay—and like Lewis Tappan and J. P. Morgan, for that matter—A. P. Giannini believed that his business was rooted in character and morality, and inconceivable except under free and accountable government. The depositor must believe that the bank which receives his or her savings is soundly managed; lenders must seek individuals who are committed to repaying their loans. A law of contract, accepted and obeyed as legitimate, and enforced by honest and reasonably swift justice administered in reasonably honest and competent courts, is even more important for a mass business dealing with hundreds of thousands of individual consumers than it is for a great institution dealing with well-known firms.

The financial infrastructure that the Anglo-Americans have built over the last three centuries helped Britain and America win wars and transform the economic and political landscape of the world. It also fostered domestic developments in the English-speaking world that helped it make a deeper cultural and social impact on the world than any culture since the dawn of history.

Eight • The Playing Fields of Eton

Imagine two farmers in the mid-nineteenth century who figure out how to build a better mousetrap: one a Connecticut Yankee and the other a rice farmer in Burma. The Connecticut Yankee takes his new design to the patent office and sets up a company to manufacture mousetraps; the Burmese farmer shows his neighbors how to build their own. Over the years, the Yankee mousetrap is improved, tinkered with, standardized. Built cheaply thanks to the factory system and to cheap rail transportation bringing raw materials from all parts of the country, distributed in national and international networks, sold if necessary on the installment plan, advertised in proliferating mass media, the Yankee mousetrap sells all over the United States, the English-speaking world, and, ultimately, Europe. All the companies engaged in this process have access to the world's most sophisticated financial markets, allowing them to leverage the smallest possible amount of capital into the most profitable configurations.

The Mousetrap King, as the farmer might become known if he prevails in the patent litigation in which his rising company would soon have been enmeshed, takes his wife and daughters on European tours, where Italian counts of dubious provenance throw themselves at the girls as society hostesses in London swallow their objections to Yankee vulgarity out of respect for Yankee money.

Meanwhile, over time, the Burmese mousetrap is also tinkered with, and new and improved versions gradually spread from village to village, house to house. The original maker is esteemed by his neighbors, but no path is beaten to his door, and his (or her) name is quickly forgotten.

Years later, Yankee traders arrive in Burma on a steamship bringing cheap Yankee mousetraps of a standard pattern. The newfangled devices are distributed on British-made and British-owned railroads to retailers all over the country. The chances are that the handmade, homegrown model will soon survive only in up-country villages and among the poor.

The Anglo-American frenzy of improvement, tinkering, and marketing was not confined to financial markets and products. New technologies, new products, new methods of organizing the work of people in corporations, new marketing strategies, new media, new methods of transportation and communication, new ways of funding and organizing and directing research: during the last three centuries a global movement centered in Anglo-American society has altered the world beyond recognition, not only transforming lives but also building new patterns in international power and trade. This has not just been a question of better mousetraps and faster Internet servers; the cultural and social changes resulting from the transformation of the material conditions of human life by Anglo-American capitalism on its increasingly global scale have helped create the first genuinely global cultures and communities.

More than that, the revolutionary capitalist societies of the Anglo-American world accomplished a revolution in political economy as important and as earthshaking as the rise of political democracy. In democracies, political power is ultimately the gift of the people. Aspiring political leaders must stoop to conquer; they must study the values, the aspirations, and even the prejudices and errors of the publics whose confidence they hope to win.

In the mass consumer societies that result from the marriage of Anglo-American finance with rapidly advancing, market-driven technological change, wealth is also a gift of the people. If ordinary consumers do not like the cars your firm produces, the firm declines. If the dogs do not like the dog food, the dog food company, its shareholders, and its executives will all suffer. In the contemporary world, everyone from Hollywood stars to clothing designers must study the masses.

In traditional monarchies and oligarchies, it is the rulers and well-born whose tastes must be studied, prejudices indulged, and caprices made much of.

The power of mass consumption, harnessed by flexible markets to the economic interest of the talented, may be the most revolutionary human discovery since the taming of fire. The changes that have come and will come from this union of the ambitions of the elites with the aspirations of the masses are incalculable. At the level of politics, the role of the English-speaking world as the chief font of techniques, products, research, and culture for three hundred years has helped establish and shape the maritime system.

Historians, including David Landes and Daniel Boorstin, have studied this process and treated various aspects of it with the attention and skill it deserves; readers should go to Landes's *The Wealth and Poverty of Nations* and Boorstin's *The Americans: The Democratic Experience* for a treatment more comprehensive and thoughtful than anything here. My goal, however, is to simply suggest that Anglo-American history, economic history, and the history of technology are interrelated and that a greater knowledge of all these subjects provides important and useful insights for, among others, students of foreign policy and the history of power.

Economic history and especially the history of the little changes that over time accumulate to change everyday life lack the drama of military history with its battles and wars. Yet they matter. The grand history of the rise and fall of great powers in modern times is based on little things rooted in ordinary lives, like the history of tea drinking and mousetraps.

To Pepsi from Pepys

The best place to start a hasty tour of the consumer-led economic revolution is the same place the tour of finance began: in the coffeehouses of seventeenth-century London where the Bank of England was debated and Lloyds of London was born. Those coffeehouses (at the time tea was seen as a more feminine drink) were not just the start of the financial revolution; they were not just the places where the English debated and to some extent made the Glorious Revolution of 1688. Those coffeehouses also both witnessed and advanced the consumer and information revolutions whose consequences only grow over time.

Coffee and tea are recreational, leisure drinks. They do not sustain life; they enhance it. And the rise of a society that was willing and able to afford such drinks, as well as their equally nonessential accompaniments like sugar, marked an important milestone. From then on, human society would be shaped less and less by the quest for the necessities of life, and more and more by a search for convenience and pleasure.

This was not always a good thing. Sugar in particular was produced under the most appalling conditions until almost the end of the nineteenth century (Brazil abolished slavery in 1888, Cuba in 1870). Even today the lot of, say, illegal Haitian workers on sugar plantations in the Dominican Republic is not a happy one.

The genteel tea-drinking ladies and vicars that Jane Austen wrote about

changed the world through their preferences and choices. Not all of the
changes they wrought were good ones—but they mattered. According to the
historian Wilfrid Prest, British sugar imports for domestic consumption
doubled between 1660 and 1700, and doubled again by the 1730s, at which
point the British were importing fifteen pounds of sugar for every man,
woman, and child in the British Isles.[1] The 10,000 tons of sugar a year
imported in 1700 would increase until it reached 150,000 tons a century
later. Over the same hundred years, tea imports rose from less than 100,000
pounds of leaves to 23 million pounds.[2] Coffee, which had never previously
amounted to a significant item of British trade, was responsible for up to
22 percent of the total revenues of the British East India Company after
1710.[3] The coffee, sugar, and tea trades were global: the ingredients came
from all over the world, and very complex networks integrating shippers,
marketers, producers, and retailers were required to supply the gentlemen
taking their refreshments in London's coffeehouses.

The first known request by any Englishman for tea came in a 1615 letter
from an agent of the East India Company based in Japan, asking a colleague
in Macao to send him some of the best-quality "chaw."[4] Samuel Pepys, an
official who helped establish the organizational and managerial basis of
Britain's world-conquering navy, confided to his extraordinarily candid and
vivid diary that he had what he called his first "Cupp" of "Tee" on September 25, 1660.[5]

Ten years earlier a Jewish man known to history only as Jacob had
opened England's first recorded coffeehouse, the Angel, in Oxford. The first
London coffeehouse opened in 1652; by 1700 there were "at least" several
hundred such establishments in London, compared to only thirty-two in
Amsterdam.[6]

Satisfying the demand for such products helped build the British companies and empire that would dominate world history for the next two
centuries. The coffee and tea trades helped make the British East India
Company supreme in India—and this company would go on to recruit and
train armies, building the British Empire in India as a kind of commercial
project.

The tobacco trade was also important, from both the imperial and the
financial points of view. Virginia and Maryland alone shipped more than
four hundred million pounds of tobacco to Britain between 1703 and 1718.[7]
The shipping costs were typically £7 per ton, meaning that tobacco represented £82,000 in business to British shipping interests.[8] Insurance premiums (which like freight costs were paid, grumbling colonials noted, by the

planters) were a substantial additional charge—and this steady income did much to establish Britain's nascent insurance industry.

There were additional advantages. About 65 percent of the tobacco that reached Britain was reexported to Europe, generating more profits, insurance premiums, and employment. The British government worked actively to promote this market, throwing its diplomatic weight around to pry open markets in, for example, Venice, Sicily, and the Austrian Netherlands.[9]

The tobacco trade turned colonies like Virginia into flourishing societies; exports of manufactured goods and luxury items to Virginia planters and the even wealthier sugar barons of the Caribbean provided the outlets for British manufacturers that stimulated rapid economic growth in war and peace for the rest of the eighteenth century. The large home market also helped British companies achieve a dominant position in many European markets: from the 1720s forward, partly because tea was replacing coffee as Britain's beverage of choice, the British coffee trade was increasingly focused on the reexport of coffee to European markets. Those who operated the fleets of ships that carried on this commerce all over the world trained the sailors who, willingly and unwillingly, would man the British naval warships against France. The skills that shipbuilders acquired and the charts and maps made by captains bent on trade helped make Britain an ever more formidable sea power—at the same time it was becoming ever richer.

Imports were as much a sign and cause of prosperity as exports. In 1725 William Defoe boasted in the *Complete English Tradesman* that

> England consumes within itself more goods of foreign growth, imported from the several countries where they are produced or wrought than any other nation in the world ... This importation consists chiefly of sugars and tobacco, of which the consumption in Great Britain is scarcely to be conceived of, besides the consumption of cotton, indigo, rice, ginger, pimento or Jamaica pepper, cocoa or chocolate, rum and molasses.[10]

The list of imports would only increase as British prosperity spread to more and more people.

If the coffeehouses were the most public and obvious sign of the consumer revolution, its influence quickly spread into other departments of life. The eighteenth century saw dramatic changes in the way ordinary middle- and lower-middle-income English people set their tables, furnished their homes, and dressed themselves and their children. As early as the 1720s studies of the movable goods people left in their wills suggest that china,

tea- and coffeepots, and other consumer articles were widely available to
the middle classes.[11] A generation later, the inauguration of mass pottery
production in Staffordshire brought new and more elegant serving ware to
an increasingly broad market. According to the historian Paul Langford, the
"carpets, wall-hangings, furnishings, kitchen and parlor ware in the homes
of many shopkeepers and tradesmen in the 1760s and 1770s would have surprised their parents and astonished their grandparents." These tradesmen
and shopkeepers were, Langford writes, enjoying a higher standard of living
in some ways than even the most aristocratic households had enjoyed only a
half century before.[12]

Already in the eighteenth century, middle- and lower-middle-income
English families were growing accustomed to the historically unprecedented idea that each generation would enjoy a standard of living visibly
higher than that of its parents.

The kitchen became the frontier of material progress for many families in
the Victorian era. When the nineteenth century began, most English
kitchens were nasty and dirty places. The closed kitchen range first
appeared about 1800, but was found originally only in wealthier homes. By
the 1860s, ranges were better designed and more widely available.
Linoleum was patented in 1860, and kitchens soon were becoming much
brighter and more easily cleaned.[13] *The Modern Householder,* a guide published in 1872, contained a list of what were deemed necessities for "cheap
kitchen furniture" that a middle-class family should have to set up a home; it
was a comprehensive list that included many items that in any previous era
would have been considered luxurious:

> Open range, fender, fire irons; 1 deal table; bracket of deal to be fastened to the
> wall, and let down when wanted; wooden chair; floor canvas; coarse canvas to
> lay before the fire when cooking; wooden tub for washing glass and china; large
> earthenware pan for washing plates; small zinc basin for washing hands; 2
> washing-tubs; clothesline; clothes horse; yellow bowl for mixing dough;
> wooden salt-box to hang up; small coffee mill; plate rack; knife-board; large
> brown earthenware pan for bread; small wooden flour kit; 3 flat irons, an Italian
> iron, and iron stand; old blanket for ironing on; 2 tin candlesticks, snuffers,
> extinguishers; 2 blacking brushes; 1 scrubbing brush; 1 carpet broom; 1 short-
> handled broom; cinder-sifter, dustpan, sieve, bucket; patent digester; tea kettle;
> toasting fork; bread grater; bottle jack (a screen can be made with the clothes-
> line covered with sheets); set of skewers; meat chopper; block-tin butter
> saucepan; colander; 3 iron saucepans; 1 iron boiling pot; 1 fish kettle; 1 flour

dredger; 1 frying pan; 1 hanging gridiron; salt and pepper boxes; rolling pin and pasteboard; 12 patty pans; 1 large tin pan; pair of scales; baking dish.[14]

The Industrial Revolution had brought an abundance of specialized products within reach of young middle-class families.

The introduction of electricity brought new waves of gadgets and tools into the average home. Toasters, irons, and hot-water heaters were on the market by 1910.[15] By 1915 a nine-pound vacuum cleaner could be had for only $25.[16] Electric washing machines were available as early as 1917. The first electric refrigerators and dishwashers had already been developed, but they were still considered playthings for the rich. By the 1950s, the standard American kitchen set included "stove, refrigerator, washing machine, vacuum cleaner, together with assorted mixers, blenders and coffee grinders."[17] In the 1970s dishwashers and televisions were standard kitchen equipment; in the 1980s microwave ovens and electric steamers and fryers jostled for space on the counter.[18]

Weaving and cloth making had long been English specialties, and by 1700 British consumers had what one observer calls an uncountable number of choices in linen fabrics.[19] Even so, historically, poor and middle-income people owned relatively few articles of clothing. Though few suspected it, there was an enormous pent-up demand for more and better clothing among working people, shopkeepers, and clerks. The textile industry was one of the first to be transformed by the Industrial Revolution. There was a vast expansion in the quality and variety of clothing that became widely available. The profits, technological innovations, financial experience, and organizational and management skills originating in the textile boom enabled the British and the Americans to move forward rapidly to the successive stages of the Industrial Revolution.

Sometimes progress was slow. Up until the middle of the nineteenth century, for example, the only shoes made by machine were called "straights"—there was no difference between the shoes intended for the right and left feet. Only after 1850 were "crooked shoes" widely available as technology and marketing combined to fill the demand for more comfortable footwear.[20]

Providing ready-made clothes for the masses posed surprisingly complex engineering and design problems. "Anthropometry" is the science of measuring the human form; it was not until the early twentieth century that the clothing industry developed the concept of standard sizes.[21] By that time even well-to-do people were comfortable buying ready-to-wear clothes.[22]

The Travel Revolution

The consumer revolution depended on and was linked to a revolution in transportation. The greater demand for goods, both domestic and imported, led to widespread investment in transportation by sea and land, and a competitive market offered rich rewards to those able to cut the cost and time required to get goods to retailers and to the final consumer.

Better ship design and larger ships cut time and costs for long-distance travel by sea. Improvements in navigation, especially the development of accurate timekeeping devices that for the first time ever allowed mariners to locate themselves by longitude as well as latitude, greatly enhanced the effectiveness of sea transport while reducing costs. There were similar improvements in coastal shipping and in the handling of cargo; rivers were dredged and canals dug to bring more and more of Britain within range of what was humanity's swiftest and most dependable form of transportation until the invention of the steam railway.

At the same time, beginning in the late seventeenth century, the British set out to improve their road network. There was great interest in improving the country's bridges. Turnpikes, roads on which the tolls from travelers supplemented local taxes to allow for better construction and maintenance, spread quickly through England after the first was established in 1685.[23] Wrote William Defoe early in the eighteenth century, "The benefit of the turnpikes appears now to be so great and the people in all places begin to be so sensible of it, that it is incredible what effect it has already had upon trade in the countries [regions of Britain] where the roads are completely finished."[24] The speed of travel grew; it took six days to get from London to Newcastle by coach in 1754; that time was cut in half by 1780.[25] By 1770 there were only a few places in England more than twenty miles from an improved turnpike, and coaches on the London–Manchester route covered more than one hundred fifty miles per day, twice the speed of any service in France.[26] Costs were lower, too.[27] The demand for travel increased; the number of coaches traveling daily from Birmingham to London rose from one per day in 1740 to thirty per day in 1763.[28] By about 1800, England had as many miles of good road as France, although it was only one-fourth the size.[29]

More than that, as David Landes notes, misguided French policy, dictated by an absence of the local leadership that in Britain made the turnpike system possible, sought to protect poor road surfaces and reduce government costs.[30] Coaches were required to observe speed limits and use broad wheels that distributed the weight of the coach over more road surface—but which slowed the coaches down, making them less efficient.[31] The Bourbons had cause to regret this poor management of the transportation system when Louis XVI and his family rode a slow coach over bad roads in a failed attempt to escape the increasingly poisonous atmosphere of revolutionary Paris.

By the time steam-powered travel began to replace animal and wind power, the United Kingdom had roughly 20,000 miles of turnpike road, 2,125 miles of navigable rivers, 2,000 miles of canals, and 1,500 miles of railway along which horses pulled carts.[32] No other country came close to matching this network for density and practicality. Relatively low transport times and costs were making Britain into a national market even as the Napoleonic Wars ground on.

Steamships had first been proposed in the late seventeenth century. As engine technology improved they gradually became feasible, then practicable, and finally profitable. Some promising early French experiments came to nothing when bureaucratic and personal rivalries prevented the Marquis d'Abban, inventor of a ship using James Watt's steam engine design, from getting government grants after a successful test before witnesses. In Britain the marquis would have been able to form a joint stock company and attract private investment whatever the government said; this was not possible in France, and D'Abban had to give the project up. Then came the revolution, and French work on steamships ground to a halt until 1816.[33] By then the steamships of Robert Fulton and others were plying major waterways in both Britain and North America, reducing shipping costs and passenger fares on the Mississippi by half.[34]

Long before steam railways appeared, the British were building rail tracks in coal mines and other locations so that animals could pull carts with grooved wheels along the track. The techniques for designing and manufacturing suitable iron rails and wheels in large quantity were already well advanced. Because many of the early uses of steam power were to replace human or animal muscle power in mining operations, it was a short step to try to power collier railways with steam engines. The first steam rail line connected a coal mine to the industrial city of Leeds in 1812.[35]

From there it seemed a natural step to use the new system for human transport; as advances in engine design made the new system safer and more reliable, the Stockton and Darlington Railway opened in 1825. When a railway between the major industrial centers of Liverpool and Manchester proved economically successful, railroads quickly became a major factor in transportation, and the economic and industrial needs of the growing rail system played a dominant role in the evolution of industrialism from the small-scale enterprises of the early nineteenth century to massive companies and factories a few decades later.

In 1830 Britain had about 100 miles of railway; by 1852 it had 6,600 miles.[36] The rail explosion would not have been possible without Britain's capital markets. By 1844 there were 104 privately financed railroad companies; there were more than 200 by 1850.[37] By the end of the century there were almost 20,000 miles of railway in the British Isles, virtually all of it privately funded and privately built.

The United States was the one country in the world that seemed to have a greater passion for railroads than Britain. The first steam locomotive seen in the United States was the Stourbridge Lion, which was brought over from Britain in 1829.[38] By then construction had already started on the Baltimore & Ohio line. Andrew Jackson was the first president to ride a steam-powered train.[39] In 1831 the House of Representatives was already debating the national future of rail transport, and the army became involved in supporting rail construction by surveying potential routes for twenty different private companies.[40]

Partly because the population was less dense and the terrain was rougher, and partly because the public clamor for railroads was so intense and the enthusiasm so high that politicians were willing to provide assistance to companies who were eager to receive it, the construction of the American railroad network received more state support than was available in Britain. A number of colorful scandals resulted. So, too, did an immense rail network. By 1860 there were 30,000 miles of rail in the country; by 1900 the United States had laid an astounding 201,000 miles of track.[41]

Financial markets in the United States, like those in Britain, were tremendously challenged and stretched by the need to fund vast investments over the extended periods of time that railroad construction required. Scoundrels and speculators abounded, but overall the financial markets managed to steer billions of dollars to the construction of the rail network. Two and a half billion dollars from British investors alone went into American railroads; capital poured into these American growth stocks from all over Europe. By 1916, U.S. railroads were capitalized at $21 billion.[42]

It is difficult to overstate the importance of the railroad boom in American history. Without its rail network, the North could not have brought to bear the concentrations of troops and supplies that enabled it to win the Civil War. Nor, without the economic advantages of the industrialization that the railroads made possible, could the North have sustained the economic burden of the conflict. The rail network allowed the opening of much of the agricultural west to settlement, not only because the railroads allowed faster transport for more people than covered wagons ever could, but because farmers who could not ship their wheat crops and cattle to eastern markets by rail would have been reduced to subsistence farming. Without access to world markets, farmers could never have purchased the heavy equipment required to convert the prairie to productive farmland, nor, without rail, could manufacturers have produced this equipment at a price and in the quantities that farmers needed. Cities like Chicago and St. Louis could not have grown anywhere near as quickly; the mineral wealth of the west would have been largely useless; it would not have been possible for John D. Rockefeller to build the American oil industry without the ability to transport oil cheaply and quickly from remote Appalachian and Texan wells to the great urban centers.

The rail network quickly created a national market, one that was even larger and richer than Britain's. Suddenly manufacturers had the whole country as a market; plants in Chicago could make goods that would be sold from San Francisco to Boston. Giant retailers were quick to capitalize on the opportunity.

The first Montgomery Ward mail-order catalogue was issued in 1872. Not much more than a listing of goods and prices, it was an immediate success, and competitors joined the fray.[43] Catalogues grew fatter and fuller, and the advertising in them grew more elaborate and enticing. Sears, Roebuck and Company first issued a catalogue in 1888; 318,000 went out in 1897, more than 3 million in 1907, and by 1927 Sears, Roebuck was distributing 75 million catalogues annually across the country.[44]

The rail system also made the modern chain department store possible. The shelves of stores thousands of miles apart could carry the same brands of goods at predictable prices with reliable delivery. Many of the techniques that Wal-Mart and other "big box" retailers now use were first pioneered in the days of rail; to build more efficient types of retail operations, these large retailers are now using new techniques in shipping and inventory management that resemble quite closely the behavior of stores like Sears, Montgomery Ward, and Woolworth's at an earlier stage.

Americans responded to the rail network in the nineteenth century in many of the ways they responded to the Internet in the late twentieth and early twenty-first. Sears and Montgomery Ward were like eBay and Amazon.com, and the experience of ordering from a catalogue in a remote farmhouse on the Dakota plain was not unlike the experience that rural and small-town Americans first had when the Internet opened up an abundance of choices they had never previously known. Internet stock promoters at the outset were almost as unscrupulous as their predecessors in the age of rail, and great fortunes were made and lost on the World Wide Web as they had once been on the railroads. Additionally, American culture responded to the Internet as eagerly as it had once greeted the railroad. With wildly varying results Americans leaped into the world of e-commerce, quitting their day jobs to trade stocks, sell memorabilia, operate or design Web sites—just as the railroad once opened up new horizons for traveling salesmen, real estate developers, magazine publishers, and tourism promoters.

The Anglo-American world was not the only place where the transportation revolution of the nineteenth century unleashed new social and economic energies. But it was the place where the potential of the new technologies was freest and quickest to develop most fully. The combination of a financial system that was ready and eager to facilitate the fast growth of both the new technology and the ancillary businesses that sought to capitalize on it, a social climate that put few obstacles in the way of the rapid and unpredictable changes that the new technology ushered in, and a widespread spontaneous public eagerness to participate in the brave new world being created and to take risks to find ways to take advantage of the new possibilities opening up all meant that the Anglo-American world made the most of its opportunities.

The pattern continued during the transportation revolutions of the twentieth century. The automobile, the truck, and the airplane have changed lives all over the world—but in each case it was the English-speaking world and, especially, the United States where the fullest consequences of the new technologies were most quickly felt. The alacrity with which Americans leaped to embrace the new possibilities, and the ability of the American political and financial systems to respond to the needs of the new technologies and industries, meant that even when the Americans didn't invent new technologies, they generally made more of them than those who did.

Americans did not, for example, invent the car, but the American manufacturing, marketing, road construction, and financial systems made the United States the place where the automobile came into its own. The first gasoline-powered car in the United States was sold in February 1896;[45] when Henry Ford's Model T first rolled off the assembly line in 1908 there were 515 automobile companies in the United States.[46] By 1910 the American automobile industry was bigger than the carriage and wagon industry,[47] and the United States had more cars than any other country in the world.[48] By 1927, 80 percent of the cars in the world were registered in the United

States, and there was one car for every 5.3 people in the country. The next three countries with the highest ratios of cars to people were New Zealand, Canada, and Australia.[49] In 1895, Germany and France produced virtually all cars made in the world; U.S. automobile output in 1912 equaled that of France, Britain, Germany, and Italy combined.[50]

An explosion of road and highway building accompanied the arrival of the automobile in the United States. As early as the 1920s, the construction of streets and highways was the second-largest government expenditure across the country.[51] The network of paved roads in the United States expanded at rates was comparable to those of the rail network.

Trucks quickly followed cars onto the roads. With greater possibilities for point-to-point delivery and faster times and costs comparable to, if not always lower than, rail freight, trucks were an attractive alternative for many shippers. Livestock, vegetables, and fruits in particular benefited from a more rapid and flexible form of transportation; by 1931, for example, almost a third of all livestock was shipped by truck.[52]

After 1909, when trucks first became a practical alternative, their numbers quickly grew—to 158,000 in 1915 and 3.5 million by 1930.[53] More than 300 firms had entered the truck manufacturing business by 1925, though, as is usual in such rapidly growing industries, only a handful went on to long-term success.[54]

For many Americans, truck ownership was a way to get into business. Independent truckers were the backbone of the early trucking industry: in the late 1920s two-thirds of the three million trucks on U.S. roads were operated by their owners.[55] What made this possible was a financial system that, as shown earlier, was uniquely adapted to the needs of small borrowers and savers. An ordinary working person with no special qualifications beyond a decent borrowing history and a driver's license could buy a truck for a down payment of a few hundred dollars, paying off the balance in installments from the income generated by the truck.

The United States held a similar position of leadership in air travel. Even today, one-third of the world's 15,000 working airports are located on American soil.[56] With airplanes and jets, as with steamboats, railroads, cars, and trucks, the United States was an early and enthusiastic adopter. In 1932, one of the worst years of the Depression, U.S. airlines reported 95 million paid passenger miles; in 1935 they had achieved 270 million revenue miles, and 677 million revenue miles in 1939.[57] By 1977, more than 63 percent of the American population had flown in a plane; the 1979 airline deregulation would set off a scramble as low-cost carriers entered the business and established names went bankrupt. Although many consequences of airline deregulation remained controversial (especially among airline employees who saw their wages, job security, and pensions decline), by 2000 governments in Europe and Asia were coming to the conclusion that the broader economic benefits of a cheaper and more flexible air transportation system outweighed the costs. Low-cost carriers like Ryan Air began to introduce the new air travel system in the European Union; prices quickly fell and traffic rose, two decades after similar changes had occurred in the United States.

Information

The seventeenth-century coffeehouse had yet another role to play in the creation of the modern world. In a generation that saw great changes in both politics and economics, timely information became increasingly valuable. Merchants needed to know if the latest tobacco convoy from Maryland had safely docked without losses to French privateers. What price did tea from the latest East India merchant ship command at the dock? What was today's price for Bank of England stock? In Addison's vision, Public Credit sat nervously on her throne compulsively snatching up newspapers and letters with information from all over the world; London's merchants and investors shared her obsession. The coffeehouse was the place where many of them came to keep up with the news.

It seems to have begun on Bread Street in 1664. A coffeehouse keeper made arrangements with a clerk at the House of Commons to get parliamentary news; for a fee, his customers could share it.[58] The phenomenon spread, and within two years King Charles II took counsel with his government to discuss the possibility of suppressing coffeehouses altogether: there was too much information circulating, and too much loose talk. No suitable response could be framed, although as of 1689 the House of Commons refused to allow printers to record and distribute its votes in order to keep this news away from coffeehouse sages and wits. All this loose information and wild talk, Charles II once complained, resulted in having "the foulest imputations laid upon the government."[59] Politicians everywhere still agree, but after the revolution of 1688–89, the British government reluctantly threw up its hands. The age of news was at hand.

It had begun tamely enough. The first news publication appeared in 1605, but until the English Civil War the Court of Star Chamber kept publishers on a short leash. Weekly news sheets were confined to foreign news, declarations and proclamations by the king, natural disasters, and crimes. After the 1641 abolition of the Star Chamber the climate relaxed somewhat, and both sides in the civil war found it convenient to publish suitably prepared mixes of propaganda and news.

With the restoration of Charles II in 1660 and the rise of a vibrant coffeehouse culture, things began to change. The *London Gazette,* an official publication of the Crown, began to appear late in 1665. Government censorship largely collapsed when Parliament failed to renew the Licensing Act between 1679 and 1685, and then let it lapse permanently in 1695. As early as 1720 there were twelve London newspapers and double that number publishing throughout the rest of the country.[60] Wilfrid Prest informs us that London had four daily newspapers by 1760, along with another half dozen which published several times a week; by 1783 it had nine daily papers, ten that came out twice or three times a week, and four weekly news publications.[61] Tax stamp sales give some idea of total circulation, as each copy of a newspaper was theoretically required to carry a stamp showing that the appropriate tax had been paid. Sales rose from 9.5 million stamps in 1760 to 12.6 million in 1775.[62] Of the two best-known newspapers in British history, what is now *The Times* of London was first published in 1785 and the *Manchester Guardian* first appeared in 1821.[63]

Just as the Bread Street coffeehouse allowed patrons to consult the parliamentary news, coffeehouses found it useful to have copies of the current newspapers on hand for the use of their customers. Coffeehouses also came to attract clienteles drawn to specific types of news or activities. There were Whig coffeehouses and Tory coffeehouses, literary coffeehouses, fashion coffeehouses, financial coffeehouses (like Lloyds), mercantile coffeehouses—551 coffeehouses in London by 1729.[64]

Coffeehouses and newspapers were also the rage in the United States. The first coffeehouse opened in Boston a year before Paris could boast such an amenity. Before the American Revolution newspapers were found wherever there was enough business to support the cumbersome and expensive printing presses of the day. By 1840 the U.S. Census counted 1,400 newspapers and periodicals, and the *New York Sun* reported a daily circulation of 40,000.[65] "In Japan papers are printed only once or twice a month, but in western countries they are printed daily," marveled a member of the first Japanese mission to the United States in 1860.[66] Fredrika Bremer, a Swedish novelist who visited the United States in 1849, pointed to the national market for periodical and popular literature that already existed: "The great diffusion of newspapers within the country, of every book which wins the love of the popular heart, of that religious popular literature which in millions of small tracts is poured forth over the nation, these all belong essentially to this life-giving circulation."[67]

Bremer noted the importance of easy communications for this national information market, praising the "free circulation and communication which is afforded by the numerous navigable rivers of North America, upon which thousands of steamboats go and come; and in still later years by the railroads and telegraphic lines which extend over all parts of America."[68]

The expanding and accelerating transportation networks and the new media that rose in the national marketplace had another important consequence: advertising and marketing became much more significant as national branding and distribution became more feasible. Spending on advertising in the United States rose tenfold, from $50 million in 1867 to $500 million in 1900. By 1950 it had reached a total of $5.5 billion a year. It would continue to grow at that rate and even faster on into the future, reaching $22.4 billion in 1972 and $263.7 billion in 2004.[69] From the rise of national magazines after the Civil War to the development of radio and both broadcast and cable television in the twentieth century to the Internet in the twenty-first century, advertising would help power the development of new media and new technologies—even as the increasingly sophisticated consumers of an advertisement-saturated environment demanded faster innovation and better quality and pricing from manufacturers.

Few observers have captured the relationship of advertising to the general economic and social dynamism of American society as well as Domingo Sarmiento, who toured the United States in 1847 and would ultimately be elected president of Argentina.

What is most characteristic of them [Americans] is their ability to appropriate for their own use, generalize, popularize, conserve, and perfect all the practices, tools, methods, and aids which the most advanced civilization has put in the hands of men. In this, the United States is unique on this earth. There are no unconquerable habits that retard for centuries the adoption of an obvious improvement, and, on the other hand, there is a predisposition to try anything. An advertisement in one newspaper for a new kind of plow, for example, is carried in every paper in the Union the next day. The day after that they are talking about it on every plantation, and the blacksmiths and manufacturers in two hundred places are at the same time considering putting out the new model. Soon the new machines are put on sale, and a year later they are in use all over the Union. You would have to wait a century for something like this to happen in Spain, or in France, or in our part of [South] America.[70]

The rising importance and value of timely information was another force driving the Anglo-American fetish for faster, better communications and transportation. From a very early date this concern showed itself in the drive to make postal service more frequent and more reliable. In 1635 Charles I had opened up the royal mails to the public; in 1660 Charles II established the general post office to facilitate both public and government mail. Various routes could be leased by private operators; in 1696 the English established the first "cross-post"—a system for routing mail so that mail not destined for London could avoid the delays and congestion of the city. By 1721, the eastern and southern counties had daily mail service; everywhere else the mail came three times a week.[71]

In the United States, the first postal service opened in a tavern in Boston in 1639. By the eighteenth century the thirteen colonies enjoyed postal service that was reasonably reliable and efficient. One sign of the importance of the postal service to the colonists was that in 1775 the Continental Congress considered postmaster general a suitable position for America's most famous scientist and man of letters and named Benjamin Franklin to the job. Reliable access to good information in the eighteenth century was seen as both an economic and a political necessity in the English-speaking world; how could people manage their business affairs or monitor their governments without accurate and up-to-date information? The U.S. Constitution gives Congress the duty of establishing and maintaining a national postal service; the present postal service was established in 1792, and for many decades postal officials were virtually the only federal employees whom most Americans ever encountered in their daily lives.

In 1840 the British introduced the world's first fixed-rate postal service along with the world's first postage stamp; the Americans followed suit in 1847. The collection, organization, and delivery of a rapidly increasing volume of mail was one of the most complex problems that the world faced. In both Britain and America postal officials and helpful outsiders were constantly suggesting and trying out new methods to move the mails more quickly and more cheaply. On the whole, they succeeded. In many ways, mail delivery in major cities like London and New York was better in the nineteenth century than it is today; letters were routinely delivered on the same day they were posted, and recipients often received two posts a day. In both countries the new postal system offered attractive rates to periodicals and newspapers; the national information market that Fredrika Bremer so admired owed much to the efficiency of the mail.

The mails provided sources of revenue for entrepreneurs working to improve the transportation networks; the post was a good customer of the turnpikes, the canals, the steamships, railroads, and, ultimately, the airlines. But no train, no homing pigeon, no plane even could deliver time-sensitive information with the speed and reliability that a world of financial markets and increasingly global enterprise demanded.

The first telegraph (literally "distance writing") system was the French optical telegraph invented in 1792 by Claude Chappe. Chappe's system involved signal towers with rotating arms that could be moved to different positions to signify different letters and codes. It was a sophisticated version of the old bonfire-on-a-mountain technique that allowed a very simple message to be transmitted quickly over long distances. Chappe's system was expensive to build, required sophisticated operators to manage the 196 different positions the arms of his semaphore system could take, and could not be operated at night. Nevertheless it worked well during France's revolutionary and Napoleonic wars and was widely imitated by other European states. An 1826 attempt by Chappe's brother Ignace to develop a commercial system to transmit commodity prices and other business collapsed when sufficient interest and financing failed to materialize.[72]

The electric telegraph that communicated signals over electric wires seems to have been invented in Germany by Carl Friedrich Gauss and Wilhelm Eduard Weber in 1833; Joseph Henry independently produced a working prototype at Princeton a little later. In February 1838 Samuel F. B. Morse demonstrated his version before President Martin Van Buren and the cabinet, and by 1844 Morse was able to send a message along electric wires from the Supreme Court chamber in Washington to a machine in Baltimore, thirty miles away. Sent in what became known as Morse code, the message quoted the Bible: What hath God wrought?

From this point, telegraph machines and telegraph wires spread explosively across North America and Europe, linking financial markets and newspaper offices and accelerating the pace of both business and politics. Two years after the message to Baltimore, there were hundreds of miles of telegraph lines reaching north to Boston and west to Harrisburg, Pennsylvania. After four years, Florida was the only state east of the Mississippi without telegraph service. President Polk's 1848 message to Congress was transmitted to St. Louis by telegraph and appeared in print there twenty-four hours after the president delivered it.[73]

Almost immediately promoters and investors began to plan underwater cable service. In 1851 T. R. Crampton laid a cable across the English Channel. For the first time investors could compare market movements in Paris and London during the same day.[74] The first transatlantic underwater cable opened in August 1858 with a message from Queen Victoria to President

Buchanan. Echoing a theme that many preachers and pundits sounded before this world-changing technology, Buchanan called the cable "an instrument designed by Providence to diffuse religion, civilization, liberty, and law throughout the world."[75] This was a little premature: the first cable broke and secure cable service would not be established until 1867. Nevertheless, the Walrus and the Carpenter were now in instantaneous communication, and, they hoped, the transformation of the world would begin. By 1914 there were a quarter of a million miles of message-bearing cables running under the oceans of the world; 75 percent of them were controlled by the British.[76] As early as the Diamond Jubilee of Queen Victoria in 1897 she sent messages by cable to the one-fourth of the world's population that acknowledged her as their sovereign. When Britain declared war against Germany in 1914, the first British military units to respond were based in Melbourne, Australia.[77]

As usual, the Anglo-Americans were enthusiastic adopters of the new technology. In 1845, the telegraph was first used for a long-distance chess game with players in Washington and Baltimore. In the same year the first credit check by wire was performed when a businessman in Baltimore verified the creditworthiness of a customer with a Washington bank.[78] The first telegraph marriage, between a bride in Boston and a groom in New York, was performed in 1848; like other long-distance contracts, the marriage was valid.[79] The first telegraphic money order was transmitted in 1851; by 1872 Western Union had developed a national system that allowed it to offer transfers of up to $6,000 between major cities and $100 anywhere in the United States.[80] By 1877 Western Union was sending almost forty thousand money orders each year.[81]

The extension of telegraph wires continued at a blistering pace. By 1850 there were twelve thousand miles of telegraph wire in the United States, compared to two thousand in the U.K.[82] The Pony Express inaugurated service between Missouri and California in April 1860, taking messages across two thousand miles of wild and mountainous frontier territory in an extraordinary ten days. After eighteen months, the service was suspended when the first transcontinental telegraph line was completed in October 1861.[83] In 1865 the line from London to Bombay was completed, and the time required to transmit a message dropped from ten weeks to four minutes.[84] Five years later, Hong Kong and Japan were wired to London.[85] The next year, the wires reached Australia.[86] The construction boom was associated with an investment boom; telegraph stocks in general and undersea cable stocks in particular ranked among the most lucrative and desirable securities of the day.[87]

Meanwhile, the number of telegraph messages carried each year in the

U.K. rose from 99,126 messages in 1851 to almost six million in 1868, and the cost per message fell by 50 percent as competition and increasing capacity brought rates down.[88] By 1889, the telegraph system was global, but the British were more "wired" than people in other European countries. According to one study, in that year there was one telegraph message in Britain for each member of the population on average; in Italy it was one for every five.

Similar contrasts still existed for the older technology of the post office. In 1889, each English person received, on average, 40 letters and postcards each year. In France, the average was 18 per year; in Italy it was 4; in Russia there were 1.3 letters and postcards per year per inhabitant.[89] The number of letters delivered each year in Britain had risen from 169 million in 1840 to more than 1.5 billion in 1889.[90]

THE TELEPHONE HAD a controversial origin, much like the telegraph's. An Italian, a German, and at least two Americans advanced claims of varying plausibility to this invention, but there is no doubt that it was American engineering, capital, and marketing that made the telephone into a world-changing technology and industry. Interestingly, it was the emperor of Brazil who gave Bell's telephone its big break. The telephone was languishing in an obscure corner at the Philadelphia Centennial Exposition in 1876 when Dom Pedro II (son of the emperor who established his throne by defending his "perpetual" trade treaty with Britain) picked up the receiver. "My God, it talks!" he said as the reporters clustered around. The wave of publicity would help launch the Bell telephone companies. By September of the following year there were more than 1,300 telephones in use, and the first long-distance telephone call had been placed between Boston and Washington.[91] There were 54,000 telephone subscribers in the U.S. in 1880, more than a million in 1900, and more than 13 million in 1920.[92] A decade after Dom Pedro discovered the telephone, American and British investors had put together twelve companies to introduce telephones across Latin America.[93]

Popular Culture

The rise of new classes to unprecedented affluence, the changed world created by emergent technologies and media, the opportunities for self-expression in a culture largely free of political (though never of cultural or moral) censorship: these helped create the popular culture of the English-speaking world that has horrified and hypnotized foreigners ever since.

Its roots can once again be dimly seen in the England of coffeehouse wits. Cheap printing, the end of formal censorship, and the rise of a mass audience with disposable income and the experience of living in a world with new possibilities created the demand for different types of literature and entertainment. Religious pamphlets and tracts supplied part of the demand; so did accounts of travels in distant lands. *The Spectator* of Joseph Addison and Richard Steele played a role not unlike that of a successful Internet weblog of our time. It was published frequently. Its authors perfected a personal voice and a personal outlook. It dealt with a wide and idiosyncratic range of subjects, including much that today we would call lifestyle journalism, and, above all, it sought to be and was entertaining. It, and its countless lesser imitators and successors, wanted to be user-friendly at a time when literature more frequently sought to be grand and impressive. It was chatty, even cheeky, and informal where others were grave. It was moral and religious, but it wore its piety and its principles lightly.

Addison's London was already full of wits aiming, with varying degrees of talent and desperation, to make a living by gratifying the taste of various audiences. They wrote ballads, lampoons, hymns, tracts, novels, works of religious disputation, essays in prose or verse, translations, histories and biographies, and anything else they or their publishers thought might catch the public fancy. Half of the public, and perhaps a larger share of the reading public, was female; increasingly both novels and nonfiction treated women's perspectives and women's concerns with great respect. Men might continue to think women were their inferiors, but as authors they saw no point in offending the public. Over time, the influence and the presence of women in Anglo-American literary culture would grow, and from the time of Jane Austen to the present day, women who were intelligent, vibrant, and self-confident would increasingly triumph over boneheaded men and the idiotic women such men tend to prefer. At least in the pages of novels, deep, troubled, and sensitive but unmistakably masculine gentlemen began to fall helplessly in love with poor and physically plain governesses as rich inner beauty began its long reign in the literary world.

The ingredients that would enable the various strands of popular culture in the Anglo-American world to triumph on a global scale are deeply rooted in the factors that enabled the Anglo-Americans to achieve such influence over the world's technological, economic, and political development under the maritime system. An intellectually and culturally open society, technological progress and mass affluence linked to capitalist development, a vigorous and rich marketplace where products are tested and where the rewards for success are great, a financial system made up of sophisticated and skillful investors and institutions ever eager to back promising new ideas and able to do so economically and efficiently: all these combined to promote the conditions for a vibrant popular culture. Vast revenues from the ever-rising tide of advertising gave the English-language print, and later radio and television, industries crucial advantages in the early stages of the development of each new form of communication. The rapid changes sweeping through the English-speaking countries stimulated people to think, write, sing, and act in fresh ways about new subjects. Because the "today" of the Anglo-American world is so often the tomorrow of its neighbors, the experiences celebrated in popular culture within that world become guidelines for those outside it who can feel their own worlds moving toward the kind of realities portrayed and discussed in, say, American movies or television. Meanwhile, as the production and distribution of popular culture required ever larger budgets, longer time horizons, and deeper pockets, the ability of American movie companies to access financing on a scale once reserved for major industrial projects would give American cinema advantages in production values that foreign rivals simply could not match.

In the end, however, while these conditions supported and strengthened the ability of American popular culture to shape attitudes and expectations all over the world—and, incidentally, to earn lots of money—it was the attitude of Addison and Steele toward their audience that best accounts for the ability of so many Anglo-American technologies and products, cultural and otherwise, to achieve so much success in so many places.

In the world of capitalism, the consumer is king. Success depends on serving the market. Powerful executives and glamorous stars may hold their audiences in contempt—but they will keep that contempt secret if they know what's good for them. Popular culture in the Anglo-American world aims to please, and its skills at pleasing have been carefully honed through centuries of experience, trial and error, and the fiercest economic competition the world has ever known.

Occam's Razor

There was another factor at work, a cultural bias of the English-speaking world best stated in philosophical form by William of Occam, a fourteenth-century Franciscan monk who was born in Surrey and educated at Oxford. William was a distinguished philosopher; he is best remembered for teaching that we should look for the simplest possible explanation for any phenomenon. The principle is known to philosophers as Occam's Razor: If something isn't needed, cut it away.

Anglo-American philosophy today is still heavily influenced by the skepticism and parsimony of William's thought. More fundamentally, this idea expresses one of the deepest impulses of Anglo-American business, culture, and entertainment. In Hollywood people say "Let's cut to the chase," meaning, let's drop all the exposition and character development and move on to the scene that draws in the crowds. This is not an expression that ever became popular in European cinema; the results at world box offices speak for themselves.

The fast-food restaurant industry also cuts to the chase. Take away everything extraneous to the meal: napkins, dishes, vegetables. Concentrate on the essentials: get as many customers in and out of the building as quickly as possible. The food itself, especially the McDonald's hamburger, the most widely dispersed recipe in the history of mankind, represents a similar paring down to the essentials of the eating experience. Hot, sweet, sour, salt: the hamburger hews closely to the four basic notes of human taste. This approach to food is not about subtlety or nuance. Like a Hollywood movie, the McDonald's hamburger gets its simple message across to the largest possible number of customers with a minimum of time and fuss.

The passion for simplicity and the belief that simple is forceful shapes Anglo-American life in many ways. Cutting to the chase, paring the fripperies and frills away to get to the essence, is not just the hallmark of American philosophy, cinema, and cuisine. This is the imagination that discovers new, cheaper, and faster ways of using a production line. This imagination develops a simple advertising message to push a new product. It cuts away the excrescence and traditions of business practice to discover the most efficient way to organize a business. In finance, it ruthlessly penetrates to the heart of a proposition.

Even in grammar the Anglophones cut to the chase. Like all Indo-European languages, English began as a highly inflected language. In the ancient Anglo-Saxon pages of *Beowulf,* every noun has its gender and takes different case endings depending on its role in the sentence. Adjectives "agree" grammatically with the noun that they modify. Verbs can take many different forms, with strict rules governing their conjugation in different tenses, voices, and moods.

Most living Indo-European languages have seen their elaborate traditional conjugations and declensions gradually erode, but English has stripped them away. Like characters in European films, the parts of speech in European languages lead much more complex lives than do their Anglo-American counterparts.

Some attribute the radical simplification of what became English to the Norman Conquest: the poor Anglo-Saxon peasants could not read and so could not master complex grammar. This seems strange; illiterate peasants maintained much more grammatically elaborate languages all through Europe despite similar waves of foreign conquest. In any case, by the fourteenth century, the English of Geoffrey Chaucer was already streamlined and sleek. From Chaucer to Shakespeare to modern times, Anglophones pruned their grammar and their rhetoric with Occam's Razor, continually making their language a more efficient way to transmit information. Nobody planned this, but English has become the McDonald's of languages. Its concision, simplicity, and ease of use (except in spelling) helped make it the business language of the world.

A League of Their Own

In the nineteenth century, Britain's lead in the early stages of the Industrial Revolution made it known as the "workshop of the world"; it was also the world's playground, and, as the Chilean sociologist Claudio Véliz has pointed out, Britain's passion for organized sport has left an indelible mark on global culture. The games the world plays today, the rules by which it plays them, the institutions by which it governs them, the corporate and business structures that finance them, and the concepts of national and international competition which turn whole societies into fanatical and devoted followers of their favorite contenders are all the products of the consumer culture of the English-speaking world.

Soccer, basketball, cricket, American football, baseball, rugby, golf, tennis, hockey, lacrosse, squash, boxing, swimming, track and field: each one of these sports today is played according to rules originating in North America or Great Britain. (The same can be said of more sedentary pastimes: Monopoly and Scrabble are the world's leading board games; poker and bridge are the two most widely played card games. All originated in either Britain or the United States.)

Some of these games, like soccer, cricket, and its American cousin, baseball, are codified and standardized versions of traditional English or even European folk pastimes. Modern golf is descended from a game played with pebbles and sticks in early modern Scotland. Modern tennis was consciously developed under the leadership of the English national croquet association from the medieval sport of kings known as real (for royal) tennis. Lacrosse and hockey are anglicized versions of games traditionally played among the indigenous peoples of North America. Boxing is mentioned in the *Iliad;* however, the modern sport descends from the rules named after the sporting English Marquess of Queensberry who gave them his sanction in the nineteenth century. The rules, a revision of codes dating to 1743, were published in 1865. Swimming is an activity older than written history, and swimming contests presumably are almost as old; yet the modern sport of competitive swimming in standardized events dates to the foundation of the first amateur swimming association in 1869 in England.[94] The rules of cricket were first codified in 1744; the first printed version of the rules ("laws" to cricket fans) appeared in 1775.[95] The Football Association was founded in 1863; to this day it is the body that governs soccer in Britain, and its rules provided the global basis for the world's most popular sport.[96] By 1877 the tennis subcommittee of the All-England Croquet Club had completed the work of developing the rules of modern tennis.[97] The first organized track and field contests in modern times were held in 1849 at the Royal Military Academy in Woolwich.[98] Basketball was invented in 1891 in Springfield, Massachusetts; baseball is widely held to have first been played in the modern form in 1839 in Cooperstown, New York.[99] Sir Alfred Willis's 1854 ascent of the Wetterhorn in Switzerland and the 1857 formation of the Alpine Skiing Club of London are held to mark the inauguration of the modern, organized form of mountaineering; of the seven highest summits in the world, six were first climbed by citizens of the English-speaking world.[100] The rules of field hockey were codified by the British Hockey Association, founded in 1886;[101] rugby in its organized form goes back to the formation of the Rugby Football Union in 1871.[102]

Even an event like the modern Olympics, a revival of an ancient Greek sporting ritual under the sponsorship of Frenchman Pierre de Coubertin, was consciously modeled on nineteenth-century British sport. According to a biographer of Coubertin, the French aristocrat believed that the British alone had "preserved and followed the true Olympian tradition."[103]

The leadership of the Anglo-Americans in the development of global sport was due to some of the same factors that contributed to the more general role of these societies in shaping the rise of modern popular culture. The relatively affluent Anglo-Saxon world had more people with more time and money to engage in such pastimes, or to pay admission fees to watch others play them. At the same time, their leadership in the transportation revolution meant that they quickly developed the rail networks which made it possible for teams to travel regularly to regional or national contests, allowing the formation of wider leagues. Thanks to the telegraph, the drama of league competition and timely accounts of distant matches could be made available on a next-day basis for anyone with access to the penny press.

Yet there is more to the story. The English-speaking athletes and sportsmen responsible for this extraordinary burst of athletic creativity combined two passions that are often opposed: the passion to compete and the passion to organize. Competition in these new sports was keener and more complete than ever; yet these sports were also far more highly regulated and controlled than the pastimes out of which they arose. Stimulating competition and excitement was the conscious goal of the organizers; they tried to develop rules that would make the games as exciting as possible. In some cases, the motive was frankly commercial. A more exciting game would draw larger audiences. In other cases, the motive was love of competition. Standardized rules would allow national and international competitions, and common rules would allow for clear, uncontested winners and losers.

The new rules were not aimed at taming sports. The Marquess of Queensberry rules in boxing, for example, provided for long matches and probably increased the likelihood of brain damage.[104] Over time, as various rule-making bodies have revised the eighteenth- and nineteenth-century rules, close attention continues to be paid to enhancing the value of the sport for spectators as well as ensuring that the rules facilitate rather than frustrate the commercial well-being of teams and leagues. Once-rigid lines between professional and amateur athletics have been blurred, even in the once-sacred Olympics. Shorter cricket matches have been designed to increase the sport's appeal to contemporary audiences; the rules of American professional football have been modified to provide an appropriate number of breaks in the play so that televised games have advertising slots to sell to sponsors.

The Anglo-American world has in fact regulated its athletic activities in much the same spirit as it has regulated its financial markets and economic life—and the results have been much the same. Like ivy staked to a trellis, the competitive spirit of the English-speaking world was bound to a regulatory framework intended to heighten and sustain competition, rather than to check and hinder it. The results speak for themselves.

While the world today carries on business and plays its games very much along lines that the Anglo-Americans sketched out, the English-speakers do not always win. The first baseball games between Americans and Japanese resulted in Japanese victories almost as sweeping as the victories Japanese car companies would later enjoy against Ford and General Motors. English teams are not often seen in the finals of the World Cup, and English cricket teams in recent history have held few terrors for competitors in the West Indies, India, or Pakistan.

Nevertheless, in a great many fields, sporting and otherwise, the world today is playing the Anglo-Saxon game by Anglo-Saxon rules, and the Duke of Wellington was speaking far more profoundly than he knew when he said that the battle of Waterloo was won on the playing fields of Eton. The way the Anglo-Americans have organized themselves for competition in business and in sport has been and remains one of the most powerful factors shaping the way the whole world lives.

Nine • Goldilocks and the West

D espite this record, when most people bother to think about modern world history at all, the Anglo-Saxons drop out. The conventional narrative assumes that the great theme of modern times is the rise and fall of Europe. Beginning with the voyages of Columbus, and picking up steam after the Turks were driven back from the gates of Vienna in 1683, the western European states gradually established world empires until at their peak in 1910 Europeans controlled almost all of the world's surface.

Then the tide turned. The twentieth century saw the Europeans waste their strength in two world wars, while independence movements in the third world gradually brought an end to the old empires. Now the world looks forward to a multicultural future, and the influence of Europe and its offspring over global culture and politics will diminish.

This is a good story with plenty of satisfying morals to draw. It flatters the vanity of Europeans, who can bask in their glorious past while assuring the third world of its coming greatness. It even has many elements of truth and plausibility in it. It has only one serious flaw: it misses the main event of the modern world. It is like a production of *Hamlet* without the prince, or like the three bears without Goldilocks.

Of course, this is not to say European civilization in 1910 hadn't reached a level of development that commanded the fascinated envy and awe of the rest of the world. Delegations from ancient empires scoured the capitals, the universities, the military academies, and the law courts of Europe to uncover the secrets of its success. The cultural and philosophical achieve-ments of nineteenth-century Europe rank with those of the Renaissance or classical antiquity. The English-speaking world was haunted, and rightly so, by a sense of provincialism and cultural inferiority through much of this time. The English novel could hold up its head in any company, but English music, painting, architecture, sculpture, philosophy, history, theology—and much more so the American versions of these—blushed and were abashed when they compared their treasures with their European counterparts. No French or Italian millionaires combed the stately homes and churches of the English-speaking world for magnificent *objets* to take home; no English or American palaces were disassembled brick by brick to be reassembled on the Loire. The dilettantish universities of the English-speaking world could not compare to seats of German learning like Tübingen, Heidelberg, and the Humboldt University in Berlin; it was also from the German-speaking world that the great scientists, philosophers, psychologists, and theologians of the age mostly came—reinforced by a respectable battalion of the French. In the cultural sphere, the old picture of the rise and fall of Europe makes a great deal of sense.

When it comes to global power politics, however, nineteenth-century Europe is almost a sideshow. Alsace changed hands as the German Empire was proclaimed in the halls of Versailles, the Papal States disappeared, the Ottoman Empire shrank in the Balkans like snowdrifts melting in springtime, the Hapsburg monarchy was driven from the Lombard plain. It was all very interesting, and forces like nationalism and socialism that were born in this turmoil would go on to have a global career, but most of these changes were minor when placed in context. Except for the moments when one or more European powers rose to mount (unsuccessful) challenges to the Anglophone order, non-British power politics in Europe had relatively little to do with the great transformations taking place in the wider world.

To the degree that the story of world power politics in the last few centuries has a single overarching plot, that plot is the long and continuing rise of the maritime system as its center shifted from the United Provinces to the United Kingdom to the United States.

The question is why. Five hundred years ago, England was by no means the leading country in the world. In Europe alone, Portugal, France, Spain, parts of Germany, the Low Countries, and some of the Italian city-states seemed well ahead of England. And Europe as a whole was by no means clearly in the vanguard of humanity's march. The Ottoman Empire was at the height of its powers, returning the ancient city of Constantinople to its former glory and harnessing the learning and energy of dozens of peoples in a polyglot culture where religious and ethnic minorities had far more rights than they enjoyed anywhere in the Christian world. The Muslim rulers were bringing order to the vast reaches of India and amassing wealth that surpassed anything Europe had accumulated. China's economy accounted for a larger percentage of world GDP than the American economy does today;[1]

its merchants, generals, artists, and scholars were perhaps the best in the world. Japanese culture, technology, and statecraft represented an acme of human accomplishment. No observer contemplating the wealth and power of the Aztec and Incan empires in the Americas would have predicted their imminent destruction at the hands of Spanish conquistadors. African potentates dealt with European visitors and merchants from a position of equality.

How Did She Do It?

As the world watched the English-speaking powers grow and gain power, both friends and enemies have noticed that, compared with other societies in Europe and beyond, the English-speaking world has seemed less bound by tradition, more willing to embrace change, tolerate dissent, and, above all, allow the chaotic and sometimes painful transformations that capitalism creates and demands. Throughout modern times, the English-speaking world has been in the vanguard of humanity's march deeper and deeper into the world of democratic capitalism.

The West is, of course, a relative term, and its precise meaning changes based on where and when you stand. Western Europe, a place which often seems hidebound and traditional to Americans, looks and feels shockingly Western to people from eastern Europe, Asia, and Africa. Chinese peasants moving east across China to seek work in Shanghai feel that they have reached the West when they see that city's glittering towers—and experience the vicissitudes of its economic competition and the freedom of its culture. Californians traveling east across the United States feel they have almost reached Europe once they reach tradition-bound cities like Boston and Savannah.

The relativity of the West has interesting political and cultural consequences. The Kurdish immigrant arriving in Berlin is certain that he or she has arrived in the West; in talking about the differences between German and Turkish society many Germans will talk about their Western identity. Yet at one and the same time, Germans will often reject the perceived excesses of American-style modernity. To visitors from Asia in 1941, Tokyo seemed on the cutting edge of Western modernity, as Singapore does today to visitors from much of Indonesia and Malaysia. Yet in Berlin, Singapore, and Tokyo, there was and is no shortage of intellectuals willing to talk about ways in which the special, non-Western, and nonmodern qualities of German, Japanese, and Singaporean society make their homes morally and culturally deeper and richer than the undesirable West of the Anglo-Saxon world.

Closer to home, fifty years ago, when the American South was much less developed than the North, many southerners congratulated themselves on their warm, human values—in contrast to the dehumanized, aggressive society of the money-obsessed North. At the same time, of course, they envied the wealth and success of the North and bitterly resented its power.

In the American North, midwesterners contrast their down-to-earth warmth and sincerity with the coldly calculating East Coasters. Up and down the East Coast, people talk about cold and artificial New Yorkers. In New York, people from Queens and Staten Island contrast their warm family lives and friendly manners with those cold fish in Manhattan—and in Manhattan everyone knows someone more careerist, more alienated, colder, and more selfish than anyone in one's own circle of friends.

Rich and free but also cold and inhuman: this is how the West looks from the East. This is how Europeans often view the Anglo-Saxon world; it is how much of the world in turn views Europe. It is how rural Thailand looks at Bangkok; it is how Swaziland looks at Johannesburg, and it is how southern Italy looks at Milan. It is, to a very large degree, how much of the Arab Middle East views the United States today.

It is what Occidentalists look at when they hate and fear the West; it is what Waspophobes are talking about when they decry the global power and influence of Britain and the United States.

Not everyone wants to embrace the Anglo-Saxon model. Throughout the history of capitalism, there has been a pervasive sense that the bargain one strikes with it is the bargain Wagner's Alberich accepted when he robbed the Rhine maidens of their gold: whoever possesses the gold must give up love.

Capitalist society is alienated society, social critics from all over the world have been saying for centuries now. Developed countries are "colder" than developing countries, the countryside is warmer than the city, and so on.

As the pace of the march increases, more and more people find themselves in a colder, more dangerous, and more inhospitable climate than they might prefer. Millions of the North African and Middle Eastern immigrants in Europe find the demands of their new homes radically incompatible with their sense of basic human values. Native-born Europeans flinch at the cold winds blowing down from the heights of Anglo-Saxon capitalism that loom above and ahead. Americans are gasping for breath and wrapping themselves more tightly against the cold winds of global competition that are making the American economy a tougher and more demanding arena all the time.

This mental picture of the world, simplistic as it may be, allows us to rephrase our question about the rise of the maritime order. How did the English-speaking countries get to the vanguard of the global caravan, and how did they stay there once they arrived? Why did they make the journey, and how can they stand the cold? The answer seems to come in two parts. On the one hand, the English-speaking world was a kind of global Goldilocks at the dawn of modern history. By luck or, as Oliver Cromwell would no doubt tell us, the providence of God, England was in the right place with the right mix of social and economic conditions at the right time. The second, much more complex part of the answer explains how Goldilocks managed to keep her lead and keep warm from the dawn of the modern age in Europe into the twenty-first century.

Getting It Right

With hindsight, we can see that the early modern world was on the verge of a great revolution: the establishment of capitalism as the driving force of history. As a social system, capitalism is much more than free markets; there have been buyers and sellers since the dawn of time. In capitalism the emphasis is less on individual economic changes than on the accumulation of great masses of productive and financial resources. Finance and money-lending is a necessary and sophisticated business in a traditional mercantile economy, but in full-fledged capitalist economies finance is the heart of the system—a cold, black heart, many would say, but the heart nonetheless.

The stakes in the race to capitalism were immense. Any country that mastered this new form of social organization and rode the tiger of capitalist development would gain a tremendous advantage over its rivals, amass great wealth, and become a great power. The Italian city-states seem to have been the first societies where the dynamics of capitalism began to appear; Venice and Genoa became great powers; other city-states grew rich enough to support the greatest cultural flowering since antiquity. Tiny Holland, fighting off first the Spanish and then the French, was larger than the city-states; at its zenith, Holland had an empire that spanned the world.

The early modern world contained many cultures and civilizations that hovered on the brink of full-fledged capitalism. Scholars have debated for decades whether and when, left to themselves, countries like China and Japan would have made the transition. Besides the Low Countries and northern Italy, the Hanseatic city-states of north Germany showed signs of leaping into capitalism in the sixteenth century. Spain's world empire depended on the capitalist skills of Italian bankers.[2] Had France not been distracted by its wars of religion, it might well have been the power that shaped the world.

England was not the first country to venture down the capitalist road, but it was the country which managed to elbow its way to the front of the procession and then hold its lead. We can see at least some of the reasons why this happened. Many of them involved luck. To a surprising degree, sixteenth- and seventeenth-century England was the Goldilocks country for capitalist development, enjoying a set of beneficial conditions which no other country could match.

At the time, England's geographic position seemed far from advantageous. On the cold and half-frozen fringes of European civilization, its ports lay far from the profitable trade routes of the Mediterranean and the South Atlantic route past the Cape of Good Hope. The stormy northern seas off its coasts offered easy transportation only to the wastelands of North America—where no great, fragile, gold-rich empires waited for the picking, where no fabulous mines lay awaiting exploitation, and where no valuable spice crops wafted their redolent perfumes over friendly harbors and bays.

Yet, as succeeding years made clear, the English had the best real estate on the planet. To begin with, they were part of Europe, where countries were kept on their toes by vigorous and dangerous competitors. The emperor of China was lord of all he could survey; Chinese civilization, incomparably stronger, more assured, and more advanced than the peoples on its borders, could rest content with its status quo as successive barbarian invasions were absorbed by China's mighty, smug, self-sufficient culture. The Ottomans, too, were rich and strong enough to ignore the unsettling possibility that their empire had much to learn from its neighbors. Even when their offensives against Christian Europe stalled, the possibility that the petty western states might threaten Constantinople could be safely dismissed. Disruptive inventions like the printing press could be banned; the state had no need to encourage scholars and generals to travel west in search of new knowledge.

The petty kings, emperors, princelings, and dukes of Germany, France, England, Italy, and Spain had no such luxury. Political, commercial, and military competition was multifaceted and relentless. English wool merchants faced competition in the Low Countries; the Holy Roman Empire and France dueled in Italy. War and economic competition drove European civilization to innovate and improve. Europe's failure to unite allowed a multipolar civilization to develop, one where more than one line of thought, more than one cultural impulse, could flourish and develop; where scholars, artists, inventors, and soldiers could leave one master for another. Those same divisions put a premium on the dissemination of successful techniques. These states were at each other's throats; if one country improved the crossbow or found a more effective method of fortification, the others had to adopt it or improve upon it.

The Europe of that era was a forcing house for political and economic growth, where competition speeded up the process of historical change. "My vegetable love should grow / Vaster than empires and more slow,"[3] Andrew Marvell wrote to his coy mistress: he was thinking of some of the great empires of the past—like China, Egypt, and Rome. Slow to rise and slow to fall, these monumental empires seemed to live on a geological time scale. By Marvell's time, history was already moving to a faster rhythm, and from his time to ours change has swept the world at an ever-accelerating pace. It was the smaller, more competitive European societies that first began to accelerate on the road to the west, and England was well positioned to experience the full force of this more dynamic and competitive environment.

Within Europe, England was in the Goldilocks spot: close enough to benefit fully from Europe's acceleration, but out of the way enough to avoid repeated invasion and ruin. While it was on the far western reaches of the European world, it was not stuck in the remote outer darkness in the manner of Scandinavia or Iceland. Unlike Russia, which many scholars argue Mongol invaders crushed, destroying a nascent civilization and leaving it permanently backward and disadvantaged in the European race for primacy, England lay on the edge of Europe surrounded by the empty sea, not the teeming Eurasian plain from which wave after wave of barbarian invaders emerged. And while the British Isles are on the edge of Europe, the mouth of the Rhine is a short and generally easy sail from the estuary of the Thames. The sea roads to Portugal were open, and the Baltic was easy to reach. When the Ottomans closed the traditional Mediterranean trade routes to the Far East, England's position was suddenly more valuable and the once-overwhelming advantages that Venice and Genoa enjoyed turned into terrible handicaps in the race for the future.

In the long run, it was probably a benefit as well that the sea routes from England did not lead so easily to the gold and silver mines of South America. The sugar islands of the Caribbean, the tobacco and cotton fields of the American South, and the naval stores of the long Atlantic seaboard ultimately proved to be more valuable than the spectacular Spanish and Portuguese conquests to the south.

Geography had another blessing for England: the island was protected from many of the worst elements in European political life by the Channel, a moat that during most of this period effectively protected England against foreign attack. Holland, Germany, and Italy all suffered in this period because they were so vulnerable to foreign invasion. Countries on the mainland had to maintain large standing armies and build massive fortifications to defend themselves. This required a strong and centralized state; few could imitate the Alpine-dwelling Swiss and reach modern times without building a crushing bureaucracy and an absolutist central government.

England was also Goldilocks-sized. It was larger than, say, the Dutch Republic or the Italian city-states and so was able to support a larger population and larger industries. On the other hand, in this era of poor communications and primitive governance, England was not such a large and heterogeneous empire that the effort to hold its divergent parts together resulted in a long series of civil wars and oppressions. Those that took place were mostly confined to what I've referred to earlier as the "Celtic fringe" and, for all their ferocity and horror, had little bearing on events in the English heartland.

The Reformation, Counter-Reformation, and the resulting wars of religion dominated European history between the sixteenth and eighteenth centuries and shaped the culture and institutions of every European state. England was lucky enough to have a Goldilocks reformation and this, like its geographical luck, helped ensure that England would win the competition to carry the capitalist revolution through. In some countries, like Germany, the Reformation was too hot—that is, the passions of Reformation and Counter-Reformation were so strong that the country exploded into ruinous civil wars. In the German case, this meant not only terrible conflicts like the sixteenth-century Peasants' Revolt and the siege of the Anabaptists in Muenster; it meant the Thirty Years' War (1618–1648), in which one-third of Germany's population died[4] and the German economy was ruined.

There were other countries in which the Reformation was too cold, where one Christian denomination established a secure position by driving out all its rivals. In southern Europe, the Counter-Reformation was able to crush the spirit of secular as well as religious innovation and freeze society into a mold that would retard the growth of capitalism. The Counter-Reformation had many valuable spiritual and cultural achievements to its credit; unfortunately, almost everywhere it triumphed the spirit of discovery, innovation, and change was crushed by the temporary imposition of a

rigid conformity. Galileo was silenced by the Inquisition; Protestant scholars and businessmen were driven into exile by Catholic France. The Scandi-
navian countries and Prussia also had cold Reformations. There, Lutheran
orthodoxy established a stale and sterile hold on public life; Prussia was in
its way as conformist and stunted as Italy under the Spanish Hapsburgs.

The English Reformation was just right—at least from the standpoint of
secular prosperity. (We must leave the judgment of its religious consequences to God.) Although its civil war and the political crises of the seventeenth century gave England a taste of religious warfare, the country never
collapsed into a German-style chaos. And while the Anglican church
emerged as the winner, it was never strong or self-confident enough to
stamp out dissent the way triumphant established religions—Protestant as
well as Catholic—usually did on the mainland. Despite the earnest efforts
of Anglican bigots like Archbishop Laud, and their success at ensuring both
that dissenting English Protestants labored under unfavorable disabilities
and that Catholic recusants suffered even more, the nation was still able to
call on the talents of its religious minorities. At the height of anti-Catholic
fervor in England, the Catholic poet Alexander Pope succeeded Catholic
convert John Dryden as the leading literary light of the kingdom. Aside
from the Bible itself, the best-selling book in eighteenth-century England
was *Pilgrim's Progress* by John Bunyan, a Baptist dissident who had been
jailed under the religious laws of Charles II. Dr. Thomas Arne, the most
important English composer of the eighteenth century next to the German-
born Handel, and author of the music for "Rule Britannia," was a Roman
Catholic. His faith made him ineligible to take a bachelor's degree, but
Oxford University recognized his achievement by awarding him an hon-
orary doctorate in music in 1759. Sir Isaac Newton and John Milton repudi-
ated basic trinitarian doctrines that had been at the heart of orthodox
Christianity since the fourth century; David Hume was at most a deist;
William Penn, adviser to two kings, was a Quaker, and so it goes. This was
not just a matter of talented individuals. Whole industries were dominated
by religious dissenters. Much of the London mercantile interest, to say
nothing of the woolen industry, was dominated by Puritans. Great aristocratic families, including the Howards, the noblest family in the land,
remained Catholic. The great coal mine developers and textile manufacturers of the north country were mostly dissenters; so was much of the rising
professional middle class. Of the twenty-two churches built in eighteenth-
century Birmingham, only five were Church of England.[5]

The English churches would probably have been less tolerant had they
been stronger or more united. In the seventeenth century the faculties of

both Oxford and Harvard viewed Copernican astronomy with suspicion, and there was a frequent agitation among the clergy to stiffen the penalties and step up enforcement of the religious conformity laws. In Ireland, where both established and dissenting Protestants were united (and massively out-numbered by Catholics), savage religious laws were introduced and enforced with a rigor that the Inquisition itself could envy. Wounds were inflicted that have still not healed in the twenty-first century. Even under William III, in the stoutly Calvinist Scots lowlands, a young university student was hanged for heresy as late as 1697,[6] and torture was used in religious cases into the eighteenth century.

Nevertheless, compared to both Catholic and Protestant countries where a single denomination managed to get something close to a religious monopoly, England's diverse religious makeup led to less stringent laws and less stringent enforcement. Among other benefits, this meant that almost uniquely in Europe, the English were able to turn their dissidents and minorities to good account. When not needed at home, sullen Puritans, restless Anabaptists, Catholics of dubious loyalty, and irritating Quakers could be allotted safe havens in the colonies, where their industry and activity created new markets, wealth, and strength for the mother country. Of the thirteen colonies that became the United States, five were founded to provide shelter to religious minorities (Massachusetts, Rhode Island, Connecticut, Pennsylvania, and Maryland). Other European states could not only not tolerate dissidents at home; they could not bear the presence of dissidence in their colonies. The Spanish felt unable to offer Moors and Jews the alternatives of a New World exile; after the failure of the ill-starred attempt at Fort Caroline to colonize what is now Georgia with Huguenots in 1565,[7] the French acted to prevent the emigration of Huguenots to French possessions abroad. These colonies therefore languished with slow population growth and chronic labor shortages as British North America spurted ahead. That counted; the large population and prosperous trade of the English colonies supported a growing fleet and, in an age when customs and excise taxes were of great importance in state finance, helped fuel the growth of England's military power.

Finally, England had a Goldilocks state: neither too soft, like early modern Germany, where the Holy Roman Empire had dissolved into hundreds of tiny local jurisdictions incapable of acting on a wide scale, nor too hard, as in Spain and France, where increasingly powerful kings and rigid bureaucracies crushed local authority and private initiative.

Again, this was not due to any superior vision or virtue of the English. In the sixteenth century, England, the Low Countries, France, Spain, and the

Italian city-states all had limited governments—the powers of the king (or other executive) were balanced and limited by the privileges and rights of the nobility, the clergy, and other estates and interest groups. As the power and needs of the state grew in the seventeenth century, rulers tried to centralize authority and crush rival centers of authority. In much of Europe they succeeded; in England and the Netherlands, they failed.

Two of England's four Stuart kings, Charles I and James II, tried to "modernize" the English monarchy by weakening Parliament. The Stuarts failed: Charles I lost his head and James II lost his throne. Under the Commonwealth, Oliver Cromwell sought to set up a new centralizing power based on the power of the Puritan army he had led to victory in the civil war. This effort, too, failed after Cromwell's death. English society did not trust the Puritans any more than it trusted its kings with absolute power.

The religious and political struggles of this era aided the early development of what later generations would call a strong civil society in England. While local officials continued to exercise civil power in their communities largely unmolested by central authority, the rise of religious denominations created a host of private corporations and organizations that were locally governed as well. Formal and informal associations of merchants protected common interests; the spread of literacy and printing combined with constant political and religious instability led to broad public engagement in the issues of the day. The Marxist historian Christopher Hill has carefully documented the importance of the religious controversies of the seventeenth century to the development of what is now called civil society; E. P. Thompson's *The Making of the English Working Class* and Robert Sencourt's *The Life of Newman* also trace the indispensable contributions of popularly led religious organizations and debate to the growing ability of English society to sustain truly democratic interchange and institutions through succeeding eras. Movements like the Wesleyan Methodists created institutions ranging from sectarian congregations to educational programs to national associations for producing and distributing both secular and religious publications.

American historians often note that the experience of self-government in the colonies prepared the people of what became the United States for their democratic experiment. It is equally true that their British cousins were preparing themselves for a more democratic and open society during the seventeenth and eighteenth centuries as clubs, chapels, philanthropic and benevolent associations, and other organizations gave a large and growing number of ordinary people new kinds of experience and self-confidence.

Yet if the governments of the English-speaking world were more flexible—softer—than the absolute monarchies of the great European empires, they were not too soft. Where states were too soft and too weak—as in Germany and Italy—independence was lost and, in some cases, society disintegrated in anarchy and blood. Where states were too hard, as in France and Spain, people lost the habit of governing themselves in a responsible fashion; they came to think of power as something that existed outside the community and was unaccountable to it. Authorities combined exalted ideas of the powers and prerogatives of the state with inefficient governance and ramshackle state structures. The state and society grew estranged and, when tested by crises of various kinds, the state was unable to stand. Louis XVI lost his head as an outraged but inexperienced, untried, and unbalanced bourgeois leadership was driven to revolution by the inability of the French state to reform. Latin societies in both Europe and the Americas would suffer greatly from the eighteenth through the twentieth centuries from an oscillation between too-rigid states and too-radical oppositions.

The English state was in a different position, as were the legislatures of the American colonies. Relatively weak states had to lean on voluntary cooperation and therefore public opinion for power and legitimacy; ultimately political leaders learned to turn that weakness into strength. Weakness forced the political leaders of the English-speaking world to heed the views of their people as expressed in the complex network of civil society and voluntary associations through which they organized themselves; as public opinion was heeded, it became responsible—and was prepared to support its leaders in peace and war. Moreover, local leaders and a broad cross-section of the population by and large supported the efforts and decisions of representative governments.

This mix of weakness and strength remains characteristic of governments in the English-speaking world today. In Britain, Canada, New Zealand, Australia, and the United States individual governments are weak and accountable to public opinion, but the state is securely grounded in the support of the people. Despite enormous changes and stresses, these countries have all had peaceful constitutional histories—in contrast to Europe, where more powerful states have been more frequently overthrown. Since 1789, France has had five republics, three monarchies, and two empires. Britain and the United States saw no changes in their basic constitutional arrangements in that same period. Since they received their founding charters, Canada, Australia, and New Zealand have also been models of constitutional stability. Since the Glorious Revolution of 1688 the American Revolution is the only instance of a violent overthrow of an existing government among these five countries. Yet these five Anglophone governments generally have had fewer military and institutional bulwarks against the wrath of the populace. The states in these countries have generally governed with a lighter hand than those of continental Europe, usually consuming a smaller share of GDP in peacetime than their counterparts and exercising less control over the social and economic development of the nation. Yet despite (or perhaps because of) this relative weakness, these states have been remarkably stable by global standards and have proved capable of summoning the immense resources needed to meet various emergencies—without crushing the life from civil society by undue preeminence in time of peace.[8]

All this helps us understand how Goldilocks broke from the historical starting gate in a good position—how the English overcame their backwardness and how their early embrace of capitalism equipped them to prevail in the early contests with, as they saw it, various axes of evil. Some of their rivals were hobbled by religious establishments that successfully prevented the wave of social and intellectual innovation that capitalism required. Others were crushed by powerful neighbors, or used up so many of their resources in defending themselves that they lacked the ability to compete. Some labored under governments that overawed the private sector and crushed initiative; some fell victim to anarchy and endless warfare because their governments could not keep order. Goldilocks dodged the bullets and hit the sweet spots, and the English-speaking world was ready to win the race for world power.

Goldilocks had another piece of luck. England's luck prepared it to rush to the head of the procession at just the time it mattered most to get in front. Full-blown capitalism was about to appear in the world; the country that mastered this new system would gather rewards that far outstripped all the treasures of any empire of the past.

Because English capitalism was inaugurated under favorable circumstances, it worked relatively well, creating great wealth and putting down deep institutional roots. The merchants of London did very well from the East India Company; holders of Bank of England stock grew rich. Political power flows to those who succeed; I have already noted that the profits of England's merchants helped Parliament prevail in its contest with the king. Had the reactionary forces been stronger or the revolutionary ones weaker, England might have moved at a slower pace and the history of the modern world been very different. There are signs that after the burst of energy in the Renaissance and the Reformation, much of Europe was ready to slow down. Spanish imperialism was a glutted, torpid force. Germany needed time to recover from the devastation of the religious wars of the seventeenth century. Had Louis XIV succeeded in installing a weak Stuart regime in England, isolating Holland and reducing the Hapsburgs, a triumphant but exhausted France might have also rested on its laurels—or concentrated on fighting the Turks. Europe might have stood pat, and the astonishing explosion of the next three centuries might never have happened. Freed from Western pressure, and faced with less challenging and aggressive pacemakers, China, the Ottomans, the Moghuls, and Japan might never have fallen so disastrously behind. Perhaps they would have faced modernity on more equal terms at a somewhat later date.

That might have led to a happier world than the one we have—or it might have exposed humanity to tyrannies and horrors from which we have thankfully been spared. In any case, we are left with a world in which the Anglophones raced ahead, defeated all challengers, and established a maritime hegemony based on global capitalism.

Early success, however, does not fully explain why the Anglophones stayed the course. Capitalism isn't easy. It unleashes one revolution after another. Take agricultural change as one example. From the time of Marx and Engels, the interaction between economic and technical changes on the farms and in the cities and transport systems of early modern England has been studied in an effort to uncover the dynamics of capitalist change. As urban markets grew and the cash economy spread, landowners were less interested in consuming the crops they produced; they wanted to sell goods in the urban markets. That meant drives for efficiency and higher profits. This led to the development of improved, scientific farming techniques—and also to the enclosure movement. Sometimes with payment and sometimes without, tenants and smallholders lost their rights to common lands, which were then enclosed in great, efficient estates. More efficient agriculture means that fewer hands are needed to do the work. Over the centuries, England's rural population was progressively driven from the land, increasing the urban population, causing great waves of crime and social unrest—but also increasing the size of the market for agricultural produce and therefore increasing the need for scientific agriculture based on enclosure and a better capitalized agricultural process.

The rise of manufacturing and mining created great wealth in formerly poor and isolated districts of the country, and created powerful new classes of magnates and entrepreneurs who wanted better representation in Parliament—and wanted changes in national economic policy that would redound to their benefit. The steam engine, the railroad, the steel mill, the automobile: each of these forced a whole series of rapid changes in English life.

Old elites lost their power, old customs their usefulness. The new realities of an increasingly mechanized, impersonal, and industrial society clashed painfully with values and habits formed in another world.

Capitalism meant conflict and change, and the more rapidly capitalism increased productivity and economic efficiency, the more conflict and change followed in its wake.

Wal-Mart cannot be content with bringing the same goods at the same prices to the same shoppers year after year. It must build new stores, find new goods and new customers, and offer better prices each year. It must constantly look for new ways to manage and train its employees, to control and shrink its inventory, to use energy more efficiently, to find cheaper designs for its stores, and above all to manage its capital more effectively if it is to remain a profitable organization.

The imperative to change and develop is what differentiates capitalism from other forms of social organization. Merchants, bankers, truckers, traders—under capitalism they are all in a Darwinian struggle. The fittest prosper and thrive; the less fit go to the wall.

As new industries and interests arise, they test the old politicians and political institutions. What had once been green meadows and sheepfolds in Britain suddenly bristled with dark, satanic mills. Those mill owners wanted a government that took their interests into account; they wanted seats in Parliament, and they wanted political parties that advocated their interests.

The large cities that capitalism created around manufacturing centers needed new networks of transportation to feed their masses of inhabitants. The new technologies required new laws to protect intellectual property; trade unions rose up to defend the interests of the workers, and new sets of laws and institutions had to be developed to balance the interests of the workers with those of the employers.

The rapid, accelerating pace of social change challenged British and American society, but somehow the English and the Americans have managed to embrace its sometimes chilly logic. The idea of laissez-faire capitalism makes most cultures nervous; the English and Americans haven't always been comfortable with it, but on balance and on the whole, British and American society has been more willing, and more able, to swim in the bracing waters toward the deep end of the laissez-faire swimming pool than have other major societies in the world. As a result, for more than two centuries, the rest of the world has looked with fascination, horror, and envy at what is still called the "Anglo-Saxon" economic model—and the powerful consequences of the model have given first the English and then the Americans an economic edge that sustained them in their battles with evil empires down the years.

Britain first and then America have helped define the reality that lies behind the geographical metaphor of "the West." In the West, markets are free and capital accumulates. People have the right to do what they want. States are relatively weak, civil society vigorous. All religions are free and people can believe or not believe as they like. On the other hand, what people gain in freedom they may lose in security. The West is a land of opportunity, but it is also the home of risk. The structures of traditional society—churches, aristocracies, guilds—lose their ability to regulate the conduct of individuals, but they also lose the power to protect them.

Apparently, on both sides of the Atlantic the rapidly expanding Anglosphere found these progressive and increasing changes easier to accommodate than did other societies. More easily and regularly than others, the Anglophone countries kept the door open to change. Although there were moments of instability in nineteenth-century England, and although the American Civil War was caused in part by the stresses of industrialization in a society that was half slave, half free, on the whole the Anglophone countries were able to keep moving toward the metaphorical West in relative calm. The path was less smooth for others; eastward-looking movements like socialism, communism, fascism, and ultratraditional monarchism were all much stronger outside the Anglophone world than inside it, and in many countries they were powerful enough to slow, halt, and even in some cases reverse their movement toward the West.

Goldilocks was not just in the right place at the right time. Somehow she managed to follow the winding, difficult, and uphill path through the woods without some of the painful encounters and detours others have experienced. Unlike poor Russian Red Riding Hood, she hasn't allowed any wolves to sweet-talk her into taking attractive but disastrous "shortcuts" on her arduous way; unlike Gretel she hasn't been lured into a *völkisch* little house in the forest where children are burned in the ovens of evil. This isn't because Goldilocks avoided the forest or stayed on its fringes; she has in fact ventured deeper and stayed longer in the woods than the other children. How did she do it?

Part Three

Anglo-Saxon Attitudes

Ten • The Wasps and the Bees

We now have some idea about what the Anglo-Saxons did; in the crucial formative years of the world capitalist economy, the Anglo-Saxons successfully mastered its dynamics and developed both a foreign policy and a domestic order that took full advantage of this new force.

But again one asks, Why? Why did the Anglo-Saxons adopt capitalism so quickly and so thoroughly? Why do they like it so much and why are they so good at it?

The answers to these questions can help us understand the course of world history, but to find them we must leave the world of geopolitics, economics, and grand global strategy to look at the social and psychological factors in Anglo-Saxon culture that made the leap to capitalism seem so relatively easy and natural for the English-speaking world.

Our quest for answers now turns to the fields of religion and philosophy, and more particularly to the work of the philosophers Henri Bergson and Karl Popper. Both men were concerned with the differences between open and closed societies (terms invented by Bergson and adopted by Popper); their work helps illuminate the cultural forces at work in the Anglo-American world.

Bergson, an evolutionary philosopher who tried to understand how the requirements of species evolution and individual survival affected the spiritual values and the psychology of individuals and groups, published *The Two Sources of Morality and Religion* in 1932. It postulated the existence of two kinds of social organization in nature. One was a community of individuals guided wholly by instinct: the beehive or the anthill. There is nothing voluntary in these societies; each individual simply fulfills an allotted role. There are less extreme forms of instinctive societies in the animal kingdom;

mountain gorillas and otters live in communities and mostly follow their instincts, but enjoy considerably more autonomy than ants and bees. Bergson supposes that our ancestors must have lived more or less in this way before the development of human consciousness. He calls this kind of instinctual society a closed society.

A closed human society is different from an anthill or even a beaver colony because human beings are conscious, aware of themselves as individuals whose wishes may differ from the behaviors that instinct mandates. Instinct cannot act directly, as it does among ants and bees. It must have a way of making itself felt in consciousness—of causing people to "choose" to behave in one way rather than another. Bergson argues that religion under certain circumstances fulfills this essentially conservative social function.

In a closed society, all the participants know their places. Custom, morality, and law all reinforce one another. The way of the tribe or the clan is the way of nature; to violate custom is to rebel against the gods.

Yet people are not ants and they are not governed solely by instinct. Moral and ethical dilemmas can appear even in a closed society. Much of Greek tragedy revolves around this kind of dilemma: Oedipus unintentionally marries his mother. When Clytemnestra murders Agamemnon, her children must choose between crimes: murdering their mother or leaving their father unavenged.

More than that, individual will creeps in. Young boys and girls do not wish to marry the person their parents have selected; love has a way of breaking the rules.

Tradition and custom defend themselves. In Bergson's analysis, religion arises as a kind of mental habit that binds human intelligence to the instinctive drive for solidarity and continuity. It is the voice of instinct sounding in consciousness. Violating a taboo causes someone to shiver and feel ill: that is the power of instinct. It causes a reaction in consciousness that impels the human being to follow instinctive drives. Bergson calls this kind of religion "static religion"; it aims to keep people and societies where they are.

Rising from a realm outside consciousness, the voice of instinct is accompanied by beauty, terror, and meaning. Myth, legend, intuition, visions, poetry, and awe all come to us from beyond our normal perceptions, and they both enrich and shape human life.

For Bergson, there is another important difference between human societies and beehives, however flourishing. If bees had a history, it would be over. The beehive as a social form works pretty well for them, but bees don't seem to be headed anywhere.

That is clearly not true for humanity. As a species, human beings are in their infancy. The brief span of recorded history, supplemented by oral tradition and the scattered evidence of archeologists and paleontologists, suggests that change and growth are as natural for humanity as stability is for bees. In a relatively short time, human beings have spread out across the whole surface of the globe, encountering varieties of habitat and challenges that demand new responses. Human culture itself has a tendency to grow and to change; techniques in hunting, agriculture, pottery, and metallurgy arise in one part of the world and spread through contact and trade.

The side of human nature that is open to learning and change pulls human societies away from the closed world of tradition and pattern. This instinct for the new, the different, and the autonomous is a necessary part of human nature without which people could not flourish or, perhaps, survive. Bergson defined "open society" as the type of society in which this human drive for change can be fulfilled. Open society is the opposite of closed society. In an open society the traditional unities break down. Custom loses its coercive power over individual lives. Women can do things formerly reserved for men, and vice versa; peasants no longer have to defer to aristocrats. Open societies base themselves on ideals and aspirations rather than, on traditions and archaic rules. Custom yields to conscience.

In Bergson's schema, every society has open and closed elements within it. Tribal peoples in small family groupings with no knowledge of the wider world nevertheless live in a social environment that is rich and complex and changes in response to external events or to social forces and the felt needs and wants of the members of the group. On the other hand, modern industrial society retains many features of a closed society. Irrational traditions and preferences shape the behavior of people who consider themselves individualists; tribal loyalties shape attitudes toward political party, nation, and hierarchies at work.

From all this it ought to be clear that what we have labeled "the West" is the world of the open society and that the journey from East to West is a journey from relatively closed to relatively open society. The open society is also higher—colder—than the closed society. In a closed society, traditional roles and family ties provide a warm if sometimes suffocating environment. In an open society individuals are less encumbered by such ties—but the absence of these certainties and relationships can be chilly and alienating.

It should also be clear that capitalism is both a product of and a motor for open society. As an economic mechanism, it enriches and empowers societies that embrace it. Closed societies that try to swim against the tide are weakened, impoverished, and eventually overcome. With the development of capitalism, something new happened: history ceased to be the record of cycles of openness followed by reaction and closure. It became instead the story of a continuing move west and a demolition of the restraining walls. Open society was beginning the transformation into dynamic society, a transformation that continues to shape our world today.

KARL POPPER BORROWED Bergson's social typology and made it a central element of his philosophy of history. For Popper, who wrote during the portion of the twentieth century that saw hundreds of millions lose their freedom to communist and fascist tyranny, the closed society exercises a powerful hold over the human mind. The open society may be free, but it is frightening. History is in large part the record of efforts, more often successful than not, of the advocates of closed society to shut down open societies. Much of Popper's groundbreaking book *The Open Society and Its Enemies* is a history of philosophy understood as a series of efforts to tame the disruptive intellectual and political forces of an open society and restore the closed society with its stability and reassuringly eternal and absolute qualities. It is a history of wall-building from the time of Plato to the time of Hitler and Stalin.

Much more of *The Open Society and Its Enemies* is devoted to the enemies rather than the friends of open societies precisely because these enemies are so numerous and so powerful. The human mind can be powerfully drawn to the concept of an open society, but open societies are destabilizing and unnerving, and the voice of instinct, in alliance with closed religion, is constantly calling the wanderers home. Popper compares the Athenian reaction against democracy, which, he argues, is expressed in the philosophy of Plato, with the reaction against the French Revolution that culminated in the thought of Hegel. In both cases, Popper saw a similar phenomenon: the forces of reaction struggle to smother an open society with the weapons of traditional religion and traditional values. Popper saw something similar at work in the Marxism of his day. In Marx's own work, Popper argued, there is a struggle between the open-society elements of liberation and justice and a closed-society tendency toward doctrines of historical determinism borrowed from Hegel and profoundly inimical to the idea of human freedom. In the communism of the Soviet Union, needless to say, Popper saw the advocates of closed society once again triumphing over the elements of enlightenment.

Popper is surely right that, historically, efforts to create open societies have usually failed or, at best, achieved partial success over time. In Greece open democratic societies had a pronounced tendency to lapse back into tyranny. In every republic, a Caesar; in every senate, a Sulla. The pattern survived antiquity, and, as we have seen, most European societies failed to move forward because the stress of dawning modernity led to absolute monarchy rather than increased democratization in the seventeenth and eighteenth centuries. The Goldilocks experience of the Anglophone world is atypical; many of the little girls setting out westward through the dark woods end up in the bellies of wolves.

The Netherlands, Britain, and the United States were not the world's first open societies. Several open societies appeared at least briefly in classical antiquity. Many of the Italian city-states could plausibly claim to be open societies, and important elements of the open society could be found among the northern trading cities of the Hanseatic League. But the form of open society that appeared in the Netherlands and the English-speaking world was more robust, expansive and long-lived than the open societies of earlier historical eras. Those early open societies were usually severely circumscribed in both time and space; they appeared in a particular city-state—usually with a population in the tens of thousands—and they disappeared before long in confrontations with foreign military powers or domestic reaction.

The societies of the modern world have had very different careers. They have not only survived where others perished; they have thrived. More than that, they have developed. Generation by generation, age by age, the open societies of the modern era have become more open. Slavery disappears; women get the vote; education becomes available to more and more people. In former times, open societies were rare and fragile blossoms that appeared when conditions were just right, but quickly faded. Today, at least in certain places, the open society is a hardy perennial, blooming from year to year, and seemingly immune to all blight.

These are not just open societies; they are dynamic. They seem to have an inner principle of development that carries them forward. Open society remains a very delicate plant in Popper's thinking; to understand dynamic societies we need to return to Henri Bergson and to another important element in his thought: the concept of dynamic religion.

Static religion, the call of instinct, is the force that holds the member of a closed society fast to its precepts and traditions. Socrates was executed for subverting religion; organized religion frequently led the ideological and political resistance to capitalism and democracy in modern European history. In much of the world we can still see static religion seeking to enforce conformity on societies increasingly stirred by capitalist influence. Fundamentalism can be the outraged reaction of static religion attempting to restore a threatened status quo.

More optimistic than Popper, Bergson was a philosopher of progress. Despite the backsliding and the triumphs of reaction, human society was, Bergson believed, becoming more open over time. The modern age permitted freedoms of thought and action that did not exist in medieval Europe. Whatever the shortcomings of human political institutions, consciousness seemed clearly more fully developed and more independent of the tyranny of superstition than in the primitive past. The world was moving west.

Bergson argued that the urge for change and development is as deeply grounded in human nature as conservatism. The transition from closed to open society is not a violation of human nature but its fulfillment, and nature is as responsible for human development and progress as it is for the forces of conformity and conservatism.

The instinct for change, like the instinct for conservatism, must act through human consciousness. Bergson's human being is like those animated cartoon figures with an angel and a devil, one on each shoulder, whispering conflicting advice—although both are, in Bergson's view, legitimate and normal expressions of human nature.

If static religion is the voice in human consciousness calling us to accept traditional social values and limits, dynamic religion is Bergson's name for the angel that calls people forward to ever more open societies. Like static religion, it can take many forms in the psychological experience of individuals: a feeling of restlessness and unease, a yearning for new experiences, a voice in the head shouting warnings or commands, visions, dreams, or ideas. Bergson, born of Jewish parents from England and Poland, had a complex relationship with organized religion. His early books were banned by the Catholic Church, but by the end of his life he and the Catholic Church had been reconciled; he refused a formal conversion only as a gesture of solidarity with Jews suffering under Vichy anti-Semitism. By his request, a Catholic priest prayed at his funeral. (Bergson, a member of the Académie Française and the holder of many other honors and appointments, renounced them all rather than petition the Vichy regime for an exemption to its laws restricting the place of Jews in French life.)

Mysticism, especially Catholic mysticism, was for Bergson the characteristic expression of dynamic religion, but for our purposes it is more useful to look at certain mystical visions and ideals that sweep through societies and call people westward. The vision of social equality for all men brought down aristocracy despite its sanction by age-old customs. The mystical ideal of democracy leveled thrones and forced the surviving monarchs to accept the reality of popular sovereignty in much of the world. The vision of racial equality drove decolonization and the American civil rights movement. The vision of gender equality has revolutionized social relations in many societies in recent decades and its work is clearly not yet done. These visions do not need to be linked to an orthodox or organized religious community to be powerful, and indeed their progress through the world seems independent of any particular sect. Yet it is also true that these visions act more powerfully when they are linked to something beyond themselves. In American history, visionary movements like abolitionism, women's suffrage, and the civil rights movement counted many secular and unchurched women and men among their leadership, but they owed their progress and, especially, they owed much of the willingness people had to suffer and if necessary fight and die for them to religious conviction that transcended their immediate object.

The most powerful of these visions, the ones Bergson calls mystical, lead to new ways of being human. A St. Francis of Assisi, a St. Catherine of Siena, a Martin Luther, a St. Ignatius Loyola, or a Martin Luther King Jr. is seized by a vision of a new way to live and, under its influence, goes on to live a different kind of human life than any seen before. One woman or one man experiences the vision directly or subjectively, but the power of the ideal is so strong that others, seeing it second- or thirdhand or reading about it in books, feel the power and are inspired to live this way themselves. They permanently enrich and deepen the world's perception of what it is to be human, and they give the rest of us new choices and new possibilities.

These visions are not always conventionally religious. The Renaissance ideal of the full human life is not classically Christian. The troubadours of the Middle Ages, with their new view of romantic love, acted in defiance of both the religious and social orders of their day, but this vision has added immeasurably to the stock of human experience. The bohemian ideal emerged from eighteenth-century Weimar and nineteenth-century Paris and for better or for worse (and perhaps for some of both) shapes the lives of tens of millions of young people and artistic strivers all over the world today.

Dynamic religion can carry people out of traditional religious structures—Ralph Waldo Emerson, Henry David Thoreau, and Abraham Lincoln all felt they were following spiritual impulses as they moved beyond the boundaries of denominations and sects. Dynamic religion gave the Wesleyans the courage to break with the Church of England and led the Latter-

Day Saints to Deseret. It can also lead people to find new meaning and possibilities in structures and dogmas that had once seemed like so many dry
bones in the dust.

But while dynamic religion may lead in a different direction from static
religion, the two kinds of religious experience have certain elements in
common. They point beyond themselves, bringing intimations of richer perceptions, broader worlds, and, above all, transcendence and meaning into
ordinary human consciousness. They are numinous and may be accompanied by visions, voices, or other manifestations of an unusual and striking nature. They carry conviction with them; to those who receive their
messages they come as authoritative pronouncements. "Saul, why do you
persecute me?" the risen Christ called on the road to Damascus. Moses saw
the bush in the wilderness. The Buddha found a new kind of existence under
the bo tree.

This concept of dynamic religion as a driving force in the creation of
open society, or in the gradual and progressive conversion of closed society
to a more open mode, is interestingly absent from Popper's adaptation of the
Bergsonian paradigm. This perhaps half-conscious rejection of the degree
to which the power of the spiritual sense can be invoked on the side of open
society presumably both reflects and strengthens Popper's bleak view of
history. For Popper, psychological forces that support open society are as
weak as reason; the deep instinctive drives pull us back to the comfortable
world of tradition and closure.

The tragic choice that many self-consciously "modern" observers see
between the black-and-white realism of open modernity and the visionary
colors and imagery of closed tradition and myth disappears if Bergson's
dynamic religion is taken into account. The great visions that light up the
western sky and drive us to pull up our stakes and move on stir human souls
to the depths—just as do those mystic chords of memory that bind us to the
past. Religion and myth are not always conservative; the follower of progress
is as god-seized as the steward of conservatism, and Socrates was (at least) as
pious as his executioners.

Karl Popper is not alone in leaving dynamic religion out of his vision of
"modernization." The idea that enlightenment implies secularization is
widely and deeply rooted, and the notion of civilization as a tragically necessary choice that inevitably cuts mankind off from the deepest elements
in its nature was one of the most common tropes in nineteenth-century
Romantic letters and in twentieth-century intellectual discourse. Yet it is
evidently true that the countries which are in most respects the most thoroughly modernized by any definition that rests on economic and technolog-

ical progress—Britain of the nineteenth century, the United States today—are significantly more religious than most.

The key to the ability of the Anglophone world to advance so far west and to maintain its lead position in the global caravan is not, then, that it is or has been more secular than other societies. Indeed, as Britain became more secular in the twentieth century, it lost its technological lead over its rivals and its drive for global power, and it fell, at least temporarily, back from the cutting edge of capitalist social change. Historian Niall Ferguson goes so far as to write that "[l]oss of faith in Empire often went hand in hand with loss of faith in God."[1] (One does not have to believe in either to see the implications of a loss of religious faith for Britain's global role.) Tony Blair, the neo-imperial prime minister who called the British people once more to a global, Gladstonian mission, was with the possible exception of Stanley Baldwin the most committed Christian at 10 Downing Street since Gladstone's resignation. As the United States widened its technological and economic advantages in the late twentieth century, it was also undergoing a religious revival which some compared to the earlier "Great Awakenings" that brought dramatic changes to American society in past centuries.

It is to dynamic religion rather than secularization that we must look for explanations of the Anglophone ascendancy. An enlightened modernity did not overcome entrenched customary religion in the Anglophone world. Rather, dynamic religion infiltrated and supplemented static religion in the religious life of the Anglophones. Goldilocks was able to follow her westward path through the dark and threatening woods so successfully because, like the Magi before her, she was following a star.

Eleven • The Vicar and the Dynamo

t first glance, the religion of the Anglo-American world seems neither particularly interesting nor particularly admirable. Its most characteristic figure is arguably the famous antihero of an eighteenth-century British lampoon, the Vicar of Bray. Coming to the pulpit after Cromwell's death brought Charles II to the throne and the clergy needed to follow the Court's political lead to win church preferment (money and position), the young vicar suited his opinions to the times:

> *In good King Charles's golden days,*
> *When Loyalty no harm meant;*
> *A furious High-Church man I was*
> *And so I gained Preferment.*
> *Unto my Flock I daily Preach'd.*
> *Kings are by God appointed,*
> *And Damn'd are those who dare resist,*
> *Or touch the Lord's anointed.*

But then the wind changed. Charles's brother James II, a Roman Catholic, inherited the throne in 1685. Using his pardoning powers, he virtually set aside the penal law that kept Catholics from holding offices in church and state, ordered a declaration to that effect to be read from every pulpit, and, until the Glorious Revolution of 1688 drove him from the kingdom, promoted Roman Catholicism by royal patronage and favor. The vicar rose to the challenge:

> *When Royal James possest the crown,*
> *And popery grew in fashion;*

> *The Penal Law I houted [hooted] down,*
> *And read the Declaration:*
> *The Church of Rome I found would fit*
> *Full well my Constitution,*
> *And I had been a Jesuit,*
> *But for the Revolution.*

The Protestant leadership of England called William of Orange to the throne. This was a revolutionary act that defied the Church of England's historic belief in nonresistance to the king and the duty of passive obedience to all his commands; a group of leading bishops and clergy refused to take the oath of allegiance to the new regime and were deprived of their offices. Not so the wily vicar:

> *When William our Deliverer came,*
> *To heal the Nation's Grievance,*
> *I turned the Cat in Pan again,*
> *And swore to him Allegiance:*
> *Old Principles I did revoke,*
> *Set conscience at a distance,*
> *Passive Obedience is a Joke,*
> *A Jest is non-resistance.*

The story continues:

> *When Royal Ann became our Queen,*
> *The Church of England's Glory,*
> *Another face of things was seen,*
> *And I became a Tory.*

This too passed.

> *When George in Pudding time came o'er,*
> *And Moderate Men looked big, Sir,*
> *My principles I chang'd once more,*
> *And so became a Whig, Sir.*

As the poem ends, the now elderly and well-established vicar swears allegiance to the new regime and repeats the refrain that states his personal credo:

The Illustrious House of Hannover,
And Protestant succession,
To these I lustily will swear,
Whilst they can keep possession:
For in my Faith and Loyalty,
I never once will falter
But George my lawful king shall be,
Unless the Times should alter.

And this is law, I will maintain
Unto my Dying Day, Sir.
That whatsoever King may reign,
I will be the Vicar of Bray, *Sir!*[1]

The song invites listeners to mock the unprincipled cleric—and themselves, as most Englishmen jumped with the vicar during the era—but it
was dexterity of this kind that saved England from bitter civil wars during
the tumultuous years of the vicar's career, roughly between 1670 and 1715.
Millions of English people accepted major changes in the governing religious and political philosophies of their national establishment in those
years. And while there were significant outbreaks of violence, English or
British (after the Act of Union in 1707 brought England and Scotland into
one political organization), society never descended into the anarchy and
open warfare of the civil war of the 1640s.

That flexibility and pragmatism was instrumental in making the greatest
event of those years—the Glorious Revolution, which replaced the monarch
but also sealed the supremacy of Parliament over the Crown as the most
powerful element in the state—as peaceful as it was. More generally, it was
the pragmatism of the Vicar of Bray—worldly, cynical, tolerant—that enabled Britain to develop a new kind of political society, one far better at
coping with the stresses and demands of an emerging capitalist system than
anything else in existence at the time.

Yet this was not, quite, secularization. Despite the exhaustion that followed the battles of the British Reformation, the new society that emerged
had changed its relationship to religion without severing its connections
with Christianity. A deep religious faith would continue to shape both popular and elite attitudes in Britain for almost two centuries after the Vicar of
Bray ascended to the Great Archdeaconry in the Sky, and both the United
States and other colonial offshoots from Britain like New Zealand and Australia remain significantly more attached to traditional religious beliefs and

practices today than most European countries. The persistence of religion in so much of the Anglo-Saxon world seems related to its ability to coexist with and even thrive on a kind of skepticism that is fatal to what Bergson would call static religion but which is characteristic of the increasingly dynamic religious orientation of the English-speaking world.

Signs of a strange new attitude toward religious dogma in the English tradition are not hard to find. "There was never anything by men so well devised or so surely established which in age and continuance of time hath not been corrupted," wrote the first Protestant Archbishop of Canterbury, Thomas Cranmer, in 1538. With a few changes that sentence survived to become the first sentence of the preface to the 1549 Book of Common Prayer, and it remains today in the prayer books current in the Anglican Communion.[2]

This is an oddly modern-sounding opening to a Reformation religious document, but it is not the only confession of uncertainty to be found in that book. All the churches have erred "not only in their living and manner of Ceremonies, but also in matters of Faith," say the Articles of Religion—for centuries the definitive statement of Church of England doctrine.[3] The Church of Rome, like all the other ancient Christian churches—Antioch, Alexandria, Jerusalem—had gone wrong. Indeed, the Church of England itself had gone wrong, and, during the two centuries following Henry VIII's break with the old religion, "official Christianity" in Britain changed doctrine almost as often as it changed sovereigns. Both the grandfather and the grandson of the Vicar of Bray would have needed his pragmatism. Slightly reformed under Henry VIII, radically reformed under Edward VI, Catholic again under Mary I, uneasily mixed under Elizabeth I, the Church of England's doctrines and practices have continued to shift with every passing wind from the age of the Stuarts to our own times, and will presumably continue to change. The heresy of today is the orthodoxy of tomorrow—and perhaps the heresy of the day after that.

There was nothing here that the Vicar of Bray would not understand (or even applaud, if the sentiment was sufficiently popular). But in the Christian tradition, this is scandalous. Christianity is about *revelation,* about God breaking into history with a definite message. Yet here are the fathers of the Anglican church plainly stating that the truth about God is unknown, perhaps unknowable. Does this mean that God tries and *fails* to reveal himself? The churches of Rome, Alexandria, Antioch, Jerusalem, and medieval England thought they had Eternal Truth; they did not, say the Anglo-Saxon divines. The kind of certainty that these churches—and that other Abrahamic dispensations like orthodox Muslims and Jews—claim for their beliefs is not, Cranmer wrote hundreds of years ago, what God intends for us to have.

What is interesting about this declaration, however, is not that the Church of England made it so early. It is that the Church took the news so phlegmatically. If no church and no book can tell us the infallible truth about God, why go to church and why read the Bible? For that matter, why do good and abstain from evil?

Not everyone questioning these certainties reacted so calmly. Dostoyevsky characters lose their faith in absolute moral orders and murder their landladies. French skeptics see through dogma and become militantly, anticlerical. *Ecrasez l'infame,* said Voltaire, and longed to see the day when the last king was strangled in the entrails of the last priest.

Others have thought that without a basis in absolute religion, no social order can stand. We still hear these worries today from conservative intellectuals who worry that without some kind of absolute, detailed, and unchanging moral code we are slouching toward Gomorrah. This fear has deep roots in human nature, but does the historical record bear it out? The English reformers may have lost their assurance that they possessed absolute truth, but they had no doubts about the need to maintain order.

English discipline hasn't always been attractive. Archbishop Cranmer, whose own convictions on sacramental theology moved from Catholicism to Lutheranism to a kind of proto-Calvinism over twenty years, burned a number of people at the stake for holding opinions that he himself had once held, or would hold very shortly. When he himself was finally burned in Queen Mary's reign, some of those who sat in judgment on him had once worked at his side for the Reformation.

In later years, the English church grew milder, but it didn't lose its spine. Its faith was defined in the Thirty-nine Articles, and until well into the nineteenth century those who refused to sign them could not take university degrees. In the 1930s, the Church that granted Henry VIII two divorces and forgave him for two more spouses beheaded forced his descendant Edward VIII to renounce the throne before he married Wallis Simpson. Prince Charles was forced to apologize to the former husband of the Duchess of Cornwall before he could marry her. The English bishops of Edward VIII's day were far more skeptical than Thomas Cranmer about the doctrines they preached. By the twenty-first century it was difficult to imagine an opinion that would force a well-connected English divine to renounce a bishopric, but doctrinal uncertainty is one thing, while unseemly royal marriages are quite another.

That is how they treated the rich. They were no less prepared to discipline the poor. The rulers of England, though deprived of the comforts of an absolute faith in an unchanging religion, nevertheless managed for four centuries to impose order on their society, often brutally. Rebels were suppressed, traitors drawn and quartered, vagrants flogged, poachers hung, thieves transported—all as if there were an unchanging moral order and the English aristocracy knew exactly what it was.

Deprived of the comforts of an absolute or closed philosophy, poor Nietzsche stared into the philosophical abyss and groaned with sick, fascinated horror: "Nothing is true and everything is permitted," he shuddered.

That hasn't been the Anglo-Saxon response. English bishops faced this truth and saw not the slightest reason to leap into any abysses, philosophical or otherwise. Instead, they went on to set out the rules for finding Easter each year. "To be sure, *in theory* nothing is true and everything is permitted," yawn the English divines with the gulf of relativism gaping beneath their slippered feet. "Now, should the Alleluia be omitted after Gospel readings in Lent? And where *is* that girl with the cucumber sandwiches?" Somehow, the choices between faith and unbelief did not appear as stark to much of the English-speaking world as they did elsewhere. The English-speaking world managed to reconcile a pragmatic and skeptical approach to history and philosophy with profound religious faith and a sense of God's providential care. Meanwhile, the chasm between religion and secular reform and modernization that dominated politics in much of Europe until the twentieth century—and dominates life in Israel and many Muslim countries today— was never as deep in the English-speaking world. Two ideas in creative tension have coexisted for half a millennium in the Anglosphere. On the one hand, God exists and reveals his will regarding moral rules and religious doctrines to human beings; on the other hand, human understanding of these revelations remains partial and subject to change.

Things Fall Apart

To bring Bergson's typology to bear on the religious experience of the Anglo-Saxon world, it appears that as its social evolution speeded up, the English-speaking world moved from an essentially static religious condition in which a stable equilibrium was periodically shaken by episodes of religious dynamism to a dynamic religious system anchored by persistent elements of stasis.

The emerging religious structure of the English-speaking world would have two outstanding features that made it particularly suitable for the growth of dynamic society. On the one hand, the English-speaking world would have a pluralistic and multipolar religious environment, with many different denominations and theological tendencies existing side by side. As Voltaire first noted, where there is one religion, there is despotism; where there are two, civil war. Let there be thirty religions and they will all live together in peace. But it was also true that the theological content of much though not all of British religion was unusually hospitable to dynamic religion.

The peculiar religious evolution of the Anglosphere doesn't seem to have happened as the result of any grand plan. When Henry VIII overthrew the pope and had himself declared the head of the Church of England, no one envisioned the change that actually occurred; almost certainly all of the major actors in the English Reformation would have been bitterly disappointed in the outcome. Perhaps Cranmer had a sense of this when he penned the preface to the Book of Common Prayer; the success of the English Reformation lay in the failure of everyone who tried to lead it into a safe harbor.

What seems to have happened is that as the framework of traditional British life dissolved and changed under the ever-deepening impact of the social changes associated with the rise of capitalism, the "closed circle" of medieval Catholic Christianity broke into pieces. Neither the towering intellectual edifices of the medieval Scholastics so beautifully synthesized by St. Thomas Aquinas and rendered in poetry by Dante nor the diffuse traditions of popular piety and folk traditions mingling Christian and pagan beliefs and stories could satisfy the whole of society. Too much was changing too rapidly; people seemed to need a stronger, more effective religion that could guide them through the social and economic changes coursing through Tudor and Stuart England and Scotland.

Some thought that the old religion, properly revitalized, could still guide British life. Under the disciplined leadership of the Jesuits and of priests sent as missionaries, a Catholic remnant labored under atrocious threats and persecution to bring England to the Counter-Reformation—a modernized and systematized Catholicism. Had they succeeded, they would have reasserted the classic pattern of humanity's long climb from closed to open society. A series of slow changes would have forced adjustments and reforms in social arrangements; an outbreak of dynamic mystical and spiritual experiences would have pointed the path to a new and richer communal life. Having made the adjustment and opened society, the energies of dynamic religion would have subsided and a new equilibrium would have lasted until new changes were necessary.

There were moments when it looked as if a Counter-Reformation could succeed. Mary I met with very little resistance initially when she reestablished the old religion. Had Mary made a more popular match (remember, she married the unpopular king of Spain), or had a child who would have carried on a Catholic succession, she might have won England back for Rome. Mary, Queen of Scots, was also a Roman Catholic; she was the grandniece of Henry VIII, and it was her son, James VI of Scotland, who inherited the English crown from Queen Elizabeth. Had Mary had better political instincts, she might have kept her Scots throne (and her head) long enough to inherit Elizabeth's crown herself, or at least long enough to raise her son as a Catholic. A century later it was too late to dream realistically of reconverting the whole country. However, if the unhappy Queen of Scots' great-grandson James II had possessed any political cunning whatever, he could probably have reestablished a Catholic party around the throne that enjoyed limited toleration and that might in time have gradually won pragmatic converts among the religiously indifferent gentry of the eighteenth century.

Nevertheless, whether by bad luck, bad judgment, or the providence of God, the Counter-Reformation failed in England. But, as it turned out, so did its rivals.

The radical Protestants wanted a more thorough reform of the church. But in the end they too believed that the result of religious reform would be a new, permanent, and all-embracing status quo. In Bergsonian terms, they agreed with the Catholics that what England needed was an essentially static, unchanging, absolute religion periodically refreshed and adjusted by dynamic episodes. Like Islamic fundamentalists today, these reformers looked at the whole world through the lens of a holy book. Like Wahhabi mullahs critiquing the idolatry of popular Islam with its saints' cults and its shrines, the reformers attacked Catholic deviations from what they believed to be the true and pure religion. The medieval church was corrupt and its traditions were often based on forged and self-serving documents like the so-called Donation of Constantine. This document purported to be a decree from the Emperor Constantine that gave the Western Roman Empire to the popes. It was used for centuries to justify papal claims. Such traditions were no guide to the religion of Christ. "Call no man your father,"[4] Christ told His disciples—yet here was the Catholic Church persecuting as heretics anyone who refused to give the forbidden title to its priests! "Suffer little children, and forbid them not, to come unto me,"[5] said Jesus—but the medieval church burned anyone at the stake who tried to translate the scriptures into a language that ordinary people could understand.

Inherent in the claim that scripture could replace the medieval synthesis was the belief that somewhere in scripture was a systematic theology that could be proved by clear, unambiguous texts. That systematic theology had to include a guide to conduct. Scripture had to be able to tell how local churches should be organized and how local congregations should be linked in broader regional groupings. Who should appoint the pastors of a church? What body of doctrine should be required of all persons seeking to belong? What standard of conduct is appropriate, and what should be done about those persons, clerical or lay, who fail to live up to it?

But surely scripture could also be interpreted to answer other questions: What allegiance do subjects owe their king? What are the duties of a king to his people? Should the law of Moses be binding on English courts? What actions should Christians take when the ruler is unjust? What should be done when a ruler like Mary I or James II attempts to force subjects to obey the old religion?

Much of English and Scottish intellectual and even political history in the seventeenth century reflected the efforts of theologians, politicians, and ultimately soldiers to work out a scriptural approach to all of life's major issues. The hope—nay, the certainty—that lay behind their efforts was that a new, purified worldview could be found, based solidly in scripture, that would replace the all-encompassing medieval synthesis. Then, with the work of discovering the true religion finally finished, society could rest.

Each in their own way, the Puritans, Presbyterians, Diggers, Levelers, Anabaptists, Lutherans, and Calvinists were working to rebase English or Scottish life on the Bible; they disagreed among themselves over many things, but they generally agreed that they weren't looking for what we would now call an open or liberal approach to life. They attacked the old, Catholic certainties—but they believed that these could and would be replaced by biblical ones.

One of those who took this logic furthest was John Milton, the poet and Puritan who rose to high office in Cromwell's Commonwealth. Milton, one of the most intelligent and learned men of his time, and perhaps the most respected Puritan scholar in the land, was convinced that a thoughtful reader, using the best manuscripts and limiting himself to simple methods of explication and interpretation, could develop a systematic theology out of the Bible that would provide political and dogmatic certainty in the storms of the age.

With great goodwill he set to work, but the manuscript he produced—in

Latin, known as *De Doctrina Christiana* (*On Christian Doctrine*)—was, by most standards, appallingly heterodox.[6] Earnestly and carefully following what he believed to be the clear meaning of undoubtedly authoritative passages, Milton denied the *homoousion,* the classic definition of Christ's relationship to God the Father that had been the centerpiece of orthodox Christianity since the Nicene Creed. In an age when wars were quickly started by theological controversy and Milton's reputation stood as high as any scholar's in Europe, this heretical manuscript must have seemed explosive. It was placed under lock and key for safekeeping, and wasn't published until the reign of George IV, by which time the English-speaking world had less to fear from doctrinal controversies.

What doomed Milton's quest for biblically based certainty was what doomed that quest generally in seventeenth-century England: people simply did not agree about what the Bible meant. This wasn't because they hadn't studied it thoroughly, or used the best sources. Serious, prayerful, educated students of the Bible disagreed radically over basic things. Was the baptism of infants required, permitted, or forbidden? Could any Christian administer the bread and wine of the Lord's Supper, or was it required that such a person be ordained? If ordination was necessary, was this the job of a local congregation or of some individual or committee with regional responsibilities? Who was qualified to preach, and how was this decided? When honest, Bible-believing Christians disagreed about a point of doctrine, what procedure should they follow to reach a resolution?

John Dryden, a younger contemporary of Milton, sought but did not quite achieve the religious dexterity of the Vicar of Bray. A good Puritan under the Commonwealth in his youth, he wrote an ode on the death of Cromwell. ("His Grandeur he deriv'd from Heav'n alone, / For he was great e're Fortune made him so," he wrote of the man who had had Charles I put to death.)[7] When Charles II was called back to the throne, Dryden quickly became a royalist and an Anglican, writing *Religio Laici,* a defense of the Church of England against its Puritan and Roman Catholic opponents in 456 lines of iambic pentameter couplets. Charles named him poet laureate in 1670. Under James II, Dryden moved a bit too quickly. By the time of the Glorious Revolution he had already converted to Catholicism, and in 1687—just a year before James fell—he published the 2,585 lines, again in iambic pentameter, of *The Hind and the Panther,* a defense of Catholic theology against its Anglican and Puritan critics.

Problems of religious authority dominate the two works: How can religious controversies be settled? When two sects or scholars disagree, how can one know whom to believe? In the later, Catholic poem, Dryden's Hind (a female deer that he uses as a symbol for the Roman Catholic Church) points to the problem of using the sacred books of scripture as the only guide to religious truth:

> *The sacred books, you say, are full and plain,*
> *And ev'ry needfull point of truth contain.*

Yet, as the Hind notes, "your sev'ral churches disagree" and

> *. . . Luther, Zuinglius [Zwingli], Calvin,*[8] *holy chiefs*
> *Have made a battle royal of beliefs;*
> *Or like wild horses sev'ral ways have whirl'd*
> *The tortur'd Text about the Christian World.*[9]

The Hind cannot be gainsaid on this point, and to this day "Bible-believing Christians" remain divided on a number of doctrinal points. What happened historically was not that people stopped looking in the scriptures for an infallible, certain, and all-inclusive guide to human conduct. That quest continues today among many Evangelical and Pentecostal Christians around the world. But English-speaking people did stop expecting that the study of the scriptures would lead to a broad social consensus about what they meant. The Reformation slogan *sola scriptura,* "scripture alone," might provide a rule by which an individual or a sect could lead a holy life, but it would not provide a safe and universal system under which the whole community could live. By the end of the seventeenth century, England's many Protestant, biblicist sects recognized that no single one of them could reasonably expect to occupy the ground of the old Catholic Church. Each could still believe that it was in possession of the full and only gospel truth, each little chapel could glory in the knowledge that beneath its humble eaves were gathered the earthly representatives of the One True Church of God—but this was a primacy that the secular world would never acknowledge.

Milton was one of the first to grasp the implications, arguing to Parliament in 1644 against government censorship of books in a famous speech, "Areopagitica," named for the hill in Athens where the judges met and where St. Paul once taught. Noting that censorship was prevalent where Catholic prelates sought to impose orthodoxy through the power of the Inquisition, and reminding his audience that he, Milton, had met Galileo, "grown old a prisoner of the Inquisition" in Italy, he urged Parliament to allow free inquiry and free publishing. Truth is revealed in a process, he said, and our knowledge of God must necessarily change over time. Citing scripture, Milton compared Truth to a fountain: "If her waters flow not in a perpetual progression, they sicken into a muddy pool of conformity and tradition."[10] Disagreement and controversy are not signs of a decadent society; they are the necessary conditions of spiritual progress. "Where there is much desire to learn, there of necessity will be much arguing, much writing, many opinions."[11] Truth requires no aid from either church or state; she will make herself known. "She needs no policies, nor stratagems, nor licensings to make her victorious; those are the shifts and defenses that error uses against her power."[12]

Moreover, our knowledge grows over time. We will know more tomorrow than we do today. Truth grows when "God shakes a kingdom with strong and healthful commotions . . . For such is the order of God's enlightening his Church, to dispense and deal out by degrees his beam, so as our earthly eyes may best sustain it."[13] Change in religion was not a necessary evil, but a necessary good.

Milton himself seems to have thought a new final synthesis would emerge in time and that the chaos of progressive discovery and revelation would come to an end. But already it seemed clear that as a practical matter, in the here and now, the only way to be faithful to God was to be open to religious change and new thinking: dynamic religion, not static, was needed as the basis for life. The search for truth through scripture led to the open seas, not to the safe harbors and estuaries the original reformers sought. Change was beginning to be seen as a permanent, necessary, and even sanctified element of true religion.

Twelve • Doxy v. Doxy

E ven before it visibly broke down into the sectarian confusion of late seventeenth-century England, the *sola scriptura* approach was not universally popular among English Protestants. A very influential section of the reforming community, heavily represented in the royal court but also among the clergy and conservative laypeople, set out to steer a middle course between what they perceived as the unacceptable extremes of scriptural literalism and Roman Catholicism. Tradition, they felt, could provide an unerring guide to at least the worst perplexities of the religious controversies.

A reliance on tradition was very congenial to the English mind. Despite the dynamism of their economy over the centuries and the degree to which the English have reshaped their ancient institutions, there is clearly a deep conservatism at work in a country whose common law rests on centuries-old precedents.

Appalled by the sectarian chaos that resulted from the Bible-thumping literalists who claimed that everything in life should be made to conform to the simple, inerrant principles of the Bible, traditionalists argued that one must look to the consensus of great thinkers and saints of the past who had reflected on these issues. How did St. Augustine interpret the Bible? What did the Council of Chalcedon teach?

When it came to the question of how to organize civil society and daily life, the Puritan enthusiasts were mocked and deplored by the students of tradition. Playwrights like Ben Jonson satirized Puritans through fictional characters like Tribulation Wholesome, Zeal-of-the-land Busy, and other busybodies with their harebrained theories.

"Dost thou think, because thou art virtuous, there shall be no more cakes and ale?"[1] Sir Toby Belch asks the puritanical steward Malvolio in *Twelfth*

Night. Puritans banned Christmas as a papist holiday with no warrant in scripture; Puritan Massachusetts levied fines on those caught celebrating these pagan rites. The traditionalist had nothing but a healthy contempt for this foolishness. Christ had to have been born sometime, no? And if scripture doesn't give us a date, why can't we celebrate when we like? And what is wrong with an annual celebration hallowed through centuries that, whatever else it may do, draws men's minds to the central mystery of the Christian faith?

More broadly, a general revelation from God to humanity cannot properly be left to the judgment of a fallible individual. God reveals himself to a wide community, and as we seek to understand what He means, we should listen to the voice of the whole community. We should interpret the scriptures in the light of historically received opinion—what has been believed in every place, at every time, by everyone.

This is all very well and all very true, but tradition proved as weak a stool as scripture. Using scripture alone led to endless theological controversy and an unpleasant, Zeal-of-the-land Busy commonwealth. On the other hand, when one tried to use tradition as a systematic guide to truth, one very serious problem emerged under two guises.

The trouble was Rome. Tradition was the glory of the Church of Rome, the bulwark of her apologists and the citadel of her claims. Although generations of English divines labored to carve out a specific Anglican tradition that could somehow show that despite centuries of more or less peaceful acceptance of papal supremacy, the truest voices of tradition not only in Britain but throughout the Western tradition opposed the pretensions of Peter's See, the case was discouragingly difficult to make.

The man who tried hardest to develop a tradition for the Church of England that both grounded it in the teaching of the apostles and liberated it from the Church of Rome was John Henry Newman, the charismatic preacher who became the public leader of the nineteenth-century Oxford Movement. That movement, whose traces can be seen throughout the Anglican Communion and the Episcopal Church to this day, sought to integrate the practice and doctrines of the Church of England with the great ceremonies, rituals, and beliefs that Newman and his like-minded colleagues found in the rich treasure-house of medieval English practice. Reverence for the saints and sacraments, respect for the priesthood, due regard for precedent and beauty in worship—all these things greatly enriched English worship, and the rediscovery of the medieval mystics would enrich English piety.

Unfortunately for English traditionalists, after twelve years as the leading voice of the Oxford Movement, Newman was received into the Roman Catholic Church and ultimately wrote an extraordinary autobiography in which he described the spiritual and intellectual logic that led to his conversion.

If one takes tradition as the ultimate judge of scripture, then one ends by accepting what might otherwise seem to be absurd ideas because tradition commands it. To Englishmen of Newman's day, the claims of Pius IX—one of the least appealing of prelates to the modern mind—to infallibility were manifestly absurd. "Before my election to the Holy See," Pius is said to have remarked to an English cardinal, "I believed the doctrine of Infallibility. Since then, I've *felt* it."[2]

Most English Protestants found these claims as superstitious and improbable as the accounts of miracles that the Catholic Church claimed marked the lives, and the relics, of the saints. Newman swallowed the camel of miracles along with the gnat of infallibility.

In *Eminent Victorians,* the sly and subversive Lytton Strachey described Newman's faith in miracles. Writing to a friend after a visit to the Chiesa Nuova in Ravello, where a vial said to contain the dried blood of St. Pantaleon was kept on the altar, Newman explained that the blood liquefied each year on the saint's feast day. This was only one of the many credible examples of this kind of miracle in the churches of Italy, he gushed. There was, of course, the well-known blood of St. Januarius, which he said liquefies in Naples each year on the saint's feast day. (The event is still celebrated annually.) There is the blood of St. Patrizia, which Newman said he saw in the process of liquefaction; the blood of the Jesuit Da Ponte, the blood of St. John the Baptist. The blood of St. Pantaleon was special, however, because, Newman said, it liquefied not just on feast days but at any time in the presence of a fragment of the True Cross. (The mother of the Emperor Constantine is said to have found, as the result of a dream, the actual cross on which Christ was crucified; for many centuries fragments purporting to come from this source were sold in suspiciously large quantities across Europe.)[3]

The liquefaction of the saint's blood in the presence of the True Cross became so distracting that the priests of Ravello, Newman relates, were forced to forbid people from bringing portions of the cross into the church. "A person I know," Newman wrote, "not knowing the prohibition, brought in a portion [of the True Cross]—and the priest suddenly said, who showed the blood, 'Who has got the Holy Cross about him?'"[4]

Newman carried more than a handful of England's best and brightest with him to Rome, but for most English minds, mooning over the liquefaction of the blood of St. Pantaleon was as foolish and besotted as the worst kind of sectarian ranting about the end of the world or the evils of beer. Tradition and superstition seemed joined at the hip; Zeal-of-the-Land Busy and Tribulation Wholesome were no worse than this.

In politics the path of tradition led to an even clearer and more dramatic dead end. The break with Rome had come over the question of royal supremacy: whether the king or the pope should be the final arbiter of doctrine in the Church of England. As the Church of England came under attack from Puritans, throne and altar turned to each other for mutual support. When Puritans lobbied James I to rid the church of the "unscriptural" hierarchy of bishops, he replied: "No bishops, no kings."[5] Crown and church would stand or fall together.

Unfortunately for the Church of England, that meant its fate was tied to the House of Stuart—perhaps the least politically gifted dynasty ever to occupy the English throne. Mary, Queen of Scots, claimed the thrones of three kingdoms—France, Scotland, and England—but she could never keep a secure hold on even one. James I was a conceited, rigid, and profoundly unattractive person whose most human character trait, a predilection for handsome young courtiers, did little to endear him to religious conservatives. James's son Charles I had such poor political judgment that he was beheaded like his grandmother, executed for treason against the realm of which he was the head.

Committed to establishing a continental-style absolute monarchy, the Stuart kings were constantly seeking ways to fund a large and powerful state without depending on Parliament. This involved them in the political conflict that led to the execution of Charles I; it led Charles II into taking bribes from France. Neither course made the Stuarts popular at home, or gave much political comfort to those Englishmen who sought to build a new synthesis based on the power of a reformed but still vital Christian tradition.

In the end, the Church of England was forced to the ultimate absurdity. Charles I had married Henrietta Maria, a French princess, who was permitted to retain her Catholic faith and chaplains. Both her sons ultimately converted to Catholicism. The politically astute Charles II waited until he was on his deathbed to take this step; his brother the Duke of York, for whom New York City is named, converted while still the heir to the throne.

At a time when across the Channel the French court was enacting some of the bloodiest persecutions of French Protestants in the sad history of the religious wars, the prospect of a Catholic king in England horrified most Protestants. The memory of "Bloody Mary," who tried to bring the old religion back into England by burning Protestants at the stake, still reverberated.

Anglican traditionalists found themselves forced into the position of supporting the divine right of a fanatically misguided Catholic to head the Church of England. They fought and defeated Whig efforts to bar the Duke of York (as James II was known before he became king) from the succession, and they rallied against rebellions led by Charles's illegitimate but Protestant son the Duke of Monmouth; unfortunately for all concerned, once enthroned James II proved to be a bigot and a fool. His one unwavering goal was to reintroduce Catholicism to England, and to this end he tried to force Catholics into the foundations of the Anglican church—the pulpits and the universities.

Intellectually committed as they were to the doctrine that it was a grievous sin to disobey God's anointed king, Anglican traditionalists faced the choice of sacrificing either their principles or their religion. They could resist the king, the head of their church, the authority in whose name the Anglican church had made the break with Rome—or they could stand by and watch as James II systematically replaced Anglicans with Catholics in all the cathedrals, colleges, and pulpits of the realm.

The Glorious Revolution marked the moment from which tradition alone could no longer make a plausible claim to stand as the basis for English life. After 1689, a few Non-jurors (Anglican divines who, by refusing to take the oath of allegiance to William III, continued to proclaim their allegiance to the House of Stuart) survived, and a broader group of sentimental Tories and high churchmen would nourish a quiet nostalgia for the old house, but none of this amounted to serious politics. In the nineteenth and early twentieth centuries, a procession of converts would follow Newman and Gladstone's friend Cardinal Manning back to Rome. This was, however, a movement, not a party: the actions of James II destroyed loyalty to the old religion and old theories of government as a serious force in two of the three kingdoms he ruled. (In Catholic Ireland, history moved very differently.)

By the final third of the seventeenth century, more and more English people lived in a mental universe in which both scripture and tradition had failed. Reliance on scripture led into endless sectarian debate, Puritanism, and that superfluity of zeal which has never greatly or for long appealed to the English public mind. Reliance on tradition led to tyranny in politics and popery in religion.

WITH BOTH SCRIPTURE and tradition in disrepute, an increasing number of Englishmen turned to a third alternative: reason. If scripture could give no conclusive answers, and tradition gave an answer that was conclusive but intolerable, human beings had no alternative but to use their best judgment to choose among divergent values and ideas.

Perhaps the most accomplished votary of reason in eighteenth-century Britain was Edward Gibbon, the historian who wrote the masterly *Decline and Fall of the Roman Empire.* Gibbon was raised by religious Protestants. His studies at university led him first to the horrid suspicion, and then to the certainty, that the Roman Catholics were right. On June 8, 1753, he was received into the Catholic Church.

This came as a terrible shock to his father. With Stuart pretenders (who invaded Britain in 1715 and 1745) still hanging around French and papal courts intriguing with coteries of British supporters, Penal Laws in the eighteenth century placed Catholics under many disabilities. Worse, perhaps, public opinion strongly condemned the old religion and its adherents. Though the Gibbon family fortunes had been substantially impaired when the historian's grandfather had been caught up in the collapse of the South Sea Bubble, the father sent Gibbon to live under strict watch in the house of a Protestant pastor in Lausanne. After a struggle, the young man returned outwardly to the profession of the Anglican religion; inwardly, he came to believe that neither the Catholic, the Protestant, nor indeed the Christian case could be proved to the satisfaction of a reasonable man.

Armed with this disillusionment, Gibbon went on to produce *The Decline and Fall,* one of the great texts of the European Enlightenment and one of the greatest monuments of English prose. It is also one of the most devastating attacks on Christian (and Jewish) piety ever written. In a dexterous, feline prose the great historian turns the cruel light of reason on traditional interpretations of religious history.

"How," Gibbon asks in mock astonishment, "shall we excuse the supine inattention of the Pagan and philosophic world to those evidences which were presented by the hand of Omnipotence, not to their reason, but to their senses?"

Great miracles, the gospels confidently tell us, accompanied Christ and his apostles in their pilgrimage through the world of the first century A.D.

> The lame walked, the blind saw, the sick were healed, the dead were raised, demons were expelled, and the laws of Nature were frequently suspended for the benefit of the church. But the sages of Greece and Rome turned aside from the awful spectacle, and, pursuing the ordinary occupations of life and study, appeared unconscious of any alterations in the moral or physical government of the world.[6]

In particular, Gibbon notes, the gospels report that at the time of the cru-
cifixion of Christ the "whole earth was covered in darkness."[7] Noting that
this eclipse was said to have lasted an extraordinary three hours, even if confined to the "whole earth" in the immediate vicinity of Jerusalem, this great
event, Gibbon marvels, "ought to have excited the wonder, the curiosity, and
the devotion of mankind."[8] Somehow, though, "it passed without notice in
an age of science and history."[9] It was not, Gibbon affects to wonder in a
puzzled way, that nobody was taking notes at the time. Two of the greatest
men of letters in the history of the world, Gibbon reminds us, Seneca and
Pliny the Elder, lived during the time of these stirring events; each of these
men eagerly collected evidence of "all the great phenomena of Nature,
earthquakes, meteors, comets, and eclipses, which his indefatigable curiosity could collect."[10] Yet, somehow, "[b]oth the one and the other have omitted to mention the greatest phenomenon to which the mortal eye has been
witness since the creation of the globe."[11]

The cool light of Gibbon's skepticism allied to his extensive learning
allowed him to review the tangled controversies between Roman Catholics,
Anglicans, and Presbyterians about the government of the ancient church.
He is able to demonstrate that by eighteenth-century standards the fathers of
the church were neither honest nor wise. He shows them to have been ridden
by absurd superstition, bigoted to the point of fanatical madness, given to
outrageous claims, and intoxicated by violent enmities and jealousies.

Gibbon made a powerful case that Christianity itself was a historical
detour—a regrettable superstition. That verdict was shared by the great figures of the French Enlightenment and has dominated much Western thinking about Christianity in the centuries since. Britain, however, did not for
many decades trust itself wholly to reason any more than to tradition or
scripture. The eighteenth century in Britain was an era of widespread quiet
deism and atheism among the governing classes, but private indifference
seldom ripened into public opposition to the church and its doctrines.
British skeptics were mostly content to keep their more controversial views
to themselves. If religion were to disappear as a powerful social force in a
Britain racked by the pangs of the Industrial Revolution, the upper classes
and much else could be swept away in a great social conflagration. No bishops, no king—and no chapels, no banks.

There were other problems with using reason as the ideological force that
holds society together. While the rules of logic promise certainty and consensus, people with every claim to be considered rational and thoughtful
often disagree—quite as much as biblical literalists dispute the meaning of
their sacred texts. In some cases, evidence or knowledge is insufficient to

give us certainty. In others, it is clear that human beings cannot separate reason from interest and passion; our minds are not soulless calculators automatically providing objective analysis like Mr. Spock on *Star Trek*. More
often than not, our minds simply dress the conclusions we would like to
reach in the colors of reason. "Opinions are like watches," wrote Alexander
Pope. "None / goes just alike, but each man trusts his own."[12]

In practice, English society decided that reason cannot stand alone as the
basis for a human society. It is not always possible to distinguish, even in
one's own mind, the degree to which bias, interest, and prejudice have
twisted reason to their own purpose. It is seldom that a nation or a class is
convinced against its own interests or passions by the power of reason.

These doubts were powerfully reinforced by events in France in the 1790s.
To much applause from enlightened circles in Britain, the French rose
against their monarchy and set about a process of building a new social order
on the basis of logic. British skeptics like Edmund Burke predicted the
experiment would end badly and at first were scoffed at—but they did not
have to wait long for vindication as the French Revolution quickly degenerated into the Reign of Terror, military despotism, and a generation of war.

Very much more rational, and very much less like a ball, as Jane Austen
would say, the French Revolution confirmed Anglo-American society in its
rejection of the rational certainties of the continental Enlightenment.

Thirteen • The White Queen

A new attitude toward religious matters began to appear after the fall of the Commonwealth. John Dryden captured it in *Absalom and Achitophel,* a satirical account of the Duke of Monmouth's abortive rebellion against his natural father, Charles II, ostensibly to protect the realm from his Catholic uncle James. This poem, which purports to be an account of the biblical story of Absalom's rebellion against his father, King David, was brilliantly successful because it brought a light touch to religious matters and suggested that a bit of skepticism might not be amiss in discussing sacred (and political) subjects. The veil was gauzy and transparent: David in the poem was Charles II. Jerusalem was London; the Jews were the English; the rabbis the Anglican clergy; the Jebusites, the original inhabitants of Jerusalem dispossessed by the Jews, were the Roman Catholics. Saul, the biblical king who preceded David, was Oliver Cromwell; Ishbosheth, Saul's son, was the weak Richard who gave up the Protectorate under pressure ("without a blow / Made foolish Ishbosheth the crown forgo"), and so on. The tone of levity and freedom with which Dryden describes both powerful politicians and religious ideas is still striking today. The poem opens with lines about David that address Charles II's well-known promiscuity and the presence of royal bastards around the court:

> *In pious times, e'r Priest-craft did begin,*
> *Before* Polygamy *was made a sin;*
> *When man, on many, multiply'd his kind,*
> *E'r one to one was, cursedly, confind:*
> *When Nature prompted, and no law deny'd*
> *Promiscuous use of Concubine and Bride;*

Then Israel's Monarch, after Heaven's own heart,
His vigorous warmth did, variously, impart
To Wives and Slaves: And, wide as his Command
Scatter'd his Maker's Image through the Land.[1]

Dryden here is mocking the Cromwellian Puritans—and perhaps hoping to bury any lingering memories of his own unfortunate ode on the death of Cromwell. "Priest-craft" was one of the terms of abuse Puritans used for the ways in which both Catholic and Anglican clergy complicated and perverted the simple religion of the Bible. The Bible itself was Puritan territory; to tell an anti-Puritan political fable using the scriptural examples and allegories that filled Puritan sermons and the speeches of men like Cromwell added what, to the Court, would have been delicious irony to the mix.

Yet the poem cuts deeper than mocking the Puritans and gently twitting, while supporting, the king. Dryden reminds his readers that at one time the God of the Bible tolerated polygamy. The great patriarchs and the kings of the Bible more often than not had more than one wife; the laws of Moses do not forbid it and the prophets generally did not preach against it. Nevertheless, today all the churches set their faces against it. On the one hand this is a point for the upholders of tradition against the supporters of the Bible as the sole authority for doctrine; on the other, it points to the inherent uncertainty in all revealed religion. If God can change His mind, or at least change His law, on something as fundamental to human life as polygamy, what else might change?

Jonathan Swift, the greatest satirist in the English language, was also inspired by the vicissitudes of the English Reformation. In *Gulliver's Travels,* today his best-known long work, he mocks both the religious fanaticism of the preceding century (the wars between the Little-Endians and the Big-Endians of Lilliput and its neighbors over which end one should use when opening eggs were an obvious parallel to the struggles between Catholics and Protestants over the meaning of the Eucharist) and the cockamamie eccentricities of those trying to reinvent human life from the ground up on the basis of Reason (the scientists of Laputa). But it is in his masterpiece, *A Tale of a Tub,* that he most fully expounds the logic—or illogic—of what became the ruling paradigm of Anglo-American civilization.

A Tale of a Tub is the story of three brothers, Peter, Martin, and Jack. According to Swift's fable, the three brothers were each left a seamless coat in their father's testament, along with a promise that the coats would never wear out so long as the brothers followed the instructions laid out in the will. These instructions were quite detailed, and they prohibited adding any ornaments to the original fabric.

All was well for some time, but then a fashion swept the town for silver embroidery on men's coats. Those without this vital accoutrement had no luck getting invitations or wooing women. The three brothers were perplexed; their father's will seemed to forbid this completely.

Fortunately the resourceful Peter (Catholics believe the pope to be the successor of St. Peter as the bishop of Rome) was able to find a tortured interpretation of the will that allowed the adornment, and in succeeding years he found ever-new if increasingly far-fetched interpretations that allowed the brothers to ornament their coats in keeping with fashion after fashion.

After some years of this, Jack and Martin noticed a change in Peter's behavior. As the eldest brother, Peter demanded more and more respect: Mr. Peter, then Lord Peter. His claims grew more and more fantastic; he expected them to kiss his foot when they entered his presence. His claims grew more and more impossible to deal with, and ultimately the two younger brothers fled—taking with them copies of the testament, which Peter had kept locked up.

On looking into their testaments, they discovered that their coats no longer bore any relationship to the unadorned state commanded by their father. Jack (so named for John Calvin and the extreme, scriptural wing of the Reformation) ripped everything off his coat. It became tattered and torn. Martin (standing for Martin Luther and the moderate reformers in the Church of England), who realized more soberly that the coat was so covered over and affected by its weight of ornament that to attempt to purge everything risked destroying the coat itself, contented himself with snipping carefully, trying to get the coat as close to its original state as possible.

Swift's allegory was like Dryden's, a complicated mix of irreverence and orthodoxy. While none of the three brothers emerge from the story with dignity—and the digressions and subplots with which Swift embellishes the story further undermine the dignity of church and state—the overall account of ecclesiastical history and the Reformation is exactly the story that the Church of England tells. If at times Martin seemed as pliable and worldly minded as the Vicar of Bray, well, that was simply the way the history of the Church of England read.

What Swift exposed is the unique mix of cynicism and faith at the heart of the Anglo-American view of the world. British society respected both tradition and scripture, and believed they were both indispensable for the good life and the good society. The word of God and the customs of the country provided valuable, indeed indispensable, order in morals and politics. But at the same time, it denied that either one of them—or any combination of both—could bring you to reliably correct answers about life's questions. It was simply no longer possible to know what the early church had been like, or what Jesus intended for it. The church had so neglected the spiritual gifts in its possession that much of God's revelation was irrevocably lost. The coat had been so altered that it could no longer be restored to its original condition. Moreover, the actions of theologians and clergy were as shortsighted as those of everyone else; human willfulness, vanity, and greed were triumphant, and the church itself could not be protected from them.

It was an Anglican bishop who summarized the state of play after Swift. In eighteenth-century English slang "doxy" meant something like "sex kitten" did at the turn of the twenty-first. In words borrowed from ancient Greek, "doxy" means teaching—so "orthodoxy" meant correct teaching and "heterodoxy" meant "other" or nonorthodox teaching, which is to say heresy.

Bishop Berkeley, an Anglican cleric who was famous as both a philosopher and a mathematician, and for whom the city of Berkeley, California, is named, gave the eighteenth-century gloss on the matter: "Orthodoxy, sir," he said, "is *my* doxy. Heterodoxy is the doxy of another."[2]

What the British ultimately did was to rely on what Burke called "convention."[3] Scripture, tradition, and reason—each had its place and each had its devotees. But all of them went wrong if you pressed them too far. You should respect the scriptures and defer to them but not interpret the scriptures in a way that led you into some weird millenarian sect or into absurd social behavior. You honored tradition but did not press it so far that it led you into the arms of royal absolutism or papal power. You can and should employ the critique of reason against the excesses of both scripture and tradition, but not press reason to the point where you ranted against all existing institutions, ate roots and bark for your health, or, worse, undermined the rights of property and the established church. One can picture John Bull scratching his head and slowly concluding that one must accept that in society there will be Bible nuts, tradition nuts, and reason nuts—fundamentalists, papists, and radicals. This is not necessarily the end of the world. To some degree they cancel one another out—the fundamentalist zealots will keep the papists down and vice versa, and the religious will keep the radicals in their place— but the competition among sects will also prevent the established church from pressing its advantages too far and from forming too exalted an idea about the proper stature, prestige, and emoluments of the clergy.

The result of all these offsetting forces, John Bull came to believe, was what he wanted all along: common sense and compromise. He wanted reasonableness, which is emphatically not the same thing as reason. Perhaps it would be a bit higgledy-piggledy from a theoretical point of view, but John Bull was very tired of the theoretical point of view by then. More than once he had let himself be persuaded by clever chaps with their books and their systems, and he regretted what it led to.

This was not merely an abstract idea; it was the approach that, after the Glorious Revolution, shaped Britain's core political institutions. As more and more Englishmen came to a consensus that James II was simply intolerable and that he would have to go, the question of his successor had to be faced. James II had a legal heir, baptized as a Roman Catholic and recognized by the Jacobites as the Prince of Wales. This prince, destined to be raised by staunch Catholics and surrounded by Jesuits from birth, was clearly as unsuitable as his father, although if there was a divine right to kingship, this child (despite certain doubts as to his legitimacy put forward by impassioned Protestant opponents of the Stuarts) was the rightful heir to the throne.

If that was unacceptable, what should England do? Puritans and Cromwellians nostalgically pined for the Commonwealth, but the results of that experiment had not been so happy that the country was eager to give it another try. Moreover, the backing of the Anglican clergy and their supporters was necessary if James was to be forced from the throne without prolonged civil war, and Anglican sentiment remained strongly royalist—if not pro-James.

The result was a solution whose only merit was pragmatic and commonsensical. It had no theoretical base. Before his conversion to the Church of Rome, James II had had a first, Protestant wife. Two daughters survived from that union. The eldest, Mary, was married to William of Orange, hereditary leader of the Dutch in their long struggle with France. After trying and failing to persuade Mary to accept the crown on her own, Parliament offered the crown jointly to William and Mary. In the not unlikely event that William should fail to produce an heir, Mary's younger (and Protestant) sister Anne would follow her sister and brother-in-law to the throne. Should Anne die without an heir, the throne would go to the next nearest Protestant relation: Sophia of Hanover, granddaughter of James I. No Catholic could inherit the throne and no future heir to the throne could marry a Roman Catholic without giving up his or her rights to the crown.

Politically, however much it wrong-footed John Dryden and however much fancy footwork was required of the clergy, it was a brilliant compromise that helped keep the peace in England for generations to come. The radical Protestants and Cromwellians accepted the monarchy and accepted some civil disabilities but assured themselves of a Protestant head of state. The Anglicans gave up the divine right of the monarchy and the legitimate heir to the throne, but saved their religion from the Catholics, preserved at least the form of monarchy for hundreds of years, and gave themselves social and economic advantages in the continuing contest with the Protestant dissenters.

Intellectually, the compromise was absurd. It threw out the baby, but hoarded the bathwater. It preserved the form of monarchy but overturned the historic grounds of its legitimacy. The British monarchy survived not because it was part of God's plan for good governance, or because the monarch had a rightful claim to the throne; it survived because the leaders of the realm felt that, on the whole, the monarchy was useful and convenient. The population was accustomed to revere the king and see the throne as a source of legitimacy and a focus of loyalty. Why trouble this sentiment and increase the chance for instability and upheaval? It was inconsistent from the standpoint of political science—but which was worse, a little inconsistency or a civil war?

Those who felt like it could argue about what it all meant. Dr. Richard Price* and the Constitutional Society could tell the world that the theory behind the revolution of 1688 was popular sovereignty; Edmund Burke could say it was monarchical legitimacy and constitutional continuity. Everyone was free to interpret it in their own way—as long as nobody tried to overturn it.

In subsequent generations, British opinion did not try to conceal the irrationalities and contradictions in British society, religion, and government. Their form of government, the Victorians endlessly proclaimed, was the best in the world because it incorporated rational and irrational elements in a happy—if logically indefensible—balance. Follow reason too far and you end up with revolutions in church and state, defaults on the national debt, and Robespierre—Carlyle's sea-green incorruptible—setting up guillotines. The British constitution, said the Victorians, can't be boiled down to legalis-

---

* Dr. Richard Price was a mild-mannered preacher. Edmund Burke strongly attacked his constitutional theories in Burke's *Reflections on the Revolution in France.*

tic formulae, and many of its elements are contradictory. It was seen as organic, growing with the needs of the British people, continually changing, continually in flux, continually seen only in its parts, never as a whole.

The British cherished those bits of the political system that testified most eloquently to the absurdity of the system. Walter Bagehot expatiated on the wonders of an increasingly ornamental and vestigial monarchy. Gilbert and Sullivan, much of whose work, like Lewis Carroll's (and, for that matter, like that of Monty Python), can be seen as a joyous celebration of the illogicalities and inconsistencies of British life, memorably celebrated the House of Lords in *Iolanthe*:

> *When Britain really ruled the waves*
> *(In good Queen Bess's time)*
> *The House of Peers made no pretence*
> *To intellectual eminence*
> *Or scholarship sublime.*
> *Yet Britain won her proudest bays*
> *In good Queen Bess's glorious days!*
>
> *When Wellington thrashed Bonaparte*
> *As every child can tell*
> *The House of Peers throughout the war*
> *Did nothing in particular*
> *And did it very well.*
> *Yet Britain set the world ablaze*
> *In good King George's glorious days.*
>
> *And while the House of Peers withholds*
> *Its legislative hand*
> *And noble statesmen do not itch*
> *To interfere in matters which*
> *They do not understand*
> *As bright will shine Great Britain's rays*
> *As in King George's glorious days.*[4]

The hereditary peers developed an irresistible itch to interfere with Lloyd George's budget in 1910 and as a result their wings were severely clipped, but the sentiments of *Iolanthe* have not yet fully disappeared. The British hold on tenaciously to the surviving inconsistencies and fictions in their form of government. The Crown can do nothing, but everything is done in its name. Tiny jurisdictions like the Isle of Man and the various Channel islands continue to flourish without the officious interventions of the modernizing, rationalizing impulse. Judges wear wigs that were fashionable in the days of Charles II, and British law still delights in its thickets of precedent. Medieval and early modern costumes and customs hang on wherever possible; the Beefeaters and the Yeomen of the Guard do nothing in particular, but do it very well. Britain, the great modernizing engine that drove all Europe and the world into the maelstrom of the Industrial Revolution, remains in some ways the most traditional of the European states.

PERHAPS THE ULTIMATE EXPRESSION of the radical worldview underlying the British establishment of the day was the provision in the Act of Union uniting England and Scotland for the establishment under the crown of an official Church of Scotland[5]—predecessors of those known as Presbyterians in England then, and in the United States now. In other words, the same person would be the head of two different religions. One of the many irritants in the perpetually difficult relationship between the high-church William Gladstone and the low-church Queen Victoria was her desire to have the prime minister accompany her to worship in the Church of Scotland while they were both in Balmoral.

For twentieth-century philosophers like Michel Foucault, it came as a great and earth-shattering discovery to find that social beliefs and institutions rested on very imperfect epistemological foundations and that relations of power played a major role in defining such basic concepts as justice or gender relations. Foucault was, in this sense, more of a Victorian than he knew. When Queen Victoria took communion in St. George's parish church in Esher and worshipped after Presbyterian forms in Balmoral, she was a living demonstration that social needs and relationships shape our ideas of religion and right conduct. Foucault felt the earth tremble beneath his feet when he reflected on the social construction of reality and the degree to which power shapes perception; Victoria was made of sterner stuff. She got in her carriage and went to church.

Lewis Carroll understood her completely. "One *can't* believe impossible things," Alice said to the White Queen.

"I daresay you haven't had much practice," the Queen replied. "When I was your age, I always did it for half an hour a day. Why, sometimes I've believed as many as six impossible things before breakfast."[6]

Dynamic Religion, Dynamic Society

Juggling scripture, tradition, and reason, the English-speaking world blun-
dered its way into an increasingly open society in which religion was constantly adjusting to the demands of social and economic change. The
religion of an open dynamic society is not necessarily Christian and it is certainly not always orthodox—except perhaps in Bishop Berkeley's "my
doxy, thy doxy" sense. But Anglo-American society was not secular. Far
from being an obstacle to the modernization of British and American society, religion became a major actor in an intensifying and accelerating process
of social change and capitalist development, accepting constant transformation as the normal and desirable human state. And as Anglo-American religion became more dynamic and less static, it also tended to become more
intense and more strongly felt.

. Adam Smith gave what is still the best description of the role of religion
in an open society. Smith, whose personal religious views seem to have
been much closer to those of Edward Gibbon than John Milton, argued in
The Wealth of Nations that religion, even fanatical religion, is necessary to
the health and happiness of society, and that free competition among religions is the best way to achieve the benefits of religion at the lowest possible
cost.

In Smith's view, there are two systems of morality and, therefore, of religion in any society. The common people, who live on an economic knife
edge, cannot afford to indulge themselves. "A single week's dissipation is
often sufficient to undo a poor workman forever," he writes, and "[t]he wiser
and better sort of the common people, therefore, have always the utmost
abhorrence and detestation of such excesses, which their experience tells
them are so immediately fatal to people of their condition."[7] They are, of
course, determined also to see that their children are brought up to fear and
abhor dissipation of all kinds. Most new sects and religions, according to
Smith, have their roots among the poor, and new sects are usually marked
by their great moral rigor.

The common people need the support of a strong religious community,
especially when they join the great capitalist migration from the countryside
to the city. In the country, the poor workman has a reputation to uphold: he
is known by all and the community judges him according to his acts. This

pressure helps keep people fulfilling the responsibilities of the place in life they were allotted in the traditional world of the village.

In the new condition of the city, however, the workman has less certainty about his role, and he needs more than ever to maintain personal discipline and to resist the temptations that from Smith's time to the present day can be found in cities. The small religious congregation—the sect—replaces the social discipline of the home community. While the manners and morals of such sects can often be, for Smith's taste, "disagreeably rigorous and unsociable," one must nevertheless concede that it is precisely their rigor and regularity that make them effective. "In little religious sects, accordingly, the morals of the common people have been almost always remarkably regular and orderly."[8]

Religion no longer opposes the modernization process. It provided the psychological strength and social support that eventually allowed tens of millions of bewildered, hopeful, frightened peasants to find a place in the teeming cities and crowded industries of the new capitalist world.

At the same time, the rise of capitalism, while destructive of religious ideas firmly based on village realities, does not subvert religion in general but can lead to a new era of religious revival—and sometimes to fanaticism. Indeed, it follows from Smith's argument that an acceleration of capitalist growth could lead to a dangerous increase in the power of religious fanaticism—that the open society could boomerang and generate a reaction strong enough to impose a new religious dictatorship. Religion could shift back to opposing society's westward march.

Smith, well aware of this danger, suggests steps governments can take to keep fanatical religion within bounds. A generally high level of education, he believes, should reduce the ability of a superstitious and fanatical clergy to impose narrow ideas on the rising generation. Government should also promote public amusements as an antidote to the gloomy fantasies of religious enthusiasts. Government should encourage the public performance of plays that mock the wiles and shortcomings of the clergy.[9]

In an aside which is full of meaning for American history, Smith also notes that the danger of religious dictatorship is much less where a multitude of religious groups already exist. The real danger of theocracy exists when a large and established church, supported by the government, can impose conformity on dissenters. When society is divided into many religious groups, with no group able to call on government power to enforce its pretensions against its rivals, society will not, Smith believes, dissolve into dueling fanaticisms. What would happen instead is that the small sects would move toward something like a religious consensus on increasingly moderate principles.

> The teachers of each little sect, finding themselves almost alone, would be obliged to respect those of almost every other sect, and the concessions which they would mutually find it both convenient and agreeable to make to one another, might in time probably reduce the doctrine of the greater part of them to that pure and rational religion, free from every mixture of absurdity, imposture, or fanaticism, such as wise men have in all ages of the world wished to see established.[10]

Relying most probably on information he obtained from Benjamin Franklin, Smith wrote that this approach "has been established in Pennsylvania, where, though the Quakers happen to be the most numerous, the law in reality favours no one sect more than another, and it is there said to have been productive of this philosophical good temper and moderation."[11] American religious history has been more colorful than Smith's analysis would suggest, but Smith's confidence that religious pluralism would guard against religious tyranny has been justified.

What Smith saw was a virtuous circle in which religion helped human beings cope with the new demands of life in an open, changing society—and in which the operation of the open society made religion continually more fit for this purpose, and less fit to lead a reaction in favor of closed-society principles. Despite the deep tensions inherent in the coexistence of closed religious systems in a dynamic society, the two realities could exist side by side and even strengthen each other.

If the history of the Anglosphere is any guide, it appears that the most vigorously open society, the society that presses hardest and fastest toward the West, is a religious society. It can even be a society strongly influenced by what Smith would call fanatical enthusiasm and what has been labeled fundamentalism in the twenty-first century.

In fact, to the degree that a secular society—one in which religion has been effectively marginalized—is shaped by reliance on reason rather than on the complex dance of conflicting elements that characterized the Anglophone powers at their various apogees, it can be less open and dynamic than one which acknowledges more fully the irrational elements of the human psyche. The "scientific" societies of the Communist world, boasting of their objective grounding in rational and scientific truth as discovered by Lenin and Marx, were considerably less flexible than the Western societies they opposed. There was less freedom in France under Robespierre and his Reign of Terror than under the less systematic and less "rational" revolutionary governments that preceded it. The ideal and rational Republic that Plato proposed would have been much less free and much less open than the messy Athenian democracy he hoped to eliminate.

This is the strength of Karl Popper's critique of the socially stifling function of total and closed philosophical systems. He was not wrong to condemn much of the Western philosophical tradition as an enemy of open society. The belief that reason can discover a substantially perfect or complete social model which philosophers functioning in the legislature can enact defies the requirements of open society as much as the belief that such a perfect model can be found in sacred writings or in ancient traditions.

In a rapidly changing society—for example, a society transforming itself under the accelerating impulses and demands of a capitalist social order— the identification of the social order with an unchanging philosophically based and rationally established set of institutions and laws can be both dangerous and obstructive. The educated and reasonable inhabitants of such a state will be profoundly conservative and averse to disruptive change. In France today, for example, resistance to the effects of globalization does not just reflect the power of entrenched interests threatened by economic change. It also reflects an ideological resistance based on the belief that the social compromises of the mid-twentieth century, however imperfect, embody the quest for a rational and just social order. For many of the French, economic change is welcome if it entrenches and extends this order and its privileges and rights: higher wages, more job security, shorter work-weeks. But when economic change undermines this old order, much of French society sees further capitalist development as a thing to be feared rather than a challenge to be enthusiastically embraced. In the end, the French are both realistic and inventive; over and over they have adapted to change. Yet over and over again this resistance and hesitation give the English-speaking world opportunities to reap the rewards of moving farther and faster into the new technologies and social relations that capitalism offers.

Pluralism, even at the cost of rational consistency, is necessary in a world of change. Countervailing forces and values must contend. Reason, scripture, tradition: they all have their uses, but any one of them, unchecked, will go too far. Moreover, without constant disputes, constant controversy, constant competition between rival ideas about how society should look and what it should do, the pace of innovation and change is likely to slow as forces of conservative inertia grow smug and unchallenged.

This is one of the reasons why the Anglophone world outpaced its continental rivals, most notably France. In France there was no multiplicity of sects like that found in Britain; besides a small leavening of Huguenots and Jews there were only the Catholic Church and the Enlightenment. Catholic France remained too fixed in the past—philosophically, institutionally, socially—to provide the framework French society would have needed to beat Britain in the race to the west. Secular, Jacobin France also had its rigidities, its fixed perspectives, its propensities to resist change rather than embrace it. The struggle between the two visions of French society did propel France westward—but never, quite, at the speed the English traveled. The westward progress of any society may well reflect the degree to which many quite different worldviews, interest groups, and subcultures find expression in its politics. Homogeneous and bipolar societies seem to be at a basic disadvantage, doomed to play catch-up in a world in which the leaders win disproportionate rewards. The social model based on the British Enlightenment and the revolution of 1688 reflects a pluralism that the political paradigms based on the French Enlightenment and the revolution of 1789 lack.

The English-speaking world emerged from the British Reformation with an ability to tolerate and even welcome the conflicts, tensions, and radical uncertainties of dynamic society. This background helps the English-speaking world cope with the risks, stresses, and other conditions of capitalist society even as they have posed barriers and obstacles for much of the rest of the world.

On a broader scale, a capitalist society is one in which the creative destruction of the market is always reshaping basic institutions. We are always saying goodbye to something we love, always leaving our fathers' homes for an unknown future. This is true of individual entrepreneurs who must risk losing the wealth they currently have in the quest for more; it is more broadly true through a changing society. *Semper eadem* was the motto of the feudal world: always the same. The church, the state, the law, the dynasty: every institution derived its authority from its antiquity. *Semper reformanda* is the motto of capitalism: everything needs to be remade over and over again. The older a machine, a firm, a factory, a product, a social compact, an idea, or a technology, the more suspect it is.

Yet at the same time, there must be room for nostalgia and a resistance to change. There must be religious voices denouncing godless secularism and calling mankind back to eternal principles—even as they denounce one another for heresy. Human society must be torn between strongly felt ideals because no one ideal can hold all the answers. Open society must be secular and religious, dogmatic and free. Doxies of all kinds must find a place there and be cherished, and the conflict and catfights between them can never end.

Fourteen • Called to the Bar

W hen I, Good Friends, Was Call'd to the Bar" is a patter song in the Gilbert and Sullivan operetta *Trial by Jury.* In it a rich and powerful judge tells the audience how, as an impecunious young barrister, he was unable to get any legal work. But although he "dances a dance of half despair" because he can't get cases, he refuses to give in to circumstance:

> *I soon got tired of third-class journeys*
> *And dinners of bread and water;*
> *So I fell in love with a rich attorney's*
> *Elderly, ugly daughter.*

The delighted father promises the young man that his good sense will be rewarded and, after telling him hopefully that "[s]he'll very well pass for forty-three in the dusk with the light behind her," ensures that a steady stream of lucrative cases goes to his future son-in-law.

The fees from these cases are so large that the young man becomes influential and powerful on his own; at that point, he breaks his engagement.

This story describes the relationship that much of the world would like to have with capitalism. In the eyes of many people and many societies, capitalism is as unattractive as the ugly daughter—but like her, capitalism is a road to riches. The goal is to gain as much money with as little congress with the daughter as possible. The best course would be to manage things as the judge did: flirt with her long enough to make money, and then push her aside. If there was absolutely no other way out, one might go through with the marriage—but even then one would see her as rarely as possible and devote a respectable part of the fortune she brought to maintaining a suitable mistress.

One might grudgingly devote some hours of the day, some years of one's life, to capitalist pursuits, but the goal would be the money, not the job or the business. It would be the leisure, the security, the power that capitalist enterprise can provide—not the enterprise itself.

Similarly, a government that notices its economy falling dangerously behind those of its rivals might grudgingly permit some capitalist reforms. It might give independence to the central bank, lower tariffs, or deregulate various industries or even its labor and financial markets. But the guiding spirit in all this for much of the world remains hesitant and reluctant. People want to do the minimum possible to achieve the desired result. The goal is intelligent conservation of the status quo: make a few unwelcome concessions to avoid the greater evils that would otherwise follow; sell the meadow to keep the cherry orchard.

Tastes differ. Samuel Johnson and Benjamin Disraeli were both married to women many years their senior, and neither Tetty Johnson nor Mary Anne Disraeli was known for beauty, breeding, wit, or even amiability. (Disraeli once said that his wife was "an excellent creature, but she could never remember who came first, the Greeks or the Romans.") Yet both men were sincerely attached, enjoyed what appear to have been extremely happy family lives, and were cast into deep mourning by the loss of their wives.[1]

The passion of English and American businessmen for their labors and the enthusiasm of Anglo-American society for capitalism have over the centuries mystified, annoyed, and amused non-Anglo-Saxon observers who can neither understand nor sympathize with this strangely tainted love.

"American life," Paul de Rousiers wrote in the late nineteenth century, "is all consecrated to business. Business! That is the word which the lips of the Yankee or the colonist pronounce the oftenest, and one reads such preoccupation on their faces. In meeting one another, the greeting is 'how's business?' It is the first subject they think of speaking about."[2]

In *Ariel,* the Uruguayan writer and anti-Yankee commentator José Enrique Rodó, both fascinated and appalled by Yankee drives, quotes Faust and Nietzsche to describe the overwhelming force of the Anglo-American will.[3] Rodó perceptively notices the predominance of Nietzschean supermen, actual or aspiring, among the characters of Edgar Allan Poe. Rodó senses there is something passionate and idealistic in Yankee society but in the end can't identify it. North American society, he concludes, is an example of Blaise Pascal's vicious circle: "the fervent pursuit of well-being that has no object beyond itself."[4] Rodó's charge remains the fundamental indictment of the Anglo-Saxon ethos: that the pursuit of business, efficiency, and the ever-rising standard of living is unconnected to any deeper vision of life or meaning.

Max Weber struggled with the same dilemma, and although even for him there was something sadly utilitarian and stunted about Yankee aspirations, he could see that the American love affair with growth and with business was more than a sordid passion for wealth. There was a kind of poetry in American life, although it was a dull and pedestrian poetry as he saw it. "When the imagination of a whole people has once been turned toward purely quantitative bigness, as in the United States, this romanticism of numbers exercises an irresistible appeal to the poets among business men."[5]

Capitalism, seen as the dedication of an entire active life to the mere acquisition of money, was so ugly and unacceptable to intellectuals and artists beyond the Anglo-American world (and, to a certain extent, within it) that even sensitive and thoughtful observers simply could not enter imaginatively into the consciousness of its devotees. The only love such an unattractive object could evoke had to be a tainted love—small, greedy, and perverse. And a society shaped by such loves and such goals must be cold, cruel, vulgar, and greedy.

Yet world history and the passions that inspire it cannot be understood without seeing that the Anglophones truly loved the elderly, ugly daughter. To many Yankee and British eyes she was transcendently beautiful, providing for the businessman a vision of the world beyond and the ultimate goal of all life.

What Beatrice was to Dante, Guinevere to Lancelot, business has been for millions of English-speakers. They have wooed her as assiduously as Paris wooed Helen.

Where the outside world sees a steely, cold businessman—a John D. Rockefeller, a Henry Ford, a Bill Gates—the inward experience is that of a dreamer. Money is not the goal; money is, as they say in the Texas oil fields, just a way of keeping score. De Rousiers knew this, even if he didn't understand it: for the American, he wrote, "Money is not so much something to enjoy as an instrument of work—a lever; not an end, but a means."[6]

The passion for growth, for achievement, for change—all to be satisfied in the competitive world of capitalist markets—marked not only individuals, but society as a whole. Since the eighteenth century the Anglophone world has been filled with what Jonathan Swift called "projectors": visionary dreamers with proposals for everything from new businesses and industries to vast schemes of social improvement and universal peace. A huge, centuries-old, and ever-growing market in self-help and self-improvement literature testifies to the passion with which individuals in every social class and walk of life have earnestly sought to retool their souls to reduce friction, enhance efficiency, and improve the results of their daily interactions with the world. Each generation sees the rise of new styles of religion, new gurus of self-improvement, new secular techniques of soul and time management spring up to assist Americans eager to keep their souls in tune with the changing times. With a handful of affluent exceptions, virtually every American hamlet, to say nothing of the larger municipalities and states, teems with enthusiasts for projects to "put our town on the map," accelerate growth, and participate more fully in the dynamism of American life. No one organizes this movement; no one coordinates or inspires it. Neither the left nor the right can lay claim to it; self-improvement and social reform inspire almost the whole of the political spectrum.

Perhaps the best and certainly the most popular evocation of this spirit of progress for decades was Henry Wadsworth Longfellow's 1841 poem "Excelsior." It captures both the passion of what we have been calling the Anglophone's rush westward—a journey that takes us up as well as west—and the radical gap of incomprehension between the Anglo-Saxon heroes of improvement and observers like Rodó.

The poem opens with a young man walking through an alpine village bearing

> *A banner with the strange device,*
> *Excelsior!*

Our determined hero presses on. He passes by happy, firelit homes toward the "spectral glaciers" beyond, heedless of warnings and entreaties, even those of a young woman who begs him to rest his weary head upon her breast. "Excelsior!" is all he can reply.

The next morning the monks at their familiar, traditional prayers in their mountain monastery hear the voice crying "Excelsior" through the "startled air"; ultimately the body of the young man is found half buried in snow, the banner with its strange device still clutched in his frozen hand.

> *There in the twilight cold and gray*
> *Lifeless, but beautiful, he lay,*
> *And from the sky, serene and far,*
> *A voice fell, like a falling star,*
> *Excelsior!*

It was the ideal of progress—the nexus of social, institutional, intellectual, economic, and moral changes that go hand in hand with the ever intensifying pursuit of capitalist development—that so resonated with Longfellow's many readers. For Longfellow's hero, the normal pursuits of human life, including the pursuit of "culture," are the vain and vicious appetites pursued to no higher end than their own satisfaction. Henry Ford did not care whether his clothes were stylish or his meals elegantly prepared; he despised any lesser concern that distracted him from his main goal of creating a new kind of automobile business. He was manifesting a passion to strip away inefficiencies, ancient cobwebs and customs, and introduce efficiency and order, one that is found among businessmen, but also among social reformers, scientists, and engineers. It scoffs at comfort and despises routine.

The Anglo-Saxons charge at progress with the same engagement of their spiritual and imaginative faculties that Don Quixote brought to his charges at windmills. Quixote saw the windmill as a giant whose defeat was a moral and spiritual necessity; John D. Rockefeller saw the organization and rationalization of the oil industry as a heroic adventure every bit as spiritually and morally necessary as Quixote's charge. Both may have mistaken the object of their attention, both may have traversed what to other eyes might seem a dreary wasteland of futility, but the imaginations of both men sprinkled fairy dust over the prospect before them.

The truth is that transcendence is where you find it. Like beauty, meaning is in the eye of the beholder. Dante's lifelong love for Beatrice might have seemed very foolish to his friends, who saw her as one attractive woman out of many; the lama's prayer wheels look like superstitious trash to the missionary.

Rodó could find no transcendent purpose in the strivings of the North Americans, and Weber could find only a sad poetry in our national life—but those directly concerned saw it otherwise. Rockefeller would probably have seen Latin American litterateurs as frittering their lives away for no serious purpose; it is hard to imagine Henry Ford thinking that Max Weber had made wise use of his God-given talents. For world history, the most important point is this: in the end the Rockefellers wind up richer and more powerful than the Quixotes—and perhaps no more deceived. Perhaps neither finds the transcendence he sought; perhaps both do.

It is attraction, not calculation or compulsion, that continually pulls the Anglosphere westward. Although there is debate, resistance, and doubt in the Anglosphere as elsewhere, on the whole attraction rules. Like Proust's Swann pursuing his beloved Odette, the English-speakers are drawn irresistibly to the beloved object. Like medieval knights caught up in the conventions of courtly love, they do her bidding gladly; they wear what she commands, spend their time at her service, reorder their priorities at her whim, and ask only that she let them serve her.

The Anglo-American world fell deeply in love with the elderly, ugly daughter. As in all great love affairs, there is something inexplicable and irreducibly mysterious at the bottom of it, and as in all great love affairs, the passions engaged were transcendent and reached the deep wellsprings of human emotion where the human spirit encounters the absolute and where religion is born.

Beginning with Adam Smith and powerfully reinforced and extended by Weber's observation, an important body of research and thought has grown up that examines the many relationships between the religious beliefs and institutions of the Anglo-American world and the form that these societies have taken over time. Most recently the French philosopher Bernard-Henri Lévy, in tracing de Tocqueville's path across the United States, followed him also in noting how American individualism, freedom of conscience and debate, pluralism, democratic opposition to natural and social hierarchies, community institutions, and a deeply grounded practice of democracy are all historically rooted in the Anglo-American Protestantism that shaped early American culture.[7]

For our purposes here, one additional element in Anglo-American Protestantism needs to be stressed. The degree to which the individualistic basis of Anglo-American religious experience links the religious life of the individual to a God who reveals Himself in the changes and upheavals of life, rather than in the stabilities and unchanging verities, has had a profound effect and continues to exercise a powerful force on the English-speaking world today. It gave a direction to the spiritual striving and self-understanding of the English-speaking world which helped ensure that over succeeding centuries, individuals and society as a whole would continue to devote their full energy to the exploration and development of the possibilities of capitalist society. Instead of resisting the dynamo of capitalist change, the English-speaking world would do its best to accelerate the process. It would not only ride the tiger of capitalist change; it would whip and spur the tiger to ever faster speeds up ever higher slopes. Excelsior!

The Call of Abraham

Ever since the sixteenth century, European observers have noted that Protestant cultures on the whole tended to do better in business than their Catholic counterparts. This was true within countries as well as between them. It was not simply that Britain prospered more than Italy, Sweden more than Spain; the northern, Protestant districts of countries were doing better than the mostly Catholic southern sections. Holland outperformed Belgium, though the two had been united for centuries before the Reformation. Within France, the Huguenot minority was disproportionately well represented among the ranks of financiers and industrialists.

There were, of course, many exceptions to a generalization this sweeping, such as the pioneering mercantile economies of Genoa, Florence, and Venice. Even so, the differences continued to be noticed and commented on until the second half of the twentieth century. (In post–Second World War Europe, with both Protestantism and Catholicism losing a great deal of their influence on much of the European population, a secular, post-Christian culture appeared and economic differences across the old religious divide seemed to be shrinking.) With the exception of Ireland, the English-speaking countries were largely Protestant; the success of the English-speaking peoples at capitalism needs to be understood at least in part in the context of this larger story.

The classic treatment of this subject is Max Weber's 1905 essay on the Protestant ethic and the spirit of capitalism. Struck by the almost monastic determination with which so many Protestants pursued their worldly interests, Weber looked for clues in Protestant doctrine that would explain this devotion. After a century of scholarly debate, Weber's findings remain important.

Weber looked to John Calvin's grim theology of predestination for explanations. The fearsome doctrine of double predestination holds that long before the creation of the world God freely chose some human beings for redemption and others (the large majority, in the view of most early modern Calvinists) for damnation. The damned souls were, as souls and as human beings, no better or worse than the saved. Thanks to original sin, *all* human souls were equally worthy of hellfire. Individual human beings cannot control or influence their fate; God chose it long before they were born. One can pray, fast, and give money to the poor and still go to Hell. On the

other hand, one can carouse till the wee hours and break all Ten Commandments every day of one's life and still go to Heaven if that is God's will. The
damned were created for the sole purpose of showing the power and majesty
of the inscrutable justice of God; the saved were created to exhibit His
mercy.

This austere doctrine, as Weber convincingly argued and as countless
obsessive diaries and letters through generations of Calvinist influence
attest, creates psychological problems for those who hold it. There is an
almost irresistible pressure for Calvinists to believe that God has in fact
chosen them for Heaven. Granted that the choice is a mystery, and that
human standards of right and wrong don't apply, are there any hints, any
clues that could help us know where we stand?

Calvinists came to believe that there are signs that God's grace is working in some people, and it is more than reasonable to believe that where we
see signs of such grace we see signs of God's intention to save their souls. In
search of these signs of grace, Calvinists began to monitor, often obses-
sively, their mental states and their behavior on a moment-by-moment basis
to see whether God was at work in their lives.

To succeed at one's occupation was clearly a sign of God's grace—one
fulfilled duties to employers, clients, family, and society at large. Calvinists
also taught a doctrine of calling—that one was "called" by God not only to
perform general religious duties as a Christian, and duties toward one's
family, but also to use one's talents in the world. Medieval Christianity,
while teaching that people should be honest and obedient in their station of
life, valued success less and tended to see the cares and occupations of daily
life as a distraction from the Kingdom of God.

Calvinism's emphasis on secular occupations as calls from God clearly
gave new dignity and importance to economic and social tasks. To serve the
world in business was to serve God. A better mousetrap would not only lead
the world to beat a path to your door; to build one was a sign that God had
chosen you for salvation.

This attitude tended to make Calvinists more successful in their worldly
occupations. At the same time, it was important to live in thrift and sobri-
ety—not to misuse the riches that worldly success brought. Intemperance
was not a sign of God's salvific grace. As a result, Calvinist communities
soon began to develop pools of capital available for investment—and dili-
gent, trustworthy young men ready to make profitable use of the savings of
others. (Weber also notes that Jewish values provided a strong foundation
for a rising capitalist economy, and from seventeenth-century Holland to
twenty-first-century North America it has often been true that Judaism and

Protestantism have been influential in some of the world's most dynamic capitalist economies.)

The habits of Calvinism persisted even when the doctrines fell into disuse. Benjamin Franklin was no Calvinist, yet the precepts of his *Autobiography* and *Poor Richard's Almanack* faithfully reproduced Calvinist strictures in a utilitarian rather than theological context. Whatever might become of us in the next world, early to bed and early to rise would make us healthy and wealthy and wise in this one. Whether one has an immortal soul, and regardless of whether this soul can be saved, a penny can be saved, and when it is, it becomes a penny earned.

In a capitalist environment, social power and wealth would flow toward those who practiced like Franklin, whether or not they believed like John Calvin; a Calvinist heritage would, Weber argued, continue to drive societies into capitalism and wealth even after the initial religious impulse had faded.

In the century since Weber's essay first appeared, a rich literature has grown up around this argument. It has been attacked, extended, qualified, and transformed—but it remains one of the central ideas in debates over modern history. Weberian arguments have even been transposed into other cultures, to see if they provide insights into such topics as the dominating role of ethnic Chinese minorities in the development of capitalism across Southeast Asia.

Anglo-American history certainly provides Weber with support. The merchants of England were much more likely to be Calvinist than the general population; in the United States it was the most Calvinist regions—like New England and its daughter communities in the Middle West—that were most responsible for America's rapid development. The anti-Calvinist Anglican plantation elites in the South lagged far behind the industrious Calvinist Presbyterians of New Jersey and Congregationalists of greater New England.

Weber's concept of calling is clearly relevant to Anglophone history, but it is not the whole story. Capitalism is about much more than hard work. It is about risk taking, embracing change, tolerating setbacks, and accepting the sometimes amoral or even immoral consequences of the impact of markets on cherished social institutions and beliefs. There is a social as well as an individual dimension to this process; institutions and customs change under its sway, not only personal habits. In Weber's view, Protestant society is driven into capitalism as much by fear as by anything else; one labors at a calling and one saves because one fears being damned. Much more than this is at work.

The connections between capitalist values and the dynamic Protestant religious culture that shaped the modern English-speaking world run deeper than the mechanisms Weber identified, creating a widespread belief that market economies and social change manifest the will of God. Social progress was a sign that leading members of a given community were the beneficiaries of God's grace—that society as a whole was on the right track. The medieval saint had been largely indifferent to external conditions and improvements. St. Francis preached God's love to the poor, but he did not concentrate on improving their housing. The Calvinist could not accept that God's grace would fail to result in visible improvements in the community at large. A region where there were many saved would be a prosperous, thrifty, progressive corner of the world.

Above all, Protestants came to believe that to live in communion with God and to experience the hope of salvation meant cooperating with and even furthering the waves of social change that capitalism unleashed on the English-speaking world. Increasingly, dynamic religion would become the only true religion for English-speakers. Religion not only had to tolerate change; it had to advance change.

The key theological reference point for this transformation of values was the biblical patriarch Abraham, and the significance his story assumed in Anglo-American religion has roots deep in Reformation theology. Martin Luther's interpretation of the theology of the biblical writings traditionally attributed to St. Paul put the figure of Abraham front and center. In the Epistle to the Romans, Paul stresses that Abraham's faithful, initial response to God's call was the basis for salvation. Justification by faith alone, that core tenet of Protestantism, was established, Luther and his followers believed, by the story of Abraham.

Over and over again, the epistles historically attributed to Paul return to the figure of Abraham and the stories associated with him. The mysterious figure of Melchizedek, a priest whom Abraham encountered following a victory in battle, becomes the central image in the discussion of Christ's priesthood in the Epistle to the Hebrews—where, again, Abraham is seen as the original hero of faith. In the Epistle to the Galatians, Abraham's saving faith is used as an argument against requiring Gentiles to accept the Jewish rite of circumcision before joining the church—perhaps the most important single doctrinal issue in the early years of Christianity.

Theologians have frequently noted that one of the distinctive marks of Reformation theology was the emphasis on the theology of Paul; given the absolutely critical role of the Abrahamic stories in the epistles, Abraham— especially the story of Abraham's receptiveness to God's call—assumes a power and centrality largely lacking in pre-Reformation piety and thought. Just as Abraham was the key figure in Paul's argument about circumcision, he became the key figure in the Protestant arguments for justification by faith: the main theological controversy of the Reformation.

Abraham believed the promises of God, and as Paul wrote in his most important theological work (the Epistle to the Romans), this faith was "reckoned to him as righteousness." Abraham's faith, his willingness to leave his home, his family ties, in obedience to a call from God, became the foundation for God's redemption of the human race. Without a doubt many Protestant converts from Catholicism were sustained by Abraham's example; they too were abandoning their fathers' beliefs in answer to what they believed was a higher calling.

The new sense of faith as a journey that required the abandonment of the familiar became a central idea in the religious and devotional literature of the time. The wildly successful *Pilgrim's Progress* is the story of how a Christian forsakes the comfortable, conventional religion of his family and community to follow a call. Next to the King James Bible, this was the most common book in English homes well into the nineteenth century; next to the Bible, it was the book most commonly owned by the American pioneers.

This faithful response of Abraham to God's promise is a deeper and more positive force than the fear that drives Weber's Calvinist analysis. It is not just that the Calvinist is running in fear from a hideous fate while the follower of Abraham is reaching out toward something positive—a haunting, transcendent call that bespeaks a reality richer and more rewarding. Embracing change becomes a kind of sacrament; moving from the known to the unknown brings one closer to God. Change has a religious sanction and a positive value; *excelsior* is the direction toward God. Change is no longer a necessary evil that must sometimes be endured; to embrace and even seek change is to encounter the meaning of life.

Where Weber, like most thinkers of the European Enlightenment, tends to see progress in terms of rationalization and the disappearance of the numinous ("magic") from ordinary existence, it may be more accurate to say that for the individualistic Anglo-American Christian, the "personal relationship with God" is a powerful and effective link with the realm of the transcendent that does not wither or fade even as the modernization and rationalization processes of capitalist society proceed and intensify. On the contrary, the experience of transcendence may become increasingly important to a population facing growing uncertainty in a world of accelerating change. The more the world changes, and the more the believer changes in response, the closer he or she comes to God.

Ecclesia semper reformanda: The church—and everything else—is always in need of renewal and change. The pull of these values has not been limited to orthodox Protestants; indeed, it is precisely this "Protestant principle" of progressive change that led men like Ralph Waldo Emerson beyond even the very capacious boundaries of the Unitarian faith. In a real sense, change—understood as progress, as response to a call whether from God or some inner, higher self—can become an object of worship in the English-speaking world.

As American religion in particular became more personalized and emotional, its identification with Abraham's faithful response to change only deepened. The distinctive American religious evolution may help explain why the United States has gone west further and faster than the other English-speaking countries. From the time of Jonathan Edwards in the early eighteenth century to the revivals of our own day, the great awakenings of American history focused on the idea of God's call. In the Kentucky revivals at the turn of the nineteenth century, where strong men and pioneer women fell to the ground and shook, when in later revivals thousands knelt in tears on the tent floors as Dwight Moody preached and Ira Sankey sang, when the fires of the Holy Spirit fell on the ecstatic worshippers at the Azusa Street church in Los Angeles in the early twentieth century, millions of Americans felt a personal call from God to leave the familiar worlds and ideas of their past, and to journey toward something unknown. In some cases, for example, the Mormons, the summons became a literal call to imitate Abraham and move to a new promised land. In others, it meant leaving established churches for fledgling denominations. Almost always, the great awakenings have come at times when Americans were either engaged in or preparing for moments of great change. The astonishing outpourings of enthusiasm that followed George Whitfield's progress across the colonies and the Great Awakening of Jonathan Edwards helped prepare the way for the American Revolution. The Kentucky revivals that followed were instrumental in the creation of a frontier society and a new kind of democratic lifestyle independent of the strictures and conventions of the East. Today's religious revivals in the South come at a time when old patterns of life based on segregation and farming have been replaced by very different conditions.

Overall, just as the proliferation of small sects helped the transplanted countrymen of Adam Smith's Britain adjust to new social patterns and work rhythms in the cities of an industrializing economy, so did the revival meetings, circuit riders, and tiny wilderness churches help Americans adapt to a succession of changes.

The belief that every Christian must have a personal experience of God's call has for more than three centuries been strengthening its hold in American life. The series of religious revivals and awakenings from the eighteenth century through the present day, the rise of Pentecostal religion in the twentieth century and the evangelical renewal of the last generation stress the importance of a personal decision for Christ and a personal relationship with God. Christianity in the American context is less and less a matter of family or ethnic identity, more and more a matter of personal choice. We must all be Abraham now. Historically, religious identity throughout the world has been largely an aspect of a broader social and ethnic identity. One is Greek Orthodox or Hindu because that is the faith one was born into. The mobility of American religious life, with frequent movement mostly among the major Protestant denominations but also beyond and across these boundaries, combined with the increasingly individualistic nature of American theology and piety, has substantially changed this picture. Religion today is increasingly part of a self-constructed, chosen identity for Americans. It is perceived as a response to a call—an inherently dynamic religious orientation, even if the doctrines embraced are venerable.

The cultural impact of this orientation goes far beyond the pulpits and the pews of American religion. The widespread American belief that each life is a kind of project to be planned, the belief that one has a unique dream which must be pursued through all hardships and reverses, and the ease with which Americans move hundreds and even thousands of miles in pursuit of opportunity or fulfillment, all testify to the power of the Abrahamic archetype in the American mind.

This Abrahamic concept of calling strengthens and intensifies the influence of Weber's "Protestant ethic" even as it extends its influence from the sphere of individual and family life into the broader society. As the Weberian Calvinist grimly works and saves, he or she generates the cash and the work habits that will make capitalism grow. The Abrahamic believer, convinced that God is leading the way to an unknown future in a new land, is ready to accept not only the personal but also the social consequences of capitalist life. Are the old folkways and habits passing away? Have strip malls and town houses sprung up in the meadows and forests where one played as a child? Are gender roles melting and changing even as new immigrant groups fill the land? Is the old industrial economy of union labor and stable employment mutating into something mysterious, complex, dynamic, and new?

For the soul grounded in static religion, such changes are hard to accept. For the dynamic believer, change is both a sign of progress and an opportunity to show the crowning virtue of faith. The many-sided tasks of modernization become channels of grace. *Excelsior! Vox mutatis vox dei*: the voice of change is the voice of God. With an energy that no central organizing power could ever summon or shape, millions of Americans through decades and centuries spontaneously turn themselves not only to improve their personal fortunes, but to make American society a more and more suitable medium for capitalist development. To engage in the struggle for change and reform is not to oppose the religious instinct, but to give it its fullest expression. Whether they were struggling to build businesses, to change social institutions to reflect the new requirements and possibilities of a capitalist system, or simply to accustom themselves to the accelerating juggernaut of change, millions of Anglo-Americans over the centuries were not trapped in a Pascalian vicious circle. They really did see something transcendent in their lives; they really did believe that they were struggling toward God. And to the degree that fulfillment comes from making a journey of faith, they didn't just seek God. They found Him.

Or, in Gilbert and Sullivan's terms, they really did love the ugly daughter, and so they won her hand, her heart, *and* her purse.

Fifteen • The Gyroscope and the Pyramid

Here thou, great Anna! whom three realms obey,
Dost sometimes Counsel take—and sometimes tea,

wrote Alexander Pope in *The Rape of the Lock.* It can be a baffling coup-
let for all except the handful of American students who enjoy the good
fortune to have been taught in the dwindling handful of schools where
British history and culture are still regarded as something worth knowing.
Most Americans would not know who Great Anna (Queen Anne) was,
what three realms (England, Scotland, and, sullenly, Ireland) obeyed her,
or that in the early eighteenth century "tea" was still pronounced so that it
rhymed with "obey." Given the enormous differences that separate the contemporary United States from Queen Anne's Britain, it seems odd to claim
that underneath the surface differences, the United States today remains in
some ways very much like British society in Anne's day—but that is the
truth.

The United States today is still a Goldilocks society, still racing westward along the old Anglo-Saxon trail, and still aiming for new summits in
the mountains. That energetic push is still transforming American society as
the technological, economic, cultural, and social changes unleashed by capitalism course through the nation.

Written with a capital letter "A," the word "Anglican" refers to the Christian churches that trace their origins to the Church of England and remain in
communion with the Archbishop of Canterbury. Written without the initial
capital, "anglican" denotes persons, places, or things who, whether or not
they belong to any of the churches in the Anglican Communion, accept that
religious and social questions should be settled on the basis of a combina-

tion of reason, revelation, and tradition.* American society today is in this sense an anglican society, and it still relies on the anglican trinity of Queen Anne's day. Reason, revelation, and tradition are the competing pluralistic sources of value and authority in American life. They are the three stars by which various elements in the country attempt to set a course and, as in the time of Queen Anne, none of them can quite crowd out or overawe the rest.

Think of a flat surface with three powerful magnets placed in a triangle. Within the triangle formed by the magnets will be a smaller, roughly triangular region on the surface where all of the magnets exert force—but where no single magnet dominates the others. The precise mix of forces will be different for every point within this smaller triangle, but within this smaller or Anglican triangle a paper clip or other magnetic object can sit without being pulled inexorably toward one of the magnets.

The effective definition of an anglican society is one which rests in the anglican triangle; it feels the effects of all of the magnets, but no single magnet is fully in control.

Since, however, anglican societies are usually dynamic, we need a livelier image. Consider a three-sided pyramid whose sides gradually become less steep until they reach a flat top. The top area will be triangular in shape; on every side of this triangle the slopes of the pyramid gradually become steeper. Now think of a gyroscope spinning on the top of the pyramid. It moves as it spins—now toward what we can call the "reason" side of the pyramid, now toward the "tradition" side, and now toward the "revelation" side. As long as the gyroscope doesn't stray too far from the flat area on top, it can move freely back and forth among the three sides. But if it strays too far, it will pass a point of no return and begin a descent toward the ground.

An anglican society is one which has not passed the point of no return; to say that America is an anglican society today means that we are still spinning at the top.

Back in Queen Anne's time, some of her subjects believed on principle that the anglican triangle was the right place to be. They believed that society should keep spinning on top of the pyramid. Some of these anglicans sympathized with what we know now as the Burkean point of view: that

* This parallels the distinction made in the use of the words "Catholic" and "catholic." Written with the capital letter, the word refers specifically to the Roman Catholic Church. Written without it, the word is used to describe persons or things who possess the leading characteristic of that church: universality.

society should spin as close as possible to the tradition side of the triangle, but without slipping past the point of no return. Others shared the rationalist views, which would later be supported by men like David Hume and Adam Smith, that society ought to spin over toward the reason line, though still without going over the edge. And finally, there were those who believed that society should get as close as it could to the revelation side—but who also didn't want to slide down the slippery slope to theocracy. But while these people all disagreed over where the gyroscope should be, they all agreed that it should stay in the anglican or, we can say, in the constitutional zone.

Others of Queen Anne's subjects loathed the anglican triangle and desperately wanted to push the gyroscope over the edge. There were the Jacobites who wanted to place the "legitimate" Stuart claimant on the throne. There were stern Puritans who yearned for something like a restoration of Oliver Cromwell's Commonwealth of saints. There were freethinking radicals and rationalists who increasingly questioned basic Christian doctrines and believed that these should no longer play any significant role in the organization of society or the state.

In Queen Anne's Britain, conscious anglicans were probably a minority in the total population. Fortunately for them, there was never an effective majority for any one of the three alternatives (although Jacobite support for the exiled Stuarts probably came closest). This multipolar dissent, even dissent that itself had revolutionary goals and sought to overthrow the status quo, functioned like an outrigger, providing additional stability and security to Queen Anne's royal barge. The Cromwellians and the rationalists accepted Queen Anne because they feared a Jacobite restoration—and a great many people preferred to live under Queen Anne than face another round of civil war.

The United States is still an anglican society in this sense, but if the shape and structure of the triangle (and the pyramid) have not changed, each leg of the triangle has undergone major changes over the years. The balance between them has also changed over time; in both Britain and the United States the gyroscope has skittered from side to side of the triangle, though it has never, so far, gone over the edge.

While in some ways the United States has stayed closer to the balance of forces that prevailed in Queen Anne's Britain, a comparison of the courses of the gyroscopes in the two countries will show both the continuity and the change in America's increasingly dynamic and West-facing society.

The Transformation of Tradition

It may seem at first that tradition is the element in the British system that is weakest and least represented in the United States. There were never very many Jacobites in the thirteen colonies, and few observers, foreign or domestic, have ever taxed the Americans with a too powerful attachment to tradition. In Britain, the power of the aristocracy and the monarchy has also inexorably declined. Queen Anne was the last British sovereign to veto an act of Parliament; three hundred years later Tony Blair drove most of the hereditary peers out of what was left of the House of Lords. A closer look, however, shows that in both the British and American cases a new kind of tradition would ultimately supplement the declining force of aristocratic and monarchical tradition.

In Queen Anne's era British tradition was seen and felt as an aristocratic and monarchical idea and it was linked to the dominant landowning class. In the United States the plantation elite of the Old South sought to keep these ideas alive. The British aristocracy never quite crossed the Atlantic. George Washington's patron and neighbor Lord Fairfax was the most important titled Briton to make a permanent home in the colonies; the convoluted table of nobility that John Locke worked out for the Carolinas never caught on. Even so, the aristocratic ethos lingered in the South. Kevin Phillips has shown in *The Cousins' Wars* how in both Northern and Southern minds the Civil War seemed like the latest replay between the Cavaliers and the Roundheads as Southerners worked to persuade themselves that slavery was somehow similar to the gentry system of the old country. David Hackett Fischer's book *Albion's Seed* notes that the settlers of the Virginia Tidewater came overwhelmingly from Wessex and other tradition-oriented parts of England that supported Charles I in the civil war—while the New Englanders came from the Puritan heartland of East Anglia.

The similarities in blood and culture were strengthened by ideological influence. Sir Robert Filmer, a seventeenth-century English political theorist who supported Charles I in his contest with Parliament, was an important influence on such pre–Civil War Southern apologists as George Fitzhugh. In Fitzhugh's work, Southern slavery was justified on the basis that despite the sentimental and unrealistic rhetoric of misguided individualists like Thomas Jefferson and Tom Paine, human beings were not and never would be equal, and that to ignore the natural inequality of the human race was a sure road to ruin. Hierarchy was the natural condition of order. As Abraham Lincoln noted, Fitzhugh's arguments would justify white slavery as well as black. It was a principled argument for human inequality—a classic argument of traditionalists who opposed the overall direction of Anglo-American society on ideological grounds.

The aristocratic traditionalism of the South lingered on after the Civil War, finding echoes in twentieth-century literature and politics, but the story of aristocratic traditionalism in both Britain and the United States was one of extended decline as the landed gentry lost economic and cultural power in both countries. However, on both sides of the Atlantic a new kind of populist traditionalism would replace the fading aristocratic legacy and create an enduring pole of politics that today still opposes the claims of both reason and religion in national life.

As conservatives in nineteenth-century Britain looked around for political allies in the face of declining aristocratic power, "neo-traditionalists" like Benjamin Disraeli grasped that populist nationalism and a kind of identity politics could and, properly managed, would rescue traditionalist politics from impotence. As progressive waves of reform extended the right to vote to more and more British workingmen, the Tories were able to appeal to popular patriotism that, like the old traditionalism, saw Britain's unique identity, forged over time, as a source of positive values. Reasonable, reform-minded liberals were horrified to discover that Tory conservatives could and did "dish the Whigs," as Disraeli put it, and outbid the reformers in the quest for public support.

The shift from the grandee Toryism of, say, Queen Anne's allies like the Earl of Oxford to the Tory populism of Margaret Thatcher has been a long and complex process, and one that is not yet completed. Tory politics in Britain still sometimes reflect these divisions. But overall, the transition has been a success. Popular nationalism is deeply and instinctively tradition-minded. It stands on what it perceives to be the historic values of the nation; it believes that values like national defense should trump, for example, civil liberties in time of danger. It is not interested in merging its own national identity in the kinds of great liberal multinational enterprises that the rational imagination favors—like the European Union.

Yet this populist nationalism is not based on religious values, either. It is sympathetic to what it believes to be the historic religious values of the nation. In Britain, this kind of opinion was a strong source of the "anti-popery" feeling that broke out into riots more than once. But populist nationalism does not usually place the nation under the authority of scripture. Jingoistic British Tories in the imperial age did not question whether

Britain's wars of imperial expansion met scriptural standards for just wars. They did not ask whether the racial hierarchies that Britain increasingly imposed on its empire were Christian. Christianity was valued insofar as it was part of the British tradition, and not vice versa.

Throughout the Western world populist nationalism has kept the influence of tradition alive into and beyond the twentieth century. This was a card that Charles de Gaulle played against the Communists in France; it has played an even greater role in the United States. Once seen as fidelity to the values and the interests of a hierarchical aristocracy centered around the throne, tradition has come to mean fidelity and allegiance to the cultural and political values of the "nation"—populist nationalism.

The source of tradition changed in the nineteenth and twentieth centuries, but this was not enough to prevent a crisis and at least a temporary weakening in the relative power of the traditional pole in anglican politics. The causes and the course of the crisis were somewhat different in the United States and the United Kingdom, but developments in the two countries continued to move in roughly parallel fashion even so.

In the United Kingdom, as in much of Europe, the catastrophe of the First World War dealt populist nationalism a succession of massive, crippling blows. The unconscionable, unbelievable slaughter of that war substantially weakened the power of traditional values in British society, such as patriotism, for generations to come. It was difficult to avoid the idea that patriotism leads to war and war leads to slaughter; it was hard to return to the old exuberance of the jingoes:

> We don't want to fight, but by jingo if we do
> We've got the men, we've got the ships, we've got the money too.

After World War I, the British had fewer men, fewer ships, less money, and, most important, far less desire for war than ever before.

Like de Gaulle, Winston Churchill was a man out of his time. Descended from the Duke of Marlborough who won the French wars for Queen Anne, Churchill wandered mystified and lost in the alien world of 1930s Britain until the threat of Adolf Hitler brought the British back, briefly, to their traditional values. He successfully rallied the British to another world war by mobilizing the still-strong forces of traditional patriotism.

After the Second World War, the fall of the British Empire undermined the politics of tradition in Britain once again. Traditionalism seemed increasingly limited to narrow minds and reactionary causes—nativist opposition to immigration from former imperial territories like Jamaica and

Pakistan, for example. Soccer hooligans and racist skinhead thugs seemed to be the repository of British populist nationalism in much of the postwar period.

More recently, there has been a revival of populist nationalism in the United Kingdom. As the memories of the slaughters in the world wars and the fall of the empire faded, the experience of membership in the European Community paradoxically revived English nationalism even as the Scots and the Welsh renewed their own sense of a national identity based on non-rational, traditional sources. The specter of European Union bureaucrats of Brussels "taking over" British life and imposing alien continental norms on English society gradually produced a new kind of English patriotism based on national identity. This patriotism was neither a longing for Britain to again rule the world nor the kind of patriotism that would lead to more massacres like those on Flanders fields. Yet it was strong and based on non-rational forces like memory and culture. The satisfyingly successful Falklands War against Argentina also contributed to the reawakening of the traditional insular nationalism. Populist nationalism and identity politics were once again forces to be reckoned with as Scotland and England entered the twenty-first century.

The crisis of American popular nationalism in the twentieth century in part reflected the forces shaping British politics but was also a product of American developments. The mass slaughter of the two world wars did have an effect on American opinion, although neither war killed as many Americans as had died in the American Civil War. Certainly the twenties and thirties were the two most pacifistic and isolationist decades in American history. However, the crisis of American populism had less to do with external wars than with internal dynamics.

Mass immigration had raised a series of questions about American identity throughout the nineteenth century, with anti-Irish and anti-Catholic feeling running high for much of the era. After the Civil War, the nature of immigration changed. Such countries as Italy, Poland, and Russia replaced the old leading sources of immigrants: Britain (including Ireland) and Germany. To much native opinion, the new immigrants seemed more alien and harder to assimilate than the old; many elite observers as well as populist demagogues warned that America's "identity" risked being submerged in this new flood of different and dangerous immigrants.

One result was to split the potential bearers of populist tradition into hostile camps. What, after all, did popular tradition mean in a country whose population came from so many different countries with so many different traditions? The twenties saw not only a popular reaction against the costs of

World War I; it also saw a resurgence of the Ku Klux Klan in the North, aimed against Catholic and Jewish immigrants.

World War II and the passage of time began to knit "traditional" American popular nationalism back together. The lingering wounds of the Civil War continued to heal. The immigrants demonstrated the sincerity of their patriotism by continuing to adapt to American values and by serving in World War II and in the Korean War. The American Catholic hierarchy encouraged the growth of a deep patriotism among its followers.

By the end of the twentieth century, American populist nationalism was well past its crisis—and had also largely sloughed off the lingering effects of the Vietnam War. The sense had reemerged among many ordinary Americans that there was a profoundly American set of values, rooted not in legal documents or in holy scripture but in the lives and sentiments of ordinary people, and that this set of values was an important source of guidance in political affairs. Once again this belief was a major factor in national politics. The tradition leg of the Anglican triangle was alive, well, and, sometimes, kicking.

The Renewal of Revelation

The pull of revealed religion on the Anglo-American world has also waxed and waned over the centuries.

After 1688, radical Protestantism lost ground in Britain. Among the better educated, the tendency of Protestantism to evanesce into rationalism meant that many of the children and grandchildren of staunchly Protestant believers became liberal agnostics. The Matthew Arnold who wrote "Dover Beach" about the slow ebbing fall of the tide of belief was the son of the Thomas Arnold who built Rugby School as a bastion of the mix of Christian piety and athleticism called muscular Christianity. The extensive and popular late-nineteenth- and early-twentieth-century literature of religious disenchantment in Britain testifies to the transmutation and decline of strong evangelical and Protestant convictions—particularly as Darwinism and modern methods of textual analysis made the historic Protestant view of the Bible as the inerrant word of God somewhat more difficult to defend.

Among less well-educated evangelicals, Catholics, and dissenters outside elite circles, additional forces were at work. Emigration removed millions of (often) pious Britons from the home islands; Australia, Canada,

New Zealand, and the United States were all to some degree more visibly influenced by religion than Britain during substantial parts of the twentieth century. The nineteenth-century Mormon missionaries brought tens of thousands of British converts to the United States; for Catholics as well as non-Anglican Protestants, the English-speaking overseas territories offered opportunities and equality that remained elusive in the homeland.

Revelation nevertheless maintained a hold on British politics. After 1837 Catholics were allowed to sit in Parliament for the first time since the coronation of William III; Catholic Ireland and a newly vocal and self-confident Catholic minority in England and Scotland continued to stand for the importance of revealed religion as a source of authority in British politics.

The continuing decline of British Protestantism in the twentieth century further weakened the Protestant side of British religious identity, while Irish independence meant that the Catholic influence in British politics was severely curtailed. An important factor in this decline was the decline of religious feeling in Scotland and Wales—citadels for centuries of Calvinist and Wesleyan piety, respectively. The rise of socialism in Britain—strongly tinged with Christianity in the beginning but increasingly secular throughout the twentieth century—further weakened the power of religious revelation as a source of legitimacy and authority in British politics.

The closing decades of the twentieth century saw a change. There was no substantial revival of religion among the native-born British; there was, however, a series of waves of migrants from former imperial lands. Muslims from the Indian subcontinent and Christians from the West Indies and Africa brought new concerns and value systems into British politics. Parliament once more began to debate subjects that enlightened British opinion had thought banished forever from politics, like the need for blasphemy laws. The presence of an organized minority that is fundamentally opposed to the status quo and that contains a smaller group that is willing under certain circumstances to shed blood to destroy it shocked many Britons in the twenty-first century. Their ancestors, familiar with religious strife between Catholics and Protestants, between different types of Protestants, and between the resentful Catholic peasants of Ireland and the British state, were rather more familiar with this sort of issue.

In the United States the politics of revelation have also had their ups and downs, but for much of the time religion has played a stronger role in American society than it has in the British Isles.

New England was the original base of those who consciously sought to make American society reflect the dictates of revelation. Settled originally by Puritans who sympathized with the parliamentary side in the English

Civil War, New England never warmed to the royal cause. Following the restoration of Charles II, the king's justice minister sought to arrest and try for treason the surviving "regicide judges" who had condemned Charles's father to death. Puritan New Haven hid three of the judges in a cave from the royal officers and later named the city's three principal avenues after the regicides.

New England's religious fervor was renewed by the Great Awakening of the eighteenth century, but by the revolutionary period New England was moving toward a more secular, rationalist perspective. Harvard Divinity School went Unitarian in 1803 as, influenced by the Enlightenment, many New Englanders saw the doctrines of the Trinity and the belief in miracles as contrary to reason and therefore unworthy of acceptance. President Timothy Dwight kept Yale orthodox, even requiring the study of Hebrew so that his undergraduates could read the Old Testament in the original—but he was fighting a rising tide. Yankee New England would gradually but persistently move steadily in the direction of rationalism from the nineteenth century until now.

Yankee secularism remains influenced by its Calvinist background, however. It is and has always been a moral, even a moralistic, secularism. This is not the easy, worldly unbelief of a Talleyrand. It is a Puritanism that has followed the Protestant principle beyond the bounds of religion. The true Yankee secularist has translated both the fervor and the certainty of ancestral New England religious convictions into a set of secular political values. The secular Yankee's reaction to southern fundamentalists is not amused and easy tolerance; it is the bitter response of a Calvinist divine to the whiff of heresy. The moralistic fervor of the secular Yankee has helped keep American life dynamic.

The South has moved in the other direction. Except for (briefly) Catholic-harboring Maryland, the southern colonies were founded for commercial purposes rather than religious ones, and the scriptures were not the central concern for a struggling plantation society brutally exploiting slave and indentured labor. Planters were known to prevent missionaries from preaching to their slaves, fearing that English common law would not recognize a right to hold baptized Christians as slaves.

The southward shift in America's center of religious gravity accompanied a profound democratization of American religious life. The colonial churches were often established churches. Prominent clerics were an integral part of the gentry leadership. The decline of the religious establishments (Massachusetts was the last state to disestablish its religion; it was not until 1833 that the Congregational Church was finally separated from the state) accelerated as populist forces took over the leadership of American religion.

American Christianity soon began to grow in other directions. The historic denominations of the so-called magisterial Reformation (Lutherans, Anglicans, Presbyterians, and Congregationalists) gradually lost ground to more populist movements like Wesleyan Methodists and Anabaptists (known, confusingly, in the United States as Baptists). These and other new denominations were known for flatter hierarchies, more congregational control over worship, weaker national organizations, less emphasis on the nuances and fine points of academic theology, and a more emotional style of worship and preaching. In retrospect it seems that the Kentucky revivals touched off a long process by which the Puritan Christianity of old New England, with its base in the magisterial Reformation, was replaced by a southern and western Christianity that stressed individual conversion and had roots in the Anabaptist movement and in German and English pietism.

Despite recurring revivals, during much of the twentieth century the United States moved in the same direction as Britain, though not as far. That is to say that the power of reason grew stronger, while the nonrational (or transrational, as their partisans would say) forces of revelation and tradition grew weaker. Darwinism and biblical criticism reduced the hold of revealed religion over many educated minds during this period, and the new sources of faith in revelation in the United States also weakened as Catholics and Jews moved out of their faith communities or into more "rational" and "enlightened" versions of their respective faiths.

The last third of the twentieth century saw a dramatic reversal of these trends. Mainline Protestantism struggled and shrank; evangelical and Pentecostal churches exploded. The liberal Catholicism that struggled to emerge after the Second Vatican Council increasingly fell victim to the disciplined and determined efforts of John Paul II and Benedict XVI to assert closer Roman control over the American church. In Judaism the Orthodox and ultra-Orthodox movements appeared to be growing—through demographics as well as through religious renewal—while more liberal forms of Judaism struggled to hold their ground against trends like secularization and intermarriage. Muslim immigrants, as in Britain though on a smaller scale, added their voices to those wanting American politics to be responsive to the laws of God rather than to the traditions and ratiocinations of human beings.

The Rise and Fall of Reason

The career of reason in Anglo-American politics has also had its ups and downs. Until quite recently, the movement was oriented strongly toward—and in some cases even beyond—the reason pole of the Anglican triangle. Particularly in Britain after World War II, but to some degree also in the United States, it appeared at times that reason had won a definitive and permanent victory in its contest with revelation and tradition.

The ascendancy of reason was due both to the weaknesses and troubles of the other two poles of attraction and to the ways in which the use of reason as a source of legitimacy and authority in politics answered the needs of modernizing societies.

The three centuries since the time of Queen Anne have seen a vast expansion of the role of instrumental reason. To maintain the infrastructure and basic services of a contemporary society requires extraordinary organizations of technically qualified personnel who are committed to acting in a rational way to achieve certain results. Those responsible for the power supply to a major city, or those who keep aircraft traffic control systems running, cannot use tradition, whether aristocratic or popular, as a guide in carrying out their responsibilities. Neither would they be well advised under most circumstances to regulate their activities by reference to fits of divine inspiration, or to seek course guidance for airplanes in the pages of scripture.

As the power of the scientific and rational professions grew, the views of those in them commanded increased respect beyond professional ranks. Women whose mothers and grandmothers trusted midwives and folk practitioners turned to the men in white coats. Against the forces of both religion and tradition, the mantras of reason proved witheringly effective: where our grandfathers *thought,* now we could *know.*

This transformation in public and popular attitudes was especially important at the level of the state and, therefore, in politics. As the career civil service was established, first in Britain and then in the United States in the latter half of the nineteenth century, government became increasingly a profession to be practiced by the trained and the qualified. The old-fashioned British belief that virtually any amateur with the right breeding could, if called upon, govern New South Wales, and the American Jacksonian belief that the average person could competently administer the affairs of government, came to look comically backward and irrelevant.

As the prestige of the natural sciences grew, the prestige of the social sciences followed. It was felt that scientific inquiry and rigorous analysis would eliminate various vexing social problems and create a new and better world. In many cases this was true. In many, it wasn't. Horrible fads and illusions alternate with important contributions to human welfare and self-understanding. Racial science, phrenology, Freudian psychology, scientific penology, planned heavy industrial economic development, Marxist-Leninist politics, eugenics, and the sterilization of the insane—each of these ideas has at various times been enthusiastically proclaimed to be scientifically true in the way that Newton's law of gravity is scientifically true. The consequences in some cases have been comical; more frequently they have been brutal and tragic. It was by social science that the best minds in England concluded that the correct response to the Irish potato famine was to avoid disturbing the Irish food market by excessive distributions of cheap or free foodstuffs.

Despite these occasionally unsettling results, over the centuries of reason-based improvements in governance and living standards, the prestige of reason as the prime source of legitimate authority grew. Progress came to be defined for many people as the continuing supplanting of irrational forms of governance (like tradition) and nonrational ideas about the world (like religion) by scientific methods and ideas.

Increasingly British politics took the form of competition between an enlightened liberalism committed to a politics of progressive improvement through a career civil service and the Labour Party's mild, distinctively British form of socialism that was coming to replace nonconformist Protestant religion as the dominant ideology of the working class. Both of these forms of politics were rational; the idea that the dictates of revealed religion should determine government policy became progressively more ridiculous in twentieth-century Britain; in the same way, the idea that "jingoistic" or chauvinist nationalism should shape the nation's political culture found no support. After the historic Labour victory under Clement Attlee in 1945, Britain set out on a generation-long attempt to put its past behind it and build a new and modern society.

Revelation and popular nationalist tradition were never quite as weak in the United States as in Britain, but the 1960s saw the apogee of reason in American politics. The civil rights movement was a powerful moral lesson that the traditional folk values of the American majority were deeply flawed; the nation had to make an enormous act of will to overcome the disfiguring and tragic racism so deeply mixed in popular values and thinking throughout American history. The economic successes of the Kennedy and early

Johnson administrations reinforced the prestige of the new, counterintuitive Keynesian economics. The Apollo program that took Americans to the moon was a success of reason that resonated at deep, prerational levels of the human personality. Further plans unveiled by the trained social and natural scientists—to conquer cancer, to abolish poverty—seemed plausible. Never had America's experts been more ambitious; never had Americans trusted them more.

The Trumpet Sounds Retreat

A generation after the Great Society of Lyndon Johnson, which represented the high-water mark of the politics of expertise in the United States, it is easy to see how the other elements of the anglican triangle have reasserted themselves in both British and American politics. But since the cause of reason had become so firmly identified with that of progress—the path of reason was seen as the only path to the west—a widespread concern has grown up that the return of the nonrational elements in politics will lead to the end of dynamic society in one or both countries.

The new balance of forces among the three poles of attraction, and the new tendency of the American gyroscope to skitter away from the reason line rather than toward or even past it, looked sinister and alarming to many thoughtful people. The latest in the country's series of religious revivals brought new power to political forces shaped by traditional American evangelical ideas, and the public arena resounded with calls for a "restoration" of the ideals of "Christian" America. American populist nationalism enjoyed a revival of its own, as the descendants of immigrants and nativist populists found common ground under politicians like Ronald Reagan. Meanwhile the forces of rationalism, still powerful, suffered a series of setbacks as society moved away from the deference to professionals, experts, and other custodians of the rational state.

By the time of George W. Bush's contested victory in the 2000 election, the retreat of the party of rationalism in American life threatened to turn into a rout. In some ways the fight over the Supreme Court epitomized the new, defensive position of the rationalist party.

In some cases, as in the civil rights cases where the courts reversed earlier decisions that had read popular American attitudes about racial inequality into the Constitution, the new jurisprudence led to important and, after a generation, noncontroversial new understandings of the legal system. In other cases, the new jurisprudence attracted increasingly bitter and focused opposition. Many scholars of the New Right believe that without the Supreme Court decisions on matters like school prayer, banning nativity scenes from town halls, overturning laws requiring parental consent before minors could get abortions, and striking down essentially all restrictions against the manufacture and distribution of pornography that didn't involve children, the vast conservative resurgence in American politics might never have happened.

The essence of the modern Supreme Court's position is that the Constitution can be interpreted only in the light of reason. The "folk beliefs" of the American people cannot be taken as providing a context that gives meaning to its tenets; neither can the Christian religious faith of the overwhelming majority be allowed to color the interpretation of constitutional law.

Rising public opposition to this approach to social issues coupled with the remarkable revival of American evangelical religion and an upsurge in nationalist Jacksonian populism has led many observers to worry that the United States might be on the verge of a kind of populist theocracy: evangelicals and conservative Catholics would merge their religious fervor with an uncritical populist nationalism. This alliance would roll back half a century of Supreme Court decisions and substitute the dictatorship of revelation for the rule of reason.

This is unlikely. The anglican triangle is more stable than it looks. Structurally, one should note that tradition and revelation work effectively as a coalition only when reason is dominant. Popular nationalists and serious biblical Christians will work together to fight the prospect of hegemonic, secular reason that opposes both folk values and Christian orthodoxy. But as that threat diminishes, it becomes clearer to all concerned that American folk values are far from identical with the teachings of the Bible. American folk values favor a live-and-let-live approach to many social issues; Christianity as understood by both evangelicals and Catholics is much more intrusive in both sexual and economic matters. Already there is talk of an emerging split in the Republican Party between the religious right and the libertarians; this is the kind of political fault line that will become more prominent and more salient as the American gyroscope spins slightly farther away from reason.

To restate an important point I made earlier about anglican societies: votaries of reason, revelation, and tradition each believe that their favorite value holds the key to a vital society, but these societies are dynamic precisely because no one vision controls them. Each of the poles, left to its own devices, would set up an absolute system. In a religious system there would be a theocracy. In a traditionalist system there would be a conservative populism that fought social and economic change. A unipolar rational system would seek to remove decisions from the popular arena as much as possible lest the populace with its "irrational" and "backward" views should bridle at the necessary reforms and improvements. In a sense, it would look more and more like the EU on steroids: an elite-driven policy system that was more and more out of touch with public sentiment even as it labored ever more earnestly for what it conceives to be the general good. Worse, it would labor as earnestly for bad things as for good ones: had American progressives enjoyed undisputed power in the 1920s, they would have introduced racially biased programs of compulsory sterilization based on very defective definitions of mental unfitness and hereditary disease.

Such systems tend to end in a crash, and the crashes are not happy. Deprived of normal political outlets and normal political responsibilities, the forces of revelation and tradition are unlikely to disappear. Instead, they reemerge as dangerous and radical forms of illiberal populism.

One may regret some of the policies that result from the cultural and political rebalancing the United States is currently witnessing, but on the whole it is more likely that we are seeing a stage in the continuing dynamic westward journey of American society than that we will soon be turning back east.

Even as populist traditionalism and "hot" religion play a greater role, it is important to note that both the traditional and the religious aspects of American life are themselves part of the process by which American society adjusted to the rapid pace of change without disrupting society. They are one aspect of the more dynamic, more open society that enables America to keep its balance as it climbs faster and faster up steeper and more difficult terrain.

Moving Forward, Looking Back

One of the oddest characteristics of the Anglo-American world is the coexistence of rapid change with the signs and trappings of unchanging tradition. The British monarchy is perhaps the most obvious example. Queen Victoria's Britain was at the forefront of the Industrial Revolution, but Victoria herself sat on a throne as secure as that of Queen Anne. After 1852, the revolutionary laws that instituted free trade and broke up the remnants of the medieval guild and welfare systems were enacted not in an aggressively and self-consciously modern structure but in the Gothic Revival Parliament building. The ability to modernize without cutting society off from its deep roots is vital to the stability the English-speaking societies have maintained despite their dynamism. The resurgence of nonrational forces in American politics is an example of this system at work, and to see how dissent and disorder still enhance both stability and dynamism, it is useful to look at the white South, the demographic slice of American society that has been the basis and spearpoint of the contemporary revivals of tradition and religion.

This is a group in the United States that sees itself as staunchly and undeviatingly conservative in its religious and social values—an estimate that nonsoutherners and nonwhites in the South largely accept. White southerners continue by and large to stand for traditional values of family and home. They pride themselves on the respect they pay to their ancestors and the way they have preserved important traditional values that the rest of the country has lost.

Yet a careful look reveals a much more complex picture in which conservatism and tradition are harder to see. Take race. I am just old enough to remember the segregated South before the Civil Rights Act of 1963 and the Voting Rights Act of 1965 ushered in a new age. I can remember when the first African American child joined my fifth-grade class in elementary school. In Chapel Hill, North Carolina, home of the University of North Carolina—then and now viewed in the rest of the South as a Gomorrah of liberalism and corruption—African Americans were banned from eating at McDonald's or Howard Johnson's, and could attend only one of the town's two movie theaters; even there, they were forced to sit in the balcony. I can remember when drinking fountains and bathrooms were marked for use by "white" or "colored" and when everything in public and private life was strictly segregated, when Jim Crow racial roles were enforced by mob violence, and when interracial marriage was against the law.

Today all that is, as Scarlett O'Hara would have put it, gone with the wind. Not all the South's whites, and especially not those of the older generations, have buried these attitudes from the bad old days, and the legacy and consequences of racism, slavery, and segregation continue to disfigure southern politics and life. But in my lifetime, the white South has gone through revolutionary social changes that earlier generations of white southerners had resisted, violently and successfully, for centuries.

Moreover, when I was born in 1952, the Deep South was still predominantly rural. In my childhood, drivers still had to watch out for mule wagons on country roads. Few farm kids, white or black, finished high school. Most people still lived in the same counties, and sometimes on the same farms, where their ancestors had lived for generations. Atlanta, the South's largest and only true city at the time, was seen as an alien place, an outpost of Yankeedom infiltrating the rural South.

Today, the South is predominantly suburban. The population mix has also changed. For the first time since before the Civil War, immigrants from other countries make up a substantial share of the southern population. In my childhood, you could often count the number of "foreign" families in a small city on the fingers of one hand. North Carolina and Georgia are home to rapidly expanding Latin American and Asian populations. Hispanics accounted for 27.5 percent of North Carolina's population growth from 1990 through 2004.

The economy has been transformed. My mother grew up in South Carolina in the 1930s; she can clearly remember when her family first got electric power. I grew up in a landscape in which many families lived in unpainted shacks with no electricity or indoor plumbing; as a teenager recruiting kids for Project Head Start in rural North Carolina, I came across families whose children were clearly malnourished and had no shoes. In 1950, the South's per capita income was 69 percent of the North's. By 2001, the region as a whole had a per capita income of $26,531—87.1 percent of the national average.[1]

Other signs of social change abound. Prohibition was still alive in my childhood; even big-city restaurants could not serve alcohol to their customers, and many rural counties were "dry," with no liquor or beer legally sold within their boundaries. "Progressives" would from time to time challenge these restrictions; voters were still voting down referenda on loosening the liquor laws. This too is now gone with the wind. Towns that once banned all sales of liquor now often have gay and lesbian bars.

The political values of the white South have also changed. Most observers look at the shift of the white South from the Democrats to the Republicans and attribute that simply to the continuing conservatism, especially on racial and cultural matters, of the white voter. Many and perhaps most white southerners share this assessment. But the change in party identification has been accompanied by a profound and even revolutionary shift in social attitudes toward the market. The old southern Democratic Party was segregationist and states' rights; it was also populist and anticapitalist. Capitalism in the South of my childhood was still seen as something of a Yankee plot. The economic populism of William Jennings Bryan helped keep the South solidly behind him during his three losing runs for the White

House near the turn of the twentieth century; family farmers in the white South saw northern corporate interests like railroads as threats to their way of life. The white South was never fond of federal regulation, and never particularly sympathetic to the labor movement—but it was also deeply suspicious of big business.

Today's white southern Republicans are pro–free markets in a far more systematic and consistent way than their Democratic parents and grandparents ever were. Thomas Jefferson's suspicions of northern mercantile interests and Andrew Jackson's hatred for the Bank of the United States were the kind of values and beliefs that shaped the old Democratic Party. To hear white southerners like Newt Gingrich, Bill Frist, and George W. Bush hailing the successes of free-market competition, urging deregulation of the trucking and transportation industries, to say nothing of electric utilities, would shock and astonish their Democratic predecessors.

Theological change among southern conservatives has been equally rapid. The Southern Baptist Convention has formally apologized for the theological support it once gave segregation. The right-to-life movement may have a conservative agenda vis-à-vis abortion, but the Catholic-Protestant alliances it has created across the white South would have been inconceivable forty years ago. In those days most southern Protestants still saw the Catholic Church as an anti-Christian cult, the whore of Babylon. Away from Louisiana and outposts of northern presence like military bases, there were almost no Catholics in the South at the time; between 1970 and 2000, the Catholic population of North Carolina grew 357 percent.[2] Now, outside the precincts of Bob Jones University (one of the few places where the genuine traditions of the old white South linger on in something close to pure form), Catholics are just another part of God's family, and a Catholic-Evangelical dialogue is replacing the Catholic–mainstream Protestant dialogue as the most dynamic arena for ecumenical relations.

America is filled with radical revolutionaries who think they are religious conservatives. Interracial Baptist congregations holding joint prayer meetings with Catholics think of themselves as warriors of reaction fighting change on every front. Suburban entrepreneurs spend their weekends dressing up as Confederate soldiers to reenact Civil War battles—while embracing classically Yankee ideas and attitudes on everything from race to economics. And overall, the white South, still billing itself to itself as the nation's most conservative, most tradition-bound force, has put its full force and weight behind the kind of revolutionary capitalist transformation of the national economy and social compact that every previous generation of white southern leadership fought with all its might.

The contemporary religious revival in the United States still seems to be governed by the social logic that Adam Smith analyzed in *The Wealth of Nations*. In a meritocratic society where everyone from junior high school on up faces increasingly stringent requirements, whether to get into a good college, to get a job, or to build and maintain a career, the abundance of temptations and opportunities that our consumer society provides can be fatally disruptive. Adolescents are constantly exposed to sexually explicit material, and to a culture which values rebellion, consumption, and sexual exploration. Adults have leisure and consumption possibilities that dwarf many of the temptations that ever enticed Roman emperors. Some Americans are wealthy or well connected enough to be able to indulge regularly in these pleasures without any significant impact on their careers or their well-being. Others, the large majority, live much narrower lives.

That majority simply cannot afford to yield to the temptations that surround it on every hand. Yet it does not live in small, rooted communities where the close observation of friends and an extended family can enforce conformity to any code of conduct. Most Americans live in suburbs; they often do not know their neighbors well. In any case, their lives are divided and compartmentalized. More often than not, their work colleagues do not live in their neighborhood; their neighbors do not work for the same company.

These are the kind of conditions Adam Smith identified as leading the Britons of his day to join intense religious fellowships. Only the combination of a strong religious belief with a strict moral code can create the inner psychological strength to lead a moral life in the face of so many temptations; only close fellowship with an intense and personal community of fellow believers can provide the support, encouragement, and accountability that sustains this kind of life. That Americans need and therefore seek to create such communities of belief for themselves and for their children is hardly surprising; centuries of experience with strong religion in the Anglo-American world should teach us that, far from being dangerous, such behavior will strengthen the basis of our society and enable it to meet new challenges ahead.

The American gyroscope may have spun away from the reason leg of the anglican triangle and moved over toward the tradition and revelation corner of its historical range; it has not, however, slowed down or tipped over. It is spinning faster than ever.

Part Four

What Hath God Wrought?

Sixteen • The Meaning of History

U p until this point, we have looked at the first three questions posed in the introduction. We have identified a distinctive Anglo-Saxon political and moral culture, looked at the economic and geopolitical strategies by which they prevailed in the long wars with various rivals to set up a global system in the last three hundred years, and examined the cultural and religious affinities with capitalism that kept first Britain and then the United States at the front of the pack for so long.

Now it is time for a shift. We have considered the "what" of Anglo-American power; it is now time to ask the "so-what" questions. We have looked at what the Anglo-Saxon powers did and how they did it; the next step is to ask what if anything their victory means for the history of the world. Are the British and American versions of the maritime system just two more examples of pointless great empires that strut their hour on the stage and are quickly forgotten—or did they actually serve some purpose beyond increasing the power and wealth of their leaders?

Anglo-American politicians and intellectuals have frequently put forward the idea that the purpose of the Anglo-Saxon ascendancy is to usher in a peaceful, liberal, and prosperous world order. The League of Nations, the United Nations, the first President Bush's proclamation of a "New World Order" after the fall of the Soviet Union: these are all examples of attempts, primarily though not exclusively proposed and brought into being by Anglo-American governments, of efforts to create the institutional basis for the peaceful and liberal world the English-speakers seek.

Yet if the history of the last hundred years teaches one lesson it is that the Anglo-Americans consistently underestimate the difficulty of establishing the global democratic and capitalist peace that they want. Whether one looks at Woodrow Wilson trying to convert World War I into the "war to end war" or at Paul Wolfowitz and Tony Blair trying to install democracy in Iraq through the overthrow of Saddam Hussein, the liberal utopia continues to elude us.

On the face of things, it appears rather unlikely that several thousand years of incessant despotism and war should come to an end anytime soon. And the Christian doctrine of original sin, which places the origin of humanity's troubles and conflicts in human nature itself rather than in bad institutions or poor economic performance, also seems to militate against an easy confidence in the imminent triumph of justice and peace. If we add not only that Anglo-Saxon political leadership has failed over and over to usher in Tennyson's parliament of man in the last one hundred years, but that the failures have been costly and expensive, a real mystery appears.

Why has something so inherently improbable as the end to tyranny and war looked so achievable to so many Anglo-American statesmen and opinion leaders in modern times? More than that, how is it that the Anglo-American world has been pragmatic and even ruthless enough to prevail over so many enemies in armed combat while a strong streak of utopian optimism remains such a powerful element in conventional Anglo-American thought?

The Walrus and the Carpenter have visited many beaches over the years, and eaten a great many oysters. Why after all this time are they still so intent on getting enough maids and enough mops to perform a task that common sense suggests can never be achieved?

Waspophobes often conclude that the zeal of men like Woodrow Wilson, Franklin Roosevelt, and Tony Blair (and George W. Bush, for that matter) to build a better world is a hypocritical mask. After all, the beaches never quite get swept, and the oysters keep on disappearing.

But that is too simple. The ever-recurring belief that the world is about to become a much better place is deeply rooted in Anglo-American culture. This optimism about the world is closely related to the positive view of change that has made such great contributions to Anglo-American success.

In this section of the book, I am going to look into the connection between the driving forces of Anglo-American culture and the bouts of optimism that, despite every discouragement and even disaster, keep springing up in our politics. The fifth and final section of the book will press these questions further, asking just why it is that the hopes of the Anglo-Saxons are so frequently frustrated. Finally, we will try to reach some kind of judgment about the meaning of the maritime system for the history of the world.

Looking at these questions is going to lead us into the roots of Anglo-American ideology. We are going to have to engage with what are known as the "grand narratives" of world history, the frameworks that give the context and background for particular events. These narratives shape the discussion of such nebulous but vital ideas as "the meaning of history," and they provide the context that enables us to understand, for example, what Oliver Cromwell and Ronald Reagan meant when they claimed that God was on their side. The way that Americans construct and interpret the grand narratives of Western and contemporary history that ultimately explains why so many of them, including those with no personal religious belief whatever, believe that God—or, for the atheists and agnostics among us, the Force—is with the Anglo-Saxon world.

Postmodernists like to believe that we live in an age when the grand narratives have "collapsed" and no single story line can capture the complexity of contemporary life. The postmodernists are partly right but largely wrong. Not too long ago, most European and American intellectuals lived in a mental world where there was just one grand narrative alive: the narrative of progress. This very encouraging narrative comes to us from the Western Enlightenment and it describes world history as the story of steady improvement based on the spread of rational, scientific thought. That narrative survives, but it no longer convinces in quite the way it used to. Today it has competition. A resurgent Islam, making itself known in European life and international politics, proposes its own grand narrative of the world's gradual conversion to the faith of the Prophet. Evangelical Christians and political conservatives in the United States have also turned their back on key Enlightenment ideas. Toxic and atavistic nationalism seems on the rise in parts of Europe, even as elements of the basic grand compromise of social democratic society are coming under increasing pressure due to global economic competition.

"Modernity" is the name for the period in history when the Enlightenment narrative of rationalist progress was the most powerful or, as many put it, the "hegemonic" intellectual force in Western life. Postmodernists are right to say that by this measure we now live in a postmodern world.

But those who say that we live in an era when all grand narratives have collapsed could not be more wrong. The grand narrative of Islam, for example, has not collapsed. Neither has the grand narrative of Pentecostal Christianity, the fastest growing religious movement in the history of the world, a movement that has gained something like half a billion followers since it broke out in Los Angeles in 1906. And if the progressive narrative of the modern enlightenment now has more competition, it is far from collapse. As a historical force, it continues to have prestige and power.

We are not in an age of collapsing grand narratives. We are in an age of competing grand narratives, and in many ways they are becoming more energetic and compelling as they react against one another in a global culture that brings them side by side.

Forces greater and more powerful than the will of any single person, and perhaps even more powerful than the wills of any combination of people, are moving through society. But billions of human beings perceive these changes as part of a narrative that extends back into the misty prehistoric past and forward to some unimaginable climax in the future. Those perceptions may be false, but true or false, they are a real force that exerts real power in world events. These stories *deserve* to be called grand or even master narratives; they reflect powers greater than those of individual or collective human wills, and they present themselves to us as givens. As individuals and even as whole national societies we do not simply shape them; they shape our times, our methods of perceiving reality, and therefore, to a significant if ultimately immeasurable degree, they shape our very selves.

The way that most Americans interpret these narratives has enormous implications in virtually every area of American politics, culture, and policy.

The oldest of these master narratives is the Abrahamic story: the spread and development of Abrahamic ideology from the ancient Middle East until today, when it covers virtually the entire world, and of the rise of its daughter religions and philosophical systems. Goethe once wrote that color is the deeds and the sufferings of light; in a very profound way, history can be called the deeds and the sufferings of the vast and quarrelsome family of Abraham.

The younger of the two narratives, and an extremely dynamic one, is the rise of capitalism. From very small beginnings, this social system has spread itself rapidly across the world, transformed cultures and social relations on every continent, and continues today—as what is often called globalization—to generate a cascade of social, technological, economic, cultural, and political revolutions in every dimension of life on every part of our planet.

These master narratives are social phenomena, but they have the force of natural events. There are many ways to describe and analyze them, and many ways to evaluate them, but there is no way to escape them. These two narratives, and the ways in which they affect one another, inevitably form the framework for questions about the meaning of American power in world history. American society is not only shaped by these narratives; the American story is a part of these unfolding narratives, and when we discuss the historical meaning of America's world role, we are essentially discussing how the American story fits the larger stories of the two master narratives.

To ask questions about "the meaning of history" it is necessary first to enter the world of Abrahamic religion and ideology.

The Father of History

History as we know it began about three or four thousand years ago when, according to the spotty and incomplete records that survive, a wandering herdsman named Abram heard what he believed to be a call from God.

As the King James Bible translates the passage, God told Abram to "[g]et thee out of thy country, and from thy kindred, and from thy father's house, unto a land that I will shew thee: And I will make of thee a great nation, and I will bless thee, and make thy name great; and thou shalt be a blessing: And I will bless them that bless thee, and curse him that curseth thee: and in thee shall all families of the earth be blessed."[1]

Later, God repeated and extended the blessing. "I will multiply thy seed as the stars of the heaven, and as the sand which [is] upon the sea shore; and thy seed shall possess the gate of his enemies; And in thy seed shall all the nations of the earth be blessed."[2]

Many scholars tell us today that this never happened or, rather, that the stories of Abraham, as Abram became known, assumed final written shape so much later than the events they describe that we can say little or nothing about the historical Abraham. Still, it would be a great mistake to think that therefore the story is pointless.

The stories about Abraham may have been pulled together at a later date, they may reflect ideas that were widely distributed at the time, and they may conflate accounts from different sources, but *somebody* in the ancient Middle East first believed that the life of his or her people was shaped by a call of God. Possibly that somebody or one of his or her followers collected scattered stories and rewrote them to express his or her intuition about the meaning of the history of his or her people. We may say with the historical critics and archeologists that it was this anonymous storyteller rather than a historical Abraham who was the founder of the Abrahamic religious tradition, and that may well be correct. But for billions of Abraham's heirs, the sacred story isn't "proven" by the antiquity of the manuscripts in which it is written, but rather by the way the fulfillment of God's promise to Abraham has dominated the history of the subsequent millennia. *Something* happened in the Middle East that has reshaped the way people think, act, hope, believe, and pray in every corner of the earth. *Some* event involving the conversion to Abrahamic monotheism by *some* group of Semites set off a series of transformations, conversions, revelations, and conflicts whose reverberations and consequences are still unfolding in our own day and dominating our times. After all, the civilizations of half the world owe their primary ideological foundations to the revolutionary idea of a single all-powerful God determined to intervene in human history, to judge every human soul, and to establish His perfect kingdom among us.

Whether we owe the monotheistic religious tradition to Abraham or to another Middle Eastern prophet of the same name, roughly half the world's population today believes that God's promise to him is the great lever of history—and the proportion of believers is growing. More than two billion Christians and more than one billion Muslims trace the origin of their faith to the desert patriarch. Add millions more Jews and members of the Bahai faith to that total, as well as uncounted millions who belong to syncretistic African, Asian, and Afro-Caribbean religions that give Abraham a special place in world history, and it is clear that more lives have been touched by the Abrahamic tradition than by any other. Sometime in the twenty-first century, conscious "Abrahamists" may come to constitute two-thirds of the human race. Unconscious Abrahamists—those whose mental and political worlds are shaped in an Abrahamic context without the influence of a conscious religious belief—make up a significant proportion of those who remain. These developments would be astonishing if there really was a historical Abraham; they are nothing short of miraculous if there wasn't.

At its simplest, the very complex Abrahamic master narrative is the story of the rise of monotheistic religions whose origins can be traced to this time-enshrouded Mesopotamian nomad. The first Abrahamists were, of course, the Jews. Abraham was first known as the ancestor of the Hebrew tribes through his son Isaac, and the Jewish scriptures recount the story of a people's encounter with Abraham's God. In the millennia since the formation of the Jewish people, their wanderings, struggles, return to their ancestral home, and above all their survival remain a distinct and unique element of the Abrahamic narrative. Apart from the significance of Jewish experience to Jews, the survival of the Jews into modern times serves for billions of non-Jews as a kind of historical proof that the God of Abraham is powerful and real. God told Abraham that he would have descendants who would remember his name—and lo! there they are. That this unique people, returning almost miraculously against all probability to the land God promised Abraham would support his descendants, is a kind of bone in the throat of the world—a people and a state that can neither be spat out nor swallowed, unable to find rest at "home" or in exile—only further shows billions of Abrahamic believers just how powerful the narrative (or the God) remains after all these millennia. That world history remains convulsed by the struggles of the Jews to make a home, and that their ethical and military successes and failures reverberate to the ends of the earth, further reinforces the most powerful cultural force that human beings know.

It is not, of course, just the Jews. When the apostle Paul made the decision to take the gospel of Christ to the Gentiles, he assured them that, through faith, they also would become children of Abraham. In the two thousand years that have passed, the growth of the Christian religion from an obscure Levantine sect into the largest community of believers in human history serves as yet another marker of the unique importance and power of the Abrahamic stories.

When the Prophet Mohammed called the Arabs to a pure faith in the One God, he too placed himself in the line of Abraham. Reminding the Arabs that tradition made Ishmael, Abraham's eldest son, the ancestor of the Arab peoples, Mohammed proposed the Koran as a return to God's pure revelation to Abraham. The Koran teaches that Abraham lived in Mecca and sacrificed at the Ka'aba; and the steps of Muslim pilgrims today on the hajj retrace the anxious wanderings of Hagar, Ishmael's mother. The faith of the Prophet serves as yet another sign of the unique power and appeal of Abrahamic monotheism.

Each of these faiths has awesome and horrifying stories to tell. The sons and daughters of Abraham have swept through the world since Moses led the Israelites out of Egypt—sometimes with fire and sword, sometimes with gentle persuasion, sometimes with a mix. Divided as Abrahamists are, most of them would agree that the unrivaled spread of Abrahamic religion proves that the God of Abraham is the true author of history. The merchants who brought Islam to Java; the missionaries who braved the febrile swamps of central Africa; the faithful rabbis who preserved Jewish learning and faith in the face of persecution and injustice; the monks and scribes who copied the holy books until the invention of printing; the travelers and scholars who collected and assessed the sayings and traditions ascribed to their prophet; the Jesuits who penetrated the inhospitable Canadian wilderness to bring the good news to the Micmacs and the Iroquois; the warriors who brought their respective faiths to the freezing Baltic coasts and the steaming banks of the Niger; the faithful and long-suffering wives who brought their royal husbands and sons to the faith among the forests of the north and the caravans of the east; the circuit-riding evangelists who brought the Wesleyan gospel to the Kentucky frontier; the Jewish, Christian, and Muslim martyrs who set their own lives at naught and held fast to the faiths they professed against torture and death: these heroes and heroines of faith transmitted and enriched the Abrahamic traditions they had received, and in the course of their deeds and their trials, and sometimes their crimes, they made the history of our world.

Millions of people each year convert to one or another of the great missionary religions. In 1900, 10 percent of Africa's 100 million people were Christians. By 2005, there were an estimated 389 million Christians out of the continent's population of roughly 900 million. At current growth rates, the Christian population will double within thirty years. The population of Muslims is also increasing; the total of Muslims worldwide has risen from 200 million to 1.3 billion since 1900.[3]

The expansion of Abrahamic religion considered as a single entity constitutes one level of the master narrative; the history of conflicts between the divided branches of the patriarch's household forms another. In much of the world the strife between branches of the Abrahamic family is a driving force in politics. According to the book of Genesis, the family of Abraham has been divided since Hagar and Ishmael were driven into the desert while Isaac grew up with Sarah in the tents of his father. Long before the birth of Christ, Samaritans and Jews argued the finer points of Abrahamic theology while Hellenized and non-Hellenized Jews debated, sometimes in bloody civil strife, how far Jews could go to participate in the culture of the wider world. Today's divisions among Jews between Orthodox and non-Orthodox, Hasidim and non-Hasidim, are business as usual for the oldest Abrahamists. Christianity's division into Orthodox, Catholic, and Protestant branches, with proliferating sub-branches shooting forth all the time, follows the same path. So, too, do the divisions tormenting Islam, which early on divided into Shi'a and Sunni wings and is convulsed today under the impact of theological and political strife.

Wars of religion are largely an Abrahamic trait, found among the Abrahamic peoples and, in self-defense, among their neighbors. Unless attacked—as India's Hindus were by Muslims—the non-Abrahamic faiths have been more pacific. Peoples with non-Abrahamic faiths fight for cows or slaves or grain or land or gold, but only rarely have they fought to compel nonbelievers to worship their gods. The Greeks and the Romans didn't fight over whether to call the father of the gods Zeus or Jupiter; they deplored but did not generally resist the spread of Eastern mystery cults through the Mediterranean world. Japanese history has not been shaped by violent, recurring struggles between different branches of Shinto; Reform and Orthodox Confucians have not made the gutters of China run red. The followers of Hanuman do not lie in wait to murder the sons of Vishnu in India. The Aztecs may have had a bloody religion, but the Native American peoples were generally content to let each people worship the Great Spirit in its own way. There have been clashes and persecutions among non-Abrahamic faiths, but such clashes generally appear as exceptions to a peaceful rule; interconfessional conflict is much more characteristic of the Abrahamists.

The children of Abraham quarrel over many things, but their areas of agreement are anything but trivial. Indeed, they quarrel *because* they agree. It is precisely because Jerusalem is a holy city to three Abrahamic religions that blood has so frequently and in such large quantities coursed through its streets. Abrahamic religion in virtually all its variety holds that history has a shape and a purpose: a beginning, a middle, and an end. Truth is universal: there is one truth and it is true everywhere and for everyone. The Abrahamic faiths all hold that there is a supreme moral order and that it is the duty of political institutions and individual human beings to reflect it. Yet they disagree over what exactly the supreme moral order is, and over what institutions and practices can establish it on earth. Whether the opposition comes from within the same religion—as between Orthodox and modernist Jews in contemporary Israel, between Sunni and Shi'a Muslims in Saudi Arabia and Iraq, or between liberal Congregationalists and conservative Southern Baptists in the United States today—or whether the conflict emerges between religions as in Nigeria and the Balkans, these disagreements have profound political consequences.

Neither the spread of Abrahamic faith nor the wars between members of rival Abrahamic traditions has come to an end. The history of the twenty-first century, like the history of so many preceding centuries, will be shaped in large part by the expansion of these quarrelling religions into new geographical zones, and by the conflicts this expansion engenders. Postmodernists can deny or deconstruct this extraordinary narrative, but it makes no difference to the narrative. It goes on all the same, shaping the world the postmodernists live in.

The Abrahamic narrative is about more than expansion and strife. Abrahamic monotheism and its offshoots have furthered intellectual and spiritual changes in human society. Important though the religious consequences of the Abrahamic revolution are, its intellectual and political consequences must also be taken into account. The idea that a single god created the entire universe and endowed human beings with the ability to understand and a mission to shape the world that we live in lies behind much ancient and most modern science. The concept of ideology—of a coherent worldview that attempts to find rational and causal connections that make human social existence comprehensible and that guides our views on how to act—also has its roots in the Abrahamic view of the world.

Islam, Christianity, and Judaism all believe that human beings can at least partially grasp the nature of the universe and, because the world is seen as the creation of a single and rational entity, that the normal course of natural events is subject to laws which can in principle be understood and ultimately predicted by human beings. Science and mathematics have flourished in non-Abrahamic as well as Abrahamic cultures, but the flowering of Western science in early modern Europe, which became the principal foundation of the scientific revolutions now sweeping the world, was clearly rooted in and related to the intellectual foundations of the Abrahamic tradition. The Inquisition may have persecuted early scientists, and the clergy opposed important ideas they considered dangerous to them, but the cultural and mental background that allowed the scientists to defy and overcome this resistance was as much a product of Abrahamic tradition as was the rigidity of the Church.

Our idea of history—the idea that the human story is a process with a purpose—is another idea that comes to us from the Abrahamic tradition. In common speech we often use "history" as a synonym for "events"; to say that France has a history means simply that France has been around for a while and things have happened there. When many people first heard the title of Francis Fukuyama's book *The End of History and the Last Man,* they assumed it was this kind of history which Fukuyama said was over, and they found his position meaningless, incomprehensible, and absurd. How could history—that is, the succession of events—be at an end? That could happen only if everyone and everything were dead, in which case there could be no books on the topic and no discussion.

This was not, of course, what Fukuyama meant. He was referring to Abrahamic history—history as the name for a period in the human story in which certain problems need to be solved. History in this sense is not synonymous with the full term of human existence. History is a period and a process through which humanity solves (or is given a solution to) certain sets of problems before moving on to the next and higher stage in its existence.

Even in everyday speech we pay lip service to this idea, distinguishing between prehistorical times (before people were civilized enough to write) and history—the story of what people did once they became organized enough to write and keep records of passing events. Posthistory is simply the next stage, when human civilization passes through changes as profound and fundamental as the invention of writing or the development of agricul-ture—or as the original call of Abraham. Thinkers like Fukuyama who speculate on the end of history are asking what the goal of the historical process is, and then looking around to see if we have reached it yet.

It is hard to overstate the importance of this idea of history to Abrahamic religion and ideology. Abrahamic religions and political movements largely define themselves by their interpretations of the meaning of history, and their approaches share a common structure. From the biblical narratives to the present day, Abrahamic cultures largely see the human story as consist-ing of three stages: prehistory, history, and posthistory.

The standard Christian story begins on a high note: the creation of the world and the placement of Adam and Eve in the prehistorical Garden of Eden. Then comes the Fall—a decline into savagery and barbarity as human crimes multiplied and ill-equipped, ignorant human beings scratched a skimpy living from the reluctant earth. For Christians, this story says that the origin of history was the Fall. Naming animals and communing with God in the garden was prehistory; scratching in fields and building cities takes us into history.

Up to this point, the trajectory of the human story has been downward. But instead of abandoning Adam, Eve, and their descendants to the conse-quences of their shortcomings, God acts to put the world back on track. He reaches out—to Noah, to Abraham, to Moses and the prophets. He builds a people for himself—the ancient Hebrews, descendants of Abraham and the ancestors of the Jews of today—and makes His will known primarily to this people, but also sends hints and intimations of His existence and His desires to all the peoples of the earth. He completes this process with the full revela-tion of His nature and plan, Christians believe, in the person, teaching, and work of Jesus of Nazareth.

In the classic Christian view, history is the record of God's action on fallen humanity. Its purpose is redemption: the return of humanity to its proper state of communion with God. As such, history divides into stages. There are the two big ones: before and after Christ, as signaled in the Chris-tian calendar's division of history into B.C. and A.D. There are also smaller subdivisions in both halves of history as the divine plan unfolds. In this view, history is not an eternal process; Christ will return to earth at some point in the future according to Christian teaching and institute the King-dom of God. That will be the end of history.

History in this view is not just the passage of time. It is the accomplish-ment of a task. Something is wrong with the world; the world has been wounded. History is the process by which what is wrong is set right, what is broken is mended. History may look chaotic and meaningless, but every-thing that happens is ultimately part of the healing process, and its culmina-tion will come with the establishment of a new world without the evil and suffering of our current existence.

While there are, of course, many important differences, in outline the Jewish and Islamic views of history are structurally very similar to the Christian plan. Both see history as a process of God's progressive self-manifestation to human beings that climaxes with a definitive revelation (on Mount Sinai to Moses and the Israelites for Orthodox Jews, with the revela-tion of the Holy Koran to the Prophet Mohammed for Muslims) and ends with a definitive act of God, still in the future, that brings history to an end by establishing God's perfect society among human beings once and for all. The three religious offspring of Abraham quarrel bitterly and frequently violently about the details, but they agree that this is the basic story that reveals the nature and the meaning of human life.

The rise of Abrahamic religion means that these ideas, too, are shaping the consciousness of more and more people in the twenty-first century of the Christian era.

The Fourth Faith

There is one more factor to take into account. Judaism, Christianity, and Islam may currently number half the world's population among their adher-ents, but this statistic, impressive as it is, does not do full justice to the unfolding importance of the ongoing Abrahamic revolution in human affairs. This revolution has not only produced religions whose vigor seems to increase through the millennia; it produces revolutionary secular ideolo-gies that have also swept the world and changed the way billions of people live and believe.

Secular modernism is the youngest member of the family of Abraham. It downplays or eliminates the idea of a personal God, but otherwise it faith-fully reproduces the most important pieces of the Abrahamic paradigm. Like Jews, Christians, and Muslims, modernists have moral values that they believe are universally valid and should be established around the world. They see history as a process that passes through the old Abrahamic stages. They believe in a prehistorical period of primeval innocence or ignorance, a process of moral and political struggle through which the truth is gradually

discovered and proclaimed, and finally they believe that the truth will triumph worldwide when history comes to a victorious close.

Believers in the fourth faith don't always like to be called believers. They
argue that unlike the superstitious and emotionally driven convictions of
religious believers, the fourth faith is based in the clear light of science and
reason. The laws of history are known and unshakable, said the Marxist-
Leninists, who believed that they had unlocked the secrets of the historical
process and discovered an infallible method for creating utopia. Human
nature is fixed and known, said the Hegelians, who have confidently proclaimed the end of history for two hundred years. Democracies don't go to
war with one another, liberal and neoconservative political scientists confidently asserted in the 1990s.

My point is not that members of the fourth faith are not as good as they
think at charting the path to utopia. After all, Christians, Muslims, and Jews
have more than once been deceived about where history is headed. My point
is that the fourth faith, like the first three, fits the definition of faith given in
the Epistle to the Hebrews in the New Testament: "Now faith is the substance of things hoped for, the evidence of things not seen." Experience,
evidence, reason, and other motives incline some to be communists, some to
be liberal Whigs, some to be progressives or socialists, in much the same
way that the same things lead others to become or to remain Jews, Christians,
and Muslims. All four faiths provide explanations of things that are seen and
known, as well as predictions concerning things that are not yet seen.

Like the three older faiths, the fourth faith has produced its share of
heroes and martyrs. Millions of women and men have suffered and died
for political beliefs they regarded as essential to fulfill human destiny. Like
the Catholic and Protestant heroes of the Reformation, communists and the
others have figured as both villains and martyrs in the holy wars of the
fourth faith. To create a future world of perfect justice and freedom that no
one has ever seen, and that can be envisioned only through faith, millions
have been slaughtered—and hundreds of thousands have gladly done the
slaughtering. The freedoms of liberal society also have their martyrs: men
and women without any theistic convictions whatever who have lived and
died for their version of political faith.

As much as any Grand Inquisitor, most devotees of the new faith believe
that their own particular version of it is the one sure way, and that history
will culminate in the triumph of the true faith. "We will bury you," Soviet
premier Nikita Khrushchev told America. "At the name of Jesus every knee
shall bow," sing the Christians. The various members of the newest branch
of Abraham's growing family may downplay or even scrap altogether the

role that God plays in this story, but they adopt the core structure of the Abrahamic idea of history to tell their own stories of the world. While some modernists see history as an open-ended sequence with no pre-scripted determination, many modernists continue to see history as the process of overcoming a problem and to assign responsibility for the forward movement of history to laws of development that are independent of the free will of individual human beings. Some modernists, like secular twelve-steppers, acknowledge a "higher power" based on natural law or human nature that shapes history even as they reject many features of traditional theism.

Modernists generally do not spend much time thinking about the history of the great world religions, Abrahamic or otherwise. The central concern for modernists is the second of the master narratives that shape the contemporary world: the story of capitalism. The various attitudes that the four faiths of Abraham and their many sects and denominations take toward that second grand narrative shapes the way both the friends and the enemies of the Anglo-Saxon powers regard the rise of the United States and its social and economic system to world power.

Seventeen • War on History

ometimes the biggest facts are the hardest to describe. The last several centuries have seen an unprecedented flowering of human knowledge. The rise of the scientific method; the development of new forms of storing and communicating knowledge, from the printing press to the Internet; the enhanced productivity of human labor as more powerful and more sophisticated machines add strength and precision to rude muscle power; new forms of social and political organization that enable new kinds of cooperation on a wider and wider scale; the creation of global markets and global networks; the tripling of life expectancies in the advanced societies; the population explosion; all these things have worked interactively to touch the lives of almost all people, and to revolutionize the way a large and growing minority of our species lives.

This explosive and ongoing revelation of the creative (and destructive) powers of the human race is unique in the life of what is still, biologically speaking, a very young species. Nothing in humanity's past prepared it for change this dramatic in so many fields over such extended periods of time.

We don't really have a word for this phenomenon. It is too big, too multifaceted, too much a part of the background of our lives. People speak of globalization today as a way of summing up the changes sweeping through the contemporary world. They use words like "development" and "modernization" to describe different aspects of the process over time. But these words evoke only parts of this process that is so profoundly altering human life.

This many-sided flowering of human potential is the other master narrative of our time. In some ways it is older even than the Abrahamic narrative. For longer than written history, human beings have been adding to their ability to understand and control the natural world, and they have been making their social world richer and more meaningful through literature, religion, culture, humor, and art.

But until relatively recently, change was slow. Since the European Middle Ages, the changes have been perceptibly deepening and accelerating. Today we reel at the speed of globalization and long for the placid, pastoral times of, say, Edwardian Britain in the years before World War I. Yet people living in those times did not think that their lives were placid or that the pace of change was slow. As suffragettes chained themselves to the fence around the House of Commons, as Lloyd George took on the House of Lords, while revolution brewed in Ireland and the ominous German naval buildup relentlessly continued across the Channel, the Edwardians longed for the pastoral, peaceful days of an earlier time—when the pace of change was slower and society was more stable. They might long for the peaceful tranquillity of Jane Austen's England—forgetting that Austen wrote during the Napoleonic Wars, when the world seemed on fire to those who lived in it.

The story of this wave of accelerating change is the second master narrative that shapes our world today. We can dispute what drives this historical tsunami; we can disagree about where it started, what it means, what to call it, and why it works. What we cannot sensibly do is deny that the phenomenon is both real and important.

The most powerful way to describe this still-developing phenomenon comes from the work of Karl Marx. He coined the term "capitalism" to describe a social system that was built on change. Marx was a materialist and an economic determinist. He called the new social system capitalism because he saw an economic dynamic driving the whole thing. But if his basic theoretical model was somewhat one-dimensional, his vision of the world was extremely complex—and in many respects it still describes our world today.

The *Communist Manifesto,* written by Marx and Friedrich Engels in 1849, offers the best available description of the new world. In a justly famous and frequently quoted section, they observe that in the new, capitalist world,

> [a]ll that is solid melts into air, all that is holy is profaned . . . All old-established national industries have been destroyed or are daily being destroyed. They are dislodged by new industries . . . that no longer work up indigenous raw material, but raw material drawn from the remotest zones; industries whose products are consumed, not only at home, but in every quarter of the globe.

Capitalism "draws all, even the most barbarian, nations into civilization . . . It compels all nations, on pain of extinction, to adopt the bourgeois mode of production [capitalism]; it compels them to introduce what it calls civilization into their midst . . . In one word, it creates a world after its own image."

The story of capitalism in this Marxian sense of a range of political, social, cultural, economic, and technological changes felt both locally and globally is the grand narrative of modern times. Whether they are Jewish, Muslim, Christian, or modernist, Abrahamic thinkers have tried to fashion ideological explanations that incorporate the rise of capitalism into Abrahamic history. American power, like British power before it, is deeply intertwined with the rise of capitalism; in the United States and abroad, the different ideological approaches to the phenomenon of capitalism in the light of Abrahamic history help shape the expectations people have of American power and the assessment they make of it. The discussion of the meaning (if any) of the rise of the capitalism-loving, capitalism-promoting maritime systems of the British and the Americans to world power is for most people finally a discussion about the role of capitalism in Abrahamic history.

Many scholars believe that what we now know as capitalism emerged in the world of the Italian city-states in the fourteenth and fifteenth centuries. As the effects of early capitalism spread through Europe, it became clear to many people that the rhythm of history was changing. The social, political, religious, economic, and cultural atmosphere had changed—and in ways that seemed like improvements. Whether it was voyages of discovery that brought new continents and civilizations into common knowledge; revolutionary inventions like the printing press that changed the rules in business, politics, religion, and law; mathematical discoveries that changed everything from accounting to theories of the universe; or the technological discoveries that brought rapid changes to whole economic and geographical sectors, observant people saw that human life was changing.

These changes took place in a culture that was deeply immersed in the intellectual habits of Abrahamic history. Reflection on the meaning of capitalism would ultimately create new kinds of Abrahamic worldviews as people interpreted the new master narrative using conceptual tools drawn from the old one.

The humanists, as they called themselves, saw the fall of Greco-Roman civilization as a kind of secular analog for the fall of Adam and Eve. The Middle Ages of ignorance and decay were a period of darkness and chaos like human history before God revealed the true religion. The rebirth of reason and humane letters, the humanists modestly suggested, was analogous to the redemption of man—the term "Renaissance" means rebirth; society was "born again" when the humanists reconnected with classical antiquity.

This born-again experience was the origin of the modern, the sense that the contemporary world was a different place from the world of even the recent past. The vision of two historical peaks—classical antiquity and Renaissance Europe—separated by the dark chasm of the Middle Ages gave rise to the idea of modern times, and reflections on the meaning of modernity generally are attempts to interpret the meaning of this historical process.

The striking thing here is that to a very large extent, the Abrahamic and capitalist narratives seem to have an affinity for each other. The intellectual and spiritual background of Abrahamic thought provides a framework for interpreting and assimilating the consequences of capitalist change. In a real sense, the second narrative reinforces the first. In many traditional, pre-capitalist societies, history was something of an abstraction. When human beings saw relatively little social change in their lives, the idea of Abrahamic big-picture history seemed distant and remote. The beginning of the world was lost in the mists of time; the divine intervention that would bring the world to an end involved dramatic events wrapped in mystery and the supernatural that were unimaginably distant from the daily concerns of most human beings.

The arrival of capitalism changed that. History became a real presence in human lives. It is not just that events and technology move faster. History moves deeper and affects more lives. In the premodern world, if a dynasty rose or fell in a far distant capital, it meant very little to the peasants who toiled in the fields and paid their taxes regardless of who sat on the throne.

There was the life of the individual, played out against the background of natural forces—the alternation of the seasons, the passing of time. "History" was really sacred history, something that had as little to do with daily life as other mysterious dogmas of religion. In Christian, premodern Europe, history was painted on church walls or portrayed in stained-glass windows. A handful of theologians and intellectuals might concern themselves with relating the great themes of sacred history to the details of secular politics, but these concerns were rarely felt by "society at large"—an entity which in any case scarcely existed before printing and mass literacy combined to create a mass public opinion that could recognize itself and feel itself affected as a mass by political events.

It is not just that capitalism makes history more palpable, and therefore makes Abrahamic religion or ideology more credible and salient in societies that are already Abrahamic. In much of the world, the arrival of capitalism led directly to the triumph of Abrahamic ideas. Marxism triumphed in so much of developing Asia and Africa because it provided a framework by which people could understand the sudden eruptions of new forces and relations that were destroying old patterns and introducing rapid, destabilizing, and often very unwelcome change.

Despite failures and setbacks, in its various forms modernism has carried the basic Abrahamic concepts of history and ideology around the world; even in countries where the impact of Abrahamic religion remains limited, the impact of modernism is increasingly reshaping preexisting ideas and values along Abrahamic lines.

Enabled by capitalism, the triumph of Abrahamic thought has no parallel in recorded human experience; no other movement has changed the world so deeply on such a broad scale. Varieties of Abrahamism rise and fall: Christianity, liberal democracy, and Islam today are surging in much of the world, while communism is only a shadow of its former self. Nevertheless, the trend of millennia continues, and has radically and dramatically accelerated in the last three centuries. We live in a world that is being continually transformed by the Abrahamic monotheisms and their secular siblings.

Like the stars in the skies your descendants will be numbered, God promised Abraham. Certainly, Abraham can claim as much as McDonald's: "Billions and billions served."

Modern History

The great Abrahamic dispensations quickly split into quarreling sects and subsects. Modernism is no exception. Moreover, the divisions among the modernists work in much the same way as those among the other tribes; differences that look clear and distinct from a distance can look much fuzzier close up.

The largest group of modernists share what we can call the progressive faith. Progressives believe that mankind is—or can be—the master of history. The laws of history are things we can deduce and understand. Having understood these laws, we can and should act to shape the future.

The distinct mark of progressive ideology is the idea that history is shaped by laws like the laws of nature. This replaces the theological idea that history is shaped by the will and purposes of God. This does not mean that all modernists or even all progressives are atheists. Devout Christians, Muslims, and Jews have all found ways to reconcile progressive ideology with theological concepts. But it does mean that modernists are likely to see God at most operating within and through nature, rather than intervening from above it.

Karl Marx is to progressivism what Thomas Aquinas is to Catholicism and John Calvin is to Protestantism. Not all progressives are Marxist any more than all Catholics are Thomists or all Protestants are Calvinists—but Aquinas, Calvin, and Marx all gave the fullest and most systematic expression to the ideas of their different forms of faith.

Just as Aquinas and Calvin built on but challenged the work of great predecessors, Marx's version of Abrahamic history essentially involved tweaking a preexisting historical model—a tweak that moved mountains and challenged a world. Marx came at the standard story of modernist history through the work of Hegel, the same philosopher who ultimately also inspired Francis Fukuyama. Hegel developed an intellectual and spiritual approach to progressive history that tried to systematize the work of the earlier enlightened thinkers who had been roughing out the idea of progress since the Renaissance.

Hegel's vision was closer to the original Christian model than the secular versions of world history that had been produced by such British writers as David Hume and various thinkers and writers associated with the Enlightenment in France. Hegel's grounding in Lutheran theology seems to have influenced his work. Like biblical history, Hegelian history begins with a naïve paradise where all human beings are equal. The fall comes very early, as human beings struggle with one another and the primeval equality is lost. The resulting inequality is for Hegel the motor of the historical process. The deepest need of human beings is to have their humanity fulfilled by being recognized as equals by other free women and men. History is the long process through which humanity, impelled by this hunger for recognition, slowly and painfully builds a society in which a new kind of equality is possible.

This picture of history includes all the core structural features of the Christian diagram of history: the garden of innocence, the fall that establishes the problem which history must then overcome, and the progressive revelation and struggle culminating in the establishment of a higher, final way of life that fully meets human goals and needs. As Marx studied Hegel, he was swept away by the grandeur of this great philosophy of history, but he thought Hegel had not gone far enough—or indeed very far at all—in differentiating his system from classic Christian history. In Marx's view, Hegel had the wrong higher power. Instead of relying on mystical mumbo jumbo and talking about the role of spirit in history, Marx wanted a driving force for history that came from natural causes and the physical world. Marx looked at how political economists like Adam Smith had substituted purely natural causes for the Christian God and set out to build a philosophy of history that was as sweeping and grand as Hegel's—but as practical and secular as British political economy.

It was one of the great intellectual achievements of all time, and even though Marx did a poor job of predicting the actual flow of future events based on his model—and those who attempted to turn his philosophy into a political handbook and economic text committed some of the greatest crimes and blunders ever recorded—Marx's work on history and society remains indispensable for anybody who wants to understand what the world's leading thinkers and writers have been concerned with for the last two hundred years.

Under the surface, Marx's great achievement was the old Abrahamic history once again. There was an early classless society of hunters and gatherers; then comes the fall into a world of oppression and the long crawling climb back up toward the light. In the end, with the triumph of the proletariat over the bourgeoisie, Marxist history ends in its own secular version of the New Jerusalem. Economic development reaches a climax in universal affluence as the proletariat takes bourgeois methods of production to new heights of efficiency while social and spiritual development climax with a society that recognizes and guarantees human equality more profoundly than any class society. Like Adam Smith's, Marx's history does not need a supernatural higher power; humanity's own propensities to produce and create drive both men's models, though they drive them in somewhat different directions.

Whether they look to Smith, Hegel, Marx, or pre-Hegelian figures for inspiration, progressive theorists of history share this basic Abrahamic framework. They also share faith that the historical process follows a set of laws that can be grasped by the human mind. At least in its broad outlines, human history is predictable. If one knew all the facts and understood the laws of history, and had a computer that could crunch the numbers fast enough, in theory one could predict significant subsequent events.

Like other Abrahamists, progressives debate questions of free will and predestination. Are the laws of history so immutable that individuals can only play their fated role? Or is there some "give" in the system so that individuals by their own choice can act to advance or retard the great human movement toward a better future? The logic of progressivism often leads toward historical determinism in some form; its ethics lead toward voluntarism. The tension is never fully resolved. Lenin and Stalin emphasized the iron laws of historical materialism even as they led Soviet society in a project that strict Marxist determinism would see as futile: trying to build the world's most advanced society in a country where industry lagged far behind countries like Germany, Britain, and the United States. Mao would do the same thing with his Great Leap Forward and his Cultural Revolution.

If history is driven by laws, and these laws can be understood, then it appears to follow that we can plan history—we can actively seek to shape it. In particular, human beings can organize in political communities to accelerate the march of progress. We can build the future. Progressives have generally interpreted this to mean that the state can and should play a decisive role in the development of human societies. It is the most powerful agent in society, and if we know what the future should look like, we should use the full powers of the state to lay its foundations.

The progressive state has been one of the major forces in world history. Building on the legacy of Colbert and Louis XIV, Jacobin and Napoleonic France first gave this state a truly modern shape. The state reshaped property rights in France, curbed the powers of the church, liquidated feudalism, laid out the great channels of national economic development, modernized the legal code, and went on to establish two of the most important forces in modern European development—universal national education and universal conscription.

Despite Napoleon's defeat, the French state he built still continues to serve both democrats and tyrants as the primary model worldwide of the progressive state. Otto von Bismarck looked to Napoleon's model even as he built imperial Germany into a more powerful, updated version. Germany and France were primary sources of inspiration for nationalist modernizers across and beyond Europe. Victor Emmanuel's Italy, the positivist founders of the Brazilian republic, the social engineers of Japan's Meiji restoration, Kemal Atatürk in Turkey, and, with modifications based on their special Bolshevik ideas, Lenin and his colleagues all saw the progressive state born on the same model.

Arab leaders like Gamal Abdel Nasser, Hafez Assad, and Saddam Hussein looked to France, often through the lenses of Atatürk's Turkey and the Bolshevik Soviet experiment. Virtually all Latin American countries from revolutionary Mexico to revolutionary Cuba have been progressive-Jacobin in the design of their state structures; so too was much of postcolonial Africa, as well as the state of Israel.

Americans in particular have a hard time realizing this, but they need to. There are two major revolutions in modern history that set the world on two competing paths. The Glorious Revolution set the course for political developments in much of the English-speaking world; the French Revolution has played a much larger and wider role in state formation. The Anglo-Americans won the military and economic contest with France for world power; when it came to exporting the political structures of modernity, however, France often prevailed.

War on History

Traditional forms of Judaism, Christianity, and Islam urge believers to cooperate with God's plan in the hope that this will speed its fulfillment for the world. But from the standpoint of the older, theistic forms of faith, the ultimate responsibility for the historical process lies mostly in God's hands, not ours. Modernists, however, feel themselves summoned to solve the problem of history and bring the historical process to its triumphant conclusion.

It was not enough for the communists to study the rise of the proletariat; they wanted to accelerate the triumph of the proletariat and build the posthistorical utopia. Non-Marxist modernists also want to do more than understand history. The application of the scientific method gives us the technological capacity for universal affluence and peace; progressive politics aims to harness these new abilities to the creation of Heaven on earth.

For modernists, perhaps the most important thing about the capitalist revolution in Abrahamic history is that the techniques, powers, and insights that human beings gain through their mastery of natural and social forces in capitalist modernity gives them both the opportunity and the duty to solve the problems of the human condition—from an Abrahamic point of view, to bring history to an end.

Because of the spread of enlightened and humanitarian principles, hundreds of millions of people no longer believe that ancient evils can be permitted to exist indefinitely into the future. Longtime assumptions and institutions have been questioned. As modernity has spread through the world there has been a humane revolution against torture and other abuses. Felons were still being broken on the wheel in eighteenth-century France.

The modern antislavery movement had its beginnings in the eighteenth century.

Beginning with a handful of reformers widely regarded by their contemporaries as crackpots and cranks, and rising throughout the nineteenth and twentieth centuries, in the Western world and beyond, the rise of modernism has led to an explosion of movements for social betterment. In the countries of western Europe where this movement has gone farthest, life has reached a level of dignity and security that has justified many of the hopes of the modernist enlightenment. Workers are protected and women emancipated. Capital punishment is abolished. European prisons of today provide better living conditions than medieval aristocrats enjoyed. Smallpox has been abolished in nature; the human life span has virtually doubled—and is increasing. Animals are the objects of benevolent and protective social action—foxes can no longer be hunted to death in Britain. We sometimes seem close to the time darkly prophesied by W. H. Auden when the world will be run by "the Society of Everyone's Aunts for the Prevention of Cruelty to Plants."

This attempted transformation of the human condition has not been fueled only by hope. Fear has also played a part. Despite all the progress, many people feel that the world as it is will just not do. The development of the terrible weapons of the twentieth century and the wholesale collapse of civilized standards in warfare have changed things. Historically, war has been both regrettable and inevitable. Wars were how states settled their differences. In a nuclear world, that is not acceptable. War is no longer a regrettable tragedy; it is a threat to existence. As John F. Kennedy once put it, "Mankind must put an end to war—or war will put an end to mankind."[1]

Because war is woven so deeply into the fabric of history, the abolition of war requires a thoroughgoing social and political revolution. In practical terms, the end of war *is* the end of history; if the human race reaches a point of development at which organized mass violence is no longer the supreme arbiter of human affairs, then we have clearly solved the fundamental problem of human society.

War is not the only ancient evil whose time has gone. The abolition of war entails so many other tasks. To abolish war, we must, surely, vanquish the causes of war. Mass poverty can clearly no longer be accepted if war is to be eliminated. The poor have too many incentives to make war on the rich; we must have a global economic system that allows the debt-bonded rice farmers of South Asia a way out of their poverty or none of us are safe.

Because Americans believe that democratic states are less likely to fight wars, Americans are now committed to the establishment of democracy worldwide. That commitment extends not only to old and long-established states like China and Morocco, but also to countries that have never had a stable state, like Afghanistan and much of sub-Saharan Africa.

Peace is impossible without justice and economic development. A world that oppresses women cannot be just; economic development is impossible without fully mobilizing their talents and safeguarding their rights. Therefore both progressive and liberal modernist countries have incorporated into their foreign as well as their domestic policies the goal of combating such undoubted evils as female genital mutilation as well as the limits on the rights of women set forth in most traditional studies of Islamic jurisprudence.

Aspirations that would once have seemed hopelessly eccentric and quixotic are now central to the foreign policy of the Western states—and many of the more modernist countries in the developing world. Woodrow Wilson electrified his own time by converting World War I into a war to end war and proposing an international organization with the authority to prevent future conflicts. Today's reformers go much farther than Wilson dared to go, and to a very large extent they have succeeded in bringing the world's leading powers into at least partial support for their ambitious reforms.

This belief that states can and should act to change the basic elements of the international system and the closely allied view that the domestic politics of each country should address and remedy some of the fundamental evils of the human condition are new by global standards. Rome's Augustus Caesar, the great Chinese emperor T'ai-tsung, and France's Louis XIV did not think that their job description included changing the nature of the world.

Britain became a global power at the time when these ideas were just taking shape. The United States came to world power as these ideas became central to world politics, and the politics of the end of history remain a basic element in international life today. Wilson wanted not simply to defeat imperial Germany but to change the human condition. American efforts between the two world wars to promote disarmament and arbitration and to outlaw war had a similarly ambitious goal. Many hoped that the United Nations would succeed where the League of Nations had failed, and abolish war among the great powers. The Cold War frustrated this hope, but it too was, among other things, an ideological war about the best way to bring history to an end. For the Soviet Union and at least some of its allies, Marxism-Leninism offered the shortest and most reliable road to a posthistorical society of universal affluence and peace. For the United States and at least some of its allies, liberal democratic society offered a surer, faster, and better road to a world in which all would have enough and war would disappear. Both sides in the Cold War shared a common belief that something basic has changed in the historical process. For policy makers and societies influenced by the fourth faith of Abraham, foreign policy isn't just about "one damn thing after another" anymore; it is about making basic changes in the human condition.

Eighteen • The Golden Meme

The belief that the stakes in world politics are high, that contemporary events involve a struggle against the limits of the human condition and age-old scourges like war, meshes very well with traditional American views about the place of the United States in world history. The idea of the war against history has deep roots in Anglo-American culture. From the time of the Reformation, English popular feeling, always insular and even xenophobic, identified the national cause with that of true religion—fighting against evil—in a simple and straightforward way that was often impossible in continental Europe (although the Spaniards and the Poles also managed this feat). Germany was religiously divided; France, though Catholic, was often allied with the pope's enemies in the interest of limiting Hapsburg power. For much of early modern European history, English support seemed essential if the Protestant cause was to survive; when Cromwell told Parliament that the cause of God's people generally depended on England, his listeners understood exactly what he meant.

The Anglo-American tradition of the war against evil shifts very easily into the idea of a war against history. History's progress toward culmination represents the will of God (or, for the secularists among us, the fulfillment of human nature). Those who try to thwart this progress are fighting God's will or blocking human nature from its right to fulfill its aspirations and achieve its justly deserved freedom—and that is the essence of evil. Woodrow Wilson and David Lloyd George made the connection explicit by making World War I a war against war as well as against the Kaiser. This is a natural and even an inevitable connection to make. Once an enlightened, modern world has taken on the task of building utopia, then any force opposed to this great effort is by definition evil. To fight for the construction of the posthistorical utopia is to fight for good and for God.

In the contemporary United States, as in Victorian Britain, many thought-ful voices are raised to challenge this basic template of history, but the most important points of ideological disagreement in American society (and in Victorian Britain before us) revolve around how best to define and then how best to win the war against history, not whether to fight one at all.

As Americans grapple with these issues, their thoughts about the histori-cal process and America's place in it are shaped by a sense of purpose and destiny rooted in the same cultural and religious complex that made the Anglo-American world such a fertile seedbed for capitalism. Whether they happen to be religious or whether they are secular, Americans tend to see world history as the unfolding of an Abrahamic process, and in interpreting that process they rely on their historical experience and their deep cultural values. The optimism rooted in Anglo-American culture and strengthened by the long record of Anglo-American political and economic success unites with the biblical roots of Anglo-American religion to create a distinct grand narrative that ties the Abrahamic story of Israel and Christ together with the intuition that capitalist modernity represents a new call from God. Thomas Jefferson's proposed Great Seal for the United States reverberates deeply in the national consciousness: Horsa and Hengist on the one side, symbols of the Anglo-Saxon conquest of England; and on the other, the chil-dren of Israel who faithfully followed God's beacon to an unknown land.

The Invisible Hand

Adam Smith's striking image of an invisible hand bringing social order out of the uncoordinated and self-interested actions of a multitude of buyers and sellers is more than a felicitous literary conceit. The idea that order and complexity emerge more or less spontaneously from the random interplay of simple forms is an insight that, one way or another, has dominated the Anglo-Saxon imagination for many centuries. The cult of the invisible hand, uniquely intense, uniquely widespread and all-pervading, may be the chief difference between the English-speaking world and the rest of the world; it is both one of the principal reasons for the Anglo-Saxon rise to world power and a leading influence in how the Anglo-Saxons have under-stood and interpreted their rise and their role.

English history and especially the history of the common law helped root this idea deep in the culture and sensibility of the English-speaking world. The primitive folk laws of the wandering Germanic tribes who founded Anglo-Saxon England grew gradually into what many English people viewed as a stately and harmonious network of jurisprudence that would ultimately grow to become the basis for the commercial laws of the most complex and dynamic economies ever known. This development did not take place as the result of a plan; it was the slow accretion of results, the outcome of tens of thousands of law cases and decisions stretching over all centuries. No single controlling intelligence orchestrated this growth, and there were blind alleys and poor decisions all along the way, but by the seventeenth century, English jurists and public opinion saw great value in the unplanned, organic growth of their common law.

More broadly, English institutions and English liberties seemed to have grown in the same way: through the jostling and collisions of barons, kings, parliaments, and burghers across the stage of medieval English history, somehow the outlines of a balanced parliamentary monarchy took form, in which subjects could not be taxed without their consent, and in which the sacred power of the Crown was hedged about with limits equally holy. The English, at least most of those rich and powerful enough to leave opinions where historians can find them, liked their system and their laws. They could see very plainly how their society and its institutions evolved and grew over time, and it was equally clear that this development had not been shaped by any overall human agency or plan. Order was inherent in the nature of their society; the task of judges and politicians was to uncover the order that was already there, not to impose a grand design on an unformed and chaotic society.

Sir Francis Bacon was a scholar and courtier under Elizabeth I and James I. His relationship with James must have been somewhat uneasy; Bacon played a significant role in the trial of James's mother that led to her execution. A small but vocal group of scholars persistently asserts that Bacon wrote the plays commonly attributed to Shakespeare; in any case Bacon's view of the scientific method reflected the processes of the common law and elevated them into a principle of reasoning. The law was not shaped by grand and sweeping abstractions. It was discovered and elucidated by the careful study of individual facts. Bacon thought that science should work more or less in this way. Theory came after experience, not before it, and theories derived by this method would ultimately be more useful, more elegant, and more accurate than theories shaped solely by a process of syllogistic reasoning. The intellect must stoop to conquer; a careful study of facts would gradually yield a clear and majestic view of the natural laws by which the world works. Behind the apparent disorder of the physical universe were great and stately truths that could be learned by carefully observing small and particular things. Bacon's method became the basis of modern science, and the confidence in that invisible order would become the foundation of Anglo-American scientific and social thought.

Like much else in Anglo-American culture, the idea of an invisible hand shaping our ends, "rough hew them how we will," received a powerful impetus during the religious tumult of the sixteenth and seventeenth centuries. From the wars, scandals, heresies, and errors of religious history, through the dynastic ambitions of a king and the greed of the laity, had, apparently, emerged an orderly, honorable, and orthodox church. That the marital adventures of Henry VIII, the ambitions of the Cecils, the shocking escapades of the Villierses, and the ups and downs of the Stuarts should have been the instruments through which Providence elected to build the Anglican church struck even its friends as peculiar.

Caroline Divines reflecting on the development of the Anglican church were driven to stress the mysterious ways in which God works His wonders to perform. Henry VIII, whom nobody has tried to canonize, was used by God to build His church and was on the side of history in a way that the admittedly saintlier Thomas More and John Fisher weren't. Like cats in a pigpen, scandalized High Anglican writers tiptoed through the mire of the Calvinist theology which so many of the early English Reformers professed to make a consoling discovery. The Prayer Book was orthodox even though those who compiled it were heretics! God writes straight with crooked lines. This perception is already very close to Adam Smith's concept of the invisible hand: the true religion emerges from the chaotic scramble of politics and appetite just as, for Smith, order and prosperity emerge from the competition and chaos of human ambition and greed.

What worked in religion and law also seemed to work in the skies. Sir Isaac Newton—astrologer extraordinaire and one of the most determined decipherers of the apocalyptic prophecies in the book of Revelation—looked into the heavens and saw something very similar to, of all things, the Anglican church and the common law. From the chaos of the cosmos, he saw particles, obeying their own rules and natures, develop into a solar system of enormous complexity and predictability. Random collisions made the stately rings of Saturn. Newton didn't use the phrase that Smith would make famous—"as if by the workings of an invisible hand"—but that, he saw, is how gravity and the laws of motion create order out of the primordial chaos of matter. Particles of matter were, he found, endowed by their creator with certain inalienable tendencies; left freely to themselves and not inter-fered with, they form the glorious and complex structures and patterns we can see in the skies.

God's order, the British came to believe, emerges over time in a process of continuing change. This was a revolution in values comparable to the ear-lier revolution caused by the discoveries of Copernicus and Galileo. The medieval picture of the universe, memorably used by Dante in *The Divine Comedy,* saw change as a mark of inferiority. Earth—which the medievals placed at the bottom of the universe—was morally as well as physically lower than the heavenly spheres because everything on earth was mutable. The lowest circle of the heavens was that of the ever-changing moon.

In Newton's cosmology we see a concept of an emergent order: change is not a defect; it is part of the process by which God's plan is fulfilled. God has become an original cause; His order is expressed in the natural constitu-tion of energy and particles, and the observed disorder and strife are an intrinsic part of God's design and, ultimately, of His order.

This perception is, of course, closely related to the shift taking place dur-ing Newton's lifetime to an Anglo-American religious consciousness based on dynamic rather than static religion. A belief in an emergent order in both the physical and social universe, and that we cooperate with God's (or Nature's) work by allowing the process of historical development to pro-ceed, powerfully reinforces the idea that change signifies progress rather than decay.

Economics followed where Newton led. The scandalous Dutch-born writer Bernard de Mandeville wrote *The Fable of the Bees* to argue that it is because, not in spite of, the faults and imperfections of human nature that human society as a whole progresses and becomes more orderly and harmo-nious. The selfish ambitions and vicious appetites of individuals produce the order and intricacy of the modern economy.

Describing Britain as a hive of bees, Mandeville satirizes the professions in turn. Lawyers swindle; doctors spend little time studying medical science so they can spend more time perfecting the art of bilking money from patients; priests are slothful hypocrites; generals take bribes; cabinet minis-ters cheat the king they are supposed to serve: from a moral point of view the hive is a mess. Yet the hive is rich—and powerful. It is the richest, most important, and most prosperous hive in all the world.

> *Thus every Part was full of Vice,*
> *Yet the whole Mass a Paradice;*
> *Flatter'd in Peace, and fear'd in Wars*

They were th'Esteem of Foreigners,
And lavish of their Wealth and Lives
The Ballance of all other Hives.
Such were the Blessings of that State;
Their Crimes conspired to make 'em Great;
And Vertue, who from Politicks
Had learn'd a Thousand cunning Tricks,
Was, by their happy Influence,
Made Friends with Vice: And ever since
The worst of all the Multitude
Did something for the common Good.[1]

It was vice, Mandeville insisted, that made the bees prosperous. The luxury, vanity, and pride of the rich gave jobs to millions of the poor and middle-class; the need to keep up with the fashions, have everything made over and redecorated when new styles came in, the need to impress the neighbors with one's taste—this is what led the rich to spend their money and therefore to allow the rest of society to make a living. Over time, the jumble of crimes and private interests made life better for everyone, even the poor.

Thus Vice nursed Ingenuity,
Which join'd with Time; and Industry
Had carry'd Life's Conveniencies,
Its real Pleasures, Comforts, Ease,
To such a Height, the very Poor
Lived better than the Rich before;
And nothing could be added more.[2]

The bees in Mandeville's fable could not leave well enough alone. Stung by moralistic reproaches, they resolved to live simply and follow virtue's dictates. The result: trade collapses, the national power collapses, and foreigners invade.

The first edition of this poem was published in 1705. Three centuries later many people think this is what Anglo-Saxon free-market economics is all about: a reversed morality in which private evil is responsible for public good.

De Mandeville's view was, however, widely denounced at the time, and Adam Smith's work on economics should be seen as a refutation rather than an endorsement. Smith was not religious, but his worldview was a moral one. Human beings have a naturally (or, for those who prefer, divinely) given nature so that when people are free to follow their own natures, they produce an orderly and affluent society without much guiding or restraining human authority. The world has been made in such a way that if we leave well enough alone, its inherent order will emerge in human economic interactions—just as it emerges in the heavens as physical bodies obey the laws of gravitation and motion.

Smith's *Wealth of Nations* was published in 1776, and the newly independent colonists in America were as profoundly shaped by faith in the invisible hand as their British cousins. Much of Jefferson's idea of democracy is an adaptation of the dynamics of the invisible hand to the political sphere: the action of individual human beings, controlled only by their sense of their own interests, will produce an orderly and harmonious society. For Jefferson, man is even more of a political animal than he was for Aristotle. Aristotle's man was a political animal because man's identity could be fulfilled only in a polis; Aristotle, however, did not think that human nature, left to itself, would necessarily create a happy or successful polis. For Jefferson, man is a political animal in a deeper sense; human nature has been constructed in such a way that the free, unforced choices of an educated majority will create a free state—as if by the workings of our old friend, the invisible hand. Once again, good order will emerge from a historical process of development and change.

The shift from the Jeffersonian ideas behind the Declaration of Independence in 1776 to the Madisonian constitutionalism of 1789 is often seen as a retreat from the radical ideas of the American Revolution to the more conservative values of the Federalist era. There was, however, no movement away from reliance on the principle of the invisible hand. The system of checks and balances among the three branches of government, between the states and the federal government, and between the representation of different classes of citizens and interests in the House of Representatives and the Senate was an attempt to create a kind of political solar system. It was believed that the interplay of the branches of government, the ambition and hopes of statesmen, the different regional perspectives, and the different economic interests would not lead to chaos and collision. It would be harmony and order, by and large: the system would be stable, kept that way as if by the workings of our favorite hand. Here Mandeville got it exactly:

> *This was the State's Craft, that maintain'd*
> *The Whole, of which each Part complain'd:*
> *This, as in Musick Harmony,*
> *Made Jarrings in the Main agree;*

Parties directly opposite
Assist each oth'r, as 'twere for Spight [spite] . . .[3]

Darwinian biology is yet another extension of the principle of the invisible hand into another field of study. From the chaotic struggle for survival comes the evolution of higher forms and, ultimately, intelligence and civilization itself. The orderly, lovely nature that we see and admire is the product of the anarchic struggle for existence in which every plant, every beetle is fighting to survive and to reproduce. From the landscapes of the South Downs to the paintings in the British Museum, every piece of order and beauty that we see has been brought out of a chaotic, ungoverned struggle of selfish elements.

To this day the Anglo-American mind approaches virtually any social, political, scientific, or economic question with the belief that, somehow, some kind of invisible hand is the answer. Academic freedom? Let the best ideas triumph in the "marketplace of ideas." Pollution? Establish a marketplace in pollution permits and rights, and let the invisible hand find the least costly, most effective solution to the problem. The problems of public education? Allow parents school choice and let the invisible hand go to work.

This predisposition to rely on the invisible hand has many consequences for Anglo-American society. Perhaps the most important is the degree to which it reinforces the cultural receptivity of Anglo-Saxon societies to the disturbing and chaotic effects of capitalism. As Joseph Schumpeter tells us, capitalism proceeds through a process of creative destruction; faith in the invisible hand gives Anglo-Saxon society more courage to accept the destruction—and therefore a greater share of the benefits of the creation.

It does not matter much that the English-speaking world is not consistent in its embrace of the idea of the invisible hand. To use contemporary American political terminology, "liberals" are suspicious of the invisible hand in the economy, but have unbridled faith in its work, say, in the arenas of civil liberties, freedom of religion, and the free press. Many "conservatives" take almost the opposite approach, placing more confidence in the economic and less in the social activities of the invisible hand. Many American Christians utterly reject the application of the invisible hand in the realm of biological evolution, while believing as firmly as Adam Smith that the free market brings the best possible order out of the chaos of human desires. While Americans and other English speakers quarrel endlessly and bitterly over specific cases, in general we mostly accept at some level that processes we don't understand but must allow to go forward are bringing greater benefits than we could gain if we attempted to rein them in. The world is benign;

human beings are fitted to their society and their environment, and vice versa. That social conviction has been and still is a major force in world history.

For all its limits, this golden meme of the invisible hand must be credited for some of the willingness Anglo-Americans have shown to accept the unfettered operations of free markets in recent centuries. Those with imaginations that have embraced this idea will find it easy and natural to attribute any stress and upheavals to a benign process which ought to be left to run its course.

The golden meme of the invisible hand sustains a powerful form of faith. This faith can be divorced not merely from orthodoxy, but from theism: the positivistic evolutionists of the nineteenth century saw rational order as inherent in the nature of the physical universe rather than as something created by a supernatural being. Yet undoubtedly millions of English-speaking people for centuries now have seen the invisible hand as God's hand at work in history, bringing good out of evil, order out of chaos, and progress out of poverty.

We cannot understand God's (or Nature's) hidden purposes; we cannot fathom the mysterious ways in which God's providence—or Nature's cunning—has ordained that good and evil must feed off each other and live side by side. Yet believers in the invisible hand are confident that the historical process is carrying forward some great if unknown purpose. We do not fight it; we believe that we must let capitalism and its revolutionary potential loose upon the world. To fight against that is to fight God and the nature of things.

Whig History

Under the influence of this faith in an emergent order arising under the ministrations of an invisible hand, the English-speaking world has constructed a grand historical narrative of its own, one that celebrates and demonstrates the rise of the Anglosphere and the moral lessons this rise holds for the rest of the world. The "whig narrative,"[4] originally the name given to the eighteenth-century Whig partisan story of the Glorious Revolution, refers today to a distinctively Anglo-American concept of history told as the story of slow, sure, and irresistible capitalist progress under the guidance of the invisible hand.

The savage individuals of the Saxon forests formed into tribes. The tribes acquired the rudiments of tradition, law, and religion. They became a rough, violent society, but there was a principle of growth and development somehow planted within. As if by the working of the usual force, the tribes formed wider communities—the seven kingdoms of eighth-century England, the united monarchy of Alfred and Edward the Confessor. Society gradually becomes wiser, milder, more enlightened and civilized. Sometimes there are throwbacks and retreats: Tudors are followed by Stuarts until Parliament can set it right. But in the end, history is moving the right way, and it is our duty and our interest to cooperate with that movement.

And history is not just moving in general to build a better world. When Britain was at the zenith of its power, the story of history was the story of Britain's rise to supremacy—how, as W. C. Sellar and R. J. Yeatman's *1066 and All That* puts it, England rose to become Top Nation.[5]

One of the greatest Whig historians, Thomas Babington Macaulay, made no bones about his intentions. Macaulay's *History of England* begins with a description of the wonders he will recount, including "how, from the auspicious union of order and freedom, sprang a prosperity of which the annals of human affairs had furnished no example; how our country . . . rapidly rose to the place of umpire among European powers; how her opulence and her martial glory grew together . . . how a gigantic commerce gave birth to a maritime power compared with which every other maritime power, ancient or modern, sinks into insignificance."[6]

The rise of Britain was not just a matter of brute strength or economic success. It was above all a moral record. While noting that disasters, follies, and crimes also formed a part of the story, Macaulay nevertheless could give a favorable reading overall. "Yet, unless I greatly deceive myself, the general effect of this chequered narrative will be to excite thankfulness in all religious minds, and hope in the breasts of all patriots. For the history of our country during the last hundred and sixty years is eminently the history of physical, of moral, and of intellectual improvement."[7]

The whig narrative is a cheerful one. The chaotic struggles of the past gradually brought about a better world—with the English-speaking powers in the lead. No human design brought this about, but the inscrutable workings of Providence. The whig narrative is a forensic study of history in quest of the fingerprints of the invisible hand, and, just as the invisible hand retains an extraordinary power in Anglophone culture, so to many English-speakers the whig narrative still seems the obvious, unquestioned form that history should take.

It is not just a British product. Winston Churchill's *History of the English Speaking Peoples* is a distinguished example, but so too in its way is

Stephen Ambrose's and Douglas Brinkley's classic study of modern American engagement in the world, *Rise to Globalism.* Samuel E. Morison and Henry Steele Commager collaborated on the authoritative and valuable text *The Growth of the American Republic.* These works and many like them see American history as "the history of physical, of moral, and of intellectual improvement," with the particular American twist that emphasizes the rise of freedom and equality. Even radical historians often share this basically Whig view of the American experience—the extension of the vote to all adult white men, to women, to minorities; the victories of the labor movement, the rise of the Progressives, the triumph of the New Deal, the civil rights movement. The victory is incomplete, say these radical Whigs, but despite the unconscionable resistance of conservatives and other backsliders, progress is the name of the game.

The invisible hand is sometimes considered an ideological prop of the rich, a convenient principle that justifies unequal wealth. It has certainly been used this way, but the whig narrative that incorporates this golden meme into a general principle of history has not had the effect of entrenching the status quo. On the contrary: faith in the invisible hand and the whig narrative has armed generations of Anglo-Saxon reformers and crusaders. Cromwell fighting Charles I, the American Founding Fathers, antislavery crusaders, those who struggled for universal adult male and, later, female suffrage, those who thirsted after the decline of the House of Lords, Prohibitionists, opponents of foxhunting: all were strengthened in their struggles by the conviction that they were the heroes of the unfolding whig narrative. Today, those who want to see democracies established throughout the third world, who work for global gender equality, who struggle against poverty, who want war criminals and dictators tried, who deplore the international arms trade—all can take comfort in the whig narrative. Smug contemporaries think such people are cranks—well, this is what they thought of William Wilberforce, but he abolished slavery in the British Empire. It is what they thought of Susan B. Anthony, but women got the vote.

But conservatives, too, can take comfort in this faith. Change will come—must come, should come—but it will come at a slow and acceptable pace. It will be domesticated; the outlandish will become familiar before we must accept it. Burke, like most of the great conservatives of the English-speaking world, wasn't a reactionary; he was a slow Whig. Burke believed that progress was the result of the slow work of history; he just thought the process was slower, less amenable to pushing, than did the eager-beaver do-gooders and constitutional reformers. And British conservatism, even in the hands of a Burke, was never grounded on the assumption that all change is bad. The heart and soul of Anglo-American conservatism is the belief that an organic process of development, even if sometimes slow in the short run, will in the long run be the most effective way of facilitating improvement and change.

The whig narrative, like Anglo-American society, is both progressive and conservative. It is progressive because it identifies progress and change ultimately with, depending on one's point of view, the will of God or the laws of nature; it is conservative because it believes that progress should come slowly and peacefully. The whig narrative is, like Victorian geology, uniformitarian. This is to say that history unfolds gradually; it comes like the Grand Canyon was carved, little by little. It moves from bare limbs to leaf buds and flowers a little at a time; each stage develops on the basis of the last. Between the primitive customs of the Anglo-Saxon heptarchy and the delicate, finely balanced tenets of the fully fledged common law of Victorian England lies an extended, sometimes inscrutable, but ultimately inexorable process of growth and development.

The whig narrative doesn't just shape the Anglo-American approach to world history; it is one of the forces that enable Anglo-Saxon success. The (relatively) early and easy acceptance of the legitimacy of political parties, and therefore of dissent, in both Britain and America rests on this foundation. Slow Whigs (aka Tories) like William F. Buckley may have loathed and opposed fast Whigs like John Kenneth Galbraith, and party spirit can run very high—but these contests are less likely to lead to blood feuds and civil wars in the English-speaking world than elsewhere. For three hundred years, the great political and cultural struggles within the English-speaking world have almost always been struggles within a framework which both sides accept—not struggles over the framework itself. The exceptions, like the American Civil War, only show how much the English-speaking world has gained by achieving broad consensus on key issues.

The struggle for the legitimacy of political parties is closely linked to the struggle for toleration in religion, and in the beginning the parties of the state were closely linked to the parties in the church. Whigs were usually dissenters or, at most, low church Anglicans; Tories were high church Anglicans and Catholics, with passions originally inflamed by taking opposite sides in the English Civil War. For many generations, political writers routinely described parties in the state (Whig and Tory), as in church (high church and low church), as illegitimate. The modern American and British idea that you need at least two parties so they can keep an eye on each other, limit corruption, and generally keep the governing authorities from getting too entrenched and too arrogant reflects, of course, the basic logic of the invisible hand. The random conflicts and controversies of parties ultimately produce the best possible order for the state.

The relatively early acceptance of the legitimacy of dissent and parties in the state among the Anglo-American societies is one of the great secrets of their success. Other cultures have had great difficulty accepting this idea; many have still not fully embraced it. Recognizing the legitimacy of political parties and an organized opposition has enormous practical consequences. Changes in the political balance no longer threaten revolution or violent change; the great competitive constitutional parties marginalize the minorities who wish to overthrow the social order.

In Wonderland there is a consensus. "We are all mad here," as the Hatter said to Alice; in the English-speaking world we are all (or nearly all) Whigs.

We need the consensus. Capitalist society is always in flux. Old industries and interests become weaker; new ones rise up and flex their muscles. Regions rise and fall: in the nineteenth century, the north of England became the workshop of the world and asserted new power in British politics. Today, the rust-belt industries and abandoned coal mines of the old industrial landscape have seen their political and economic fortunes diminish.

This change means that politics will always be tense. The landed proprietors will want tariffs on imported grain to maintain their crop prices. The manufacturing interests will want to abolish these tariffs so that their workers can buy food cheaply—and, therefore, be satisfied with lower wages.

New immigrant groups will muscle in on the turf of old ones as the old ones escape to the suburbs: Hispanics will replace Jews on the Lower East Side; Irishmen will yield to Italians, and in turn Little Italy will be absorbed by Chinatown.

A capitalist society needs a political system and a set of political values that can accommodate the clashes of opposed interests without blowing up. That is what a party system provides. If the Irish dominate the city under the Democratic banner, the Italians can organize as Republicans and carve out a niche. Industries that benefit from protection can struggle peacefully against industries dependent on free trade. Class tensions can be ventilated and adjusted; after a Gilded Age of robber barons, a progressive income tax can, if the majority wishes, redress the social balance.

A capitalist society that does not have a viable party system is a crisis waiting to happen. It is like a crab that cannot grow unless it throws off its shell from time to time. Social conditions and power relations are changing, but there is no way for these changes to work their way slowly into legislation and reform. Pressure for change builds until it becomes irresistible, and change when it comes can be abrupt and destabilizing.

The rise of the party system has helped the English-speaking world achieve its astonishing record of political continuity mixed with rapid social and economic change. Since 1689, the Anglosphere has witnessed more radical and sweeping changes than most of the world because capitalism has had a freer hand there. Yet politically, these countries remain what they have long been: among the most stable regimes in the modern world. If history in the Anglosphere looks more like the whig narrative's picture of uniformitarian progress toward Elysium than does the history of much of the world, the "golden meme" of the invisible hand can claim some of the credit.

All this testifies to the importance of the whig narrative in Anglo-American society. It also reinforces the confidence which the Anglo-Americans place in it. Three hundred years of almost unbroken domestic peace and prosperity, combined with three hundred years of almost constantly growing success in reshaping the international environment, have helped make Whig history the default history for most Americans today.

The whig narrative is a powerful and all-embracing synthesis of the Abrahamic narrative and the story of capitalism. It links capitalist development to the unfolding will of God, reconciling those who accept it to the changes and upheavals of capitalist life, even as it promotes the ideas and practices that tend to make capitalism successful. But the ideological forces that propelled first the British and then the Americans to world power have still another dimension. Americans, whether or not they have followed Paul Tillich's* Protestant principle so far that they have transcended faith in a personal God, generally believe that their country has a covenanted relationship with the power or person who directs the historical process. America is on a mission from God—and the well-being of the United States depends on how faithful Americans are to their mission.

The Chosen People

The idea of a covenant enters American history very early. The Puritans carried the idea to Plymouth on the *Mayflower,* and it was one of the central animating ideas in the Calvinist theology that so profoundly shaped the Anglo-American mind in the seventeenth century. A covenant is an agree-

---

* Tillich held that Protestants must always be able to discard traditions and creeds, however hallowed, to seek a God Who transcends all human understanding.

ment between two parties, one weak and one strong. Calvinists in particular read the Bible as the story of God's successive covenants with human beings climaxing in the new covenant He made through Jesus.

The keystone of a covenant is election, in the old sense meaning "choice." God as the stronger party cannot be compelled to make agreements with human beings; He chooses His partners and He dictates the terms. The Jews are the Chosen People because God chose—elected—them for a special relationship.

For Americans, there was very little doubt from the beginning that they were chosen by God. The Puritans believed themselves to be the elect of the elect. English Protestantism was the fullest flowering of God's true religion; the Puritans who left England to build a purified commonwealth in the New World saw a need to do more than could ever be accomplished in a corrupt and backsliding England.

That initial sense of election was then reinforced by the evidence that God was pouring out blessings on His elect. They had expected their New World exile to be a tough and a bitter one, with much privation and many sacrifices. For the first few years it was, but very quickly the colonies began to enjoy an extraordinary and sustained rise in living standards, which still continues today. Living in smaller, newer, and therefore healthier cities than the fever-ridden pestholes of the Old World, enjoying the benefits of a healthy climate, good harbors, and available land (as plagues had conveniently or, New Englanders might have felt, providentially killed off most of the native Indians), the transplanted Puritans soon grew to have one of the world's highest standards of living. Their descendants still do. The country they helped to found has enjoyed centuries of relative peace, rising prosperity, and rising power. Almost everything in the experience of the American people points to the belief that they are either unusually lucky or unusually blessed; the continuing flow of good fortune deeply reinforces the belief that the United States stands in some special relationship to the powers that be.

Foreigners and some Americans often see this claim to a special place in God's plan as the swaggering arrogance of a rich bully. Victorian Britain often produced the same impression. Understandable as this feeling may be, Anglo-American psychology will remain impenetrable to those who do not see that this sense of election and calling reflects (possibly poorly, often tactlessly) a sense of humility. It is precisely when Americans are most conscious that they are no better than other people that they turn to the idea that God, for inscrutable reasons, has chosen Americans to lead His work at this stage in history. "We speak it not with vanity," said Cromwell. Shakespeare's Henry V leads his soldiers singing *"Non Nobis, Domine"* after the battle of Agincourt: Not unto us the glory, O Lord, but to Thy Name.

In any case, the United States is, Americans tend to feel, not just another country, one that happens to be bigger and richer than most. Americans don't expect moral leadership to come from Russia, China, or France. They aren't waiting for Japan to turn into a city on the hill, a light to enlighten the Gentiles. That job is already taken, and America has it.

Much of the Old Testament concerns the workings out of the covenant God made with the ancient Hebrews. The books of law like Leviticus and Deuteronomy lay out the obligations of the Hebrews and record the solemn acceptance of the terms of the covenant by the Hebrew people at Sinai. Historical books like Judges and Kings are written to show how, when the Hebrews obey God, He rescues them from their enemies and makes them victorious in battle. The books of the prophets are filled with dire warnings of what will happen if the people and rulers don't fulfill their obligations to God. They depict Him raising up the Assyrians, Babylonians, and other enemies to smite a nation which has turned its back on Him.

Ever since the first settlements in New England, Americans have interpreted history through the spectacles of covenantal theology. Was the soil fertile and the voyage a success? God blessed us. Was the weather dry and did the weevils blight the corn crop? Someone had sinned.

Americans have done more than read themselves into the covenantal patterns of Old Testament history. They have turned their own founding documents into the scriptures of a civil religion. The Declaration of Independence, the Constitution, and the Bill of Rights: Americans do not simply feel that these are useful and even time-hallowed documents which have a certain utilitarian value because they tend to be effective.

No, the great founding documents of the American republic are a kind of holy writ. Judges are supposed to search and interpret the Constitution as preachers search and preach scripture. Constitutional scholars quarrel over principles of interpretation as intensely as theologians quarrel over the interpretation of the Bible. More than that, the principles of these guiding documents are held to be timelessly valid, rather than historical records of beliefs people once held.

And Americans, religious and secular, generally believe that the covenant includes these founding documents and their principles. We have our Ark of the Covenant. If we stick with the commandments, we prosper. If we violate them, we suffer.

This is the framework that most Americans still use to understand America's place in world history. For soi-disant sophisticated secularists as well as for Holy Rollers shouting and steaming at the revival meeting down in the creek bottom, America's relationship with its higher power is a covenantal one. From the Christian Coalition's point of view, we cannot allow gay marriage and take the Ten Commandments out of our courtrooms. From the ACLU's point of view, we cannot safely betray our civil-libertarian principles in an ill-advised crackdown against those who hold unpopular views. Secularists often don't realize they are still using this category, but in both cases these actions constitute sin: an act which is contrary to the will of God or to the law of nature. Such acts are bad in themselves because, depending on the point of view, either the will of God or the natural order is our measure of moral good. Acts that go against the grain in this way are also bad for those who commit them: God's commands are there to help us live happy and contented lives, and when we break the moral law we suffer consequences. To live in a way contrary to the dictates of nature will only bring misery and regret.

To keep on the right side of reality and to fulfill our side of the covenant, it is not enough to avoid sin. We must actively do good.

This is partly about domestic development. For Americans, continually reinventing the country and pressing forward to new and more adventurous forms of capitalist enterprise and social change is more than a way to make money. It is equated with a religious duty. The covenantal relationship calls for Americans to climb new peaks and surmount new heights on the long march to the west.

These treasures, these values, are not to be selfishly hoarded. They must be shared. We must spread the principles that our higher power has vouchsafed to us. Feminists believe that it is not enough that we safeguard the rights of women at home. We must empower and assist women abroad. The U.S. must use its economic and diplomatic power to end discrimination against women worldwide; we must ensure that women abroad have access to family planning information and the right to abortion on demand. The AFL-CIO and others argue that the United States must stand up for the rights of workers in other countries to organize unions. Our economists want to spread the benefits of Anglo-American economics to the world. Our military works to professionalize and upgrade the militaries of other countries. Even the postmodernists in our universities think that the New Zion of the American university system is a light to the heathen all over the red states and to at least most of the non-Francophone world.

This is the mood in which the Walrus and the Carpenter took their Anglo-Saxon consciences to the beach. The beaches should be swept clear. Democracy, feminism, the environment, antismoking—American society is not true to itself unless we are trying to change the world. And as long as we are working to fulfill this mission, God is on our side.

Like Abraham, we must have faith. When we falter or fall short, God may smite us to get us moving in the right direction again, but if we keep pressing forward on the right path, He and we will succeed. The invisible hand is bringing order out of chaos; the irresistible powers of Nature and God are working to bring about precisely the kind of world we seek.

This entrenched faith in the whig narrative and the pervasive cultural importance of the idea of a covenant with God or, at least, history, make plain the answer to the fourth question I've attempted to address in this book: why the Anglo-Americans have been so frequently convinced that the end of history has been reached. Optimism is the default mode of Anglo-American historical thought. How could it not be? The whig narrative teaches us plainly that God is on our side, and centuries of victorious experience and economic progress confirm that the message is right.

Yet the answer to the fourth question leads immediately to the fifth and sixth. After every new success, after the collapse of every great enemy, the Anglo-Saxon world proclaims that history has finally come to an end. The fall of Napoleon, the fall of the Kaiser, the fall of Hitler, the fall of the Soviet Union—at each of these moments leading voices in the Anglo-American world were heard to proclaim, ever more sweepingly and confidently, that history with its dismal struggles and miseries was finally behind us, and the bright new day was at hand.

Yet, so far at least, each time these confident predictions have ended in failure and a renewed cycle of war. Tennyson's vision in "Locksley Hall" has never come to pass; Norman Angell died before the illusion of war and the era of soldiers came to an end; the League of Nations failed; the United Nations has yet to build a lasting peace. Whig history is supposed to be more than just a chronicle of British and American military victories; it is supposed to climax with Victorian Britain and contemporary America changing and converting the world. Why isn't it happening? And why does the world sometimes seem to be getting worse? The heyday of British power ended in the carnage of World War I and the chaos of the interwar years; after sixty years of American leadership, the world, though by many if not all measures richer and more democratic than ever, faces unprecedented dangers from new types of superempowered terrorists, even as "rogue states" seek more and more horrifying weapons.

What is going on? Why do the Americans, whose political and economic skills are plainly keen enough to have allowed them to dominate world history in the twentieth century, so persistently mistake the meaning of events they themselves have done so much to shape? And, finally, if the Americans are wrong about where history is going and we aren't on the threshold of a long and stable peace under liberal capitalism, what is going on in the world and where are we headed?

Nineteen • Whig Babylon

The morning after the fall of the Berlin Wall in 1989, I was sitting at a sidewalk café in Rio de Janeiro, straining my rudimentary Portuguese by trying to decipher the news in *O Globo*. "*O Triunfo do Capitalismo!*" the headline screamed over a picture of jubilant Germans dancing on the top of the once-formidable wall. As I was reading, I felt a tug on my shirt and looked down. A four-year-old child from one of Rio's favelas was begging for the scraps from my plate. The triumph of capitalism, I began to suspect, might not be *entirely* completed just yet.

Faith in the whig narrative has helped the Anglo-Saxons dominate modern history, but it hasn't always helped them understand the world they are shaping. In particular, Anglo-Americans have historically found it difficult to understand why so many foreigners despise, reject, and resist (or misuse) the blessings of free markets and democratic government. From the eighteenth century to the present day, British and American thinkers and policy makers have repeatedly underestimated the difficulties and obstacles of establishing a stable world order on Anglo-Saxon lines. Americans sometimes seem incapable of appreciating the obstacles other societies must overcome before they can play the Anglo-Saxon game of free politics and free markets, and they have failed to grasp the sometimes profoundly destabilizing and unjust consequences of the sudden intrusion of liberal capitalist methods and competition in other societies.

Following the fall of the Soviet Union, Americans congratulated themselves for their success and celebrated an era of unipolar power and universal esteem of one sort or another for American values right up until the morning of September 11, 2001. Yes, there were inconsistencies and contradictions. Yes, there were still a few valleys that needed to be exalted, a few rough places left to make plain. But the real work of history was already done, and humanity, with a little nudging and coaxing, was ready to move into the house the Americans had built for it.

That was not, of course, the way much of the world saw the global situation. To many others throughout a troubled world, it was not the inconsistencies, hypocrisies, and failures that accompanied the American march to world power that they hated. It was the ideals and the goals. For these principled, frightened, and enraged opponents of the Anglo-Saxon juggernaut, what the Walrus and the Carpenter were so industriously and irresistibly building wasn't Jerusalem, the City of God; it was Babylon, the Mesopotamian metropolis that became to the biblical writers a symbol for an evil, crushing power. And many of the critics of the Pax Americana, such as it was, weren't angry primarily because the city wasn't quite finished yet, or because some of the neighborhoods were nicer than others, or even because the police sometimes used excessive force, especially in the bad neighborhoods where many of the critics lived; they were angry because they rejected and even loathed the project as a whole.

To those whose cultural or religious values were threatened or crushed by the bright lights of the capitalist order, to those who were excluded from its glittering prosperity, to those who feared or hated the power of the United States of America, the country which its inhabitants considered a city on the hill and the citadel of freedom was the new and terrible Babylon.

Different Rules

Non–Anglo-American observers through the centuries have tended to see the emerging maritime system from a perspective very different from that of most English-speaking observers. This is partly because they usually come from societies where the gap between the religious, economic, social, and cultural presuppositions of liberal capitalism and local values is greater than in the English-speaking world. Not sharing the specific historical experiences that shaped the dynamic, future-oriented religious atmosphere of the English-speaking world, much less the series of historical events that drove Britain (very unwillingly for the most part) toward a political culture based on compromise and tolerance, foreigners have often found liberal capitalism both morally and culturally repugnant. Today's Waspophobic Muslims are by no means the first to see things in this way: Catholic and Orthodox opinion in Europe and Latin America for centuries drew the same conclusions; principled critiques of this social system continue to emerge from East and South Asia as well.

It is not just that liberal capitalism looks different to people who approach it with different cultural and religious views. It actually behaves differently in different parts of the world. Perversely, over time it moves more slowly and smoothly in the cultures that have a greater tolerance for it, while it appears more rapidly and behaves more disruptively in cultures that have a greater resistance to it. As cutting-edge countries, the United States and Great Britain have tended to progress at something close to the overall speed of technological and economic progress. That is, they began to deal with the steam engine in the eighteenth century; the mechanization of textiles hit them both in the decades before and after 1800; the railroads appeared a generation later, and the consequences of the financial and communications revolutions that ensued gradually made themselves felt in the subsequent years. The radio and the automobile appeared early in the twentieth century and gradually caused various changes to work through society; the consequences of television and mass air travel were felt after World War II, and the computer and Internet revolutions have been transforming our societies since the end of the Cold War.

The Anglo-American world has not thought it was living through a slow-motion transformation to modern capitalism, but in fact its progress has been leisurely compared to what people all over the world have faced. Industrial and social revolutions that took decades or even generations to unwind in the Anglo-American world suddenly appear in far less developed countries where the consequences of several revolutions must be digested all at once. Children whose parents lived by subsistence agriculture in culturally isolated villages use the Internet in their schoolwork. Villagers who never saw a train are suddenly able to buy motorcycles. Young men who grow up in the rural hinterlands of Senegal make their way into the underground labor markets of Europe and find themselves in Paris or Brussels. Financial markets and practices that grew up over centuries of trial and error in the metropolitan centers of capitalist enterprises are imported complete and wholesale into countries whose publics a few years ago did not know what a stock was.

The capitalism that much of the world sees is a far more dynamic and voracious force than the capitalism whose evolution Anglo-Americans have lived through. The consequences for social stability and well-being are exacerbated by the way that this much more rapid transformation challenges and often overwhelms the institutions charged with managing the consequences and making appropriate decisions among conflicting interests as the transformation unfolds.

The Anglo-American world tends to forget how hard it was and how long it took to build institutions and develop the habits needed to make capitalism work. By modern standards, eighteenth-century English governments were staggeringly incompetent and corrupt. High government officials considered bribery and theft part of the job. As even Winston Churchill conceded, in a biography written to vindicate his ancestor against the vitriolic attacks made on him in Macaulay's *History of England,* John Churchill, the first Duke of Marlborough, regularly engaged in confidential communications with Britain's archenemy France while he commanded British forces in the field, and among the subjects of this correspondence was a fabulous bribe from Louis XIV that was promised to him on the conclusion of a peace treaty between Britain and France. Throughout the army, officers bought and sold their commissions, and resorted to tricks and dodges of every kind to cheat the treasury of money intended to provision and pay the ordinary soldiers.

Corruption started at the top. Sir Robert Walpole is often considered the first prime minister in British history, exercising power from 1721 through 1742. He developed a formidable parliamentary machine resting openly on the bribery of members, often through offering them lucrative sinecures. As late as 1816, British taxpayers were supporting a "Hereditary Grand Falconer," although neither the government nor the king kept any falcons. Walpole himself made a substantial fortune in office; questioned on the subject by the House of Commons, he saw nothing to deny. "Of course," he said, he had acquired a fortune. "[H]aving held some of the most lucrative offices for nearly twenty years what could anyone expect, unless it was a crime to get estates by great offices."[1]

Seats in the House of Commons were openly bought and sold, as were the votes of the electors. In 1734 Anthony Henley, a British MP from Southampton, wrote a letter in answer to constituents' complaints about his support of the excise tax:

Gentlemen:

I received yours and I am surprised at your insolence in troubling me about the excise. You know what I very well know, that I bought you. And I know well what perhaps you think I don't know, that you are now selling yourselves to somebody else. And I know something you don't know, that I am buying another borough. May God's curse light on you all. May your houses be as open

and as common to all excise officers as your wives and daughters were to me
when I stood for your scoundrel corporation [as a candidate for Parliament].[2]

In nineteenth-century America, corruption and incompetence proliferated luxuriantly at every level of government. Between 1869 and 1871 a
single municipal courthouse in New York City ended up costing taxpayers
four times as much as Britain's Houses of Parliament—and the building
remained unfinished.[3] The Credit Mobilier scandal involved approximately
$20 million in illegitimate profits connected with construction contracts for
the Union Pacific Railroad company. The cost of the contracts was covered
by federal subsidies, and the company distributed stock to politicians in
both parties to secure their support.

On a smaller scale, Mark Twain follows a trail of corruption and incompetence through more than a generation to tell the story of the politically
well-connected Fisher family and its quest for bogus war damages following their loss of a field of standing corn to Indian raiders during the Florida
Creek War of 1813. Lobbying to get one law after another through Congress, the Fishers ultimately collected the equivalent of one million dollars
in today's money—and were lobbying for still more when the Civil War
intervened.

Elections in nineteenth-century America were disorganized, dangerous,
and notoriously corrupt. In *Age of Betrayal: The Triumph of Money in
America, 1865–1900,* Jack Beatty reports that the going prices for votes
($14 to $27) were printed in the newspapers of upstate New York; that
African-American voters in the South were literally herded into pens so that
their votes could be sold to the highest bidder; that 85 percent of the voters
in Adams County, Ohio, and 42 percent of the voters in Cape May County,
New Jersey, sold their votes during the period. When it was too expensive to
buy votes, political operators stuffed the ballot boxes with fakes. In 1868,
Tammany Hall printed 45,000 fake ballots to carry an election. A suspicious
political reformer sent letters to each registered voter in one of Philadelphia's election districts; 63 percent of the certified letters were returned with
notes that the addressee was deceased, had moved away, or could otherwise
not be reached.[4]

Corruption was far from the greatest problem that the Walrus and the
Carpenter had to deal with as the continuing capitalist revolution presented
inept and incompetent governments with one problem after another. The
rise of London and New York, the two great metropolitan centers of the
Anglo-American world, set problems that were far beyond the capacity of
the Anglo-Americans to solve. A flood of migrants from the countryside

and, in the case of New York, from all over Europe combined with the growing density and size of the urban area completely overwhelmed the ability of authorities to cope. For more than two centuries urban conditions in both cities were almost indescribably squalid and dangerous.

London had had a population of up to 50,000 people during the Roman Empire, a figure that would not be reached again until the fourteenth century. By 1600 it was home to approximately 200,000; that number continued to grow, and there were more than half a million Londoners by the Glorious Revolution.[5]

The city authorities were completely unable to manage. Police and fire services were almost nonexistent, and the poorly trained, poorly educated, and poorly supervised watchmen and constables in eighteenth-century London were more like Shakespeare's Constable Dogberry than a modern police force. Not until 1829 would London have a regular professional police force. The laws were savage, but the courts were so poorly organized and the jails so poorly managed that thieves and murderers often felt they had little to fear from the law. Public prosecutors scarcely functioned; criminal prosecutions were brought by individuals. Jonathan Swift satirized jailhouse conditions in his poem on morning in London:

> *The Turnkey now his Flock returning sees*
> *Duly let out a' Nights to steal for Fees.*[6]

Samuel Johnson found the city fascinating and disturbing:

> *Here malice, rapine, accident, conspire,*
> *And now a rabble rages, now a fire;*
> *Their ambush here relentless ruffians lay,*
> *And here the fell attorney prowls for prey;*
> *Here falling houses thunder on your head,*
> *And here a female atheist talks you dead.*[7]

With about one million inhabitants in 1800, London gained six million more in the nineteenth century. Key services, and especially sewer and water services, found it hard to keep pace. For much of the century, they failed.

Londoners had long dug cesspits for human waste; by the middle of the nineteenth century there were more than 200,000 of these unpleasant holes, many full and flowing over. The Thames stank with its burden of human and industrial waste. The water in the city, either pumped in from the Thames or supplied by wells and pipes, became increasingly polluted as the cesspits, dug ever deeper and larger to accommodate the growing volume of human and animal waste, leaked their contents into the water supply. Leaky sewer and water pipes ran side by side; their contents often mingled.[8]

It was the smells rather than the bells of London that most impressed travelers at this time. Besides the cesspits and the Thames, more than 75,000 tons of animal dung each year ended up on London's streets from the horses who pulled the city's wagons and carriages, and the sheep, oxen, and pigs brought to market from the surrounding countryside.[9] Chamber pots were still being emptied from upper-story windows, with predictably unsavory consequences for the pedestrians below.

The consequences were severe. Plague and pestilence swept through London in the seventeenth and eighteenth centuries. The Great Plague of 1665 killed an estimated 100,000 Londoners. Even after the Great Fire of 1666 purged London of the plague, other diseases continued to ravage it, and mortality rates were far higher than in the countryside. Cholera arrived from India in 1832, and this disease took full advantage of London's horrendous sanitation. Recurring outbreaks drove the rich to the country and decimated the poor; the month of January 1849 saw more than 14,000 deaths from this disease.

New York fared little better. Population growth was also rapid. As late as 1790 the combined population of what became the five boroughs of New York City stood just under 50,000. In 1850 the census counted almost 700,000 New Yorkers; in 1900 there were 3.4 million. Most of them lived in squalor.

Pigs roamed the muddy, often unpaved streets of nineteenth-century New York; sanitary conditions quickly approached those of London. Charles Dickens watched groups of hogs roaming the streets as late as 1842; as David Reynolds tells us, Henry David Thoreau thought that the pigs were the "most respectable part of the population" of the burgeoning metropolis. Frederick Law Olmsted started to plan Central Park before the Civil War; he found that the city north of 59th Street was "steeped in overflow and mush of pig sties, slaughter houses, and bone boiling works, and the stench was sickening."[10] Cholera was no stranger in New York, either. In 1849, roughly 5,000 New Yorkers died of this dreadful disease.

The point is that the rush of capitalist development and change presented both Britain and the United States with problems that they could not quickly solve. Huge flows of immigrants, the rise of new industries, new problems in health and sanitation came at the bewildered authorities faster than they could respond. Sprawling slums, crime, unsafe living conditions:

all these proliferated in the two metropolitan centers of the Anglo-American world.—

This is what happened in the two countries which were best placed to manage capitalist change. Britain and the United States had relatively responsive political systems. They had active civil societies alongside a steady and growing stream of private philanthropists searching to improve the lives of their fellow citizens. They had a lively religious culture that sought pragmatic solutions to the problems of this world. Both countries adopted capitalism early, enjoying almost unbroken economic success as their technological and financial skills enabled them to triumph in global competition.

It is small wonder then that so many countries today are having a hard time making the adjustments and improvements that the accelerating pace of global change demands. The urban conglomerations of the contemporary world have grown much faster than the Anglo-Saxon cities ever did. Since 1950, São Paulo has gained more than 15 million inhabitants, and Mumbai has gained about 15 million.[11] Urban inflows like this would have utterly overwhelmed the municipal governments of London and New York, but these are the challenges that today face the developing world.

It is also no wonder that corruption is such a problem in so much of the world. Many politicians share Sir Robert Walpole's untroubled belief that riches should be the reward of office. Often, their views are formed by a context not very different from that in which Walpole operated. Right up until the Glorious Revolution, many people in the British Isles saw the state as the property of the king. The ideal, seldom achieved, was that the king should manage the state and pay for its upkeep out of his own income from land and fees. Officials received their jobs from the king, and the fees and other benefits that came from the job were part of the deal. Even in the United States remnants of this old system could be found in the nineteenth century; American consuls overseas, for example, received a percentage of the duties they levied on U.S.-bound commerce as part of their official and legal pay.

This kind of personal state is clearly not suitable to the conditions of the modern world, where government jobs demand much more independence, professionalism, and expertise than the old system could reliably provide. Yet for people brought up in the moral universe of an old-fashioned state, much of what contemporary Americans see as corruption does not feel wrong—any more than it felt wrong to Sir Robert Walpole or the Duke of Marlborough. Complex ties of tribal and dynastic obligations, traditional forms of deference, and habits left over from an era of weaker, less responsible government continue to shape the expectations of both the governed and the governors in much of the world today.

The explosion of cities like Lagos and Nairobi is one example; but urban overcrowding and slums are only one aspect of this problem.

Take, for example, shrimp farms.

Oysters, it turns out, are not the only crustacean on the Carpenter's food list. More than a billion pounds of shrimp disappear down American throats every year; roughly nine-tenths of them are imported. Shrimp are prolific breeders and grow very quickly to edible size; they are easily harvested and frozen, and they bring a good price.

Word got out very quickly, and people living on the coasts of countries like Thailand rushed to convert worthless mangrove swamps into lucrative shrimp ponds. Production shot up, jobs were created, fortunes were made, profits flooded into formerly poor and isolated villages on forgotten coastal backwaters.

Properly managed, this could have been a godsend. But the boom was too fast and too big for that. Soon the bills started to come due.

Coastal mangrove swamps look worthless to farmers, but marine ecosystems depend on the shelter they provide baby fish. As habitat disappears, yields in other fisheries plummet even as shrimp output rises. Then farmers made some painful discoveries. Large populations of shrimp and the food they require pollute waterways, killing the shrimp along with everything else.[12] And large concentrations of shrimp are susceptible to various viral diseases. In the crowded pools, healthy shrimp eat the sick ones, absorbing the virus and passing it on. Birds eat the shrimp they see struggling feebly on the surface of the pond, then go on to excrete the dead shrimp in another pond area, perhaps, miles away. Terrified farmers, fighting the mass die-offs taking place in their shrimp ponds, begin flushing them out with clean seawater—spreading the virus and the pollution into surrounding waters. Epidemics spread, wiping out the shrimp and savings of the farmers who had invested in this promising new crop. One year alone saw 80 percent of the shrimp farms near Bangkok go bankrupt.

Inefficient, underfunded, untrained, or corrupt, governments largely failed to cope. Proper regulations could neither be written nor enforced; officials were bribed to look the other way; powerful politicians protected special interests.

It is a sad story but not an unusual one. Confronted with rapid growth on a scale that Britain and the United States never had to face even in the most intense periods of their industrial revolutions, developing countries have incurred immense costs and liabilities that will dog them long into the future. Council on Foreign Relations senior fellow Elizabeth Economy estimates that pollution and related problems cost China the equivalent of 8 to 12 percent of GDP each year. The rate of desertification in northern China has doubled in the last generation. The deforestation of Sichuan Province has been rapid and radical; nine-tenths of the province's original forest cover has disappeared—driven by demand for everything from furniture and paper to chopsticks. According to Economy, deforestation and the uncontrolled destruction of wetlands caused the devastating Yangtze River floods of 1998, leaving three thousand dead, five million homeless, more than fifty-two million acres of land flooded, and causing more than $20 billion in damage.[13]

Earthquakes in the developing world are vastly more devastating because so much urban housing is built in violation of building codes, if building codes exist at all. Air pollution kills tens of thousands of people each year as drivers swelter and stall in the vast, chaotic traffic jams of cities like Jakarta and Mumbai. Fire, ambulance, and other services are utterly overwhelmed by the rapid, unplanned, and uncontrolled growth of urban conglomerations.

It is easy to miss the human dimension of the problems caused by countries attempting to face an onrushing wave of change and to catch up to the world's leading economies. It is not just a matter of inadequate urban planning and devastating pollution. Gilles Kepel, one of the world's leading experts in radical Islamic movements, traces a significant share of Egypt's political, economic, and social problems to its poorly funded, poorly staffed, poorly conceived, and poorly organized system of higher education.

"Establishments of long-term instruction" is a better name for these institutions than universities, wrote Kepel. More than half a million students enroll in programs that are "rigidly compartmentalized into narrow disciplines and offering degrees governed by an examination that yields little to the Koranic schools in its exclusive reliance on the routine memorization of manuals." When Kepel studied the system, poorly paid professors required students to buy poorly produced booklets containing the materials they would be required to memorize to get their degrees.[14]

Students who attend these institutions are told—and a few may actually believe—that what they are getting is a professional education to fit them for the modern world. In fact, they are prepared for little more than the underpaid make-work jobs that the overstaffed and incompetent Egyptian government provides university graduates. In Kepel's view, the situation of these students, and the fact that Islamist political movements organized to help students with the problems they faced—such as providing cheap copies of the "manuals" containing required course material and allowing students

to circumvent the high prices professors were charging—contributed significantly to the rise of radical Islam in Egypt.[15]

The last thing Egypt needs is more restless, half-educated young people
sullenly seeking poorly paid jobs in an overstaffed, underfunctioning government; at the same time it desperately needs qualified university graduates in a wide variety of fields. The current system, set up as part of
the modernizing rush that Nasser hoped would transform the country, costs
money that Egypt does not have, to provide services the country does
not need.

Meanwhile, the rich have their children educated abroad.

Egypt's university system is not uniquely bad; far from it. Nigerian universities are worse off; Mexican universities are in some respects little better. But all around the world today, in some of the countries that most need
to equip the rising generation with modern skills, eager and talented young
people are crammed into institutions of this kind.

None of these problems are new, and it seems likely that over time much
of the developing world will grow out of them. As societies get richer and
gather more experience dealing with the upheavals that capitalism brings in
its train, they are willing and able to do more to improve air and water quality, attend to health and safety issues, and so on.

Yet for now and perhaps for the foreseeable future, these countries face
different and in some ways more difficult challenges that the West ever did,
and the ultimate cost in squandered resources, environmental damage, and
lost lives will be higher than anything the West had to pay.

It is very easy for Anglo-Saxons to establish anticorruption panels, to
bemoan bad governance in many countries, and call for more maids with
more mops, and such measures are no doubt in many cases exactly what
would help. But none of this changes a basic and to some degree unfair fact
about the world we live in today: others must change and adjust much faster
and in far more difficult circumstances than the Anglo-Saxons ever had
to do.

The Anglo-Americans had another advantage. Today's modernizing
societies adopt capitalism in a world marketplace that is already filled with
powerful companies, sophisticated technologies, and financial markets of
great complexity and global reach. India today is struggling to open its retail
sector to chain stores and large supermarkets. This is a necessary step; large
and efficient retailers create national markets and reduce the cost of key
goods. The United States has excelled in the creation and development of
these chains since Sears, Roebuck and Montgomery Ward took advantage
of the railroads to build national systems of marketing and distribution.

India today has a retail landscape dominated by small mom-and-pop retailers. These retailers, ranging from the owners of grocery and hardware stores to pushcart vendors and itinerant salespeople, stand to lose their livelihoods if forced to compete with more efficient and better capitalized chain stores. These mom-and-pop retailers do something else that is very important in a democratic society: they vote.

The American debate today over super-retailers like Wal-Mart contains many of the elements of the Indian debate. But there is a key difference: the Indian debate triggers memories of foreign exploitation that is centuries old. Are we really going to let Wal-Mart and Home Depot into our country, opponents warn, and destroy the livelihood of millions of hardworking Indians so that foreign stockholders can get larger dividends? The British destroyed the Indian textile industry in the nineteenth century, nationalists point out. Are we going to stand by while Americans destroy Indian retailing?

Nationalist passions inflame American debates on issues like immigration and trade, and political firestorms sometimes erupt over issues like the 2006 proposed transfer of security responsibilities at U.S. ports to a firm headquartered in Dubai. The nationalist emotions rarely improve policy outcomes, and the result can often be expensive and self-defeating mistakes.

The United States is fortunate that such eruptions are relatively rare. In countries like Argentina, Venezuela, Turkey, and France, virtually every serious economic issue is also a nationalist issue, although as in the United States the economically advisable choice is very often not the choice that automatically commends itself to populist, nationalist opinion.

Such countries find themselves impaled, over and over, on the sharp horns of a very unpleasant dilemma. The choice that gratifies nationalist opinion in the short run will weaken the country in the long term; the "right" long-term choices are usually politically costly and sometimes ruinous for those who must make them.

Economists, both Anglo-Saxon and otherwise, are quite fond of lecturing developing countries about their shortcomings, and especially the over-staffed and underperforming governments so prevalent in so much of the world. How much better, we artlessly observe, are the sleek, well-managed governments of our own happy lands. Small enough to support a vibrant private sector, strong and active enough to regulate the dynamic economy, our Goldilocks governments are a model for the world.

And why, these economists and development specialists ask, do so many developing countries build these corrupt, inefficient states—too large and too grasping in some ways and too weak and too ineffective in others? Ignorance, prejudice, blind adherence to tradition, and the devious machinations of rent-seeking elites who hope to feather their nests in various unsavory ways.

What Anglo-Saxon opinion often misses is that the preference among many developing societies to build the largest and most powerful governments they can reflects several pressures. One is the well-grounded fear that without large powers these governments will be too weak—to stand up to powerful foreign countries, to preserve national unity in new and ethnically diverse countries, and to manage the disruptive consequences of capitalism. Thus the leaders of Meiji-era Japan believed with some reason that they needed a stronger and more active state than the Anglo-Saxon countries had at comparable stages of development. As Kemal Atatürk sought to bring order to the remnant of the Ottoman Empire that became modern Turkey, he contended with ethnic minorities at home, with religious traditionalists opposed to his modernization program, with invading Greek and Italian forces intent on territorial expansion, with Communist Russia to the north, and with a hostile Great Britain. Neither he nor the military leaders with whom he chiefly worked believed that a small, Anglo-Saxon–style state was the answer to Turkey's problems. Few could disagree.

Another reason is to provide employment. The spectacle of undereducated Egyptian graduates taking poorly paid jobs in an overstaffed government is depressing, but from the standpoint of the Egyptian government it is possibly not as depressing as millions of restless students and recent graduates who have no jobs at all.

There is another factor at work. The (relatively) small but (relatively) honest and competent governments of the Anglo-Saxon world do not exist in isolation. They grew out of a specific set of cultural and historical circumstances. They work for the Anglo-Saxon world as well as they do because the division of labor between civil society and government reflects our preferences and makes sense to us. Crucially, the government we have depends on the ability of Anglo-American society to govern itself in many respects, and especially in a capitalist context.

Americans need a less powerful federal government because at all levels of society business interests, state and local governments, civil society, families and individuals are constantly involved in making plans and decisions. Every county and municipality in the country is trying to attract business. Virtually every college and university is looking for ways to attract students by developing degree programs that help graduates get good jobs. Churches, synagogues, and mosques are setting to work to address social problems, feed the hungry, and meet the housing needs of the poor. Jealous politicians are hunting for scandals and abuses committed by their opponents—while also trying to develop policy proposals that win varying degrees of public and business support. Armies of PTA mothers and fathers besiege school administrators to demand new programs and facilities. Yet this dynamism is not anarchy; by and large, Americans respect and obey the law—even when no one is watching.

The greatest wealth of countries like the United States and Great Britain is not their mineral deposits or their agricultural land. It is not the money that they have in the bank. It is the mentality and habits of the nation at large. These are peoples accustomed to governing themselves, accustomed to promoting enterprise, ready to join in spontaneous and private activities of all kinds—but also accustomed to an ordered liberty whose roots now are many centuries old. This human and social capital is by far the most valuable to have—and by far the hardest to get.

In much of the world today, powerful states represent attempts to overcome the absence of this dynamism and order. The central government must be strong because local government is both feeble and corrupt. The state must play a leading role in economic development because the society at large lacks the education, life experience, or orientation for large-scale economic activities.

In many countries, economic know-how has been concentrated in a small group: a group of families who had close relations with the former colonial power, or in an ethnic minority—Chinese in Indonesia, Malaysia, and Thailand; Indians in East Africa; Germans in the Balkans; Greeks, Jews, and Armenians in much of the old Ottoman Empire including Egypt; Germans and Jews in eastern Europe. The nationalist struggles of the twentieth century often resulted in the expulsion or persecution of minorities who were both rich and unpopular. The majority had political power, but little understanding of economic life. Hastily and poorly educated government bureaucrats attempt to fill the vacancy—to substitute planned government activity for what was formerly a vibrant and private economy. The results are almost always bad.

Unfortunately, just because a strong state is necessary does not make it beneficial. The lesser of two evils is still an evil. The strong states that many countries adopted to help them make the transition to capitalism may have started out with high ideals. In some cases, they preserved those ideals for many years. Yet the disadvantages that have led the Anglo-Americans to favor relatively small governments that play only limited roles in economic planning are serious ones, and most developing countries have paid the full price for their choice. In many cases, rent-seeking elites *do* end up monopolizing and abusing the economic power of the state—and, often enough, they use that economic power to build lasting one-party autocracies. In many others, bureaucrats make vast and tragically mistaken development decisions.

The developing world is also littered with white elephants—ambitious development projects that went badly awry. Fidel Castro's Cuba is a grave-yard of impractical schemes: plans to boost sugar production to record levels with misguided and unworkable methods, to breed herds of super-productive cows, to create a world-class biotech industry, and so forth. The three-thousand-room Yu Kyong Hotel in Pyongyang, North Korea, is 105 stories tall but has never opened for business. Not only did the tourists never arrive; the building has reportedly begun to sag and the elevators cannot be used. Africa is littered with the rusted-out hulks of industrial facilities that were once-hopeful symbols of progress.[16] The Gezhouba Dam on the Yangtze River was built during the Cultural Revolution as a "birthday pres-ent" for Chairman Mao; during its construction half of China's total invest-ments in the sector went to this project. Now completed, the dam backs up river traffic due to a poorly planned and inadequate lock system, fails to generate enough electricity in much of the year, and its reservoir has become polluted enough to drive important species toward extinction.[17]

While Anglo-Saxon economists often yield to the temptation to issue familiar sermons about the inevitable failure of planned economies, it is more important to reflect on the way that history gives so many countries less attractive options than those the Anglo-Americans have had at key stages in their history.

To make matters worse, the geopolitics are different. For the Anglo-Americans, the process of capitalist development coincided with and rein-forced a great transformation of the global political and security climate in ways they fundamentally liked and understood. It brought both countries to pinnacles of power and prestige. The maritime system was a good thing. For others, beginning with France, the experience has been much more prob-lematic. Russia, Germany, China, Japan, the Arab world: so many areas of the world have seen their plans for order and domination thrust aside, even as the world within their borders has been changed in deeply unwelcome ways by the values, practices, and influence of the Anglophones and of the foreigners who have learned to succeed in their system. The Anglo-American order and the liberal capitalism it brings have been the harbingers of failure, marginalization, defeat, and frustration for much of the world.

Like beavers, the Anglophones have been building a dam; as the dam rises and the pond grows, the beavers see a world that is getting better and better. They see plenty of food, security for all. But not all the animals are happy. There are some who manage well enough, the fish and the salamanders and perhaps the raccoons, but the squirrels, red and black, are not thrilled about the destruction of trees; the rabbits lose their nests and the foxes their dens.

Culture Clash

As Americans tried to grapple with a world moving in odd and contradictory directions after the end of the Cold War, two leading schools of thought emerged. One saw the triumph of liberal politics, capitalist economics, and American power, and projected the inevitable and continuing rise of the maritime system. This perception contributed to the enthusiastic reception that Francis Fukuyama received when he speculated that the world had reached the "end of history." Others noted the persistent and even growing opposition to key American values and policies in much of the world and speculated with Samuel Huntington that the world might be headed for a "clash of civilizations." The debate between supporters of the Fukuyama and the Huntington theses was a contemporary form of a very old debate in Western history.

When Fukuyama asked whether the end of the Cold War was the end of history, he consciously placed the idea in the long tradition of the Western enlightenment which holds that events are ultimately guided by universal reason. What is true in France is, or soon will be, true in Germany and China. Humanity is the same everywhere; the cultural differences that we see are accidental, not essential; as human societies develop according to the universal laws of nature they will tend to converge in their political and economic arrangements and in their ideological beliefs. Cultural differences will persist, but they will be trivial—Italians prefer pasta, Swedes herring, Singaporeans fish-head curry. On the important issues, however, they will all be the same: postreligious, democratic, liberal, capitalist.

Huntington's world is a world of irrepressible conflicts and irreconcilable logics. Religion and culture make people responsive to different incentives and ideas. Muslims do not want to live like Westerners; Hindus do not want to live like Confucians. The Serbs do not wish that Serbia was more like France. What is true in Baghdad is false in Delhi.

Fukuyama's world culminates in a secular version of the city of God, with all mankind living reasonably happily under a single set of laws. In Huntington's world, we have the Tower of Babel: God has "confused the tongues" of the world's peoples and we may never agree on a single framework that can govern us all.

These recent debates echoed the conflicts that appeared in nineteenth-century European politics between those whose first loyalties were with a universal, worldwide revolution (whether bourgeois or socialist in inspiration) and the nationalists whose concern was for the liberation and development of their own peoples. Fukuyama stands in the line of Kant, Hegel, Marx, and Manchester School economists like Richard Cobden and John Bright; Huntington is the successor of Giambattista Vico, Johann Gottfried Herder, the nineteenth-century Romantics, and Isaiah Berlin.

The debate between universal reason and cultural particularity has greatly enriched Western intellectual life. Elements of both positions make sense. On the one hand, a kind of universal logic informs the process of globalization, and there is visible convergence taking place in many countries as the needs of economic and social development force institutional changes and reforms. On the other hand, there are a great many facts that the cultural paradigm covers much better than the idea that universal reason has triumphed by bringing the historical process to its close. We did not need 9/11 to remind us that culturally rooted conflict does not seem on the verge of disappearing from our world.

In raising the prospect of a clash of civilizations, Huntington was neither arguing that such a clash was inevitable nor advocating that we have one. He hoped that an analysis of the forces driving the world in this direction would help guide actions in ways that make such clashes less likely. To carry out this analysis, he finds himself using ideas about history and culture that originated to a large extent with the work of Herder and went on to influence a series of Romantic and nationalist writers in eighteenth- and nineteenth-century Europe.

Although he attacked Kant and his cosmopolitan vision of a postpatriotic world order, Herder was in many ways a figure of the Enlightenment. He was liberal, republican, and even egalitarian—things that were much harder to be in eighteenth-century Germany than today. He was also Abrahamic: he believed that the historical process is one of development leading humanity from a lower level to a glorious culmination. But Herder's understanding of the path toward that final stage was distinctly different from the vision that was and remains most prevalent among modernists.

From Immanuel Kant through Alexandre Kojève, the Hegelian philosopher immediately responsible for the concept of the end of history as it appears in Fukuyama's book, the interpreters of progressive modernism have been cosmopolitan. That is, they have assigned at most a passing importance to the cultural differences among human societies. The drivers of history, the big forces that actually make things happen, are universal: common values, laws of economics, the structure of human nature itself. This is universal history, a view of history that concentrates on the forces that transcend geographical, cultural, and civilizational boundaries. This is a cosmopolitan view of the world: what matters most are the things we have in common.

Herder, though himself largely sympathetic to the French Revolution, wrote at a time when many German patriots were reacting against what they saw as the arrogant universalism of that revolution. Like many Germans of his day, Herder envisioned a different path to the end of history, one less cosmopolitan and less focused on reason. Whether you speak of folk traditions and customs or religion with its appeal to the deepest, preconscious recesses of the human soul, culture in Herder's view is an essential part of humanity. This means that while all people may be equal, they are not the same. The German is not the same as the Frenchman, and what is true for Parisians is not necessarily true for Bavarians.

Herder was a student of both ancient and modern languages; he laid great stress on the way that language shapes thought and perception. Those who speak different languages don't just use different words; they see different things. Those distinct perceptions and the cultures that form around them are not, as cosmopolitans tend to think, secondary phenomena of only minor importance. They are the stuff and substance of human nature; diversity is an essential part of what it means to be human.

Herder did not believe that people could, should, or would "overcome" their cultural differences over time: when the end of history came we would not all be speaking Esperanto. Instead, he believed that the diversity of perspectives would persist and deepen as humanity moved toward the culmination of history. His vision of the end of history was not of a human community sharing a single culture and set of institutions, but of a family of different and sometimes competing perceptions and ideas. This is particular history; all humanity may be moving in the same general direction, but each nation, each culture, and each civilization rises on its own path and in its own particular way. And while human history will reach a posthistorical state of universal peace, that peace would be based on many different ideas, values, institutions, and priorities as expressed by the different cultures of the world.

Both views can go wrong. Fascism is a perversion of Herder's view that nationality is an essential feature of human identity; Marxism-Leninism is a perversion of universal cosmopolitan logic. One cannot quite divide the two schools neatly into left and right. Today's leftist multiculturalists stand in Herder's tradition, as do Burkean conservatives on the right. At the same time, American neoconservatives as well as most liberal internationalists follow the universal and cosmopolitan traditions of Hegel and Kant.

Those who believe that Anglo-American economic and political liberalism are sweeping the world clearly take their stand on the ground of universal history. They believe that the cultural differences between, say, Muslim Arabs in the Middle East and evangelical Christians in Texas are ultimately not very important. Given the chance, Arab Muslims will swiftly embrace certain core values and practices of Fort Worth. Others, who think in the categories of particular history, believe the Anglo-American Whigs are trying to impose a uniform ideology on a complex world that will never accept it. Many multiculturalists and postmodernists, for example, hold that the influence of culture on human nature is so profound and inescapable that far from moving toward a grand convergence around liberal democratic capitalism, the world is permanently divided into radically different cultural and/or civilizational zones. People don't all want the same thing, and therefore people throughout the world will never finally agree to buy what the Whigs want to sell.

WHILE SOME THINKERS BELIEVE the two modes of historical thought are mutually exclusive, it is useful to keep both dimensions in mind when trying to analyze the way that the capitalist world, and especially the Anglo-American portion of it, interacts with the rest of the world. Capitalism considered as a social and economic force works along the lines of universal history: it cuts across cultural and civilizational boundaries and imposes its own logic and realities on people everywhere, regardless of what they think or want. That is, once one country or one part of the world goes capitalist in a serious way, others must either match the technological, economic, and social development of the world capitalist leaders or lose their ability to control their own destiny as power flows rapidly and irresistibly to those able to master the new dynamics. The Japanese were able to master the system and hold their own in the nineteenth century; the Chinese, among many others, were unable to do it and endured decades of humiliation and loss. The different abilities of China and Japan to meet the test of the nineteenth century may have been rooted in the history and culture of those two countries, but the challenge they both faced was an objective one which they had to encounter, like it or not.

What convinced so many Americans in particular, but others too, that history might have come to an end after the Cold War was the evidence that liberal capitalist democracy on the Anglo-American model was demonstrably more effective as an economic model than any existing rival. Whiggery achieved (or many thought it had) a perfect match between its ethical and spiritual values and its economic and geopolitical goals. Its approach to secular economic issues was seen as so effective that anyone who wanted to avoid falling into backwardness and helplessness had no choice but to follow the Anglo-American way. For the most part, God's blessings rain down in buckets on those who follow the Walrus and the Carpenter; those who don't must make do with much, much less.

Following Kojève, Fukuyama grounded his political analysis in the force that Hegel believed drove history: the human need for recognition. For orthodox Hegelians, the desire to be accepted and respected as an equal, as a full human being, is the motor driving political, religious, and cultural history. Originally our ancestors might have once all been equal in the primitive, prehistorical era, but as population increased and people began to compete over resources, the world divided between winners and losers—between the masters, who dominated their societies and forced the losers to work for and serve them, and the slaves, who lost the competition but preferred to stay alive as slaves rather than die fighting.

This was, of course, much nicer for the masters than the slaves, but both sides of the human race were less than fulfilled by this division. The slaves were considered less than human and were reduced to the status of things. Obviously, their desire for recognition was not met. But the masters, too, encountered problems. You can be recognized as an equal only by your equals; slaves can work for you and tremble with fear when you want them to, but they cannot provide the free and unforced recognition of your equal humanity that you most deeply desire.

Hegel saw the eras of human history as eras in a long process through which the slaves and the masters gradually moved beyond this original division. Christianity, for example, proclaimed that the slaves and masters were both fully human in God's eyes. They were equal in theory, even if practice lagged behind.

In Fukuyama's view, liberal democratic society finally achieved the goal that all humanity has been seeking for thousands of years. This is not because it produces a cornucopia of very attractive consumer goods. It is because liberal democracy provides a solution to the problem of recognition. Liberal democracy honors the equality and dignity of all people—unlike earlier systems of feudalism or slave societies. People in Western societies are not just equal in theory; they are equal at the polls and equal before the law.

But people don't just want to be recognized as equal, Fukuyama notes. They also want to compete, to win, and to enjoy the rewards of success. Liberal democratic society squares the circle; it allows people to compete for honor, glory, and wealth in political and economic competition—but losers aren't utterly crushed.

Liberal capitalist democracy is a better fit for human nature than competing economic and political systems; that is why it wins. The collapse of the Soviet Union represented, Fukuyama argued, the last attempt by a great power to organize itself on any other basis than liberal democratic capitalism. The Soviet defeat showed the futility of trying to oppose the system once and for all.

This argument makes a great deal of sense; as far as it goes, it cannot be refuted. Yet for a social system that meets every human need, liberal democracy has a lot of enemies. If liberal capitalist democracy meets human needs so perfectly, why do so many people hate it and fight against it?

From Herder forward, students of culture and particular history have had an answer: the problem of collective recognition. Individuals don't just want to be recognized as equal on an individual basis. People derive their sense of identity in part from the important groups to which they belong (a race, a tribe, a nationality, a religion). Their individual drive for recognition is not over until their faith or their nation has achieved recognition as well.

For Herder, human beings need to belong to a group, and the identity of an individual is necessarily rooted in that sense of belonging. From this perspective, the distinction between individual and group rights that cosmopolitan thinkers and Anglo-American individualists often draw begins to look a little fuzzy. An insult to a collective of which I feel myself to be part is not just an insult to the collective. It is an insult to me, and my need for recognition has not been met until the groups of which I am part have been given their due.

This is not just a theoretical issue. In the real world, people are not presented with an ideal "liberal society"; they are presented with something very concrete: the maritime order. To accept liberal society one must not only accept the ideas and values of capitalism as an ideal system; one must also accept, or at least be prepared to tolerate, the international system that has brought liberal capitalism to its current stage of development. The maritime order, the unique position of the United States, the privileged position of the various Western states that were quick to master its techniques along with other and often unpleasing aspects of the current global system, are inextricably entwined with the abstract concept of liberal society in the here and now.

This is a version of the problem that Germans faced in Herder's day, and is why so many leading German intellectuals and artists rejected the French Revolution despite their sympathy for some of its values. In their specific historical situation, they were not faced simply with the question of democracy values versus royal autocracy. The French Revolution might be welcome in some ways, but arrogant and extortionate occupations by the French army and subjugation to schemes to advance the personal and dynastic interests of Napoleon Bonaparte were completely unacceptable to many Germans. The abstract system might be appealing; the only concrete package on offer was not. German nationalism became linked with anti-Enlightenment values, a development whose fateful consequences troubled Europe for many generations.

Germans rejected the French Revolution if that meant accepting permanent French supremacy in Europe. There are many people today who reject liberal capitalism if that means accepting American leadership in the world.

There is more to it than that. Liberal democratic capitalism today is not just an expression of American culture. As we have seen, it is deeply rooted in the heritage of the West as a whole, and more especially Christianity. Does accepting liberal capitalist democracy mean living in a world in which the Christian religion is acknowledged as the leading religion, and in which Western history, Western ideals, and Western powers have a special role? A great many people in a great many countries today will not freely accept a world order that seems to entail these consequences.

More than this, culture shapes the way we understand and define our individual desires and goals. For many people in the world, equality among human beings implies more equality of income than it does for many people in the Anglo-Saxon world. Americans still debate what equality means between women and men; globally there is very little consensus on what this might mean. Contemporary Westerners believe that equality means the full equality of women; sentiment on what equality means for illegal aliens is rather more divided, and many Westerners are quite comfortable with a legal system which systematically marginalizes and otherwise penalizes illegal aliens. In much of the world, the feeling is just the opposite, and people feel that it is natural and proper to have different rules and requirements for women and for men, while Western immigration rules and the West's legal discrimination against "illegal" aliens are profoundly and unacceptably unjust. The quest for equality and freedom may well be universal; these values, however, are defined and sought in particular contexts and people often do not agree on what they mean.

For global society to meet my need for recognition, it must do more than offer me legal equality. I must have what I feel to be cultural equality as well. If I live in a world order that does not respect my religious faith and does not honor my moral intuitions about the way a just world should work, my demand for recognition has not yet been met.

Culture does not just shape our attitudes toward the values and power patterns of liberal democratic society as it actually exists in the maritime order; it also affects our ability to flourish in it. Unfortunately, being good or being bad at capitalism has enormous consequences for the international position of any nation or culture. It doesn't matter much that Japan and Cuba like baseball while Germany and Nigeria don't. It matters a great deal that Germany and Japan are pretty good at capitalism while, so far, Cuba and Nigeria aren't.

This effect can be self-reinforcing. A culture that doesn't like capitalism to begin with or isn't well equipped to play this particular game will be less and less happy with the way the world is going. Countries who don't like Anglo-Saxon capitalism and Anglo-Saxon culture to begin with will not like a world order that is dominated by Anglo-Saxon power and Anglo-Saxon values. They will also fall behind, failing to adopt new technologies or develop new industries and companies that can benefit from the opportunities of the global system. They become poorer and less powerful compared to cultures that are better at playing this particular game. All this is likely to make them like capitalism even less, and to make it harder to play the game well. It is frighteningly easy for countries to be caught up in a vicious circle of alienation and failure.

The result is a paradox. Universal Hegelian history and the forces of particular history and cultural difference have teamed up to shape the world that we live in. The ability to compete in the emerging capitalistic framework is the most important force in the global distribution of power and wealth. Since culture does so much to shape the individual desires and perceptions on which the affinity for and ability at capitalist competition depends, the advance of capitalism makes culture an ever more powerful factor in determining the global power structure.

It is a frustrating paradox for those expecting the end of history and the reign of peace after every Anglo-American triumph. Liberal capitalism is a force of universal history if ever there was one. It cuts like a scythe across every barrier between cultures and civilizations to impose its own logic across the world. But the result, so far, has not been the universal democratic peace that the Anglo-Americans keep looking for.

Au contraire: the triumph of liberal democratic capitalism has given new power and new energy to the forces that oppose it. When liberal capitalism shapes the flow of world history, and culture shapes the ability of different states and societies to manage capitalist development, culture becomes increasingly important as a factor in world politics and power.

Far from satisfying the deepest desires of human beings, the present world system and world order frustrate and enrage many people. Hegelians can still argue that at some future point the misguided enemies of capitalism will overcome the backward values and ideas that they have imbibed from their culture and join the supporters of the world system. This could well happen, but there is no guarantee that it will happen soon.

Americans will not understand their role in the world until they have fully grasped the paradoxical relationship between the success of American society at home and even internationally and the level of global unhappiness with the American project and the American way. Success builds American confidence in the whig narrative and the American project; it creates resistance to it as well. The bigger the dam, the bigger the pond; that makes the beavers happy and smug, but the squirrels, foxes, and rabbits become angrier and more alarmed.

The first five questions that opened this book have now received at least partial answers. We have looked at the distinctive cultural and political agenda that the Anglo-Americans bring to world politics. We have examined the geopolitical and economic strategies that enabled them to prevail in the power politics of the last three hundred years. We have seen how they built two successive versions of the maritime system. We have reviewed the distinctive view the Anglo-Americans have of the historical process as a whole and of their place in it—and we have seen why their expectations of universal peace have been so frequently and so painfully disappointed. One final question remains. If the Anglo-American expectation that the maritime system is leading the world to an era of peaceful prosperity is, to say the least, premature, what then is the point of Anglo-American power? What does all this history mean, and what can it teach us today—both about the likely prospects of the maritime order and about the meaning of Anglo-American power in the larger human story?

Part Five

The Lessons of History

Twenty • The Future of Sea Power

T his book is a thought experiment, twisting the knobs on the telescope of history to see what new patterns emerge when we shift from the more usual focus on "European civilization" or "the West" as the chief protagonist in the three hundred years since the Glorious Revolution and concentrate instead on the rise of the maritime order, largely though not exclusively based on the power of the English-speaking world. From this point of view, the English Channel seems wider and deeper than usual—and the Atlantic seems smaller and less deep.

Our twist of the telescope, the shift from an emphasis on a united West to the maritime system and the English-speaking world as the chief hero (and sometimes villain) of the story, is intended less as a refutation of the conventional story than a refinement of it. I do not advocate discarding the concept of a Western civilization that has played a crucial role in the most recent centuries of world history, but I do think we should look more deeply into the structure of the West.

Up until this point, I have described what happened in modern history, asked why it happened, and examined how the English-speaking world has interpreted and understood its experience to show the geopolitical, economic, and ultimately cultural foundations of Anglo-American power during the last three centuries. This is the long view of American power: instead of seeing the last sixty years of American primacy as an isolated period in world history, we can see it as the latest stage in the long-term development of the maritime order.

As we shift from developing and exploring this perspective on American power to exploring the uses of that perspective for Americans and others in the world of today, a new question appears. How should a knowledge of the history of the maritime order and the long view of American power influence debates over American grand strategy and over key issues in American foreign policy?

History does not give policy makers infallible answers, but carefully used it provides a context that makes our debates sharper and smarter. To ground the discussion of American foreign policy in the long-term history of the maritime order highlights the geopolitical, economic, and cultural foundations of America's global position. This focus promotes a clearer discussion of the issues and priorities that really matter, while simultaneously providing a deeper, wider, richer, and ultimately more useful context for discussions of American policy and power. I would go further still. It is impossible to think clearly about questions of American power and world order today without grasping the story of the long rise of the maritime system. The history of the maritime system is the best available guide to America's history, its current situation, and the choices that confront it; at least in the United States the study of that history ought to become the foundation of world and American history curricula. More broadly, the knowledge of this history needs to become a part of the intellectual equipment of everyone, Americans and foreigners alike, involved in the formation and discussion of American foreign policy. It may not be universally popular to argue that "Wasp studies," so to speak, should return to center stage, but this is a perspective that those who care about power—whether they wish to reform, overthrow, or perpetuate the global power system unchanged—need to study.

The long view can often put contemporary debates in perspective. The antiterror and security legislation in both Britain and the United States after 9/11, for example, is clearly the latest stage in a long tradition of such laws in times of real or perceived threat. This is, on the one hand, reassuring. Those who fight these laws in the belief that they represent a permanent loss of freedom are probably wrong. For the last four hundred years, the English-speaking world has been generally moving in the direction of allowing individuals greater and greater personal and political freedom. That progress has frequently been suspended and even reversed in time of war, but the restrictions have, so far, always been lifted when the danger is past. On the other hand, the record also shows clearly that these laws have sometimes been more severe than needed, and individuals and groups have suffered serious injustice as a result.

The long view can also enhance our understanding of alliance and coalition politics. For those who consider only America's history as a world power, history began in the 1940s; only World War II and the Cold War can serve as examples of how international partnerships and coalitions work—

or fail. Both of these alliances were, by the standards of the maritime system, relatively straightforward. The Cold War alliances forged in the late
1940s survived for forty years with little change; the World War II alliance
with the Soviet Union was more tempestuous, but American involvement in
the war lasted less than four years. These unusually benign experiences may
have left Americans unprepared for the twists and turns more characteristic of multipower coalitions in long wars. The wars against Louis XIV
and Napoleon featured complex and fractious coalitions in which the different agendas and priorities of the coalition partners had serious and sometimes, from the British point of view, very unfortunate consequences for the
course of the war. The war on terror is still relatively young, but already
its international politics look more like the politics of the older and more
complex partnerships than like the relatively simple international coalitions of the last fifty years. A deeper awareness of these dynamics would
have helped the Bush administration in the years after 9/11 and enabled
both the administration's critics and its supporters to make more thoughtful and appropriate policy recommendations during that confused and
difficult time.

The domestic politics of the Cold War and World War II were also more
straightforward than those of earlier international conflicts. During the wars
against France, British politicians were often deeply divided not only on
the strategy but on the necessity and the morality of the conflicts. Many
of Britain's most famous political and intellectual leaders sided with the
Americans during the American Revolution and with the French during
much of the French Revolution. It was domestic politics more than developments on the battlefield that brought Britain to the negotiating table to end
the War of the Spanish Succession and the Seven Years' War.

A better knowledge of the history of the maritime order would have stood
the United States in good stead after the fall of the Soviet Union in 1989.
Not only would this knowledge have helped limit the illusion that history
was over and that the nation could safely withdraw its attention from international affairs; it would have also helped Americans recognize the changes
that were taking place and think more clearly about the choices they had.
Over the last three hundred years, the maritime order has existed under two
very different sets of conditions. Both Britain and the United States at various times have been actively defending a maritime system against direct
attack by a power or coalition of powers seeking to overturn its foundations;
sometimes they have found themselves trying to manage an order that is not
being attacked. The two tasks require quite different priorities and outlooks,
but they are both difficult and demanding. Better understanding of the diffi-

culties and responsibilities of managing a world system in relatively peaceful times would have helped the United States after 1989; a deeper understanding of the dynamics and dangers of defending the system against an
attack would have helped the Bush administration avoid some of the expensive errors it made after 9/11. Whether at war or at peace, future generations
of American leaders are likely to benefit from a deeper appreciation of the
tasks and accomplishments of their predecessors.

In addition to casting light on particular policy questions, the long view
helps us make sense of the big questions we face: on the prospects for
American power and on how to meet the challenges of this, in the fourth
century of the Anglo-American era.

America in Decline?

Since the end of the Cold War, policy makers and engaged thinkers in the
United States and elsewhere have debated the future course of American
power. Broadly speaking, there are two principal positions in the debate.
Some argue that the United States has already begun or is about to begin a
process of inexorable decline. Others argue that the "unipolar" world
described by Charles Krauthammer in 1990 is likely to endure and that
American power may be destined to become even greater as time goes by. In
the context of maritime history, this debate appears too stark. Decline and
continuing unipolarity are both possible futures; neither, however, appears
likely.

Declinist arguments generally proceed from one of two standpoints: a
general argument about the rise and fall of civilizations, or analogies, either
explicit or implied, between the United States and Great Britain.

The civilization argument rests primarily on a loose syllogism and an
identification. First, its proponents argue from history that all civilizations
decline. The United States, they go on to say, is a part of Western civilization, whose decline is plain to see. The United States not only must decline;
its decline is already upon us. This is the argument that Sam Huntington
makes in the last chapter of *The Clash of Civilizations*. A second generic
argument is like unto it: All empires decline. The United States is an empire.
Therefore, the United States will decline.

These arguments are less reliable than they are sometimes thought to be,
and not just because proving that something must someday decline is very

different from proving that it is currently declining. Rooted in the work of thinkers like Oswald Spengler and Arnold Toynbee, these arguments reflect ideas about civilizations and history that looked more probable in the early and middle years of the twentieth century than they do today. Consider the idea that all civilizations decline. Fifty or one hundred years ago, perhaps, China looked like an example of a formerly great civilization (and empire) that had fallen into contemptible weakness and backwardness. Does it still look that way today? What about India? These are among the world's most ancient civilizations and they don't rise and fall so much as they wax and wane, and then wax again. They have good times and bad times, but they recover from their setbacks and go on—much as they have been doing back to the earliest written records we have. Some civilizations do fall; others pass through one crisis after another. The idea that there is some sort of inexorable law of aging and decline to which all civilizations are somehow subject looked quite compelling in 1920, when all the world's civilizations except for those with roots in western Europe (and Japan) appeared to be tottering toward their doom.

Today, these civilizations no longer seem to be ready for the graveyard. This fact should and perhaps ultimately will discredit the idea that civilizations are analogous to individuals with birth, youth, maturity, and decline in inevitable sequence. For now, however, the faith in decline remains strong, but the location of decline has changed. China, India, and Islam are rising and today are held out as examples of vigorous and expanding civilizations; it is Europe that is often seen as the one tottering into an assisted-living facility, and this decline is held to reflect the inexorable processes of historical necessity.

The real lesson here should be that there is nothing inevitable about the decline and fall of civilizations, and that the outlook for civilizations and cultures can be transformed on short notice. It is true that great civilizations have fallen, but this is the exception rather than the rule. Invasions whether by barbarian tribes or by "civilized" people behaving very badly, demographic or ecological catastrophes, or religious conversion can lead to cultural changes so profound that later observers speak of the fall of a given civilization—but this perhaps was never very common and is becoming rarer today. All the world's great civilizations now are very ancient, and all of them have survived many shocks and many winters. Great civilizations don't fall; they are pushed, and it takes an unusual combination of circumstances for a whole civilization to be pushed past its breaking point.

Even granting the premises that the United States remains part of Western civilization and that Western civilization as a whole is on the decline, one must also ask how closely America's political fate is tied to that of the rest of the West—and especially that of western Europe. For Huntington and for other culturally focused analysts like Robert Merry, they are joined at the hip. The West despite its differences is a unit in world politics, and an alliance between the United States and Europe against the world's rising civilizations is our only real choice. Tragically, such analysts generally conclude, this alliance will only prolong and delay the inevitable fall of the aging West in the face of competition from more vigorous civilizations.

Perhaps—but the historical record seems to show that the British triumphed over the Spanish and the French because they had different concepts of religion, different social values, and different ideas about the relationship between government and society. World history seems to confirm that this was no fluke; the differences within major civilizations are often more important than similarities when it comes to the political destinies of states and empires.

The two ancient halves of the Greco-Roman civilization shared many values and ideas, and Greek philosophy and culture were decisive elements in Roman cultural life. Yet from a political standpoint their destinies were not linked. The high point of Athenian power was touched in about 430 B.C., close to the start of the Peloponnesian War. Arguably the high point of Greek power more generally came with Alexander the Great's conquest of Egypt and Persia one hundred years later. The decline and fall of Greece did not cause the fall of Rome. On the contrary: Roman power rose as Greek power declined, and it was Roman arms that put an end to the power of some of the chief Hellenistic kingdoms. Not until four hundred years after Alexander's death did the emperor Trajan expand the Roman Empire's boundaries to their greatest extent—and three more centuries passed before the Goths sacked Rome.

There are many other cases in which different parts of the world's great civilizations have faced very different political outlooks at the same time. In the Islamic world, Arab power was collapsing in Spain and declining in the western Mediterranean as the Ottoman, Persian, and Moghul empires were rising to new heights of glory in the early modern world. At the start of the twentieth century Japan established itself as a great power even as China, the source of Japanese culture and civilization, entered what seemed to most observers like the final stages of collapse and decrepitude.

I am not among those who see Europe doomed to inexorable decline. The Old World has the resources to address and overcome its problems should it choose to do so. But even if the European decline continues, this does not mean that some inner weakness or exhaustion in Western civilization will drag the United States down as well. The differences between Europe and the English-speaking world, not the similarities, continue to shape events in the Atlantic world today, as they have done since the seventeenth century. Europe's decline—if Europe does not emerge from its current doldrums and the decline continues—does not imply a similar decline for the United States or the collapse of the maritime system, any more than the decline of the Hellenistic kingdoms after the death of Alexander implied the fall of Rome.

THE SECOND FAMILY of declinist arguments tends to emerge from relatively unsophisticated and unsystematic readings of maritime history and the dynamics of sea power. One of the most common is the argument that colossal budget and/or trade deficits are about to cause the collapse of the American economy and therefore of the American world position.

The observers making these arguments are not entirely misguided. The economic dynamism of the United States remains the key to its global position, and anything that threatens that dynamism poses, potentially, a mortal threat to American power. But the relationship between debt, even very high levels of debt, and economic dynamism is not as simple as it looks.

As we have seen, as early as 1850 Macaulay was able to point to more than 150 years of dire prophecy about the national debt and national ruin when he described the foundation of the Bank of England. Since Macaulay's time, 150 more years have passed, years that have rung and rung again with dire prophecies of ruin. Yet, so far, the ruin has not come. The United States was a debtor nation through the nineteenth century; it was a much greater and richer country after one hundred years of debt. The American national debt was far higher as a percentage of GDP after World War II than it was sixty years later. The ruin did not come. The press echoed and re-echoed through the Reagan administration that the unprecedented budget and trade deficits of those years—hundred-billion-dollar-plus deficits stretching ahead "as far as the eye can see"—meant that ruin was at hand.

The result? Between 1983 and 2006 the American economy enjoyed the two longest expansions in its history, punctuated only by short and mild recessions. The European and Japanese competitors who seemed on the point of overtaking the American economy in 1983 spent the next generation anxiously studying and seeking to replicate the extraordinary successes the American economy went on to enjoy. Far from staggering under the hideous mountains of Reagan-era debt, the Clinton administration went on to bask in a prosperity unmatched in the history of the world.

The history of the maritime order suggests that the Anglo-Americans have not excelled at staying out of debt. On the contrary, they have often had larger debts than other people. But they have historically been better than others at managing debt through creative finance and flexible markets, and they have been unusually successful at making good use of borrowed money. The ability to bear staggering, unprecedented levels of debt while continuing to prosper and to grow has been the hallmark of the Anglo-Saxons since they borrowed the techniques of "Dutch finance" in the late seventeenth century. They may someday lose this knack, but so far they seem to be managing.

Prosperity and power in the shadow of debt is now more than three hundred years old, yet the cries continue to draw the same attention and alarm as if the phenomenon and the warning were new. At each stage in the rise of the various debt mountains of the English-speaking world, there have always been voices ready to point out that the new debts are greater than the old, and that the danger of collapse is therefore greater than ever before.

Perhaps, but it may also be true that the recurring cries of alarm are part of the cultural processes which, for over three hundred years now, have enabled the English speakers to manage their financial affairs. Over that time prophecies of imminent financial doom have been brought forward by thoughtful, well-educated, and well-respected figures who have managed to assemble powerful arguments well fortified with bristling bulwarks of fact; they have led public and elite opinion into one bout after another of panic, pessimism, and gloom—and have been profoundly and perpetually wrong.

A STRONGER SET OF ARGUMENTS arises from comparisons between the American world position today and that of Britain one hundred years ago. Just as Britain was ultimately surpassed by rising powers like Russia, Germany, and the United States, the argument runs, the United States today will be left behind by rising superpowers in Asia. China and India are now achieving growth rates three to four times greater than those of the United States. Fairly quickly on the basis of purchasing power parity and more slowly on the basis of market exchange rates, the economies of these countries may match and surpass the American economy in size and technological sophistication. When that happens, the United States will be in a position like that of Great Britain in 1910: facing economic and political rivals with larger populations and larger economies than its own. In such a world, the United States, as the argument goes, would have no choice but to follow Britain's long path of decline. This kind of logic underpins part of Yale scholar Paul Kennedy's argument that the United States may be facing "imperial overstretch," a condition in which our commitments outrun our ability to maintain them.

This analogy on its face seems both accurate and inevitable; it is probably the chief intellectual pillar supporting the view that some form of American decline is inevitable in the twenty-first century. But a closer look at even this analogy in the light of the history of the maritime system suggests that the forces supporting the unique American position in the world may be appreciably stronger than they appear at first glance.

To begin, Britain achieved its unique global position at a time when it had less than a third of France's population—and about half of its estimated GDP. In 1700 the U.K. is believed to have had a population of about 6 million; France had 21 million. British GDP at that time is estimated at around $10.6 million in 2006 values; the French GDP was $19.5 million.[1]

The same pattern held true on a global scale. In 1820, China is believed to have had the largest economy in the world, accounting for 33 percent of global GDP.[2] Economically, Britain's acquisition of its Indian empire was like a toad swallowing a cow; Britain's share of global GDP in those years was only 5 percent,[3] and the Indian economy remained significantly larger than Britain's through the end of the nineteenth century.[4] Britain's GDP as a percentage of global GDP is believed to have peaked in about 1870 at 9 percent of total world output—almost two hundred years *after* Britain began its rise to world power, and at a time when some scholars believe Britain's decline had already begun.[5]

Clearly, the relationship between the relative sizes of economies and the political role of countries is not simple. Britain became a world power with an economy much smaller than some of the countries that opposed it. It is therefore not obvious that a decline in the relative size of a country's economy translates automatically into a declining political position. India's economy today is significantly smaller as a share of global GDP than it was in 1800, but today's united, democratic India is a far more effective force on the world stage than it was when the British were extending their authority across the subcontinent, two hundred years ago.

In any case, for the foreseeable future, America's economy will account for a substantially larger percentage of global GDP than Britain's ever did. According to the World Bank, the United States currently accounts for about 28 percent of global output, and there is no sign that the U.S. will sink to anything like the single-digit percentage of global output that Britain claimed even at its peak.[6]

. . .

THE GEOPOLITICAL OUTLOOK PROVIDES additional reason to believe that the maritime order remains stably based. Some point to the European Union and some to Asia to find the powers that will one day overturn the maritime order or replace the Americans as its guiding power. This looks premature. Conditions in both Asia and Europe seem broadly favorable to the continuation of a unique American global role and to the absence (or the failure) of great-power challenges to the maritime system.

Memories of the long wars between the British and their continental rivals help shape the fear occasionally voiced even today that the European continent will be the source for a new and potentially successful assault on the foundations of the maritime system. This is partly due to a sense, felt more strongly among anti-EU forces in the U.K. perhaps than in the U.S., that the integration of Europe under Franco-German leadership represents a strategic defeat for the balance-of-power politics that the English-speaking world has followed on the European mainland since the time of the Tudors.

From an American point of view the outlook is substantially brighter. The European Union is not the triumphant Continental System of Napoleon's dreams. The finely balanced European political system provides binding legal assurances that no single country can use European institutions to impose its will on the rest. The multiple centers of power in the vast and complex Brussels bureaucracy, the tradition of collegial decision making in many European institutions, the existence of both national and EU-wide judicial systems able to check the actions of executive and legislative powers, the democratic traditions and different political cultures within each member state, and the continuing disagreements among the members about foreign policy priorities all combine to make very unlikely the emergence of a single-minded, aggressive, and strategic power from the present-day EU. This is not the overthrow of the European balance of power; it is the institutionalization of the "liberties of Europe" for which the British once fought.

Despite occasional transatlantic spats on everything from trade to security policy, the development of the European Union is fundamentally compatible with the continuing success of the maritime order. In many ways the European Union remains the crowning achievement of American foreign policy, and Europe, once the source of one challenge after another to the liberal democratic and maritime order, is now one of its chief pillars.

Outside the EU, Russia is the most important country in Europe, and those who envision an anti-American or anti–maritime system alliance in the twenty-first century look to some combination of Germany, Russia, and China. This grand land alliance would attempt to balance against the United States and, in particular, would seek to profit from American vulnerabilities in the Middle East.

As many world leaders have discovered, this alliance is easier to envision than to consolidate. The politics of the European Union, in which many countries and smaller nationalities associate German-Russian partnerships with some of the saddest hours in their long histories, will present one important obstacle to this kind of alliance, but the most important obstacle may be Russia's vulnerabilities. The demographic and social collapse of Russia casts a heavy shadow over that country's future. The rise in mortality and the fall in birthrates since the demise of the Soviet Union have seen Russia's population fall from 148 million to 143 million between 1990 and 2006. Currently, the fertility rate is too low to maintain the existing level of population.[7] From 1987 to 1999, the yearly number of births in Russia plummeted from 2.5 million to 1.2 million.[8] According to official Russian projections as well as U.N. forecasts, Russia's population may decline below 100 million by 2050.[9]

From the Kremlin's perspective these numbers are even worse than they look. The population crisis in Russia is almost entirely concentrated among ethnic Russians. The Muslim minorities in Russia are gaining population, and the birthrates in the north Caucasus are markedly higher than in the Slavic parts of Russia. Since 1989 Russia's Muslim population has grown 40 percent to more than 25 million people.[10] The non-Muslim population of the country fell by roughly 13 million people after 1990, a 10 percent decline in less than a generation. Given these trends, at least one former U.S. government official has suggested that Russia may have a Muslim majority within thirty years.[11]

The Russian Far East is another major area of vulnerability. The sparsely populated, resource-rich territories of Asian Russia are potentially a major flash point in international politics. Today the always meager Russian population of the region is in retreat. The smaller towns and northern settlements were always heavily dependent on government subsidies and the Soviet system of control and internal exile; without these props many people are migrating back toward the heartland of European Russia. As a result, the Russian population of the Far East is falling even faster than the overall demographic level. According to demographer V. F. Galetskii, the region's population of 6.6 million in 2006 marked a drop-off of 16.5 percent since 1989, and the decline is projected to continue at least through 2025.[12]

The ethnic Chinese population of the region is another matter. Hundreds of thousands, perhaps millions, of Chinese may move north as the Russians move west. From a population of several thousand in the 1980s to over 250,000 today, this rapidly growing minority is projected by some to become the largest ethnic group in the Russian Far East by 2025.[13] Meanwhile, China's economic success and growing political and military power make it an increasingly intimidating neighbor for an overstretched, underpopulated, and underperforming Russia.

Bitter and resentful, still unreconciled to the loss of its superpower status after the Cold War, today's Russia is an angry, dissatisfied power that blames the United States for many of its troubles. At the same time, the failure of post-Soviet Russia to develop, so far, a viable system of liberal or even quasi-liberal capitalism means that it is unable to receive many of the economic benefits that the maritime system offers to those willing and able to play by its rules. Yet Russia's need for help containing unrest and rebellion among some of its Muslim minorities, its desire for economic cooperation, and its weak and deteriorating position in the Far East, place sharp limits on its ability to embark on a wholesale and determined policy of strategic anti-Americanism. Until and unless the wounds of the Cold War heal and Russia develops the institutional and cultural foundations for a more successful participation in the maritime system and finds a stable and satisfactory framework for its relations with former Soviet republics like Ukraine and Georgia, Americans should expect that Russia will be quick to oppose the United States where it can. It must, however, overcome daunting obstacles to become a strategic competitor like the Soviet Union, or to form a key link in an effective and enduring anti-American, anti–maritime system alliance of hostile land powers.

ATTENTION TO ASIAN THREATS to the future of American power usually focuses on China. The signs of growing Chinese influence in Latin America, Africa, and the Middle East are often seen as indicators of trends that will ultimately result in the sharp reduction in American power throughout the world. Additionally, the rise of other great Asian economic and political powers such as India, combined with the increasing power and independence of Japan and others, look to many like early stages in a general erosion of the American world position.

A look at the history of the maritime system suggests that this approach is both too simplistic and too gloomy. Indeed, looking at world history over the longer term suggests that far from being a danger to the maritime order and to America's unique world role, an emerging match between American national interests and the complex strategic geometry of a changing Asia presents the United States with an extraordinary set of opportunities in the twenty-first century. With three great powers (China, Japan, India), a traditional fourth (Russia), and currently or potentially significant regional powers like Indonesia, Australia, Vietnam, Thailand, and Pakistan, the world's fastest-developing region offers many favorable prospects for the key strategic, economic, and political concerns of the United States and the maritime order it seeks to preserve.

Overall, Asia seems to be moving toward a complex balance of power, something like the European system that emerged after the Congress of Vienna. In this system, an offshore balancing power—Britain in 1815, the United States today—can exercise great influence and protect its vital interests at a relatively low cost, even if other powers in the system have larger populations or economies, or even, by some measures, stronger military forces.

From the classic point of view of maritime balancing powers like Britain and America, the first key feature of this situation is that it begins to look impossible for any single country realistically to aspire to an Asian hegemony. Not only does the United States stand offshore ready to build coalitions against any threatening power, the Asian powers look increasingly able to keep a rough balance on their own. Even though the rise of India and China over the long term poses a threat to Japan's standing as Asia's preeminent economic and technological power, for the foreseeable future the three great Asian powers form a potentially stable triangle. Either India or China, *plus Japan,* is likely to be strong enough to make it unrealistic for the third power in the triangle to seek to dominate the other two. With the United States as a second balancing power available to counter any aspiring hegemon, the path to an Asian supremacy for India, China, or Japan seems difficult if not impossible to navigate—always assuming that the other powers, including the United States, recognize and act on their national interests. (This cannot always be counted on: France and Britain could have stopped Hitler easily in the early 1930s; by 1939 it was too late.)

In the past, American policy in Asia has been haunted by the wobbly nature of the regional balance of power. Before the rise of Japan, no Asian power was developing in ways that could prevent the British and/or other Europeans from carving the region up. When Japan began its extraordinary modernization, the failure of China to follow suit (while British power waned) created an intrinsically unbalanced and dangerous situation and ultimately led to the Pacific war. For the first time in modern history, Asia today seems to have all the elements of a potentially stable balance of power.

China is developing and modernizing, so is India, so are many of the (relatively) middle-size regional powers, and Japan is not fading away.

In fact, the greatest danger to the United States in Asia does not come
from the prospect that India and China will continue to modernize and grow;
it lies in the possibility that one or both of them may fail. The economic and
social transformations now sweeping through these countries make an awesome sight. Never in the history of the world have so many people experienced so much change. Despite continuing issues and problems, thus far
India and China have managed this process with extraordinary success. It is
less clear that their political systems can remain coherent and effective as
pressures and changes accumulate. Environmental problems and social pressures could drastically affect the outlook for India, China, or both. From an
American point of view, anything that interrupts their progress is a problem.
If one country should falter while the other surges ahead, defending the balance of power in Asia would require a more active and perhaps risky American policy. If both countries should falter, the region could be engulfed by
political, military, and economic chaos with unpredictable consequences on
a global as well as a regional scale. America's strategic interests lead it to
wish all Asian countries well, to support the development of major and
minor powers in the region, and to promote integration and cooperation
among the major Asian powers. Here Richard Haass's characterization of
the coming era for the United States as one of opportunity is surely the right
one. The United States is uniquely positioned to play an extraordinary and
positive role in Asian politics in the twenty-first century; the consequences
for Asia, for world politics, and for the United States itself if we take full
advantage of this great opportunity will be truly historic.

THE LONG VIEW of Anglo-American history makes inexorable decline
look unlikely; it does not, however, support the opinion held by some commentators that the United States will remain the "unipolar" center of world
politics.

There have been unipolar and bipolar moments during the history of
the maritime system. After Britain's 1763 victory in the Seven Years' War, it
had achieved a recognized position as the leading hegemonic power in the
Mediterranean basin, the Americas, and Asia. After the fall of Napoleon,
only Russia could match Britain's influence—and even then, Russia was
largely a European power, while Britain was unchallenged as the leading
global power. Through much of the nineteenth century, Britain's prestige,
wealth, and global reach put it in a league of its own.

Yet there were also moments when Britain could be better described as the first among equals in a world of more balanced competition and power—or when it was able to hold its own against powers like Spain or France only because it joined coalitions that it could not always control.

In the shorter period of American leadership since the end of World War II, the position of the United States in the international system has moved through different phases. Immediately after the Second World War, the United States enjoyed overwhelming economic advantages: it was the world's largest and most advanced producer and exporter of oil and of most agricultural commodities in a world facing famine, as well as the leading manufacturing power from the standpoint of both quantity and technological sophistication; in its communications and financial capacities it towered above all possible rivals. In the military sphere it was the world's only nuclear power, and no other country could match America's ability to send conventional forces to all corners of the earth and then support them. Indeed, for some years after World War II, no other power was capable of sustaining overseas military adventures without the blessing and even the support of the United States.

Not even after the Cold War would the United States enjoy this kind of global primacy, but is decline really the best word to describe what happened to American power between 1945 and 1989? There were terrible setbacks in those years: the rising Communist tide in so many developing countries including, most tragically, China; the inconclusive war in Korea; the defeat in Vietnam; the continuing decline of Britain; the Soviet Union's successful drive for nuclear and strategic parity; the peak, followed by the gradual decline, of America's oil production; the Iranian revolution; growing anti-Americanism in Latin America, Africa, and the Middle East; the rise of powerful and successful technological and economic rivals to American firms first in Europe and Japan, then throughout the developing world. The list can be extended—but surely America was richer and its key interests more secure after the Cold War than in 1945, when Europe teetered on the brink of starvation and Communist takeovers, the global economy lay in ruins, and against the hard-eyed certainty of Communism and its acolytes neither the Americans nor anyone else had a clear idea about a path forward.

The real question about the future of American power is less whether the world will be more or less unipolar in 2015 or 2050 than it was in 1946 or even 1989 than whether the United States will be able to secure and promote the maritime system as time goes by. For some, this will seem like a counterintuitive proposition, but there are many circumstances in which a reduction of American unipolarity will actually promote the defense and development of the maritime system rather than undermine it.

Developments in Europe after both the Napoleonic Wars and World War II illustrate this point. After the fall of Napoleon, only Russia could match British prestige and influence. France was defeated, Austria had been shaken to the core, Prussia had yet to recover from the shocks and traumas of the war. All over Europe, trembling monarchs on their shaky thrones waited with bated breath in fear that the revolutionary forces unleashed in France would explode once again and plunge Europe into another generation of ruinous conflict. As France, Prussia, Austria, and the lesser powers stabilized after the Congress of Vienna, and as the continental economies recovered from war and began to master the techniques of the Industrial Revolution, Britain's ability to influence events on the European mainland tended to diminish. Yet Britain was clearly safer and richer, and its global position clearly more comfortable and sustainable as Europe "normalized" after the wars. After 1815 it would be many decades before the rise of other European powers posed a serious threat to Great Britain, and even then the dynamism and power of the United States meant that the maritime system was becoming more deeply entrenched as the unipolar and bipolar eras of the early nineteenth century yielded to a more multipolar world.

Indeed, the growing multipolarity of post-Napoleonic Europe strengthened Britain's world position. The return of a balance-of-power system in Europe, especially one that was—at least until the time of Bismarck's wars—accepted as necessary and even legitimate by all the European powers, including the strongest one, was a great strategic asset for Britain's world role. It was a good thing that British fleets had been able to blockade the continent during the wars, and that Wellington's forces could defeat Napoleon in pitched battles. It was, however, much better not to have to mount the blockades or fight the battles and to enjoy the benefits of a European order that safeguarded British interests without sustained British involvement.

Events after World War II have followed a somewhat similar course in Europe. The strategic goals of American policy (preventing one strong country from controlling the rest, an end to generations of warfare, promotion of liberal political and economic models, market access for American producers and investors, cooperation in facing regional security challenges) have been greatly advanced even as direct American political power has diminished.

A similar trade-off in Asia would strengthen rather than erode the foundations of the maritime system and secure vital American interests at steadily diminishing cost. The long view tells us that unipolarity is neither the most desirable nor the most typical form that Anglo-American power has taken during the history of the maritime system; in the past, a shift from a unipolar world to a world order compatible with the maritime system in which many powers have voices has not represented a decline in Anglo-American power. Rather, it is a sign of successful diplomacy and of a fortunate tide in world affairs.

This is why the emergence of a multipolar international system in Asia can be an extraordinary opportunity for the United States and its maritime system. The interests of the key Asian powers appear to be aligned with those of the United States and of the liberal capitalist order; American interests are never more secure than when multiple pillars support the system. This ability to match strategic and economic interests with those of important countries around the world is one of the core advantages of sea-power strategies. The offshore balancing power that is interested in an open global trading system poses less threat and offers more opportunity to more partners than traditional land powers can usually match.

"How to Be Topp"

A narrow focus on the American world role gives something like sixty years of precedent and experience, from World War II through the "war on terror." But if we look back at the whole rise of the maritime system we find a much richer historical memory; American power seems more deeply rooted in the structure of world politics than it does when one looks at the United States alone. The United States is the leading state in a power system with a three-hundred-year history, one that has flourished under many different sets of conditions. It rose when both the Netherlands and Britain had smaller populations and fewer natural resources than rivals they ultimately defeated; it has weathered many storms and surmounted many challenges. It has fought many different kinds of wars with many different coalitions; it has pursued its basic goals in many different ways under changing conditions. America's world role is not a mushroom that sprang up suddenly, almost by accident, after World War II devastated potential rivals; it was not improbably revived once more when the Soviet Union collapsed. It is the result of processes that have been shaping world history since the time of Louis XIV. The forces that support both the maritime system and American power are durable and strong.

The military and political ordeals that the maritime system endured under Dutch and British leadership were far more severe and testing than anything Americans have yet to endure. The Dutch saw their homeland invaded, their cities razed; they were forced to open the dikes to flood their low-lying farms in order to keep their enemies at bay. Philip II at one point put all the Dutch under a universal sentence of death for the crimes of heresy and rebellion. In 1588, 1803, and again in 1940 Britain awaited a possible invasion by powerful forces that if they weren't stopped at sea could not be stopped at all.

This history suggests rather dismally that the Americans need to prepare themselves for greater and sterner tests than they have so far endured. Yet should the world darken and the threats grow until the United States stands alone or almost so against large and fanatical enemies, the British and Dutch victories in those earlier conflicts will be beacons of hope in trials yet to come.

Above all, history teaches the vital importance of sea power in the broadest sense for both the domestic prosperity and the international position of the United States. The combination of geopolitical and economic strategies with an enduring domestic commitment to a dynamic society powered the Dutch and British versions of the maritime system for centuries. This combination remains, or always ought to remain, the central concern of American statesmanship today.

The protocols of the elders of Greenwich remain the key to world power. Develop and maintain an open, dynamic society at home; turn the economic energy of that society out into world trade; protect commerce throughout the world and defend the balance of power in the world's chief geopolitical theaters; open the global system to others, even to potential competitors in time of peace; turn the system against one's opponents in war; promote liberal values and institutions wherever one can.

This sea-power strategy remains, in the words of Ronald Searle's fictional English schoolboy Nigel Molesworth, "how to be topp" in the global power competition, and the United States remains a sea power in the fullest sense of the phrase. Maintaining the health and the vitality of the maritime order is the primary task facing American leaders in the twenty-first century. Debates over American grand strategy, international economic policy, and domestic policy need to be set in this context, and policy alternatives evaluated in terms of whether their likely outcomes will shore up and extend or weaken and diminish this order.

To the degree that American foreign policy debates take the health of the maritime order into account, these debates will have greater coherence than they often do now. Both expert and lay opinion will incorporate a set of common ideas about the structure of American interests, and the advocates of different policy prescriptions will be able to build greater support for their proposals to the degree that they can convincingly show how their prescriptions will advance a set of interests that are generally understood.

The Five-Point Plan

For Americans today, the chief lesson of the last three hundred years is easy to state as a principle, but much more difficult to put into practice.

Here is the lesson: the plan works. Stick to the plan. The "protocols of the elders of Greenwich" are still the best guide to grand strategy. For almost four hundred years, taking the Dutch experience into account, the countries that have been willing and able to follow this strategy consistently have prospered, even triumphed. Such a heritage should not be lightly cast aside. Spain, France, Germany, Japan, the Soviet Union: all these great powers once fought great wars against the maritime order. Once each of these powers seemed wrapped in an air of power and triumph; their armies bristled with advanced weapons, their military leadership included men of great courage and wisdom; their brilliant diplomats dominated world politics and they assembled great and intimidating alliances; often, the world's leading intellectuals sang hosannas to the glory and the wonder of the philosophy or religion in whose name they marched.

More than once, the maritime powers have been foolish and divided. At times they have been late to recognize danger and slow to act. At other times they have rashly embarked on campaigns that increased the dangers they faced and strengthened the coalitions they fought. Greed, cowardice, arrogance, complacency, sloth, and self-righteousness: every vice known to history has flourished in the politics and policy of the maritime states. They have committed almost every possible folly and crime. They have neglected the rise of great and dangerous rivals. They have antagonized vast swaths of the world population through cruelty and injustice. They have suffered staggering defeats. They periodically lost their grip on the stubborn realities of international life and squandered great opportunities to make the world better in an ill-advised rush to make it perfect.

And yet, despite these failings and more, three centuries have seen the Walrus and the Carpenter advance toward more democratic, more affluent, and more open societies at home, while defending and developing the maritime system abroad.

If history teaches anything at all, it should teach Americans that this grand strategy works, that we should remain what Admiral Mahan would call a sea power in the fullest sense of the term, and that in the United States of the twenty-first century, Thomas Pelhan-Holles's comments about British policy in the eighteenth century still hold true: "Ministers in this country, where every part of the World affects us, in some way or another, should consider the whole Globe."

The greatest disasters that came upon the United States—and indeed the whole world—in the last one hundred years did not come from the many American blunders in carrying out a sea-power program. The intervention in Vietnam, the rash invasion of Saddam Hussein's Iraq: these were disasters that brought untold grief and pain to innocent victims, that sacrificed the lives of honorable and patriotic soldiers, that squandered American treasure and damaged America's standing. Yet these disasters pale before the horrors brought on by isolation, abstention, and the foolish neglect of our responsibilities abroad.

George Kennan, the scholar and diplomat credited with the development of the containment strategy that guided American foreign policy during the Cold War, was a bitter critic of both the Vietnam and Iraq wars. Yet Kennan's history of American foreign policy from 1900 through 1950 makes much harsher judgments about America's failure to engage comprehensively, globally, and, at times, to use force. Kennan argues that America's neglect of the deteriorating European balance of power before World War I encouraged Germany on the road to war, and that America's vacillation and delay before entering the conflict made that war longer and uglier than it had to be.

This is almost certainly true; had America recognized Britain's increasing need for assistance in managing the maritime order and responded to it earlier, that war and its attendant horrors might well have been avoided. Nazism and Communism might never have come to power; hundreds of millions of lives could have been saved.

America compounded its failures and folly after that war. Wilson's tragically flawed peace proposals, the American withdrawal not only from the League of Nations but also from the European security system after the failure of the Treaty of Versailles, the willful American blindness to the danger posed by the rise of Nazi and Stalinist power: these helped make World War II inevitable in Europe and contributed to some of the darkest hours and darkest deeds the world has ever known. American folly and complacency were equally disastrous for Asia, Kennan notes, where American diplomacy feebly opposed Japanese aggression with pious sentiments, and American passivity and blindness helped bring on the agonies of the war in the Pacific and its terrible aftermath in China.

No blunder, no folly, no crime, no sin of commission by American foreign policy since has been as devastating and costly as the silent sins of omission that so marked and marred the first half of the twentieth century. This, too, is a lesson of history. Americans need to be cautious and prudent, but above all they must be globally engaged. And the business on which they must be engaged is the old business of the old firm: the creation and development of a world system based on the five-point program that the Dutch first dimly envisioned.

The protocols of the elders of Greenwich are not only the most effective grand strategy the United States can pursue in the international arena; they are also our best guide to a genuinely moral and progressive stance in the world. They integrate our security needs, our economic interests and our ideals more fully than any alternative we have. The maintenance of global geopolitical stability; the growth of global commerce and the rising prosperity of the poor; the spread of liberal and democratic institutions and practices around the world: American grand strategy must always concern itself with these goals.

To the Waspophobic imagination, this strategy looks a little Mordoresque ("One Ring to rule them all, one Ring to find them, one Ring to bring them all and in the darkness bind them"). Yet for Americans today there is no alternative. There can and should be strong debate over how, exactly, this grand strategy can best be carried out in the changing circumstances of the contemporary world, but the strategy itself, tested and tempered by time, reflects the American character and serves the nation's and indeed humanity's interest far better than anything else we could do.

IF HISTORY TEACHES that this grand strategy should not be discarded, it also teaches that it should not be mechanically and ritualistically worshipped. The world changes. War changes. The relationships between cultures and civilizations change.

There was in fact an almost ritualistic quality to the old European wars.

Some wicked war leader—emperor, king, führer—would cross some line in the sand, usually invading the Low Countries in violation of various solemn treaties. The British would be appalled. While intellectuals and prelates on both sides of the contest uttered threats, imprecations, and anathemas at one another, the British cracked down on whatever "fifth column" within seemed particularly troublesome at the moment and tightened their links with current or potential Continental allies and conducted various military activities in and around Europe. The European struggle spread into a world war. Britain sought to deny its enemy access to world markets and the enemy vainly sought to counter Britain's sea power. There were various disastrous expeditions, failed campaigns, episodes of gross incompetence among politicians and military leaders alike. Public opinion turned sullen. Each side industriously publicized various allegations of atrocities, a disheartening number of which were based on fact. A bidding auction broke out to lure neutral powers, however odious, onto the different sides. The enemy played the Celtic card, supporting rebellions in Scotland and/or Ireland.* The Celtic card failed, and Britain's superior economic strength gradually made itself felt. Often, this happened even as Britain and its allies were soundly and repeatedly bested in various land campaigns. But in the end the sea power system prevailed, the British won, and the old saws were heard yet again: Britain muddles through. Britain loses every battle but the last. A peace of sorts was scratched up, and the various participants licked their wounds and prepared for the next round.

This pattern played itself out and the era of great European wars seems to have come to an end. As the center of world politics shifts from the Atlantic to the Pacific, the conflicts of the future are extremely unlikely to follow the traditional pattern, and we do not need to guard against the possibility that either China or Al-Qaeda will invade the Low Countries.

Nevertheless, the key principles of international relations that Americans and their allies need to review and update rather than discard the traditional five-point strategy as they prepare for the future.

---

* The Celtic card, originating in the medieval "auld alliance" between Scotland and France, gained new prominence as Catholic Irish and Scots Highlanders continued to support the deposed Stuart dynasty. Napoleon supported Wolfe Tone's rebellion in Ireland and the card was still being played in World War I as Germany ferried the Irish republican leader Sir Roger Casement to Ireland in a submarine. Under Norwegian colors the Germans sent a surface ship with weapons for an Irish rising; the ship was intercepted and the Easter Rising of 1916 was easily crushed. Perhaps the last example of this traditional gambit came in World War II when Germany vigorously courted the Irish government and when Rudolf Hess parachuted into Scotland to meet what he hoped was an anti-Churchill member of the Scottish nobility.

. . .

THE FIRST PIECE OF THE STRATEGY, the creation and preservation of an open and dynamic society at home, remains the foundation of America's domestic prosperity, liberty, and international position. Any diminution in America's cultural vitality, commitment to liberty and enterprise, social mobility, and pluralism, and any serious decline in either the creativity of American religious faith or its denominational and theological diversity would make the United States a less dynamic society, sap its energy, reduce its wealth, and impair its ability to carry out the remaining elements of the national strategy.

The second, third, and fourth steps of the maritime strategy will continue to influence world politics and power moving forward. The engagement of American society with the rest of the world, economically, culturally, religiously, and politically, will remain a crucial dimension of America's standing in the world. The management of American geopolitical strategy in the emerging world of great Asian powers will require all the diplomatic and military skills that Anglo-Americans have learned through centuries of international life. And the further development of an integrated global economy that serves American interests while drawing others into a deepening participation in this key feature of the maritime system will require constant thought, creative policy, and serious work in both domestic and international politics. These are serious challenges, but I am relatively confident that the United States is ready for them.

It is to the fifth point of the traditional sea-power strategy, the promotion of policies, practices, institutions, and values around the world and in key partner countries where the United States risks failure, that I now wish to turn.

Twenty-one • Dancing with Ghosts

T he mix of policy missteps, adventures gone awry, rising anti-Americanism, and growing estrangement between the Arab world and the United States that marked the George W. Bush administration are matters of grave concern, but this is far from the greatest crisis in the long history of the maritime system.

The study of the history of the maritime order can help us think more clearly about the relationship between the Anglo-Saxon powers and the world of Islam. This is not the first time that waves of Waspophobia have swept large parts of the world; it is not the first time that foolish and imprudent policies of Anglo-American governments have made a bad situation worse; it is not the first time that atrocities committed by Anglo-Saxon forces have ignited international outrage; it is not the first time that countries seeking to oppose the maritime order have been able to tap into widespread world sentiment favoring their cause. It is not even the first time all this has happened while the Walrus and the Carpenter were cluelessly congratulating themselves on the imminent global triumph of their ideas and their order.

From its emergence in the revolt of Dutch Protestants against the Catholic empire of Spain, through the long struggles between Britain and France, and on through the wars of the twentieth century, the maritime order repeatedly found itself engaged in conflicts which have been, among other things, wars of religion. While each struggle has its unique features, a look back at the long history of these conflicts can help us now as we seek to avoid a great confrontation with Islam, and to help the world of Islam find an appropriate and satisfactory place in the global system.

The chief lesson history offers is that this does not have to be a struggle to the death. Protestantism and Catholicism today are well integrated into the religious life of the maritime order, and endless contrasts are drawn in the Western media between Christian values, which are believed to be compatible with the liberal ideal of the open society, and the supposedly closed and unenlightened values that are seen as part of the essence of Islam.

This is almost surely wrong. Catholicism had a long and bitter history of opposing the values of the open society before finally making peace with it. Even Protestantism did not at first accept the open society, and when some observers call wistfully for an "Islamic Reformation" so that Islam will become a more tolerant and open faith, they miss both the nature of the Reformation and the current condition of Islam.

Every culture has its own unique characteristics, but the Wahhabi and Salafist movements in Islam, as well as the political movements rooted in them, bear an almost eerie resemblance to some of the most radical Protestant groups in the Reformation. The Wahhabis and other contemporary Muslim reformers want to return to the original sources of Islam, just as the Puritans wanted to restore the pure Christianity of apostolic times. The Wahhabis denounce medieval theology and tradition, arguing that the only source of religious authority in Islam is the word of God in the Holy Koran. Substitute the "Bible" for "Koran," and this was the program of the Puritan party in England. Wahhabis seek to suppress the popular cults associated with saints and others traditionally believed to intercede for believers with God. Every soul is accountable to God for its own acts, and there is no human mediator. Puritans similarly attacked the cults of the Christian saints, and argued that it was vain and unbiblical to pray to the Virgin and the saints for their intercession with God. To make sure such cults are suppressed, the Saudi government under Wahhabi influence has recently destroyed mosques and monuments in Mecca and Medina that had become associated with cults and customs considered un-Islamic. Puritans, like many radical Protestants across northern Europe, destroyed altar screens, stained glass, statues, and other church furnishings which, in their judgment, distracted the people from the worship of the one true God. For Puritans and Wahhabis, the law of the land should be based explicitly on God's law. Both groups reject traditional political arrangements in order to build a godly commonwealth in which the legitimacy of rulers is based on their adherence to the revealed word of God. They both believe that God is intimately involved and concerned with current events, that God has predestined all that has happened or will happen, and that traditional forms of piety have failed to give due acknowledgment to God's utter and absolute control of all human events. Both groups are intolerant of what they consider heresy and apostasy, and are quick to read rival theological traditions out of their religion. The Puritans considered Catholicism a Satanic cult; many Wahhabis believe that the Shi'a are not truly Muslim. Both groups believe all truth is found in God's revealed word; that the word has been infallibly communicated in a holy book; and that the words of that book, properly understood, contain all that is needed to order man's political, moral, and spiritual affairs. Yet neither group is anti-intellectual; they reject the emotionalism and mysticism of rival religious movements. They believe that the words of the holy book demand to be read with profound attention and interpreted with precise and careful logic. Both movements aspire to grow and to transform their entire culture, and they see their religious destiny in a global context. Ready to tear down old governments and to build up new states, both are ready to coexist with monarchs, yet both are suspicious of monarchs' intentions and will sanction the overthrow of political rulers seen as disloyal to religion. Both are ready to defend and to spread their religion by war and consider war to be an inescapable religious duty under certain circumstances.

Whatever their doctrinal differences with the Wahhabis and with one another, Martin Luther, John Calvin, and Oliver Cromwell would find much to admire in the spirit and the theology of today's reformists in Islam.

In the medium to long term, these are hopeful signs. The Protestant Reformation, whatever its shortcomings, was the milieu out of which modern dynamic society grew. The religious struggles, revolutions in doctrine, individual conversion experiences, persecutions, crimes, and political struggles that grew out of this movement testified to an outbreak of what Bergson called dynamic religion, which would ultimately allow for the birth of a new kind of society. Islam today is a living religion, struggling to find its authentic voice in a rapidly changing world. This may be an uncomfortable, and sometimes frightening and dangerous, phenomenon for Muslims and non-Muslims alike, but it is also an important sign of the vitality and engagement of a great civilization.

The Puritan movement in British and American history was a critical factor in the development of Anglo-American liberalism and democracy. Religious movements that trace their origins back to Puritanism or similar strands of Reformation theology continue to play a vital role in American democracy and society today. But the Puritans themselves were neither liberal nor tolerant, and it was only their failure to establish a permanent theocracy in Britain that enabled British society to take the next step forward.

It may seem presumptuous to say so, but the Wahhabi movement and related currents of Islamic reform seem headed for a similar fate. The reformers are unlikely to achieve their ambition to remake the entire religious landscape of the Islamic world. Not only are the Shi'a bound to resist, there are many rival traditions of great antiquity that are deeply rooted in the affections and customs of many pious people throughout the Muslim world. It also seems likely that the intensity of Wahhabi piety will wax and wane over the generations, as has been true in the past for reform movements in both the Christian and Muslim worlds. Additionally, just as printing democratized Christian theology by giving millions of ordinary believers direct access to sacred scripture, the Internet is making the great works of Islamic scholarship available to tens of millions of Muslims, including women, who can and will be free to draw their own conclusions about what their faith means and how it should be lived. Theological diversity within Islam seems bound to increase; as it does, we shall see whether growing pluralism within Islam leads to an acceptance of that pluralism, however grudging, and from there to a gradually widening recognition of the positive value of pluralism in human life.

THE HISTORY OF CHRISTIANITY and its relationship with dynamic society shows many more parallels with contemporary Muslim values and ideas. Most Catholics and most Anglo-Americans once believed that Catholic theology could not be reconciled with liberal democratic society, and many observers believed that Catholic societies in southern Europe and Latin America would remain backward and poor because of cultural habits stemming from their religion.

Today we hear the same things said about Islam. Islam, we are told, is fundamentally and irrevocably opposed to the key tenets of dynamic society. Unlike Christianity, we hear, Islam is intolerant of other faiths and rejects the separation of church and state as it has developed in the West. Tied to literalistic and legalistic interpretations of its scriptures and traditions, Islam seeks a theocratic legal system that, among other things, forbids lending money at interest and denies equal rights to women. Moreover, we are told, Islamic culture is incompatible with the cultural values necessary for success in building capitalist and democratic societies.

It is not only Westerners who profess these views. It is not hard to find Islamic scholars and teachers, present and past, who agree that Islam is irreconcilable with liberal society. Yet even a quick survey of Christian history, Catholic and Protestant, reveals very little that is distinctively Islamic about these values and ideas. For example, usury was long prohibited in Christian teaching, and the very orthodox Dante placed bankers next to sodomites in the fifth circle of Hell because both groups committed what

Catholic teaching regarded as sins against nature. In Christian history it was groups of monks who gradually found ways around the traditional prohibition until a richer theological understanding emerged; today Islamic clerics are finding ever more sophisticated methods by which financial institutions can provide flexible services in global financial markets.

Religious persecution and discrimination remained features of British life long after the passions of the Reformation subsided. Catholics and Jews were not allowed to sit in Parliament or take degrees from Oxford and Cambridge until well into the nineteenth century. Blasphemy still remains a prosecutable offense in Britain. In 1977 the publication *Gay News* was successfully prosecuted for printing a poem in which Jesus was portrayed as a homosexual, and as recently as January 2007 a Christian group sought (unsuccessfully) to bring a blasphemy charge against the British Broadcasting Corporation after it aired the comic musical *Jerry Springer: The Opera*.[1] After due consideration, the "New Labour" government of Tony Blair decided not to seek repeal of the British law that makes blasphemy against the doctrines of the state church illegal—although, for now, the British remain free to blaspheme against the religions of pagans and dissenters as much as they like.

Catholicism was long opposed to religious pluralism. In 1864, Pope Pius IX explicitly condemned belief in religious freedom as a heresy that no Catholic could accept. Specifically denounced as an intolerable error was the proposition "Every man is free to embrace that religion which, guided by the light of reason, he shall consider true."

Not until the Second Vatican Council in 1965 did the church formally accept that freedom of religion was a moral principle. Under the Franco regime in Spain, Protestants and Jews could not hold public ceremonies (such as weddings and funerals) or proselytize. As late as 1946 a mathematics professor was fired from a Spanish university because of his Protestant faith. Mobs of fanatical Catholic youth, often tolerated or even encouraged by zealous local officials, attacked Protestant houses of worship. In one case, a mob attacked a Protestant chapel, smashing and burning furniture and causing other damage because their religious sensibilities had been, they said, gravely wounded by a leaflet allegedly distributed by the Protestants which insulted the Virgin Mary.

The concept of a strict separation of church and state is also much less deeply rooted in Christian history than many believe. The traditional Roman Catholic view of the subject was most clearly set forward by Pope Innocent III (1160–1216). In his *Venerabilem* decree (1202), he asserted the divine right of popes to anoint and depose kings and rulers. He compared the church to the sun and the state to the moon, and argued that just as the moon gets its light from the sun, so the power and legitimacy of secular rulers comes solely from God and, therefore, the church. Many Protestants shared this basic view. Bishop Hugh Latimer, who was later burned at the stake under Mary I for his Protestant beliefs, preached in a 1549 sermon to the young king Edward VI that kings and emperors were not only bound to obey God and his book, but "also the minister of the same."[2] In 1864 Pius IX condemned as heretical the proposition "The Church ought to be separated from the State, and the State from the Church."[3]

The Preamble to the Irish Constitution of 1937 shows little desire to separate the two spheres, as it begins with the words: "In the Name of the Most Holy Trinity, from Whom is all authority and to Whom, as our final end, all actions both of men and States must be referred . . ."[4]

In practice, American Protestants rather than European Catholics have been the most eager to base their civil codes directly on sacred texts and divine revelation. Puritan New England consciously and deliberately set about basing its legal codes on the provisions of the laws of Moses in the Hebrew scripture. In Massachusetts this led, among other things, to the passage of laws punishing adultery by death. The process of adopting the Christian equivalent of Sharia law went the farthest in the then independent colony of New Haven, where voters unanimously adopted a 1655 resolution that the Bible "shall be the only rule to be attended unto in organizing the affairs of government in this plantation." Not to be outdone, Massachusetts acknowledged itself to be a "theocracy," and its statutes included the relevant biblical citations to show the authority and principles on which they were based.

Religion long retained special privileges and position under American law. In a case argued by Daniel Webster in 1844, the U.S. Supreme Court affirmed that "Christianity is part of the common law of Pennsylvania," and specifically found that the "divine origin and truth" of Christianity are part of Pennsylvania law. This precedent still stood as late as 1927, when the Pennsylvania Supreme Court upheld a law against professional baseball on Sunday because it was an "unholy" activity that defiled the Christian Sabbath. In deciding against Sunday baseball, the Supreme Court ruled that "no one . . . would contend that professional baseball partakes in any way of the nature of holiness. . . . We cannot imagine anything more worldly or unreligious in the way of employment than the playing of professional baseball."[5]

Countless Christians have agreed, and many still do, with what we are sometimes told is the uniquely Islamic position that the status of women is defined by God's holy book—and is inferior to that of men. The great Scottish reformer John Knox made the point very eloquently in his monumental *First Blast of the Trumpet Against the Monstrous Regiment of Women.* Woman, he writes, "was made to serve and obey man." His proof? The words of St. Paul in the Bible: "And man was not created for the cause of the woman, but the woman for the cause of man."[6]

While some of these tendencies are clearly stronger in contemporary Islam than in much of the world of Western Christianity and Judaism, it is hard to argue that there is something peculiarly or uniquely Islamic about opposing the separation of church and state, wanting to base legal codes on divine revelation, or believing that religion mandates different roles and different rights for women and men.

THE HISTORY OF THE ENCOUNTERS of religious faith with the dynamic society of the maritime world suggests that neither Islam nor religion should be seen as the enemy. Not even terrorism is distinctively Islamic; both Catholic and Protestant fanatics stooped to terrorist tactics during the long wars of religion out of which the dynamic society ultimately rose. There is as yet no good historical argument to back the belief that as its encounter with dynamic society proceeds, Islam will ultimately prove to be less dynamic and less adaptable than Christianity has been.

In the end, when and if Islam makes its peace with the dynamic society, it will do so in the only way possible. It will not "secularize" itself into a mild form of atheism. It will not blend into a postconfessional unity religion that sees all religions as being fundamentally the same. Rather, pious Muslims of unimpeachable orthodoxy, conspicuous virtue, conservative principles, and great passion for their faith will show the world what dynamic Islam can be. Inspired by their example, vision, and teaching, Muslims all over the world will move more deeply into the world of their religion even as they find themselves increasingly at home in a dynamic, liberal, and capitalist world that is full of many faiths and many cultures.

History offers no certainties, but it does give grounds for hope.

The Cattle Killing

Even the radical terror movements associated with Osama bin Laden and
Al-Qaeda have close parallels with non-Islamic movements of resistance
against the Walrus and/or the Carpenter in the past.

The year 1856 was one of crisis for the Xhosa people in what is now the
Republic of South Africa. A long series of wars with Dutch and British
colonists led to the progressive loss of Xhosa territory. Most recently, the
Xhosa had suffered a shattering defeat in the War of the Axe and seen
British forts established in their territory. A devastating cattle disease had
decimated the herds on which they depended. With former allies weakened,
and a British military presence that appeared to be growing stronger and
more insolent, the Xhosa leadership saw few positive options.

At this moment, in May 1856, a young girl had a vision as she went down
to fetch water from a pool by the river. Nongquawusa came back from the
river and told her uncle that the gods had appeared to her and promised that
if the Xhosa sacrificed all their cattle and destroyed all their crops, the gods
would replace all the lost goods and more. Moreover, the British and indeed
all the whites would die or leave the country, and the old prosperity would
return. Her uncle believed her, and repeated the story to the paramount chief
of the Xhosa. He, too, believed, and the word went out to the villages and
tribes of the people.

Some believed that this was a clever strategy to unite the people in a last
great war against the British. With no food or cattle to rely on, the people
would have no choice but to fall on the British settlements in a do-or-die
battle. Others appear to have believed the prophecy. Eagerly awaiting the
promised bounty, many built new corrals and prepared storage facilities for
the expected grain. The Xhosa systematically slaughtered their cattle;
300,000 head are estimated to have been killed, and uncounted quantities of
grain and other foodstuffs were destroyed. When the new cattle and grain
promised by the gods failed to appear, the spirit of resistance was crushed. A
famine is believed to have killed half of the Xhosa population; Nongquawusa
survived, though her uncle did not.

Other cultures under this kind of stress have found similar beliefs attractive. We are in trouble, the reasoning goes, because we have not fully trusted
or fully followed the righteous ways of our ancestors. Charismatic figures
have visions, revelations, and dreams which promise that the old religion

and old gods (or God) will deliver us from the hated foreigner if we truly
repent and return. Our religion, our culture, is far more powerful than we
realize, they say. If we just fully trust and believe, the hidden powers will
manifest themselves, cleansing the world of our foes and restoring a righteous order to mankind.

Prophets of this kind arose among the American Indians at various points
in their long and losing struggles with the whites. The Shawnee prophet
Tenskwatawa (1775–1836) urged members of many of the native nations to
purify themselves of European influence, and give up the use of European
goods, and, especially, avoid substances like alcohol. Strengthened and
united, they would be able to resist the settlers then pouring into the Ohio
Valley. Indians who favored cooperation with the whites were accused of
witchcraft; some were executed. Indians from many tribes gathered with
Tenskwatawa at the settlement of Prophetstown, which flourished until a
preemptive attack against United States forces under William Henry Harrison failed. Tenskwatawa's religious renewal collapsed, and Harrison went
on to be elected president of the United States because of his victory over
the prophet's forces at the battle of Tippecanoe.

In 1890, when Harrison's grandson Benjamin was president of the United
States, another movement inspired by another prophet spurred the Lakota
(Sioux) people to a final struggle. At that time, the Sioux faced a major crisis as American authorities divided the Great Sioux Reservation into five
smaller territories and forced Sioux families to live as farmers. A religious
revival based on visions spread not only through the Sioux but through other
tribal peoples of the west. The original form of the revival was syncretistic
and pacifist; the Paiute prophet Wovoka (also known as Jack Wilson)
reported a vision of the whites disappearing from the prairie and the return
of the buffalo and the antelope—if the Indians would dance a variant of a
traditional Spirit Ghost Dance. In Wovoka's vision, if the Indians lived in
peace and followed the ancestral ways, God would divide the continent,
making Harrison his deputy to rule the east, and putting Wovoka in charge
of the west.

The new movement spread throughout the West; members of the various
tribes came to hear Wovoka as others had come to Tenskwatawa.

Among the Sioux the pacific aspect of the revival disappeared. A belief
grew up that it was not enough to dance the Ghost Dance and wait for the
whites to abandon tribal lands. It would be necessary to drive them out. Fortunately, dancers wearing Spirit or Ghost Shirts would be invulnerable to
the weapons of the whites. Inspired by their version of Wovoka's message,

some of the Sioux refused to accept the increasingly unbearable treaty terms dictated by American forces. This resistance would end tragically at the Wounded Knee massacre.

Such movements are not confined to small nations on the fringes of expanding civilizations. The Righteous Harmony Movement in China— followers were known among Westerners as "Boxers," and the movement is called the Boxer Rebellion—involved a widespread belief that magic shirts would defend the wearers against bullets and that the purity and rigor with which traditional Chinese beliefs were followed would endow the practitioners with a supernatural ability to drive the foreigners away. In European history, Carlist soldiers fighting against what they saw as a secular and antireligious Spanish government believed that specially blessed images of the Blessed Heart of Jesus would protect them from the bullets of the unrighteous but well-equipped (and British-backed) enemy. As Japan faced defeat during the Second World War, there were factions in the armed forces and the government who similarly believed that a return to a (hypothetical and unhistorical) purity would yet lead the country to victory. The cult of the kamikaze pilots, the first organized corps of suicide bombers, was part of this movement. There are many other examples of a desperate culture or subculture that, on the cusp of an overwhelming and destructive encounter with a dynamic and overpowering foreign culture, came to believe that a return to its pure roots would provide a miraculous path out of an unsustainable situation.

Movements like Al-Qaeda clearly share many traits with these earlier examples. Like Tenskwatawa's followers, modern Islamic ghost dancers brand leaders who favor compromise with the foreigners as religious deviants. Visions and dreams were prevalent among the followers of Osama bin Laden during the Afghan war against the Soviets, and presumably still continue to inspire resistance today. Members of these movements believe that if they and the Muslim peoples as a whole throw off foreign and Western customs, and truly embrace the righteous ways of the early followers of Islam, God will give them victory over their enemies, however intimidating the odds may seem. Suicide bombers, hijackers on missions like the 9/11 attacks, and the human waves of enthusiastic young men charging the Iraqi front lines during the Iran-Iraq war all show the power of these beliefs to inspire people—especially young people—to face death for them.

Unfortunately, ghost dancers do not always remain marginalized outsiders in the political or literal wilderness. Nongquawusa quickly gained the support of the Xhosa leaders. Tenskwatawa's movement attracted many powerful leaders and talented individuals and helped Tenskwatawa's brother Tecumseh organize one of the most effective coalitions that the American Indians ever achieved. The dowager empress Cixi supported the Boxers against foreign forces. Adolf Hitler started his political career among the isolated and marginalized ultranationalist ghost dancers of Weimar Germany and brought a ragbag collection of fanatics, lunatics, thugs, and crackpot intellectuals to power in one of the world's most powerful states. The ghost-dancing Ayatollah Khomeini took the helm in the venerable state of Iran.

On the other hand, the arrival of the ghost dancers is often a sign that the struggles within a culture or civilization are reaching their climax. The most important result of the Ghost Dance movement among the American Indians was not the massacre at Wounded Knee; it was the discovery of the cultural resources and strengths that allowed Native Americans all over the country to preserve their languages and pride in the face of defeat. The most famous name in the political history of the Xhosa is Nelson Mandela, not Nongquawusa. With the defeat of the Boxers, China began the process of revolution and modernization which, through a century of horror and bloodshed, has finally seen that country moving to find a place at the center of global history. The historical fate of most ghost dancers is to illustrate by the futility of their actions that the path of rejection is closed. Once they are out of the way, the real business of renewal and adjustment can begin.

WE SHOULD NOT DELUDE ourselves with easy optimism. Isaiah Berlin was a deep student and serious proponent of cultural diversity, but he warned that a collective whose feelings have been deeply outraged by historical developments changes in ways that make healing harder. Reflecting on the poisonous and genocidal nationalisms that tortured twentieth-century Europe, Berlin located the root problems in historical suffering and insult imposed by stronger, outside powers.

German nationalism took its disastrous turn toward anti-Semitism and chauvinism following centuries of insult and domination, especially at the hands of the French. "To be the object of contempt or patronizing tolerance on the part of proud neighbors," he wrote, "is one of the most traumatic experiences that individuals or societies can suffer. The response, as often as not, is pathological exaggeration of one's real or imaginary virtues, as resentment and hostility towards the proud, the happy, the successful. . . . Those who cannot boast of great political, military or economic achievements . . . seek comfort and strength in the notion of the free and creative life of the spirit within them, uncorrupted by the vices of power or sophistication."[7]

Berlin shares Herder's belief that it is the success of expansive societies, embarked on ambitious projects of global transformation that helps create bitterness and animosity. Writing more than two hundred years ago, Herder attacked the consequences of European colonialism and trade around the world. "Do not all these lands," he asked, "more or less cry for revenge?" The cruelty of the Spaniards, the greed of the English, the "cold impudence" of the Dutch have conquered much of the world and spread what we call civilization: we "blasphemously pretend that through these acts of injury to the world is fulfilled the purpose of providence."[8]

From these acts of oppression and conquest, Herder writes, flows a long train of destructive consequences. The Roman conquests of the "barbarians" destroyed their native civilizations and cultures and forced the subject people to develop in an alien framework unsuited to their native genius and culture. This was true even though Roman conquest brought a "higher" culture and the enforced conversion to Christianity. The incalculable harm by such universalizing conquerors echoes and re-echoes down the ages, and the British generals, merchants, and missionaries industriously spreading their values through Asia and the Americas were no better.

The consequences of centuries of conquest and war reverberate today in the foundations of the world order and in the consciousness of most of the world's peoples. Due recognition for the world's different cultures, collectivities, and nations is a necessary task for any order with aspirations to endure. That centuries of inequality and oppression have produced a true witch's brew of just demands for equality, grandiose and unrealistic demands, and perceptions, envy, hatred, and a bitter desire for revenge vastly complicates what is already a difficult and delicate task.

Dealing with those who rightly or wrongly believe that their just and legitimate aspirations cannot be realized within the existing framework of the maritime system will remain a principal concern of world politics and American foreign policy for a long time. As the world's cultures and civilizations come into ever-closer contact with one another, and as the stresses and tensions that inevitably result from those contacts grow, the diplomacy of civilizations will become an essential dimension of international life.

Crisis of Civilizations

The imperatives of history force the world's civilizations into contact with one another. Whether they like it or not, all civilizations today are condemned to live in close contact, to deal with one another, and to affect one another. This is one of the ways in which liberal capitalist society imposes its own preferences on the rest of the globe: mass travel, instant communications technology, and global economic integration are products of the maritime system produced by the liberal capitalist realm to serve its own purposes, and the rest of the earth's other cultures have no choice but to address the challenges posed by a shrinking world.

Both to prevent the rise and spread of terrorism and more broadly to promote the peaceful development of global society along lines favorable to the security and the interests of dynamic society, managing the relationship between the maritime system and the cultures and civilizations affected by it may well be the primary task of American foreign policy in the decades to come.

The first four years of the administration of George W. Bush were almost a textbook example of the dangers that American foreign policy faces when it ignores the enduring importance of collective recognition in international life. Its European policy trampled openly on the sensibilities of Cold War allies, raising questions about the structure of the Atlantic alliance in ways that seriously reduced public support for that alliance in much of Europe. At times the Bush administration seemed to glory in its relative isolation and its capacity for unilateral action, and it was only too happy to remind countries like Germany and France that they were not the great powers they had once been.

What proved to be an unnecessary and poorly planned war in Iraq reminded America's allies of the limits on America's wisdom. With gratuitous slights and grandiose posturing, men like former defense secretary Donald Rumsfeld made American power odious in much of the world. This was not wise; it risked waking old memories and disturbing old ghosts best left to slumber in peace. The chief European allies of the United States today are to a large degree former foes: Satans or aspiring Satans brought low by the crushing power of the maritime system.

"What though the field be lost?" Milton's Satan muses as from Hell he contemplates the unbearable spectacle of God.

> *Who now triumphs, and in the excess of joy*
> *Sole reigning holds the tyranny of heaven.*

Milton's Satan has lost a battle, but he is resolved to continue resisting:

> *All is not lost—the unconquerable will,*
> *And study of revenge, immortal hate,*
> *And courage never to submit or yield . . .*
> *To bow and sue for grace*
> *With suppliant knee, and deify his power*
> *Who, from the terror of this arm, so late*
> *Doubted his empire—that were low indeed . . .*

These Miltonic sentiments have lodged in French bosoms since Louis XVI supported the American colonials as a way of revenging himself on Britain for its triumph in the Seven Years' War. They were the animating passion in German nationalist politics in the twenty years between the two world wars and, barely acknowledged, they continue to bubble under the surface among some Germans today. And revenge and resistance today are never far from the thoughts of the Kremlin.

Let sleeping Satans lie; that is, or ought to be, one of the first rules for American officials dealing with Europe—and Japan, for that matter. As William Faulkner's character Gavin Stevens puts it in *Requiem for a Nun,* "The past isn't dead; it isn't even past."

The need for tact does not mean that the Europeans or the Japanese are immoral and ungrateful wretches who long to return to their former wicked ways and fail to appreciate the blessings that the Anglo-Saxon triumph has brought them; it means that Europeans are human beings who want their societies and cultures recognized as equals.

Contrary to what many Americans unreflectively suppose, dynamic society in its actually existing form is not simply the triumph of certain principles and values; it rests on the triumph of one power over others in the long and bitter battles to shape the future of the world. It is not just a *pax*; it is a *pax Americana,* and the current world order rests on the power of the United States and is more responsive to American interests and values than to those of other nations. Not everyone enjoys being reminded of this.

Turning to the Arab world, one finds that the issues of collective recognition play much more decisive roles in complicating and even poisoning the relationship between much of Arab culture and geopolitical, economic, and cultural elements of the maritime order—and it was in dealing with the Arab world that the Bush administration's inability to practice the diplomacy of civilizations led to the most serious problems.

As I have argued, there is no reason in principle to believe that Islam as a religion will ultimately prove to be incompatible with the economic and political realities of dynamic society. And there are clear signs that much opinion in the Islamic world is moving toward an approach to the faith that would build on these prospects to find ways of being authentically Muslim that work in a liberal world.

But the maritime order and American power frustrate the demands of the Arab world for collective recognition so harshly and on so many levels that the successful practice of a diplomacy of civilizations between the maritime order and the Arab world is one of the most difficult as well as one of the most important jobs on the planet.

We do not start with a blank slate. It is impossible for many Arabs and Christians not to regard the present clashes between their civilizations as continuations of a centuries-old struggle between two great faiths. Each Western outrage to Muslim sensibilities, each terror bombing by a fanatic, confirms this impression among millions of ordinary people—and not all diplomats and policy makers are exempt from this popular feeling.

The Muslim and Anglophone worlds approach this common past in very different ways. Before 9/11, the wars of religion between Christians and Muslims had largely grown foggy and dim in the Anglo-Saxon mind. *1066 and All That* is a book that purports to tell history as it is remembered by British adults rather than the boring record that pedantic scholars reconstruct from mildewed parchments and heavy books with tiny print. Its account of the Crusades is fuzzy and short. Richard I "went roaring about the Desert making ferocious attacks on the Saladins and the Paladins. . . ."[9]

That is not much and it is not accurate, but it is probably not far from what most twentieth-century Britons remembered about the Crusades, and it is rather more than most Americans knew—or cared to know. Of the episodes of religious warfare before and after the Crusades—the Islamic expansion through North Africa and the Middle East under the early caliphs, the war of reconquest by Spanish Christians culminating in the fall of Grenada in 1492, the siege of Vienna in 1683—even well-educated Americans and Britons thought very little. Neither the defeats nor the victories of the Christians in their wars against Muslims stirred much popular or scholarly interest; bishops and preachers paid virtually no attention to the whole subject other than to voice vague regrets about the bad conduct of the Crusaders at various points in the saga.

This reflects victor's amnesia, a condition I first encountered when, as a young boy from the Carolinas, I was sent to Massachusetts for school. This came at the end of the observations of the centennial of the Civil War; most white Southerners at the time could recite long lists of battles lost and won and argue over the relative merits of Confederate generals. In the North, nobody knew or cared very much about the war, even in a school where many of the students bore surnames made glorious by the exploits of their ancestors in Union arms. Currently, victor's amnesia blinds most Americans to the real nature of the problems we face in the Middle East; the Bush administration's comprehensive and catastrophic failure to engage in a diplomacy of civilizations with this vital and aggrieved region is in part a consequence of a failure to grasp the degree to which the last three hundred years look very different to Anglo-Saxon and Arab eyes.

Many Arabs think the Crusades never ended because, for them, they haven't. For the last three hundred years, the Christian powers have been carving up the Islamic world, and first the Walrus and now the Carpenter have been the powers with the sharpest carving knives and the longest reach. The stunning reversal of Muslim history since about 1700, and the rise of the Christian West as a whole and especially of the maritime system to power over the Muslim world are the defining facts of the contemporary world for many Muslims, particularly Arabs.

Many historians date the turning point from the 1699 Treaty of Karlowitz. For the first time the mighty Ottoman Empire had to yield; Russia and Poland made territorial gains, and the Austrian Hapsburgs received a right to intervene in Ottoman affairs to protect the rights of Roman Catholics. Since that time, a tsunami of Christian conquest has swept over the Muslim world. First the outlying and contestable lands fell—the khanates of Russia, the most extreme Ottoman conquests like Budapest. But the tide of disaster continued.

The Dutch overcame Islamic resistance in the East Indies; Muslim power collapsed in much of Ukraine and into the Caucasus as the Orthodox Russian armies advanced. The British put increasing pressure on the Muslim states of India.

The eighteenth century witnessed the decline of Muslim power, the years from 1800 to 1920 saw the fall. North Africa fell to the French and the Italians, and Muslims encountered systematic discrimination in their homelands. Tens of thousands of European settlers planted themselves

on the best agricultural land and built exclusive neighborhoods like the
Israeli settlements on the West Bank. Muslims paid extra taxes but could not
attend good schools; native Algerian Jews received automatic French citizenship but Muslims were barred unless they abjured the use of Muslim religious law. The British brought the once-powerful Moghul Empire
in India to an end, reducing the emperors to puppets before deposing
the last.

The Muslim emirates and sultanates of sub-Saharan Africa were crushed
by European forces (mainly British and French). The Ottoman Empire itself
came under more and more vigorous and unremitting attack. Christian powers vied to be named "protectors" of various Christian minorities in the
empire to give their governments the right to intervene in Ottoman politics.
Encouraged and often armed and supplied by Christian powers, the Christian minorities of Europe rose to fight for independence.

The most bitter wars of the era were fought in modern-day Greece and
the Balkans. These were wars of ethnicity and wars of religion; grievances
ran deep on both sides. Over the centuries, many Greeks and Slavs had converted to Islam, while Turks and other Muslims had settled throughout the
empire. As the Greeks, Bulgarians, Romanians, Croats, and Serbs sought to
regain their independence in the nineteenth century, supported by one or
more of the European Christian powers, savage and brutal warfare spread
throughout the region. Hundreds of thousands of civilians on both sides
were killed in one vicious atrocity after another. Muslims killed Christians,
Christians killed Muslims—and often killed Jews for good measure. When
Russian forces drove the Turks out of Bulgaria in the 1870s, panicky Bul-
garian Jews fled with the Muslims, fearing the attacks of their Christian
neighbors and the forces of the Russian tsar.

According to historian Justin McCarthy's *Death and Exile: The Ethnic
Cleansing of Ottoman Muslims, 1821–1922,* approximately five million
European Muslims were driven from their homes between 1821 and 1922 in
the greatest movement of ethnic cleansing in Europe until the forced
removals of Germans from Poland and Czechoslovakia following World
War II. A century of ethnic cleansing and murder converted the former territories of the Ottoman Empire in Europe from a population with an absolute
majority of Muslims to a region with a Christian majority. Between 1912
and 1920 alone, an estimated 62 percent of the Muslim population of south-
eastern Europe (excluding Albania) disappeared, fled, or was killed or
driven into exile.[10] Twenty-seven percent of the original Muslim population
died. Many of the survivors fled to what became Turkey;[11] one-fifth of Turks
today are descended from Balkan refugees, and no doubt they receive both

pleasure and instruction from the many lectures showered on them by earnest Western politicians urging Turkey to live up to European values.*

The final stage came with World War I. The British had previously made themselves the paramount power in the Persian Gulf, imposing themselves on Persians and Arabs alike—even before the region's oil was discovered. The Ottomans held the British off at Gallipoli, but across the Arab Middle East British armies advanced into the Arab heartland of Islam almost at will.

The Crusaders briefly emerged from historical obscurity in Britain in 1917, when joyful Britons hailed General (later Field Marshal) Edmund Allenby, who entered Jerusalem on December 9, 1917. After the war, virtually the entire Arab world was divided among the European powers, with Britain having by far the largest share, and France coming second. By 1920, when the British Empire reached its geographical peak, more Muslims lived under British rule than had ever lived under any Muslim caliph or sultan. An empire that included one-fourth of the world's people and one-fourth of its land surface ruled over more than half of the world's Muslims, and in much of the world, Britain was seen as the leading imperialist power and the greatest threat to the freedom and the religion of Muslims.

"We certainly do not want to administer their disgusting territories and people," the British "political advisor" in Bahrain stated at one point.[12] The British preferred to rule indirectly through local elites and royal families. Some of these families still sit on Middle Eastern thrones today; many Middle Easterners believe that the United States is pursuing a slightly modernized version of Britain's traditional practice of indirect rule.

From the standpoint of the Arab world, then, the Crusades are not an ancient and misty memory of Saladins and Paladins whacking away. The last three hundred years have seen one invasion after another by the Christian powers of lands that the Muslim world considered part of its own territory. No corner of the Muslim world was or is safe from this unrelenting onslaught. Since Allenby's entry into Jerusalem, the third holiest city in Islam has been mostly under either Christian or Jewish rule. At the time of this writing, the seat of the first great caliphate in Baghdad is patrolled by American troops. The dependence of Saudi Arabia, site of the holiest places

---

* Balkan history in this period is, of course, a controversial subject. I do not wish to imply that the Ottomans and the Muslims were innocent of atrocities; all sides sometimes behaved badly in a century of vicious and bitter conflict. My goal here is not to balance the accounts and give a dispassionate and evenhanded account of the period; my goal is to help a Western and non-Muslim audience understand the perceptions behind contemporary Muslim attitudes toward the West.

in Islam, on the American military for its security has been demonstrated over and over.

Decolonization has not given Muslims the recognition they hoped for. Muslim power in India was not restored when the British left; most of British India has become an aggressive and growing Hindu power. Muslims are left as minorities in India, or as citizens in troubled and less powerful Pakistan and Bangladesh. No Arab state outside the tiny sheikhdoms of the Gulf has achieved European or American standards of affluence. Worse, East Asia has long passed the Arab world as China, Korea, and other Asian countries advance.

This is the context in which Arab opinion (and indeed much Muslim opinion throughout the world) views American foreign policy and the state of Israel. Israel is simply the latest in a long line of incursions into Muslim territories; Muslims are shoved aside and Europeans (and Middle Eastern Jews) are preferred, just as they were in Algeria. The Muslims huddle in miserable camps, as they did in Anatolia after the various ethnic cleansings of the Balkan Wars. Arrogant Christian powers lecture Muslims on moral and civilizational values as they recklessly play with the fates of Muslim peoples for the sake of their own imperial games.

The Americans, like the British, are utterly inflexible where their national interests are concerned and where oil is at stake. And American power is even more omnipresent than British power used to be.

On top of all that, the secrets of economic success still seem hidden away. The Israelis are prospering more on their strip of worthless sand than the Egyptians or the Syrians, to say nothing of the Iraqis, with their oil and water riches.

This is not a complete and is certainly not an unbiased account of the last three hundred years of Muslim-Christian relations, and it does not include other, more positive elements in the relationship, but the context described here is an important fact with which American foreign policy in the region must work. In Arab eyes, the maritime system and the European civilization from which it sprang lack legitimacy from almost every point of view. Religiously it is both alien and hostile. Geopolitically it is responsible for centuries of wrong, and today its power is seen as continuing to block the aspirations of Muslim states. Its firm support of Israel is not an isolated instance; it is part of a long established pattern of anti-Muslim, anti-Arab foreign policy.

Into this charged environment came Bush and Blair, intoning pieties about individual rights, the virtues of liberal economic policy, the need for massive revolutionary upheaval in the Arab world, and the universal principles of moral law. Many Arabs dismissed this as simply the usual happy-clappy Anglo-Saxon hypocrisy, meaningless background noise for the invasion of Iraq. Others saw it as an attempt to undermine Arab cohesion and resistance in the service of some sinister plot connected either to Israeli expansionism, oil, or both. Still others saw it as the latest stage of a conscious and well-developed plan to undermine Islam, hatched by the enemies of God.

Americans will have to go well beyond diplomacy as usual to address the deep differences that divide the Arab world from the United States, especially since the United States is committed and will remain committed both to the security of the state of Israel and to the orderly functioning of the international markets in oil and natural gas. The maritime system has interests that require continued and even deepening U.S. engagement in the Middle East, but the historic relationship of the maritime system with the Arabs makes that engagement very difficult to sustain.

There is no way forward without a much deeper encounter between the United States and the Arab world, and this encounter cannot succeed unless the Carpenter can learn to talk less and listen more.

Twenty-two • The Diplomacy of Civilizations

I n the years ahead, we can expect some significant and hopefully benign changes in American policy and attitude, but these will fall well short of what America's most impassioned critics want, and they are unlikely to address what many Muslims and Arabs consider the roots of their grievances against the maritime system and the contemporary world.

To some degree, this cannot be helped. Americans cannot become less Anglo-Saxon. They may well reform their capitalist system, but they will not abandon it, nor will they abandon the attempt to make the maritime system work. And as long as Americans are concerned with the health of the world economy and the state of world politics, they cannot look with indifference on the state of Middle Eastern oil markets. American culture will not stop creating attractive and, to some people, disturbing cultural products, and technology will not stop making these products ever more cheaply and easily available all over the world. As an increasing number of countries masters the secrets of participating in the maritime system, the competition will become steadily tougher. The maritime system will not stop becoming more tightly connected, and the pace of economic and cultural change will not slow.

These developments elsewhere will not stop setting the agenda for the Arab world and for other societies struggling to keep up. As Herder observed in 1793,

[When] one or two nations accomplish steps of progress in a short time for which formerly centuries were required, then other nations cannot, and may not, want to set themselves back by centuries without thereby doing themselves painful damage. They *must* advance with those others; in our times one can no longer be a barbarian; as a barbarian one gets cheated, trodden on, despised, abused. The epochs of the world form a moving chain which no individual ring can in the end resist even if it wanted to.[1]

"It takes all the running you can do to stay in the same place," said the Red Queen to Alice. But what happens to those who run as hard as they can and are still falling behind?

It appears very unlikely that the Arab world will quickly develop the ability to surf the waves of global change. And what is true of the Arab world is true also of a number of other Muslim societies, of Russia, and of substantial portions of Latin America and Africa. And there will be conflicts within societies between ethnic groups and between elites and the masses as some groups run faster than others within individual countries. Even those countries like India and China that have found new success are likely to face increasing challenges as the pace of change accelerates, and social pressures and conflicts arise.

We will have a situation that satisfies no one. The Whigs will not build a global Tower of Babel, a single set of laws and values that overshadow the whole world, but those who resist and oppose Whig civilization will be unable to free themselves from its presence.

This does not look like a calm world, but it looks like the world we will have.

AS AMERICANS SEEK WAYS to come to terms with this difficult and occasionally quite dangerous set of forces, increasing numbers are likely to turn to the intellectual and theologian whose insight contributed so much to America's moral and political self-understanding in the Cold War: Reinhold Niebuhr. No twentieth-century American so fully and completely articulated and simultaneously critiqued the core elements of the Anglo-American worldview as this intellectual Protestant clergyman. Trained as a Lutheran, Niebuhr was powerfully drawn to the Anglican faith and particularly to the *Book of Common Prayer* so heavily stamped with the radical religious ideas of Thomas Cranmer. The exquisite balance of conviction and uncertainty, faith and self-questioning found in the Prayer Book resonated with Niebuhr's deepest convictions about the nature of human society and politics.

Niebuhr's central accomplishment was to apply a core Christian doctrine to the predicament of contemporary humanity: original sin. This doctrine, dismissed by optimistic Christian liberals confident that the war on history could be won and that human striving was rapidly bringing us to the golden age, accounted in Niebuhr's view for the repeated disappointments encountered by the would-be architects of the Whig utopia. More than that, Niebuhr believed that the presence and power of original sin was a key driving force in human society as a whole.

The doctrine has a strong religious pedigree; it is solidly rooted in the epistles of Paul, and profoundly influenced the work of St. Augustine of Hippo—still the most important historical thinker in the western Christian tradition. Martin Luther's appropriation of this doctrine helped shape the Reformation understanding of redemption through faith—a concept that, as we have seen, plays a continuing and even growing role in Anglo-American culture. In placing this doctrine in the foreground of his analysis, Niebuhr was enlisting one of the major building blocks of the Reformation and the Anglo-American worldview into his project.

Niebuhr's project was classically Anglo-American in another way. The idea of original sin emerged as a religious doctrine in the Christian faith; Niebuhr, sometimes praised and sometimes derided as the favorite theologian of atheists and non-Christians, reconceived the idea so that without losing its religious salience it became available as an analytical tool for students of foreign policy regardless of faith.

Niebuhr's approach to the idea of original sin was not through a literal reading of the Book of Genesis. Rather Niebuhr understood original sin as a universal element of the human condition, a systematic failure that all of us share to have a truly unbiased view of the world. Original sin in this view is a serious disturbance in human moral life, one that created problems for individuals in their daily lives, but had an even greater effect at the level of social life, politics, and relations between nations and cultures.

Individuals in Niebuhr's view have a natural tendency to exaggerate their own importance in the scheme of things, to view themselves as the moral center of their world. Individuals struggle to overcome this and to achieve a more balanced and less narcissistic approach to the world, and while they may never fully succeed, they do make some progress. (This account is surprisingly similar to the description of human nature that Adam Smith presents in *The Theory of Moral Sentiments*.) But the isolated individual is only part of the story.

Like Herder and Berlin, Niebuhr saw that human beings derive significant parts of their individual identity from the social groups to which they belong. Niebuhr notes, however, that the process of learning to question and check our own sense of self-importance that operates at the level of individual life does not apply to the collective dimension of our identities. The claims made for these collective selves are more far-reaching and grandiose than the ones we make for ourselves. We feel embarrassed if our claims on our own individual behalf are larger than life, but it is far more acceptable to make such claims on behalf of the various groups to which we belong. As Niebuhr wrote in *Moral Man and Immoral Society,* most of us make our claims to absolute power and importance through group identities rather than on our own individual behalf. Our egotism and self-centeredness find expression in the collective claims we make on behalf of the "community of which we are part: a tribe, family, religion, nation, race, gender, profession, or church."[2]

"Serious sins are mostly communal sins," wrote Niebuhr, and this is because "we give ourselves with all our loyalty and power to our group, to its security and success, and to its conquest and domination of competing groups."[3] Groups such as labor unions and corporations are quicker to fight hard for their claims, less concerned about the justice of any of their adversary's point of view, and less scrupulous about the tactics they use than their individual members usually are in their private lives.

For all their many fine qualities, neither General Motors nor the United Auto Workers possesses a soul or a moral consciousness. The stockholders who control the one and the voting union employees who control the other look at their relationship in a purely pragmatic way. Neither expects its adversary to extend justice or show mercy; and neither party considers doing so on its own.

The situation becomes more dire at the international level. The larger and grander the abstraction, the less critical we are of the claims, and the less need we feel to recognize the just claims of those who belong to competing camps. It is patriotic to make large claims for our nation, pious to make them for our faith. Great powers exhibit the arrogance of power, trampling over the rights and concerns of smaller peoples and weaker nations with little real awareness of what they have done. But there is also an arrogance of impotence; wronged peoples attach a cosmic importance to those wrongs, demand impossible things, and reject realistic compromises out of a romantic attachment to "ideals" they feel to be nonnegotiable. Into all this comes the mix of anger, resentment, blindness, and bigotry that Herder and Berlin found among nations who are or perceive themselves to be victims, and the weak with their own bitterness and limits then engage with the blindness, arrogance, self-centeredness, and self-righteousness of the strong.

The larger and more abstract an entity, the more unbalanced it can become. In Niebuhr's day, social class was the most prominent example of a collective identity in whose names great crimes and gross tyrannies were justified. Today, religion seems to have taken on this role for some people.

And religion is possibly the most dangerous of all the collectives. The grandeur of its claims are the greatest: what could possibly be more important that to defend, honor, and advance the one true religion? And in the meantime, all the egotism and pride that have been frustrated in my daily life, all the fury at humiliations, all the impatience at having to adjust to the wishes of others, all the grandeur in which I wish to be wrapped is projected onto my faith. And when I want my faith to dominate the world I am actually not hating the heathen: I am seeking on their behalf the highest blessing of all by bringing them into God's true fold.

The greatest conflicts and the greatest crimes often stem from the noblest aspirations, and the same collectivities that give life meaning and offer opportunities for solidarity serve also as the seedbeds of conflict. This is both a tragic and an ironic view of the world. It is tragic because the noblest human aspirations are undermined by the flaw deep in our nature. It is ironic because it is when we are most confident that we are acting righteously, most sure of the moral ground beneath our feet that we are in the greatest danger.

To achieve such a rich and paradoxical view of the world using the classic elements of Anglo-American thought is a remarkable thing, and Niebuhr can justly be ranked among the greatest and most profound thinkers twentieth-century America produced.

NIEBUHR FIRST ADVANCED HIS VISION during the Depression; with the approach of World War II and then the outbreak of the Cold War, he applied his approach to the international situation. In some ways Niebuhr's analysis of the Cold War was not far from Oliver Cromwell's description of the contest with Spain. "[W]e are embattled with a foe who embodies all the evils of demonic religion. . . . We will probably be at sword's point with this foe for generations to come. . . ." And like Cromwell, Niebuhr warned against the dangers of subversion at home, denounced the despotism and faithlessness of the enemy, supported alliances even with dubious and immoral partners in the great contest, maintained that the United States was fighting for a cause greater than its own interest, and argued that the struggle had to be prosecuted to the end.

But he did more. Evil was not only resident among our enemies; it was among us as well—and not just as a fifth column of potential traitors within. America itself was subject to evil; Americans themselves could be and sometimes were guilty. "We will incarnate the democratic cause the more truly," Niebuhr wrote, "the more we can overcome the pretension of embodying it perfectly."[4]

While the struggles against these two foes were necessary and needed to be engaged with all that we could bring to bear, the internal struggle would ultimately have the greatest consequence. "The pivotal problem in our national destiny," according to Niebuhr, was whether the United States could maintain an appropriate humility before God and man even as it embarked on a life-and-death struggle with the Soviet Union.[5] "We know that we have the position which we hold in the world today, partly by reason of factors and forces in the complex pattern of history which we did not create and from which we do not deserve to benefit. If we apprehend this religiously, the sense of destiny ceases to be a vehicle of pride and becomes the occasion for a new sense of responsibility."[6]

Niebuhr told Cold War America that it needed both to combat communism and Soviet influence around the world and to maintain a critical stance toward its own moral and political claims. It needed to understand the elements of justice, however twisted and perverted, in the claims of its foes. It could not confuse its own aspirations, however noble they appeared or however virtuous it felt to revel in them, with the good of all mankind. It had to recognize a complex mix of evil and good in its own motivations and acts, and yet not be paralyzed by this realization into passivity and inaction. Americans, imperfect themselves, were at war with an evil (though not perfectly evil) enemy in an imperfect world. Not all the means the Americans used would be pure, and victory in the Cold War would not usher in either the Whig utopia or the Kingdom of God. But even a partial and imperfect victory was worth having: we are not going to establish perfect justice or abolish coercion and power relations in international life. But perhaps we can have "enough justice" and coercion can be "sufficiently non-violent" to prevent the complete breakdown and disaster of human civilization. To achieve this limited goal, Niebuhr not only supported the development of nuclear weapons; he believed that under certain circumstances nuclear weapons could appropriately be used in a just war.[7]

AS AMERICANS STRIVE TO UNDERSTAND the nature of the threat revealed by the terror attacks of 9/11 and to develop a foreign policy stance that can guide them through this latest challenge to the maritime order, Niebuhr's ideas seem more compelling and vital than ever. More even than in the Cold War, the United States will have to combine a capacity for action and assertion with a capacity for reflection and self-criticism. The world of religiously motivated Middle Eastern terrorists is far more alien to most Americans than was communism. Marxism, after all, is a product of the same Western civilization that produced the United States, and the worldview of its Soviet adherents was recognizable and comprehensible though repugnant to many Americans. Niebuhr himself had been a socialist and was a serious student both of Marx and of the intellectual history that shaped his worldview.

To understand the terrorists, and to understand the shades of opinion surrounding the movement, much less to learn how to operate effectively in the political and cultural environment of the modern Middle East, the United States must make larger intellectual and cultural leaps than it did in the Cold War. It will have to come to terms with rage and frustration that is more deeply seated, more diffuse, and harder to reconcile than the mix of anti-capitalism, Occidentalism, and Russian nationalism that powered the Soviet Union.

The task will be all the more difficult in that the religious overtones and connotations of the terror threat invoke deeply seated collective identities both in the mostly Muslim Middle East and in the mostly Christian United States. For both sides the greatest possible disaster would be to regard one another as enemies in an escalating spiral of misunderstanding, provocation, violence, and retaliation. Given the history, and given the religious and cultural differences, this would be a dangerous possibility under any circumstances; with disciplined, highly trained terrorists seeking to bring about just such an outcome a worst-case scenario can look ominously likely.

But if Niebuhr urges self-examination, an awareness of the ironies of history, and recognition of the imperfection of one's own side, he demands action in an imperfect world. As a Christian theologian who supported continuing development of nuclear weapons during the Cold War, he had no illusions about the need for force and compulsion in the service of causes considerably less noble than the war against history. Many Anglo-Americans have only been able to talk themselves into support for the use of force by persuading themselves that the alternatives were stark: Heaven or Hell, utopia or the destruction of every civilized value in the world.

Niebuhr will not allow us the comfort of that illusion. We may have to fight even though the world that emerges from a given war will still be deeply flawed. Looking back to the first Gulf War under the first President Bush, a Niebuhrian adviser might call for clarity as well as resolution. Driving Saddam Hussein out of Kuwait, he could have said, might not usher in a new world order based on peace and cooperative security arrangements under the auspices of the Security Council—but we might have to drive him out anyway. We might even have to admit to ourselves that while the principles of international order are part of our motivation for freeing Kuwait, so too is our determination to prevent Saddam from getting a stranglehold on the world's oil supply. Going further, we might even have to acknowledge the truth that for many Arabs, the American commitment to the independence of the Gulf emirates and sheikhdoms has the effect of frustrating Arab nationalism whether secular or religious, and that for more than a generation the United States has opposed not only Saddam Hussein, but every leader—and every movement—who aspired to unite the Arab world. We must come to terms with the very complex ways that our support for Israel affects the way that Arabs interpret American motives and actions. And yet, knowing all this, we might still have to drive Saddam Hussein from Kuwait—and defend an imperfect Israel while supporting the independence of the Gulf states even if they show few signs of evolving into secular, democratic polities. Yet we must do all this without losing our grip on our ideals and our values.

To broaden our horizon from the Middle East to the world at large, the diplomacy of civilizations involves handling the relationship between capitalism, a system with global implications that forces every country to adjust and respond, and the separate identities, aspirations, and attitudes of the many different societies affected by the maritime system. And in a world where many countries already feel with the Red Queen that they are running as fast as they can, capitalism is a relentless taskmaster demanding that everyone go faster and faster.

Our successors are very likely to believe that even with all the problems we face in the Middle East today, our time remains a benign one. At the moment, for example, the vast and revolutionary changes sweeping through Asia manifest themselves to Americans chiefly in the form of bargain products at Wal-Mart. We are sometimes sentimentally sorry for those who work long hours at low pay in dangerous factories to create these bargains, and for Americans whose jobs are at risk because of foreign competition, but any serious discontent among those workers has yet to affect us.

This is unlikely to last. The first generation of urban factory workers may be grateful enough to escape from rural poverty and preoccupied enough by problems of survival to limit their political involvement. It is unlikely that their children and grandchildren will accept the same treatment with the same relative forbearance. Yet the economic forces that keep factory wages low in the developing world are likely to last. As coastal Chinese wages rise, industry moves inland, or relocates to Vietnam and India. Bangladesh and Africa beckon beyond.

When these workers bring their grievances about their wages and their working conditions into politics, and China already experiences something like 150,000 demonstrations and strikes a year, both Chinese life and international politics will be seriously affected. A complex, volatile, and dangerous mix of class resentment, ethnic and regional strife, and cultural, national, and racial anger with roots deep in the past could explode onto the Chinese and world stages. Frustrated demands for both individual and collective recognition and rights will contend with one another in ways that test China's political wisdom and cultural values.

In India it is also unlikely that the wider dispersal of capitalism will be a magic elixir that resolves all disputes and ends all dissension. Capitalism increases inequality, increases the value of certain privileges (like access to high-quality instruction in English), and characteristically brings greater benefits to some regions and subcultures than to others. India's political system is flexible and resilient; those strengths will be tested as one wave of change after another spreads more and more widely through the most complex and diverse political society on the face of the earth.

I argued above that the strategic geometry of Asia in the twenty-first century favors the emergence of a relatively peaceful and stable political system based on a rough balance of power. This is true, but for that system to come into being, Asian countries and their international partners are going to have to ride out some storms. The industrial revolution in Europe produced communism and fascism and episode after episode of murderous nationalist violence; today's economic and social revolutions in Asia are politically bigger, faster, and more disruptive than anything in Europe.

The legacy of Reinhold Niebuhr is not something Americans need to pick up in order to manage their relationship with the Muslim world, to be rapidly discarded once the worst of that battle is over. The diplomacy of civilizations and Niebuhr's approach to it will become increasingly necessary as this new and explosive century unfolds.

We face a quintessentially Niebuhrian situation. The Anglo-American Whigs, caught up in enthusiasm for their global project of liberation and development, cannot lose sight either of the ways their project affects others, or of the roots of their ideology in their own cultural values and, indeed, their interests. And yet their awareness of the conditionality of that project and of its actual and potential drawbacks and limitations cannot and should not affect their core commitment to their values—and those values continue to power the global activities and transformational agenda of the maritime order. As long as the diplomacy of civilizations and the problems of collective recognition dominate world politics, Americans will need to subject themselves to the bracing if sometimes astringent effects of Niebuhr's thought.

BUT WILL THEY? In a country never noted for the respect it pays intellectuals, Niebuhr was a towering intellect whose engagement with social problems reflected lifelong engagement with dauntingly recondite ideas and philosophers. In a country whose religious landscape is currently dominated by evangelical churches, Niebuhr was a frankly and staunchly liberal Protestant who once famously refused to meet with the evangelist Billy Graham because Graham had preached before racially segregated audiences. And in a foreign policy climate that seems torn between liberal utopians (whether of the traditional internationalist or of the neo-conservative varieties of the breed), isolationists, and angry, combative nationalists, the outlook seems poor for the kind of foreign policy to which Niebuhrian analysis leads.

Meanwhile, the gap between the foreign policy elite (or the intellectual elite more generally in the United States) and the broader society appears to be widening. Whether on the left or on the right, Americans are increasingly skeptical of experts and establishments of all kinds.

The traditional source of support for Niebuhr's thought is the old liberal wing of the Democratic Party. Martin Luther King, Jr. read Niebuhr closely and often. Cold War liberals like Arthur Schlesinger, who once called for the formation of "Atheists for Niebuhr," George Kennan (who called Niebuhr "the father of us all"), and two-time presidential candidate Adlai Stevenson were deeply versed in Niebuhr's thought. President Jimmy Carter has often spoken of his intellectual debt to Niebuhr.[8] Today writers like Peter Beinart, Leon Wieseltier, and E. J. Dionne call for a Niebuhrian renaissance, and Senator Barack Obama has spoken to journalists about Niebuhr's influence on his thought.

Largely marginalized in American politics during the first six years of the George W. Bush administration, centrist Democrats regained significant influence when the elections of November 2006 returned Democratic majorities in both houses of Congress. When and if Democrats regain the White House, it seems likely that Niebuhr will once again loom as an important point of reference for many of those entrusted with the formation and execution of American foreign policy.

Yet this to some degree is a case of those who need Niebuhr the least liking him the most—he is in the position of a minister preaching to the choir. The United States does not just need a handful of thinkers and even leaders in a particular political party to think in Niebuhrian terms, though that is a good thing as far as it goes.

The diplomacy of civilizations is much larger than government policy and, in any case, in a country like the United States where even transient waves of public sentiment frequently have large consequences for foreign policy, Niebuhrian policies can only be sustained when they have wide and deep support. Conservatives as well as liberals need to internalize the Niebuhrian stance, and mass public opinion as well as elite debates should reflect these values. In particular, American populist nationalism, the Jacksonian school of foreign policy, must develop a more Niebuhrian understanding of its place in the world.

Particularly as disillusionment with the Bush foreign policy spread through conservative ranks, a number of writers, most prominently David Brooks of *The New York Times,* looked to Niebuhr for explanations about why the neo-conservative experiment went so badly awry. If Republican as well as Democratic intellectuals come to foreign policy with ideas and sensibilities that have been shaped in part by their encounter with Niebuhr's thought, this is a better thing than having only one party's thinkers engaged with him. But this is still very far from planting a deeper self-awareness in the American body politic at large.

Evangelical Protestantism is the one social movement in the United States that has the presence and power to create a significant new mass of public opinion that is responsive to Niebuhrian ideals. Evangelical religion is strongest precisely in the states whose voters supported Bush in 2000 and 2004; evangelical religion has a strong presence in the armed forces; evangelical religion has a long history as the dominant form of American folk religion.

More than this, evangelical America is often considered—as it has often been—the section of the population most committed to uncritical flag waving, to simplistic understandings of foreign peoples and culture, and resistant to complex and nuanced discussions of the international issues facing the United States. This is the group in the population that most needs the message of Reinhold Niebuhr; but on the face of things it is the least likely to get it. For several centuries, evangelicals have been criticized by other conservative as well as liberal Christians for an anti-intellectual approach to life and for a theological stance that is characterized as "cheap grace": that stresses the ease of repentance and promises a simple and happy walk with the Lord. That a large evangelical following could be found for a dense and often dour thinker who emphasizes the element of constant moral struggle in the Christian life has always seemed unlikely. Unfortunately, without some development of this kind, the American public and therefore its leaders are likely to be inadequately prepared for the diplomacy of civilizations that their interests increasingly require.

TRANSFORMATIONS OF THIS KIND do not come often and they do not come quickly. Yet there are definite signs that the contemporary American evangelical community is becoming significantly more receptive to a Niebuhrian vision of the world.

What is happening is that what theologians call the *"Sitz im Leben,"* the life-situation, of the American evangelical community has changed. From a defensive and dwindling community of survivors huddled together for protection after the first two decades of the twentieth century, evangelicals have gradually become more powerful, assured, and outward looking. The nature of the evangelical community, its relationship to American society, and its relationship beyond that to the world at large have changed in fundamental ways that are creating a new type of American evangelical.

These new evangelicals are not the answer to a liberal secularist's prayer. They are significantly more conservative on most social issues, and especially on abortion, than most liberals, secular or religious, would like. While most are willing to consider intermediary positions between what they consider scientifically reductionist forms of evolutionary theory and an excessively and unimaginatively literal reading of the Genesis creation account, they are committed to the supremacy of scripture and to the idea of a God who acts, sometimes miraculously, in history. While they think of novels like the Left Behind series more as popular entertainment than serious theological statement, they believe that the prophecies of the Bible, Delphic as they sometimes appear to be, remain valid pointers to a future that will include a literal return of Christ to judge the whole earth. They are, generally speaking, uncompromisingly opposed to the idea that any religions except Christianity are true, and believe that whatever elements of truth and insight these faiths contain pale before their errors and omissions. They believe in a literal Hell and take seriously the so-called Great Commission, Christ's command to His disciples to spread the true faith throughout the world.

Yet despite all this, they bring a very different set of attitudes and ideas into the American political process than their immediate predecessors. In past generations, young evangelicals often attended small religious colleges where they could be protected by vigilant teachers from dangerous and disturbing currents of thought. With increasing numbers of evangelical young people graduating from colleges like Harvard and Yale and attending top professional schools, the new evangelical generation is far better integrated into the various wings of the American establishment than at any time since World War I. Scholars such as Mark Noll, Nathan Hatch, George Marsden, Richard Mouw, and Miroslav Volf are held in respect far beyond the bounds of the evangelical world. Whether or not they attend secular schools, young evangelical students and pastors are enthusiastically grappling with serious contemporary thought. More than that, serious theological studies that engage nonpolemically with liberal Protestant theologians and ideas have enjoyed a substantial boom on evangelical college and seminary campuses. In that boom, the names of Reinhold Niebuhr and his onetime student Dietrich Bonhoeffer are among the most prominent heroes for the new evangelical leaders. When Dr. Richard Land, president of the Southern Baptist Convention's Ethics and Religious Liberty Commission, cites Niebuhr and Bonhoeffer as major influences on his thought and urges American religious conservatives to learn from Bonhoeffer's resistance to an idolatrous form of nationalism in Hitler's Germany and refrain from idolatrously identifying American culture and values with the gospel, interesting changes are clearly under way.

Beyond the intellectual revival, today's evangelicals are far more engaged with nonevangelical and non-American counterparts than in the past. Partly due to common opposition to abortion and among other factors partly due to a common desire to defend the place of religion in American society, evangelicals and Catholics today are far more closely connected than ever before. Partly through the influence of Niebuhr, evangelicals have increasingly familiarized themselves with Catholic teaching on just wars. The encounter with Catholicism, both at a personal and at an intellectual level, has also exposed many evangelicals to a much richer and more complex body of Christian thought and social reflection than they have previously known.

The rise of flourishing evangelical and Pentecostal churches in Africa, Asia, and Latin America has contributed to a significant broadening of the cultural horizons of American evangelicals as well. The increased ease of travel has opened the doors to a new kind of "mass mission" as well, in which scores and even hundreds of American evangelicals travel overseas for short-term voluntary work either directly in missions or providing relief and assistance in various ways. The American evangelical community has never been as internationally experienced and traveled as it is today. And relations with African Christians in particular are far less paternalistic than they used to be. At a time when Anglican bishops in Rwanda and Nigeria are establishing missionary outreach in the United States to minister to conservative white Episcopalians alienated by that church's liberal stand on gay rights, among other issues, American evangelicals have lost both the ability and the will to condescend to African Christians.

Finally, the civil rights movement, the most important social movement in twentieth-century America, and one whose consequences are still reverberating today in virtually every dimension of American life, is also—if perhaps a little belatedly—transforming the world of American evangelical religion. Following Martin Luther King Jr., two generations of African American pastors and intellectuals have found guidance in Niebuhr's work. The African American experience is perhaps particularly conducive to an intuitive understanding of the ambiguities of culture and identity with which so much of Niebuhr's thought is concerned. In any case, African American pastors and intellectuals such as the Reverend Eugene Rivers of the historically black Church of God in Christ have developed a significant profile in the white evangelical world, and evangelical congregations are more racially mixed and more comfortable about it than they were a generation ago.

Contributing to the change in racial attitudes in the evangelical world has been the arrival of large numbers of non-white, non-Western immigrants, many of whom now reach this country as evangelicals while others convert once they have arrived. Asian, Afro-Caribbean, sub-Saharan African, and Latino Christians are increasingly significant elements among American evangelicals, both changing the context in which native-born black and white evangelicals encounter one another and bringing new perspectives and new cultural diversity into what was once a relatively homogeneous religious community.

Perhaps even more significantly for the prospects of a Niebuhrian revival in American politics, theological reflection on the civil rights movement and on the long and sad history of so many prominent evangelical religious groups in support of segregation and even of slavery is leading evangelicals to examine the influence of culture on theology in a new and vital way. Grant the evangelical assumption that the Bible is the inerrant Word of God; how then does one account for generations of false teaching by well-educated and pious evangelicals who defended segregation as God's will? Almost inevitably one is forced to conclude that cultural habits and assumptions creep in and distort one's interpretation of the holy books. God's revelation is everlasting and secure; man's reception of that revelation is something else.

Niebuhr's work and his stance are profoundly relevant to an evangelical community wrestling with issues of this kind. They are in fact almost unavoidable. The need to be firm in our convictions even as we test their foundations and search for the hidden assumptions and secret flaws that lead us into error is strongly felt among contemporary evangelicals; few thinkers can address these problems as clearly and as seriously as Niebuhr.

Meanwhile, the foreign policy problems that face the United States are not lost on the evangelical community. Evangelicals are well represented in the armed forces, including the reserves. Congregations all over the country include members cycling through tours of duty in Iraq. The importance of Israel in evangelical theology generally and also for various schools of interpretation of biblical prophecy should also not be underestimated. Many evangelicals are following news from the Middle East with great attention. It can hardly escape their notice that matters there are not going well.

In these circumstances, well-known and well-respected evangelical leaders and preachers have a historic opportunity to help the faith communities they serve engage more intelligently, compassionately, and effectively with the world. In an era of social as well as political polarization when popular suspicion of establishments and experts runs very high, evangelical and Pentecostal clergy are among a relative handful of trusted voices who can help public opinion at large appreciate the complex issues the country currently faces. The clergy and the lay leaders of these churches not only remain important channels of information and ideas that go well beyond Sunday morning sermons. Through programs of adult and youth education, study and reading groups, and both accredited and nonaccredited programs of intensive education, American evangelical churches provide the channels through which millions of politically active and engaged Americans receive much of their intellectual and cultural education. Many of those who benefit from these programs will never read a word of Niebuhr or even know his name; but if his insights help inform the way they approach critical matters of national identity, cultural values, and foreign policy no one, least of all Niebuhr, would object.

As is inevitable with a thinker as subtle, difficult, and paradoxical as Niebuhr, many of those who brandish his name will fall well short of comprehending much less deploying his ideas. And American foreign policy will never be as nuanced, well articulated, and thoughtful as intellectual and conscientious philosophers would wish. But incomplete and unsatisfactory as the results sometimes will be, a distinctly Niebuhrian influence is likely to make itself increasingly felt in America's encounter with the world to the extent that evangelicals begin however tentatively and inconsistently to work on these questions.

. . .

THERE IS ANOTHER REASON for regarding the potential for change in evangelical America with a certain cautious optimism. I alluded above to the close similarity between Niebuhr's account of human nature and Adam Smith's. That is, both thinkers believe that individual human beings have an inborn disposition to place themselves at the center of the universe. I am more distracted by my own sprained ankle than by the news of your broken leg. Both thinkers see that in private life these tendencies are somewhat checked. Niebuhr characteristically stresses the moral dimension of this process; equally characteristically Smith looks to automatic and natural process to account for it. In both cases, however, the result of encountering other selves is a kind of education: we learn to limit our pretensions and to develop greater respect for the feelings of others. Perhaps in the beginning this perception isn't very noble; children in kindergarten learn, slowly and painfully, to play with each other. Yet over time we learn to rub along with one another, and more sophisticated and far-reaching forms of trust, friendship, and solidarity ultimately emerge from the education that began in the sandbox.

It is not unreasonable to see a similar process taking place at the level of collective identity. A labor union and a manufacturer might learn that neither can serve its interest without understanding the situation and motivations of the other. They are still not precisely what Niebuhr would call moral actors, consciously seeking to serve higher ideals in their mutual intercourse. But they do become more effectively pragmatic. Democratic society would be impossible without this education in pragmatic cooperation.

Nations also seem capable of the same kind of behavior, though few ever learn these lessons as well as collective entities based within a common national society. After centuries of war, France and Germany have learned new ways to work with each other; even Britain and France, no closer than ever to true friendship, have learned to get along better than formerly.

It would be tempting to resurrect Whig optimism on this basis, and many try. We will all learn to cooperate better and better as our self-interest binds us into tighter and tighter relationships. History will end when we all gather round the campfire and sing "Kumbayah."   ·

But surely a little caution is in order. Domestic political interest groups learn moral lessons more slowly and less completely than individuals. Nations learn these lessons more slowly and less fully still. Cultures, civilizations, and religious faiths, it seems reasonable to suppose, make even less progress and take even longer to get there. Perhaps the reason the world's civilizations are in such a state of crisis and chaos is that until quite recently in historic terms they had so little contact with one another. In recent centuries, the scope and depth of that contact has rapidly grown— more rapidly, it seems, than the capacities of Americans and possibly also others to handle them well.

The worldview that emerges from this picture is not one of unrelieved darkness and gloom. There is real room for improvement. Not just individuals, but nations and civilizations can learn from mistakes. The diplomacy of civilizations is not just an eternal and desperate attempt to stave off a perpetually threatening set of conflicts. Good policy and thoughtful global engagement on our part can reduce the likelihood of such conflicts. Utopia is not just around the corner, but we can and should work for modest improvements. Here one returns to Niebuhr's idea of "just enough": just enough national and cultural growth to better fit us for the diplomacy of civilizations; just enough success in that diplomacy to prevent the collisions and clashes between the world's classes and cultures from plunging us all into a bottomless pit of destruction and war. Even this may be more than we get, but it is well worth the try.

As Niebuhr would certainly insist, it would be worse than foolish to regard this process of learning and accommodation as a task primarily for other cultures and civilizations. We are not the adult keeping watch over the squabbling children in the sandbox. We are down in the sand with everybody else, fighting over whose turn it is to play with the truck.

From this standpoint one can see the more culturally open and internationally engaged evangelicalism of the present day as one, though certainly not the only, dimension in which American society is gradually gaining the capacity to play the global role to which its economic and geopolitical success has called it. And while I do not know to what degree Americans can gain the ability to conduct a more fruitful diplomacy of civilizations, I am certain it is our duty as well as in our interest to try.

Twenty-three • The Meaning of It All

Whatever we say about the maritime order, it is not just another empire and it won't be remembered that way. Like the Greeks and the Romans, like the ancient Chinese, the maritime powers have left an indelible mark on history, and unlike those and other great ancient human societies, the maritime powers have made their imprint worldwide. For the first time ever, human beings all around the world are part of the same political and economic order. They travel and trade with one another across oceans and deserts on an unprecedented scale and over unprecedented distances, and, ever since the undersea cable boom of the nineteenth century, they have had access to virtually instant information about what people are doing on the other side of the world. The archeologists of the future are going to find Coca-Cola bottles in trash dumps all over the world; they will see "made in China" on trade goods everywhere they look, and they will find, along with millions of discarded pieces of Japanese-designed "Hello Kitty"–branded memorabilia, evidence of global consumer and cultural fads that sweep the entire planet almost overnight. There will be the traces of golden arches in the ruins of Beijing, and evidence of Chinese restaurants in the half-buried remnants of Manhattan. Archeological architects will be able to trace the rise and fall of international building styles that show techniques and designs leaping from continent to continent; such basic features as freeway exits and on-ramps will look similar whether found in Stockholm or Santiago de Chile. Linguistic evidence will show the spread of English words, especially in sports, medicine, business, and technology. The archeologists will painstakingly track flows of migrants that overshadow anything found in earlier eras; mass graveyards in Europe, Africa, and Asia will point to an era more explosive and murderous than anything found in the past. The layers of ash scattered across the urban cores of Eurasia will, along with the traces of radiation still detectable in the ruins of Hiroshima and Nagasaki, document a horrifying spasm of destruction. And unless these archeologists are extraterrestrials picking through the ruins of a dead planet, or unless humanity undergoes a catastrophe and recovery far more sweeping than anything known in our past—that is, if these hypothetical archeologists come from a future shaped in any meaningful way by the long human story of which the maritime order is the latest episode—their own languages, cultures, arts, religions, and sciences will bear the impress of the Anglo-American era at least as much as today's cultures are variously marked with the stamp of the great empires and cultures of the past. The Tower of London may be as much of a ruin as the Forum of Rome, and the interstate highway system may decay as much as the great network of Roman roads that once fanned across Europe, but in the culture, religion, law, finance, science, and mathematics of the future the Anglo-American legacy will remain a living presence and spirit long after the physical monuments of their accomplishments share the fate of the statue of Ozymandias, king of kings. Whatever else they have done, and however many oysters they have eaten, the Walrus and the Carpenter have left deep and durable footprints in the sands of time.

But is that all they have done? Have the Anglo-Saxons simply created another big and brawling civilization that will do nothing more than leave some impressive ruins behind? That is the final question we are left with: What is the place of the Anglo-Saxon era in the long human story? We've seen that many Anglo-Saxon politicians and sages have believed for several centuries that they were fighting and winning a war against history. They believed that the American and British world goals were to establish just, orderly, prosperous, stable, and free world societies on the basis of liberal and democratic capitalism.

They may not have built a utopia, but even so, the Anglo-Saxon era has produced changes that are as profound as they are enduring. For all its injustices and imperfections, the creation of the first truly global society is a substantial achievement; the maritime powers have effected a transformation of international relations whose consequences will be felt as long as the current civilization endures.

The rise of the Dutch witnessed the first world wars in which conflicts among European powers were fought out in Asia, Africa, and both North and South America. During the British era, the world became a single economic system, and the railroad, the steamship, and the undersea cable brought the far-flung branches of the human family into closer association than ever before. In the American era this accelerating process of global integration proceeded farther and faster than ever. Although the poor remain largely excluded from it, this rapidly expanding global society is nevertheless an extraordinary development.

In a very odd way, this emerging global society shares some key traits with the dynamic societies that grew up in the English-speaking world. Most of the countries and cultures in the world today are not very much like Queen Anne's England. But the world as a whole is. That is, today's world is divided among three competing sets of visions, and no one vision can impose its values on global society as a whole. In one group are the advocates of reason, who believe that universal logic, principles, and law are the only suitable or even feasible basis for an international system. This approach is particularly influential in Europe, but also has its advocates in the United States and elsewhere. For this group, the establishment of a powerful system of institutions that can enforce the global rule of law is the obvious and natural goal of international society. Whether inspired primarily by the French or by the Anglo-American revolutions, advocates of this position believe that universal human rights, universally valid legal principles, and the ideals of the Western Enlightenment should shape international institutions and domestic policy all around the world.

A second group is composed of the advocates of religion: people who believe that one of the world's great religions (as they understand it) is the necessary foundation for any just international order. For some, this foundation is Wahhabi Islam; for others it is the Shi'a faith that was taught by Ayatollah Khomeini. For others it is the Roman Catholic faith; still others believe that Pentecostal or evangelical Protestant Christianity is what the whole world needs in order to prosper and to stay at peace. Like the quarreling Christian sects in Queen Anne's Britain, the advocates of a religion-based international order disagree on the details, but share a common commitment to base both international and domestic society on the precepts of revealed religion. While such groups may, depending on their understanding of religious truth, accept larger or smaller portions of the "Enlightenment agenda" proposed by the votaries of reason, they insist that religion must have the last word, and they are determined to resist any efforts, however well intentioned, to build a rationalistic and secular international system according to Enlightenment principles.

Finally, there are the devotees of tradition, partisans of various forms of cultural and identity politics. These are often populist nationalists who believe that their own values and culture ought to be the basis for international life or at least that they must be protected from the soulless internationalism of others. I have written elsewhere of the Jacksonians, populist

American nationalists who often resist the transfer of power to international institutions because they do not trust foreigners and see these institutions as threatening deeply held American values. The United States is not the only country in the world where such views are popular. Across much of Asia many people can be found who are suspicious of international organizations as disguised forms of colonialism that seek to perpetuate European or Western power. Powerful and prominent people attack the idea that the French and American Enlightenment ideals constitute a universally valid approach to human rights. They argue that "Asian values," generally seen as more communal and less confrontational, must also be taken into account. The West should not use international institutions as vehicles to impose Western ideas on Asian societies. Issues connected with the rights of women also elicit opposition from those who claim that it is illegitimate for the West to impose its own models of appropriate gender relations on different societies with different roots.

Often these arguments lack credibility in Western ears. When Robert Mugabe defended his increasingly brutal and destructive misrule of Zimbabwe by invoking African identity politics against Anglo-American and European calls on his government to respect human rights, few Western observers were convinced by what they perceived as his self-serving rhetoric. Yet Mugabe's rhetoric continued to resonate in much of postcolonial Africa. This was not a tribute to Mugabe's economic management, and most of those who applauded his rhetoric had no interest in living under his rule; but identity politics remains a potent force throughout much of Africa today. From Argentina northward, Latin America also has strong traditions of populist nationalism whose adherents reject the universal applicability of ideals and ideas rooted in the Anglo-American Enlightenment.

Global society is as divided among the three poles of attraction today as Britain was in Queen Anne's time. Furthermore, as in Queen Anne's Britain, no one tendency in the world is strong enough to compel the others to conform. Radical Islam cannot conquer the world through jihad and impose a universal caliphate and Sharia law. The European Union cannot impose the rule of reason and of civil law on the affairs of nations. The United States cannot impose either the Christian religion or its own folk and cultural values on humanity at large. China and Japan can and will successfully resist the Westernization of international life, but they cannot impose Asian values as a replacement.

What this means is that to the degree a global society can establish itself and common institutions can serve the needs of the world's different societies and cultures, that society and those institutions will have to be anglican. That is, they will be limited in power; they will proceed from sometimes contradictory assumptions; they will be built in such a way that they can be interpreted and justified from opposed points of view. They will be a hodgepodge, not a systematic whole.

The world of global institutions and international law already seems to be based, like English common law, more on precedent and historical accident than the result of rational principles consistently applied. The most conscious proponents of a law-based and institutionally defined international system generally deplore this condition, hoping instead for a more rational system. That is probably a mistake. Tolerating and even welcoming a more diverse and less uniform approach to international life and global governance is likely over time to lead to more effective and widely accepted institutions. This will partly be expressed by a shift of power to regional institutions where specific cultural values and circumstances can be better accommodated than in global and universal ones. Looking ahead, the path to a more effective and just international society is likely to be at least as crooked and devious as the road the English-speaking societies took toward the development of their own unique blending of the values of reason, tradition, and religion.

In any case, the English-speaking countries have led the effort to create the first global society, created the economic and political systems that have sought and at least to some degree succeeded at keeping pace with its rapid development, and found ways that people with radically different values and priorities can work together in an open and dynamic system. This is not a bad showing for three hundred years; the English-speaking world has already had an influence over the human story as profound as that achieved by the great civilizations, east and west, which laid the foundations for the modern world, and the story of the maritime system does not yet appear to be drawing to a close.

The Permanent Revolution

But what is the point of Anglo-Saxon power?

G. K. Chesterton once wrote, "Cows may be purely economic, in the sense that we cannot see that they do much beyond grazing and seeking better grazing grounds; and that is why a history of cows in twelve volumes would not be very lively reading."[1] Cattle are also all equal; bulls may vie for dominance in a particular herd, but there are no oppressed races or castes of cows stewing over their historical grievances and plotting to overthrow bovine tyrants. The Guernsey cows do not envy the Angus; the oxen are not agitating for their rights; the Herefords do not resent the special status of the Brahman, and the Texas Longhorns do not frighten and offend the rest by unpredictable displays of unilateralism in their foreign policy. This is all very soothing, but how much like cattle do people want to be?

The problem of the cows haunts liberal, open society. Rodó, the Uruguayan critic who called Yankee society an example of Pascal's vicious circle, a society with no purpose higher than mere affluence, made the lack of higher, noneconomic values the centerpiece of his attack on Yankee civilization. The human spirit, argued Rodó, is greater than this. The Yankee fixation on prosperity makes for a society that is materially strong, but intellectually and morally weak. He compared this society to Caliban, the brawny but stupid servant in Shakespeare's *Tempest*. He compared Latin American society, less economically developed but more intellectual and cultivated, with the noble and brilliant spirit Ariel in the same play.

The issue is bigger than Rodó's critique of Yankee values, and cuts to the heart of the project of the Western Enlightenment. The liberal Enlightenment promises personal freedom and material abundance to all. That might be an adequate goal—if people were cows. But if the project of material betterment is really the only thing that liberal society offers mankind, then what becomes of qualities like self-sacrifice, nobility, courage, and honor?

As Francis Fukuyama noted in *The End of History,* there has always been something sad and unfulfilling about the Hegelian picture of the end of history. After all the fire and storm of the historical process, the struggles between good and evil, progress and reaction, the long and difficult climb from barbarism and slavery up into the light of civilization and finally of free civil society, at last and at length we struggle up to the peak of the mountain to encounter the culmination of generations of human striving: Homer Simpson. We are left with a humanity that has joined the cows and, like the inhabitants of John Lennon's imagined utopia, has "nothing to kill or die for." The world turns into a big mall, and we all go shopping: forever. Nietzsche called the inhabitants of this peaceful shopping paradise the "last men" and devoted some of his harshest polemics to the kind of human being who would be satisfied by this type of world.

This is a more cheerful future than one in which the human race goes extinct in a nuclear holocaust—but it remains, at best, painfully anticlimactic. Were all the heroism of the past, all the suffering, all the passionate faith, the sacrifice, the religious and political contests simply to build a shopper's paradise? Does liberal society really stand for nothing more than the accumulation of material possessions? This is the deepest critique of the American project in the world: that it is mere "busyness," sound and fury signifying nothing.

From this point of view, America is not only an empty society of ice-cold businessmen pursuing their dreary tasks. It is the enemy of meaning, morality, and authenticity wherever such things still exist. As American economic, social, and political values spread around the world, and as American consumer culture insinuates itself into the global consensus, everything that makes human life worth living, that makes people nobler and more interesting than cows, begins to disappear. The triumph of America is the death of humanity: that perception is what can unite a not-very-ex-Nazi like Martin Heidegger with not-very-ex-Stalinists like Jean-Paul Sartre, and unites both these men with Latin American humanists like Rodó and with both Sunni and Shi'a radicals in the Islamic world. "We worship God by hating America," as Tareq Hilmi puts it. To fight America and its insidious influence is to fight for the survival of authentic human experience and values, however we may construe them.

The best and I think the decisive response to this critique takes us back to the work of Henri Bergson. Bergson argued that humanity has an instinct for growth and change. This instinct is not a temporary aspect of human character, but a permanent feature of our identities. If Bergson is right, the Hegelians are wrong. In the classic Hegelian view, humans make history for the same reason that oysters make pearls. Something, a grain of sand in the case of the oysters and a social disequilibrium in the case of the humans, is causing discomfort; we do what we can to make the discomfort go away. Oysters secrete soothing layers of slime to cover the irritating sand; people have struggled to overcome the social imbalance and establish a just society. In both cases, we'll stop if the pain goes away.

To believe this is to miss the essential point of the Anglo-American project and, more broadly, to miss the grandeur of the human race. The open-ended dynamism that powers Anglo-American and capitalist society owes more to Bergson than to Hegel. The quest for more scientific and technical knowledge, and for the application of the fruits of that knowledge to ordinary human life, is not simply a quest for faster cars and better television reception. It is a quest to fulfill the human instinct for change, arising out of a deep and apparently built-in human belief that through change we encounter the transcendent and the divine. The material and social progress that is such a basic feature of Anglo-American society and of the broader world community gradually taking shape within the framework the Anglo-

Americans have constructed ultimately reflects a quest for meaning, not a quest for comfort and wealth. And unlike Hegelian history, this quest has no foreseeable ending point because the quest itself is a permanent feature of human nature.

If this is true, society will never reach a final stage, politics will never stop changing, and human beings will continue to reinvent themselves and to quarrel as long as humanity exists. We remain the heirs of Abraham, called to an encounter with transcendence that requires us to leave the familiar and embrace the challenge of a new kind of life in an ever-developing world. From the Anglo-Saxon point of view, participating in this adventure is not materialistic, even if the quest brings material benefits. *Abandoning* the quest is materialistic; to turn aside from this challenge is to embrace a merely material existence and to abandon the spiritual values that make human life truly human.

This transcendent call into an unknown future is what men like Andrew Carnegie, John D. Rockefeller, and Henry Ford were responding to when they poured their life's energy into business enterprise. Carnegie and Ford were both political as well as business visionaries; Carnegie's vast philanthropies included an endowment for peace that continues today to fund projects aimed at building a new and better world; Ford's peace ship was a well-intentioned if much-mocked effort to bring the slaughter of World War I to an end through private activism and moral suasion. (I am not defending the business methods or the political vision of either man; I am merely trying to understand what these men and others like them believed they were doing. Carnegie's labor practices were reprehensible; Ford's anti-Semitism even more so. Nevertheless both men were driven by much larger passions than mere greed.)

Capitalism gives full expression to the side of human nature that responds to this Abrahamic call to embrace dynamic religion with all its perils and its risks. This is why the Anglo-Americans under the influence of a culture and psychology shaped by the dynamic religious movements emerging from the various phases of the English and Scottish reformations have been so strongly drawn to capitalism and why they have worked so persistently to give it full scope.

This Promethean drive to acquire all the power that can be acquired, to do everything it is possible for humanity to do, to learn what can be learned, to build what can be built, and to change what can be changed is the force that impelled the three maritime powers to their global position. Societies that grasp this dynamic and embrace it become wealthier and more powerful; those that reject it or fail to handle its challenges become weaker. Within

societies something similar happens: the more dynamically oriented individuals, regions, institutions, and industries tend to gain power at the
expense of those who prefer a slower and safer path. The unique role of the
Anglo-Americans in modern times stems in part from the way in which
these societies have come to believe that dynamism is their tradition: that
they honor their past and acknowledge their roots by pressing on into the
future.

Unlike the Hegelian oyster seeking quiet and peace, the Walrus and the
Carpenter want a permanent revolution. There is no resting place, no final
destination for this process, and the real goal of Anglo-American civilization is to get the permanent revolution well and truly under way. We are
launching a space ship, not building a rest home.

We do not yet know what humanity is capable of, what intellectual, spiritual, technological, and cultural limits—if any—there are on humanity's
abilities. The maritime order represents at the deepest level an organization
of human abilities and societies, open to all nations and all cultures, for a
voyage of exploration into unknown waters.

This voyage, I think, is both our destiny and our duty even though we do
not, and cannot, know how or when it will end.

IT WILL NOT BE a restful voyage. In Bergson's model the instinct for tradition and stasis is also built into human nature. Static religion, religious and
transcendent experiences and beliefs that affirm the power and the necessity
of stability and continuity, will not go away. And people responsive to its call
will oppose the forces that seek to dismantle old traditions. The permanent
revolution which dynamic religion seeks will, it appears, generate equally
permanent resistance from static religion and the forces of tradition.

The struggle between the two forms of religion is largely responsible for
the struggle between universal and particularist history. Dynamic religion
corresponds to universal history, the expression in politics and culture of the
call to transform the world. Static religion corresponds to particular history,
the call to remain loyal to the roots of who we are and to bear witness to the
human achievements and transcendent values that are expressed in the sacred
past behind the particular society and faith tradition in which we stand.

We have noted that the maritime system has not been able to meet the
collective demands of many of the world's cultures and civilizations for
equality and respect; this conflict, we can now see, springs in part from the
two opposed sets of instincts that Bergson described and reflects the clash
between the universal and the particular visions of history.

If all this is true, the end of history may indeed be upon us—but the end of history is not an era of stagnation and stability. For Hegel and his followers, the end of history meant that humanity had built the right social system, a social system that met the deepest requirements of human nature.

I think we may have done this, and that we have built a world system that corresponds to human nature, but the results have been, to say the least, surprising. It turns out that human nature demands conflict and competition, not tranquillity and sloth. A society that fits human nature will not be a placid place; it will be a society in perpetual turmoil. On the one hand, the permanent revolution of capitalist society is the only form of human society that fully answers the instinctive human drive for development and growth. On the other hand, human nature requires continuity, and humanity will struggle to hold on to its particularity and its past. This conflict is probably not capable of resolution; to participate in this conflict and to be shaped by it is a large part of what it means to be human.

A hymn by William A. Percy used in Anglican worship today expresses this idea, that the goal toward which humanity strives is more complex than many think. Recalling how the "happy, simple fisher folk" Jesus called to be his apostles ended up, the hymn describes how

> *Young John who trimmed the flapping sails*
> *Homeless in Patmos died;*
> *Peter who hauled the teeming nets*
> *Head down was crucified.*

Looking back over the lives of the fisher folk before and after they knew "the Peace of God which filled their hearts / Brimful, and broke them, too," the hymn concludes:

> *The Peace of God it is no peace*
> *But strife closed with the sod*
> *Yet brothers pray for but one thing:*
> *The wondrous Peace of God.*

The end of history is, I think, this peace of God, and like the peace of God it is not something that we enter totally and at once. It is a beginning, not an end; we will be moving into it more and more deeply, and learning more about what it means as time goes on.

We must always bear in mind that the revolutionary transformation of the human condition by advancing technology is still in its early stages. As hundreds of millions of people in countries like China and India enjoy greater opportunities for education, as faster and smarter computers become more widely available, and as more companies and countries are able to pour greater sums into scientific research, we are likely to see a tremendous surge in scientific discoveries. The ever more flexible and deeper capital markets in the world, and the ever larger numbers of profit-seeking enterprises eager to exploit new scientific discoveries to provide new products or to enhance the productivity of their workforces, will work together to ensure that the results of this flood of discovery will pour more quickly and efficiently than ever into world markets.

Capitalism is taking us toward a future of accelerating change. The first twenty years of the twentieth century saw as much technological progress as the entire nineteenth century. Currently, industrial societies appear to be doubling their rate of technological progress every ten years. If this continues, and there is every reason to suppose that it will, the twenty-first century will experience the equivalent of twenty thousand years of "normal" human progress.[2]

This suggests the tide of social change will continue, that economic and political relationships around the world will be in constant flux, and that the cultures that dislike dynamic capitalism or are unable to manage it well will suffer even greater difficulties than they now face. New armies of ghost dancers are likely to sweep down from the hills, and, as technology creates new and cheaper biological and other weapons of mass destruction, they are likely to wield more terrible weapons than ever.

I cannot predict how this will end. But it seems likely that even as the historical process continues to accelerate, and even as dangers surround us on every hand, much of American society is going to approach this new and so far rather unsettling century with the optimistic faith in the invisible hand that has long been our hallmark. One way or another, large numbers of Americans are likely to continue to believe that the values that have shaped the Anglo-American world and by which the Anglo-Americans have gone on to take the lead in the last three tumultuous centuries remain the values that bring success in their daily economic and political pursuits. They will also continue to believe that these values are leading us westward and upward. Like the young man in Longfellow's poem, America will continue rushing forward, however steep the slope or forbidding the terrain, bearing its banner with the strange device: *Excelsior!*

Acknowledgments

As usual, there are many people to whom acknowledgment is due. First and foremost is Richard Haass, whose unstinting support made it possible for me to write this book, and whose wise counsel made it better. I also want to thank Richard for everything he has done to make the Council on Foreign Relations such an extraordinary place for scholars to work. Jan Murray, chief operating officer, and Jeff Reinke, chief of staff, share Richard's commitment to the institution and to the fellow. Thanks to both of them for many years of friendship and help.

I would also like to acknowledge those whose advice and insight helped me shape (and in some cases, reshape) the core ideas of this book, and who called various matters of interpretation and fact to my attention. Two study groups provided ongoing comment and advice. One, based in Washington, D.C., was made possible by the generosity of the Pew Forum on Religion and Public Life. The other was based in Los Angeles, and was underwritten by a generous gift from Robert J. Abernethy.

I am grateful to all who attended the sessions of these two groups and who helped me with their advice and their criticism; I am particularly grateful to Luis Lugo and Tim Shah at Pew. They were more than funders; they were intellectual partners. Also at the Washington meetings, contributions from Francis Fukuyama, Peter Berger, Adrian Wooldridge, Leon Fuerth, Andy Kohut, Bryan Hehir, Adam Garfinkle, Elisabeth Bumiller, James Kurth, Richard John Neuhaus, John Judis, Richard Land, Husain Haqqani, Reuel Marc Gerecht, Terry Lautz, and Moses Naim were particularly useful.

In Los Angeles, I'd like to thank Robert J. Abernethy, Jonathan D. Aronson, Cody D. Burke, Dan Caldwell, Arthur N. Greenberg, Edwin O. Guthman, James P. Halper, Ann Z. Kerr, Heather S. Greys, Robert J. Lempert,

Thomas F. Kranz, Robert M. Macy, Victor H. Palmieri, Barry A. Sanders, Charles Wolf, Curtis A. Hessler, Michael D. Intriligator, John Shu, Edwin M. Smith, David R. Ayón, Gregory Frye Treverton, Jason R. Wolff, and John N. Yochelson. Many members went well beyond the call of duty, sharing written responses and making detailed notes on the manuscript. This group, which met regularly during the full period I worked on the book, was an invaluable sounding board. I am grateful for your help and support.

There are others whose generous personal and financial support made it possible for me to work on the book. Mark Fisch's support and advice were very timely and welcome. John Guth and the Woodcock Foundation surprised me again and again with the constancy and generosity of their support. Allen Adler, Frances Beatty, and Mark Berner continued to offer helpful counsel. I would also like to thank The Henry Luce Foundation for its support. I am grateful to you all.

The Council on Foreign Relations remains a great place for scholars in large part because of the people who work there. James Lindsay and Gary Samore, the two directors of studies, who served during the time I worked on this manuscript, gave me every possible support and encouragement. Janine Hill, the deputy director for studies administration, has become a good friend as well as a valued colleague. The fellows at the council represent a remarkable range of views combined with enormous talent. My conversations with my immediate neighbors Laurie Garrett, Max Boot, and Isabel Coleman have over the years been enlightening as well as enjoyable. I'm also grateful to a number of current and former colleagues in the studies program, among them Lee Feinstein, Julia Sweig, Michael Levi, Steve Cook, Rachel Bronson, and Jagdish Bhagwati, for their friendship and counsel. I'm also grateful to the military, diplomacy, and intelligence fellows detailed to the council from the U.S. government over the years. They have been more than willing to share their expertise with me; in many ways this book reflects insights and reflections that were stimulated by my encounters with people like Helima Croft, Christopher LaFleur, Evans Revere, James Creighton, Steven Busby, Thomas Culora, John Newell, and Pete Mansoor.

Beyond the studies department, I've also benefited from the insights and efforts of many colleagues throughout the council. Jim Hoge and Gideon Rose at *Foreign Affairs* are an extraordinary team, and I'm grateful for their insight and wisdom. David Kellogg has more than once served as a sounding board for ideas that went on to become part of the book. Nancy Roman in the Washington office of the council has been a friend as well as a colleague. Suzanne Helm of the development program has provided help and advice as

I've sought funding for my research. The council's phenomenal team of librarians—Marcia Sprules, Michelle Baute, Connie Stagnaro, Erika Anderson, and Nick Fokas—under Leigh Gusts's leadership were enormously helpful every step of the way. Nancy Bodurtha, Jan Hughes, Irina Faskianos, and Lisa Shields and their teams have provided all kinds of advice, help, and support. I continue to be grateful for everything they do and for all the support I receive from their staffs. Dan Kurtz-Phelan at *Foreign Affairs* has kept a steady stream of books coming to my office. Charlie Day, Robert Osoria, Virginia Parrott, and Deepak Trivedi in the information services offices pooled their talents to keep my computer working, and more than once saved files that appeared to be forever lost. I also want to thank Ian Noray and Frank Alvarez, who keep the council running from day to day.

No list of my debts at the council would be complete without mentioning the role of Les Gelb. Les brought me to the council ten years ago, and ever since then he has continued to advise, support, and inspire me. His comments on this manuscript were extremely helpful; more helpful still has been his example of intelligent patriotism, integrity, loyalty, and friendship.

Jonathan Segal, my editor at Knopf, has been a patient and able editor whose support for the book never wavered, and whose insights have made a real difference. Geri Thoma continues to be both a dear friend and an astute agent. My parents read every word of this manuscript in several different drafts; their support and suggestions greatly helped.

I'm also grateful to my students at Bard College. They were the first audience for some of the ideas and text of the manuscript; their reactions and their comments have greatly helped. I'm particularly grateful to Jake Nabel for his thoughtful comments and also for suggesting that I consult Reginald Horsman's *Race and Manifest Destiny.* Thanks to Leon Bottstein for bringing me to Bard, to Jonathan Becker for everything he has done to make my teaching experience positive for both me and the students, and to George Soros for introducing me to Leon.

I also want to thank George Soros for the work he has done on Karl Popper and the open society. Astute readers of *God and Gold* will have no trouble recognizing my considerable debt to George's work, and some of the ideas in this book were first broached in conversations at his dinner table.

Last but not least, I want to thank the remarkable procession of young people who over the years have served as my research associates. Without their intelligence and diligence this book would be far less interesting and accurate. Benjamin Skinner, Derek Lundy, and Daniel Dolgin provided some of the initial research; Ben Skinner continued to provide feedback and helpful suggestions long after he left the council's employ. Charles Edel, Bryan Gunderson, and Scott Erwin carried much of the burden during the years in which the bulk of the manuscript was written. All three remain good friends, and I thank them for that as well as for their help with the book. Eitan Goldstein and Eliana Johnson came on board for the final stage of work on the book. Assisted by our hardworking intern, Ivan Lidarev, they overcame great obstacles and challenging deadlines, and by Benjamin Wise, who volunteered to join us for the final push. Thanks, Eitan and Eliana, and well-done! Eitan, Eliana, and the rest haven't just been researchers and fact-checkers; they have been thoughtful and careful readers whose suggestions and ideas have in many cases helped shape the final form of the book. Responsibility for any errors of fact or interpretation is, of course, mine.

Kigali, Rwanda
July 2007

Notes

INTRODUCTION

1. Arthur Schlesinger, "Bye, Bye, Woodrow," *Wall Street Journal,* October 27, 1993.
2. Paul Kennedy, *The Parliament of Man: The Past, the Present, and the Future of the United Nations* (Toronto: HarperCollins, 2006), xi.
3. David Patterson, "Andrew Carnegie's Quest for World Peace," *Proceedings of the American Historical Society* 114, no. 5 (October 20, 1970): 371–383.
4. Douglas Brinkley, *Wheels of the World: Henry Ford, His Company, and a Century of Progress* (New York: Penguin Books, 2003), 197.
5. Harry Kantor and Howard J. Wiarda, eds., *The Continuing Struggle for Democracy in Latin America* (Boulder, Colo.: Westview Press, 1980), 41–43.

CHAPTER ONE

1. *Speeches of Oliver Cromwell,* ed. Ivan Roots (London: J. M. Dent & Sons, 1989), 80.
2. Ibid., 80.
3. Ibid., 81.
4. "Remarks at the Annual Convention of the National Association of Evangelicals in Orlando, Florida," The Public Papers of Ronald Reagan, Ronald Reagan Presidential Library, http://www.reagan .utexas.edu/search/speeches/speech_ srch.html (accessed July 10, 2007).
5. Ibid., 364.
6. Ibid.
7. Roots, 83.
8. "Remarks at the Annual Convention of the National Association of Evangelicals in Orlando, Florida."
9. Roots, 82.
10. Ibid., 82–83.
11. Ibid., 84.
12. "Remarks at the Annual Convention of the National Association of Evangelicals in Orlando, Florida."
13. Roots, 85.
14. R. B. Merriam, "Some Notes on the Treatment of the English Catholics in the Reign of Elizabeth," *American Historical Review* 13, no. 3 (April 1908): 481.
15. *The Catholic Encyclopedia,* s.v. "Edward Bradshaigh."
16. Godfrey Davies, *The Early Stuarts, 1603–1660* (Oxford: Oxford University Press, 1959), 211.
17. Patrick Francis Moran, *Historical Sketch of the Persecutions Suffered by the Catholics of Ireland Under the Rule of Oliver Cromwell* (Dublin: Callan, 1903), ch. 8, point 2.

18. Thomas Burton, *Diary of Thomas Burton, esq., April 1657–February 1658,* http://www.british-history.ac.uk/report.asp?compid=36843 (accessed February 12, 2007), 153.

19. Roots, 83.

20. *The Works of Joseph Addison,* vol. 2, ed. George Washington Greene (Philadelphia: J. B. Lippincott & Co., 1870), 553.

21. Joseph Addison, *A Letter from Italy to the Right Honorable Charles Lord Halifax in the Year MDCCI,* in *A Collection of English Poems, 1660–1800,* ed. Ronald S. Crane (New York: Harper and Brothers, 1932), 280.

22. Ibid., 280.

23. Davies, 211.

24. William Hague, *William Pitt the Younger* (New York: Knopf, 2005), 145.

25. *The Speeches of the Right Honorable William Pitt in the House of Commons,* vol. 4 (London: Longman, Hurst, Ree and Orme, 1806), 28.

26. Charles F. Horne and Walter F. Austin, *Source Records of the Great War,* vol. 1 (New York: National Alumni, 1923), 398–404.

27. "A War for Honor, Lloyd George Says," *New York Times,* special cable, September 19, 1914.

28. James Bryce, ed., *Report of the Committee on Alleged German Outrages Appointed by His Britannic Majesty's Government and Presided Over by the Right Hon. Viscount Bryce, Committee on Alleged German Outrages* (N.P.: Kessinger Publishing, 2004), 23.

29. Ibid., 48.

30. Priscilla Roberts, "Benjamin Strong, the Federal Reserve, and the Limits to the Interwar American Nationalism," *Economic Quarterly* 86, no. 2 (Spring 2000): 10.

31. William Appleman Williams, ed., *The Shaping of American Diplomacy* (Chicago: Rand McNally, 1956), 582.

32. President Woodrow Wilson, War Message to Congress, on April 2, 1917, to Joint Houses of Congress, 65th Cong., 1st Sess.

33. George M. Marsden, *Understanding Fundamentalism and Evangelicals* (Grand Rapids, Mich.: W. B. Eerdmans, 1991), 51.

34. Marsden, 52.

35. "Proclamation of Additional Regulations Prescribing the Conduct of Alien Enemies." *American Journal of International Law* 12, no. 1, Supplement: Official Documents (January 1918): 6.

36. "Espionage Act, Title XII, Sections 1 and 2," *American Journal of International Law* 11, no. 4, Supplement: Official Documents (October 1917): 197.

37. Donald Johnson, "Wilson, Burleson, and the Censorship of the First World War," *Journal of Southern History* 28, no. 1 (February 1962): 51–52.

38. President George W. Bush, Address to a Joint Session of Congress and the American People, on September 20, 2001, to Joint Houses of Congress, 105th Cong., 1st Sess., http://www.whitehouse.gov/news/releases/2001/09/print/20010920-8.html (accessed January 5, 2005).

39. Ibid.

CHAPTER TWO

1. Angela Partington, ed., *Oxford Dictionary of Quotations* (New York: Oxford University Press, 1992), 317. Probably an oral rendition of words that appear in Bede's *Historia Ecclesiastica Gentis Anglorum: History of the English Church and People* (bk. 2, sec. 1; completed 731).

2. Lewis Carroll, "The Walrus and the Carpenter," *Through the Looking-Glass: And What Alice Found There* (New York: Macmillan, 1906), 73.

3. Ibid., 73–74.
4. Ibid., 75.
5. Ibid., 77.
6. Ibid., 78.
7. Dating from the first attempted English settlement in the New World in 1587 through the Treaty of Paris in 1783 by which Britain recognized American independence, the eight kings are James I, Charles I, Charles II, James II, William III, George I, George II, and George III; the two reigning queens were Mary II and Anne; the two lords protector were Oliver Cromwell and his son Richard.
8. James Boswell, *Life of Johnson,* vol. 2 (London: Oxford University Press, 1927), 155.
9. Daniel Defoe, *The Earlier Life and the Chief Earlier Works of Daniel Defoe,* ed. Henry Morley (London: Routledge, 1889), 186.
10. David Landes, *The Wealth and Poverty of Nations* (New York: W. W. Norton, 1999), 223.
11. Reginald Horsman, *Race and Manifest Destiny: The Origins of American Racial Anglo-Saxonism* (Cambridge, Mass.: Harvard University Press, 1981), 18.
12. Ibid., 17.
13. Ibid., 19.
14. Ibid., 22.
15. Ibid.
16. Ibid., 174.
17. Ibid., 292.
18. Ibid.
19. Ibid., 293.

CHAPTER THREE

1. Josef Joffe, *Uberpower: The Imperial Temptation of America* (New York: W. W. Norton, 2006), 88.
2. "Russian Squirrel Pack 'Kills Dog,'" BBC, December 1, 2005, http://news.bbc.co.uk/2/hi/europe/4489792.stm (accessed March 18, 2005).

3. See the *sus scrofa* and others at the U.S. Department of Agriculture's National Invasive Species Information Center, http://www.invasivespeciesinfo.gov/index.shtml (accessed July 12, 2007).
4. Robert Ley, "Roosevelt Betrays America!" http://www.calvin.edu/academic/cas/gpa/ley1.htm.
5. Lance Morrow, "Oh, Shut Up! The Uses of Ranting," *Time,* March 18, 2005.
6. Eberhard Richter and Ruth Fuchs, "Rhine Capitalism, Anglo-Saxon Capitalism and Redistribution," *Indymedia UK,* October 10, 2004, http://www.indymedia.org.uk/en/2004/10/299588.html (accessed October 22, 2005).
7. H. L. Mencken, ed., *A New Dictionary of Quotations on Historical Principles from Ancient & Modern Sources* (New York: Knopf, 1991), 343.
8. Ibid.
9. Norman Hampson, *The Perfidy of Albion: French Perceptions of England During the French Revolution* (New York: St. Martin's Press, 1998), 30.
10. Ibid. 133.
11. H. D. Schmidt, "The Idea and Slogan of 'Perfidious Albion,'" *Journal of the History of Ideas* 14, issue 4 (October 1953): 610–611.
12. J. Christopher Herold, ed., *The Mind of Napoleon: A Selection of His Written and Spoken Words* (New York: Columbia University Press, 1955), 125.
13. Philippe Roger, *The American Enemy* (Chicago: University of Chicago Press, 2005), 356.
14. David Strauss, *Menace in the West: The Rise of French Anti-Americanism in Modern Times* (Westport, Conn.: Greenwood Press, 1978), 51.
15. Ibid., 39.
16. Roger, 159.
17. Gerald Emanuel Stearn, *Broken Image: Foreign Critics of America* (New York: Random House, 1972), 175.
18. Ibid., 221–222.
19. Ibid., 175.

20. G. Jenner, "A Spanish Account of Drake's Voyages," *English Historical Review* 16, no. 61 (January 1901), 46–66. Pedro Simon's 1623 Spanish biography of Drake, *Noticias Historiales de las Conquistas de Tierra Firme,* includes accounts of how Drake robbed, pillaged, and held ransom Spanish settlements (including churches) in South America.

21. Harry Kelsey, *Sir John Hawkins: Queen Elizabeth's Slave Trader* (New Haven, Conn.: Yale University Press), 26–27.

22. Robert Gibson, *Best Enemies: Anglo-French Relations Since the Norman Conquest* (Exeter: Impress, 2004), 33.

23. Jenner, 57.

24. "Iranian President Mahmoud Ahmadinejad in Bushehr Responds to President Bush: Superpowers Made of Straw Are Behind All Wars and Conspiracies in the World," *MEMRI Special Dispatch Series,* no. 1084, February 1, 2006, http://memri.org/bin/articles.cgi?Page=archives&Area=sd&ID=SP108406 (accessed November 3, 2005).

25. Husnu Mahalli, "'USA—the God-Damned Country'; 'Murdering Is Genetically Ingrained in American Culture,'" *MEMRI Special Dispatch Series,* no. 857, February 2, 2005, http://memri.org/bin/articles.cgi?Page=archives&Area=sd&ID=SP85705 (accessed November 3, 2005).

26. Marivilia Carrasco, "Beslan: Responsibility of Slaughter Points Towards the Anglosaxons," *Non-Aligned Press Network,* http://www.voltairenet.org/article30021.html (accessed January 7, 2006).

27. Gibson, 137.

28. Alexis de Tocqueville, *Democracy in America* (New York: Harper Perennial, 1969), 615.

29. Ibid., 621.

30. Stearn, 17.

31. Gibson, 138.

32. H. L. Mencken, *A New Dictionary of Quotations* (New York: Knopf, 1991), 344.

33. "Maximilien de Bethune Sully on England," http://encarta.msn.com/quote_561549110/England_The_English_take_their_pleasures_sadly_.html (accessed July 12, 2007).

34. J. Herold Christopher, *The Mind of Napoleon: A Selection of His Written and Spoken Words* (New York: Columbia University Press, 1955), 156.

35. Gibson, 137.

36. José Enrique Rodó, *Ariel* (Austin: University of Texas Press, 1998), 80.

37. Stephen P. Gibert, *Soviet Images of America* (New York: Crane, Russak, 1977), 57.

38. Ibid.

39. Aleksander Solzhenitsyn, *East and West* (New York: Harper and Row, 1980), 58.

40. David Von Drehle, "A Lesson in Hate," *Smithsonian* 36, no. 11 (February 2006): 96–101.

41. Strauss, 208.

42. Stearn, 246.

43. Knut Hamsun, *The Cultural Life of Modern America* (Cambridge, Mass.: Harvard University Press, 1969), 144.

44. Uta G. Poiger, "Rock 'n' Roll, Female Sexuality, and the Cold War Battle over German Identities," *Journal of Modern History* 68, no. 3 (September 1996): 577.

45. Joffe, 77.

46. Von Drehle, 96–101.

47. Theodor Adorno, *Prisms* (Cambridge, Mass.: MIT Press, 1981), 127–128.

48. "Syrian MP Dr. Muhammad Habash Denounces the American Culture of 'Violence' and 'Cruelty'" MEMRI Special Dispatch Series, no. 832, December 22, 2004, http://memri.org/bin/articles.cgi?Page=archives&Area=sd&ID=SP83204 (accessed January 7, 2006).

49. Ibid.

50. Roger, 159.

51. Michael McMenamin, "Churchill and the Litigious Lord," *Finest Hour,* no. 95 (Summer 1997).

52. Ibid.

53. Dr. E. J. Dillon, *The Inside Story of the Peace Conference* (New York: Harper and Brothers, 1920), 497; now found at the Web site of Radio Islam: http://abbc .com/quotes/q601-650.htm.

54. Josh Pollock, "Anti-Americanism in Contemporary Saudi Arabia," *Middle Review of International Affairs* 7, no. 4 (December 2003): 33.

55. Tareq Hilmi, "America That We Hate," *Al-Sha'b,* October 17, 2003.

56. Bruce Lawrence, ed., *Messages to the World* (London: Verso, 2005), 160–171.

57. Ibid.

58. Ibid.

59. "Iran's Revolutionary Guards Official Threatens Suicide Operations: 'Our Missiles Are Ready to Strike at Anglo-Saxon Culture . . . There Are 29 Sensitive Sites in the U.S. and the West . . . ,'" *MEMRI Special Dispatch Series,* no. 723, May 28, 2004, http://memri.org/bin/articles.cgi?Page= archives&Area=sd&ID=SP72304 (accessed January 10, 2006).

60. Sarah Baxter, "UN Imposes Nuclear Sanctions on Angry Iran," *Sunday Times* (London), December 24, 2006.

CHAPTER FOUR

1. A. T. Mahan, *The Influence of Sea Power upon History, 1660–1783* (New York: Dover Publications, 1987), 63.

2. Ibid., 96.

3. Landes, 223.

4. John Brewer, *Sinews of Power: War, Money and the English State, 1688–1783* (New York: Knopf, 1989), 181.

CHAPTER FIVE

1. Landes, 234.

CHAPTER SIX

1. John Gallagher and Ronald Robinson, "The Imperialism of Free Trade," *Economic History Review,* vol. 6, no. 1 (1953): 5.

2. Ibid., 8.

3. Alan Manchester, *British Preeminence in Brazil* (New York: Octagon Books, 1972), 69.

4. Gallagher and Robinson, 5.

CHAPTER SEVEN

1. Niall Ferguson, *The Cash Nexus: Money and Power in the Modern World* (New York: Basic Books, 2001), 128–129.

2. Ibid., 124–125.

3. Brewer, 38.

4. Ibid., 122.

5. Ferguson, 113.

6. Donald Winch and Patrick O'Brien, eds., *The Political Economy of British Historical Experience* (New York: Oxford University Press, 2002), 69–70.

7. Brewer, 90–91.

8. Winch and O'Brien, 251.

9. John Steele Gordon, *Hamilton's Blessing: Extraordinary Life and Times of Our National Debt* (New York: Walker, 1997), 41.

10. Frances M. A. Voltaire, *Letters on the English* (New York: P. F. Coller and Son, 1909–1914), vol. 34, part 2, letter 10, "On Trade."

11. P. G. M. Dickson, *The Financial Revolution in England* (New York: St. Martin's Press, 1967), 11.

12. "Fortis Bank and ING Group Celebrate Bicentennial of Historic Louisiana Purchase Bond Transaction," *Business Wire,* June 3, 2004, http://www .findarticles.com/p/articles/mi_m0EIN/ is_2004_June_3/ai_n6053882 (accessed April 10, 2007).

13. Ron Chernow, *The House of Morgan: An American Banking Dynasty and*

the Rise of Modern Finance
(New York: Atlantic Monthly
Press, 1990), 26.

14. Ibid., 111.

15. Ibid., 197.

16. Philip Ziegler, *The Sixth Great Power*
(New York: Knopf, 1988), 216, 293.

17. Niall McKay, "Playing with Plastic,
How It Works in the Rest of the
World," *PBS Frontline,*
http://www.pbs.org/wgbh//pages/
frontline/shows/credit/more/world
.html (accessed April 10, 2004).

18. Daniel Boorstin, *The Americans: The
Democratic Experience* (New York:
Vintage, 1974), 186.

19. Lendol G. Calder, *Financing the
American Dream: A Cultural History of
Consumer Credit* (Princeton, N.J.:
Princeton University Press, 1999), 158.

20. Ibid., 164.

21. Ibid.

22. Ibid., 165.

23. Ibid., 18.

24. Ibid.

25. Ibid., 28.

26. Ibid., 118.

27. Ibid., 147.

28. Benjamin Schwartz, "Born Losers,"
Atlantic Monthly (January–February
2005), 159.

29. Calder, 161.

CHAPTER EIGHT

1. Wilfrid Prest, *Albion Ascendant:
English History, 1660–1815* (New York:
Oxford University Press, 1998), 50.

2. Roy Moxham, *Tea: Addiction,
Exploitation and Empire* (New York:
Carroll and Graf, 2003), 31.

3. Brian Cowan, *The Social Life of Coffee*
(New Haven, Conn.: Yale University
Press, 2005), 65.

4. Claire Tomalin, *Samuel Pepys* (London:
Viking, 2002), 374.

5. Cowan, 22, 28.

6. Curtis P. Nettels, *The Money Supply of*

the American Colonies Before 1720
(Madison: University of Wisconsin
Press, 1934), 53–54.

7. Ibid.

8. Ibid., 60, 62.

9. Ferguson, 14.

10. Prest, 154.

11. Paul Langford, *A Polite and
Commercial People* (New York: Oxford
University Press, 1989), 61.

12. Ibid., 61.

13. Judith Flanders, *Inside the Victorian
Home* (New York: W. W. Norton, 2003),
26, 35.

14. Ibid., 111–112.

15. James Norris, *Advertising and the
Transformation of American Society,
1862–1920* (New York: Greenwood
Press, 1990), 86.

16. Ibid., 86, 88.

17. Victoria de Grazia, *Irresistible Empire*
(Cambridge, Mass.: Harvard University
Press, 2005), 418.

18. Ibid., 418–419.

19. Prest, 152–153.

20. Boorstin, 100.

21. Ibid., 189.

22. Ibid.

23. Prest, 244.

24. Ibid.

25. Rick Szostak, *The Role of Transporta-
tion in the Industrial Revolution*
(Buffalo, N.Y.: McGill–Queen's
University Press, 1991), 62.

26. Szostak, 70.

27. Ibid., 61, 72.

28. Ibid., 77.

29. Szostak, 68.

30. Landes, 215.

31. Landes, 224.

32. *Catholic Encyclopedia,* vol. 8, s.v.
"Claude-François-Dorothée de
Jouffroy, Duc d'Abbans."

33. Prest, 245–246.

34. David Oliver, *The History of American
Technology* (New York: Ronald Press,
1956), 193.

35. Lance Day and Ian McNeil,

NOTES TO PAGES 154–163 425

Biographical Dictionary of the History of Technology (London: Routledge, 1998), 509.

36. Michael J. Freeman, *Railways and the Victorian Imagination* (New Haven, Conn.: Yale University Press, 1999), 1.

37. Ibid., 2.

38. Oliver, 251.

39. John Stover, *American Railroads* (Chicago: University of Chicago Press, 1997), 31.

40. Robert G. Angevine, *The Railroad and the State: War, Politics, and Technology in Nineteenth-Century America* (Stanford, Calif.: Stanford University Press, 2004), 58, 64.

41. Railway Statistics Before 1890, U.S. Interstate Commerce Commission.

42. Stephen Goddard, *Getting There: The Epic Struggle Between Road and Rail in the American Century* (New York: Basic Books, 1999), 14.

43. Norris, 15.

44. Boorstin, 128.

45. James Flink, *America Adopts the Automobile* (Cambridge, Mass.: MIT Press, 1970), 25.

46. Ibid., 42.

47. James Flink, *The Car Culture* (Cambridge, Mass.: MIT Press, 1975), 18.

48. Ibid.

49. Ibid., 70.

50. Goddard, 49.

51. Flink, 141.

52. William Childs, *Trucking and the Public Interest* (Knoxville: University of Tennessee Press, 1985), 21–22.

53. Kenneth Jackson, *Crabgrass Frontier: The Suburbanization of the United States* (New York: Oxford University Press, 1985), 184.

54. Childs, 10.

55. Goddard, 86.

56. CIA World Factbook, s.v. "United States," https://www.cia.gov/cia/publications/factbook/geos/US.html (accessed April 6, 2007).

57. Roger Bilstein, *Flight in America* (Baltimore: Johns Hopkins University Press, 2001), 104.

58. Brian Cowan, "The Rise of the Coffeehouse Reconsidered," *Historical Journal* 47, no. 1 (2004): 35.

59. Cowan, 36.

60. Harold Herd, *The March of Journalism: The Story of the British Press from 1622 to the Present Day* (London: Allen and Unwin, 1952), 39–43.

61. Prest, 193–194.

62. Ibid., 193.

63. British Library, s.v. "Concise History of the British Newspaper Since 1620," http://www.bl.uk/collections/britnews.html (accessed February 17, 2004).

64. Angela Todd, "Your Humble Servant Shows Himself: Don Saltero and Public Coffeehouse Space," *Journal of International Women's Studies* 6, no. 2 (June 2005): 121.

65. Oliver, 214.

66. M. G. Mori, ed., *The First Japanese Mission to America* (Wilmington, Del.: Scholarly Resources, 1973), 42.

67. Oscar Handlin, ed., *This Was America* (Cambridge, Mass.: Harvard University Press, 1949), 231.

68. Handlin, 231.

69. Boorstin, 146.

70. Domingo Sarmiento, *Travels in the United States in 1847* (Princeton, N.J.: Princeton University Press, 1970), 123–133.

71. Szostak, 75.

72. Daniel R. Headrick, *When Information Came of Age: Technologies of Knowledge in the Age of Reason and Revolution, 1700–1815* (Oxford: Oxford University Press, 2000), 193–215.

73. Oliver, 219.

74. Day, 174.

75. Oliver, 434.

76. "Telegraphy," www.britishempire.co.uk/science/communications/telegraph.htm (accessed June 13, 2005).

77. Oliver, 78.

78. Tom Standage, *The Victorian Internet: The Remarkable Story of the Telegraph and the Nineteenth Century's Online Pioneers* (New York: Berkley, 1998), 52.

79. Ibid., 127.

80. Ibid., 119.

81. Ibid., 120.

82. Ibid., 61.

83. Clark Manning, *A Short History of Australia* (Victoria, Australia: Penguin Books, 1989), 145.

84. Standage, 102.

85. Ibid.

86. Ibid.

87. Ibid., 102.

88. Mackenzie, 373, 392.

89. Floud, 88.

90. Ibid., 88.

91. Hugh Thomas, *An Unfinished History of the World* (London: Macmillan, 1995), 395.

92. Susan B. Carter and others, eds., *Historical Statistics of the United States* (Cambridge: Cambridge University Press, 1996), 783.

93. J. Fred Rippy, "Notes on the Early Telephone Companies of Latin America." *Hispanic American Historical Review* 26, no. 1 (1946): 118.

94. John Cannon, ed., *The Oxford Companion to British History* (Oxford: Oxford University Press, 1997), 906.

95. Ibid., 259.

96. Ibid.

97. Ibid.

98. Ibid., 565.

99. Claudio Véliz, *The New World of the Gothic Fox* (Los Angeles: University of California Press, 1994), 136.

100. *Columbia Encyclopedia,* 6th ed., s.v. "Baseball." *Encyclopaedia Britannica Online,* s.v. "Basketball," www.search.eb.com/eb/article-9108493 (accessed January 10, 2007).

101. "The Seven Summits," www.pbs.org/wgbh/nova/kilimanjaro/seve-nf.html (accessed May 4, 2006).

102. Cannon, 482.

103. Véliz, 142.

104. Eric Dunning, Dominic Malcolm, and Ivan Waddington, eds., *Sports Histories* (New York: Routledge, 2004), 25.

CHAPTER NINE

1. Angus Maddison, Historical Statistics, GDP and Per Capita GDP, http://www.ggdc.net/maddison/ (accessed August 23, 2006).

2. Henry Kamen, *Empire: How Spain Became a World Power* (New York: HarperPerennial, 2004), 13.

3. Arthur Quiller-Couch, ed., *The Oxford Book of English Verse, 1250–1918* (New York: Oxford University Press, 1939), 399.

4. Michael Clodfelter, ed., *Warfare and Armed Conflicts: A Statistical Reference to Casualty and Other Figures, 1500–2000* (Jefferson, N.C.: McFarland, 2001), 38.

5. William Hutton, *History of Birmingham* (Birmingham, UK: Thomas Pearson, 1839).

6. Arthur Herman, *How the Scots Invented the Modern World* (New York: Crown Publishers, 2001), 7.
On January 8, 1697, theology student Thomas Aikenhead was executed for heresy by hanging on the road between Edinburgh and Leith.

7. Kamen, 249.

8. B. R. Mitchell, ed., *International Historical Statistics: Europe, 1750–1993* (New York: Stockton Press, 1998), 674.

CHAPTER TEN

1. Niall Ferguson, *Empire: The Rise and the Demise of the British World Order and the Lessons for Global Power* (New York: Basic Books, 2003), 317.

CHAPTER ELEVEN

1. "The Vicar of Bray," in *A Collection of English Poems, 1660–1800,* ed. Ronald S. Crane (New York: Harper and Brothers, 1932), 693–694.
2. Diarmaid MacCulloch, *Thomas Cranmer* (New Haven, Conn.: Yale University Press, 1996), 225.
3. John H. Leith, ed., *Creeds of the Churches: A Reader in Christian Doctrine from the Bible to the Present* (Louisville, Ky.: John Knox Press, 1982), 273.
4. Matthew 23:9 (Authorized Version).
5. Matthew 19:14 (AV).
6. There is some doubt about the authorship of the manuscript, which was found in 1823. However, the theological views expressed in the manuscript are so close to those expressed in *Paradise Lost* that the attribution appears likely.
7. James Kinsley, ed., *The Poems and Fables of John Dryden* (New York: Oxford University Press, 1970), 7.
8. Luther, Zwingli, and Calvin were three leading Protestant reformers. Their theological conclusions often differed not only from Roman Catholic dogma but also from one another.
9. Kinsley, 372–373.
10. John Milton, *Complete English Poems, of Education, Areopagitica,* ed. Gordon Campbell (New York: Everyman's Library, 1993), 604.
11. Ibid., 610.
12. Ibid., 614.
13. Ibid., 615.

CHAPTER TWELVE

1. William Shakespeare, *Twelfth Night,* ed. Arthur Henry Bullen (New York: Oxford University Press, 1938), III.ii.58.
2. Lytton Strachey, *Eminent Victorians* (New York: Capricorn Books, 1963), 96.
3. It should, however, be noted that a careful inventory of all registered fragments of the True Cross in reliquaries and other collections existing today would, according to the *Catholic Encyclopedia,* not amount to, as some writers attest, the size of a battleship, but would be equal to roughly one third of the wood to be found on a first-century Roman cross. No studies exist to show how many of these fragments can be shown to come from the same tree.
4. Strachey, 32.
5. Angela Partington, ed. *The Oxford Dictionary of Quotations* (New York: Oxford University Press, 1992), 362.
6. Edward Gibbon, *The Decline and Fall of the Roman Empire,* vol. 1, ed. Hans-Friedrich Mueller (New York: Modern Library, 2003), 444.
7. Ibid.
8. Ibid.
9. Ibid.
10. Ibid.
11. Ibid.
12. Alexander Pope, *Essay on Criticism* (New York: Dover Publications, 1994), 9–10.

CHAPTER THIRTEEN

1. John Dryden, *Absalom and Achitophel,* ed. James Kinsley (New York: Oxford University Press, 1962), 1–10.
2. Partington, 721.
3. Edmund Burke, *Reflections on the Revolution in France,* ed. L. D. Mitchell (New York: Oxford University Press, 1999), 150.
4. Arthur Sullivan and W. S. Gilbert, *Iolanthe,* ed. Ian Bradley (New York: Penguin Books, 1982), II.86–100.
5. According to *Encyclopaedia Britannica Online,* "By separate statutes annexed to the treaty, the Presbyterian Church of Scotland and the Episcopal Church of England were secured against change."
6. Lewis Carroll, *Alice's Adventures in*

Wonderland; and, Through the Looking Glass (New York: Knopf, 1992), 238.

7. Adam Smith, *Wealth of Nations,* ed. Edward Cannon (New York: Modern Library, 1937), 746.

8. Ibid., 748

9. Ibid.

10. Ibid., 745.

11. Ibid.

CHAPTER FOURTEEN

1. Hesketh Pearson, *Dizzy: The Life and Personality of Benjamin Disraeli, Earl of Beaconsfield* (New York: Harper and Brothers, 1951), 135. On pp. 75–76, Pearson writes, "Their life together was serenely happy, wholly unmarred by the egotistical quarrels of most married people, his unvarying affection, patience and gentleness, her high spirits, shrewdness and impulsiveness, contributing to a harmony as rare as their natures were remarkable." Concerning Mary Anne Disraeli's death, on p. 215 Pearson quotes Disraeli as saying, "[T]o witness this gradual death of one who has shared so long, and so completely, my life, entirely unmans me." According to Christopher Hibbert in *The Personal History of Samuel Johnson* (New York: Harper and Row, 1971): "Yet, for all their petty bickering Johnson was fond of Tetty to the end, and became so accustomed, perhaps, to her complaints that he did not even notice them any more . . . During Tetty's last illness her husband nursed her tenderly; but it was not until she died, on 17 March 1752, that he realized just how much she had meant to him. His grief was overwhelming . . . he felt beyond the reach of comfort."

2. Paul de Rousiers, *American Life* (New York: Firmin-Didot and Co., 1892), 13.

3. Rodó, 77.

4. Ibid., 79.

5. Max Weber, *The Protestant Ethic and the Spirit of Capitalism* (New York: Charles Scribner, 1958), 71.

6. Rousiers, 14.

7. Bernard Henri-Lévy, *American Vertigo: Traveling America in the Footsteps of Tocqueville* (New York: Random House, 2006), 276.

CHAPTER FIFTEEN

1. Alfred E. Eckes, "The South and Economic Globalization, 1950 to the Future," in *Globalization and the American South,* ed. James Cobb and William Stueck (Athens: University of Georgia Press, 2005), 39.

2. John Quinterno, "Tar Heel Catholics," *Southern Cultures* 10, no. 4 (Winter 2004): 92.

CHAPTER SIXTEEN

1. Genesis 12:1–3 (AV).

2. Genesis 22:17–18 (AV).

3. Philip Jenkins, "Believing in the Global South," *First Things* (December 2006): 12–13.

CHAPTER SEVENTEEN

1. "'. . . to a World of Peace'—Text of the President's Address," *Washington Post,* September 25, 1961.

CHAPTER EIGHTEEN

1. Bernard Mandeville, *The Fable of the Bees* (London: Penguin Books, 1989), 67–68.

2. Ibid., 69.

3. Ibid., 68.

4. The capital letter is omitted; "whig" is used here as the name of a political and cultural tendency, not the name of either the British or the American parties which once bore this label. When the parties are meant, a capital letter will be used.

5. Walter Sellar and Robert Yeatman, *1066 and All That* (New York: E. P. Dutton, 1931), 115.

6. Thomas Babington Macaulay, *The History of England* (New York: Penguin Books, 1986), 51.

7. Ibid., 52.

CHAPTER NINETEEN

1. Robert Neilds, *Public Corruption: The Dark Side of Social Evolution* (London: Anthem Press, 2002), 62.

2. Jeremy Paxman, *The Political Animal* (London: Penguin, 2002), 132.

3. Morton Keller, *Affairs of State: Public Life in Late-Nineteenth-Century America* (Cambridge, Mass.: Harvard University Press, 1977), 240.

4. Jack Beatty, *Age of Betrayal: The Triumph of Money in American Politics, 1865–1900* (New York: Knopf, 2007), 215–217.

5. George V. Zito, "A Note on the Population of London," *Demography* 9 no. 3 (August 1972): 512.

6. Jonathan Swift, *Satire and Personal Writings* (New York: Oxford University Press, 1932), 452.

7. Robert D. Spector, *Samuel Johnson and the Critical Essay* (Westport, Conn.: Greenwood Press, 1997), 55.

8. Liza Picard, *Victorian London: The Tale of a City, 1840–1870* (New York: St. Martins Press, 2007), 64.

9. Ibid., 1–3.

10. Phillip Lopate, ed., *Writing New York* (New York: Washington Square Press, 2000), 58, 68, 249.

11. "UN Agglomerations 2005," http://www.un.org.osa/population/publications/WUP2005/2005urban_agglo.htm (accessed July 14, 2007); "Sao Paulo Statistics," http://megacities.uni-koeln.de/documentation/saop (accessed July 14, 2007); "Population Growth in Cities," http://www.un.org./sa/population/publications/wup2001/wup2001_CH6.pdf (accessed July 14, 2007).

12. Jagdish Bhagwati, *In Defense of Globalization* (New York: Oxford University Press, 2004), 32–33, 140.

13. Elizabeth Economy, *The River Runs Black* (Ithaca, N.Y.: Cornell University Press, 2004), 9, 88.

14. Gibs Kepel, *Muslim Extremism in Egypt* (Berkeley and Los Angeles: University of California Press, 2003), 155.

15. Ibid., 136–137.

16. Gavin McCormack, "Hard Times in North Korea," *New Left Review* A, no. 198 (1993): 35

17. Dai Qing and Lawrence R. Sullivan, "The Three Gorges Dam and China's Energy Dilemma," *Journal of International Affairs* 53, no. 1 (Fall, 1999).

CHAPTER TWENTY

1. Angus Maddison, *The World Economy: A Millennial Perspective* (Paris: Development Center of the Organization for Economic Cooperation and Development, 2001), 261.

2. Ibid.

3. Ibid.

4. Ibid.

5. Ibid.

6. World Development Indicators Database, World Bank, July 1, 2006, http://siteresources.worldbank.org/DATASTATISTICS/Resources/GDP.pdf (accessed March 10, 2005).

7. Julie DaVanzo and Clifford Grammich, "Dire Demographics: Population Trends in the Russian Federation," RAND Corporation (2001), 21.

8. Ibid.

9. Steven Eke, "Russia Faces Demographic Disaster," *BBC,* June 7, 2006, http://news.bbc.co.uk/2/hi/europe/5056672.stm (accessed March 20, 2007).

10. Jonah Hull, "Russia Sees Muslim Population Boom," *Al Jazeera,* January 13, 2007, http://english.aljazeera.net/NR/exeres/F8C5F608-FA29-4BB3-A7CA-A6F05B98BE23.htm (accessed March 22, 2007).

11. Kim Murphy, "The Future Looks a Lot More Diverse," *Los Angeles Times,* October 10, 2006.

12. V. F. Galetskii, "The Russian Far East: Searching for a Demographic Development Strategy," *Studies on Russian Economic Development* 17, no. 6 (December 2006), 655.

13. Guy Chazan, "Giant Neighbors Russia, China See Fault Lines Start to Appear," *Wall Street Journal,* November 16, 2006.

CHAPTER TWENTY-ONE

1. "Group to Get Over Springer Drama," BBC, January 10, 2005, http://news.bbc.co.uk/2/hi/entertainment/4161104.stm (accessed July 14, 2007).

2. Abraham Katsch, *The Biblical Heritage of American Democracy* (New York: Ktav Publishing, 1977), 97.

3. Katsch, 98.

4. Thomas Robbins, ed., *Church-State Relations* (New Brunswick, N.J.: Transaction Publishers, 1987), 169.

5. Harold Seymour, *Baseball: The Golden Age* (New York: Oxford University Press, 1989), 365.

6. "The First Blasts of the Trumpet," http://www.swiob.com/newslett/actual/nls/firstblast.htm (accessed July 17, 2007).

7. Isiaih Berlin, *The Crooked Timber of Humanity* (Princeton, N.J.: Princeton University Press, 1990), 246.

8. Johann Herder, *Philosophical Writings,* ed. Michael N. Forster (New York: Cambridge University Pres, 2002), 380–382.

9. Sellars and Yeatman, 30.

10. Justin McCarthy, *Death and Exile: The Ethnic Cleansing of Ottoman Muslims, 1821–1922* (Princeton, N.J.: Darwin Press, 1995), 164.

11. Ibid.

12. Simon C. Smith, *Britain's Revival and Fall in the Gulf* (New York: Routledge, 2004), 3.

CHAPTER TWENTY-TWO

1. Johann Herder, *Philosophical Writings,* ed. Michael N. Forster (New York: Cambridge University Press, 2002), 377.

2. Reinhold Niebuhr, *Moral Man and Immoral Society* (Lexington, Ky.: John Knox Press, 2001), xix.

3. Ibid.

4. *Reinhold Niebuhr on Politics,* eds. Harry Davis and Robert Good (New York: Charles Scribner's Son, 1960), 279.

5. Ibid.

6. Ibid., 280.

7. Campbell Craig, *Glimmer of a New Leviathan* (New York: Columbia University Press, 2003), 80.

8. Wilson Miscamble, "Kennan Through His Texts," *The Review of Politics* 52, no. 2 (Spring 1990): 307.

CHAPTER TWENTY-THREE

1. G. K. Chesterton, *The Everlasting Man* (Garden City, N.Y.: Image Books, 1955), 137.

2. Ray Kurzweil and Michael Dertouzos, "Kurzweil vs. Dertouzos," *Technology Review* (January 10, 2001), http://www.technologyreview.com/Infotech/12228/ (accessed March 25, 2007). See also: Ray Kurzweil, "The Law of Accelerating Returns," March 7, 2001, http://www.kurzweilai.net/articles/art0134.html?printable=1 (accessed March 25, 2007), 3.

Index

A Note on the Type

The text of this book was set in a typeface called Times New Roman, designed by Stanley Morison (1889–1967) for The Times (London) and first introduced by that newspaper in 1932.

Among typographers and designers of the twentieth century, Stanley Morison was a strong forming influence—as a typogrpahical adviser to the Monotype Corporation, as a director of two distinguished publishing houses, and as a writer of sensibility, erudition, and keen practical sense.

Composed by
Stratford Publishing Services, Inc., Brattleboro, Vermont

Printed and bound by
Berryville Graphics, Berryville, Virginia

Designed by
Iris Weinstein

A Note About the Author

Walter Russell Mead is the Henry A. Kissinger Senior Fellow in
U.S. Foreign Policy at the Council on Foreign Relations. He is a regular
book reviewer for *Foreign Affairs,* a member of the editorial board of
The American Interest, and a founding board member of the New
America Foundation. His books include *Special Providence,* which won
the Lionel Gelber Award in 2002, and *Power, Terror, Peace, and War*.
He lives in Jackson Heights, New York.